God's Sabbath with Creation

God's Sabbath with Creation

Vocations Fulfilled, the Glory Unveiled

JAMES W. SKILLEN

WIPF & STOCK · Eugene, Oregon

GOD'S SABBATH WITH CREATION
Vocations Fulfilled, the Glory Unveiled

Wipf & Stock
An Imprint of Wipf and Stock Publishers
199 W. 8th Ave., Suite 3
Eugene, OR 97401

www.wipfandstock.com

PAPERBACK ISBN: 978-1-5326-5949-2
HARDCOVER ISBN: 978-1-5326-5950-8
EBOOK ISBN: 978-1-5326-5951-5

Manufactured in the U.S.A.   APRIL 5, 2019

For Doreen

her love

and the inspiration of her life of service

Contents

Preface

WHEN I WAS GROWING up, the Christian messages I heard in church were built around the sin-and-salvation story: humans are sinners alienated from God and headed for destruction; the only remedy for sinners is God's saving grace and forgiveness of sin in Jesus Christ who offers eternal life. As I grew older and became acquainted with different traditions of Christian worship and witness, I realized that the preaching, church liturgies, creeds, and most hymns and educational classes are built around that story. Over time, two questions grew on me: 1) is the fundamental identity of humans their sinfulness?, and 2) is the fundamental identity of Jesus that he is the savior of sinners? In taking these questions to the Scriptures, I gradually became convinced that the sin-and-salvation story is an insufficient abstraction from the larger biblical story.

The Bible tells us that humans are creatures made in the image and likeness of God and commissioned for the high-level responsibility of governing and stewarding the earth in service to God. That is the fundamental identity and vocation of humans, and that is why their fall into sin is of such immense significance. Jesus, according to the Bible, is not first of all the savior of sinners but the Son of God incarnate, through whom all things are created and in whom all things hold together. That is what the openings of the Gospel of John, the letter to the Colossians, and the Letter to the Hebrews tell us. The New Testament does indeed tell the story of Jesus—Israel's Messiah—coming to save sinners. But that saving work is accomplished by the one who upholds the creation and has come to redeem and reconcile the sinfully disordered creation to God in fulfillment of God's creation purposes. The story of sinners and the savior, therefore, depends on God's purpose for creation.

The question that follows is this: what is the meaning of God's creation? Why did God create everything, including humans, in the first place? Why has God created us for such a high level of responsibility? What is God's intended destiny for human creatures and the creation as a whole? Has that goal changed because of human sin or is it still the same? Through the course of my life, these questions led to this book. They set the course for my years of study and teaching in biblical, philosophical, and political fields as well as my full-time work for thirty years in the civic arena.

My aim in what follows is to offer an interpretation of the biblical story that shows, on a textual basis, how the sin-and-salvation story unfolds *within* God's seven-day creation order, culminating in the celebration of the divine glory in God's sabbath with creation. This interpretation comes from examining what the biblical writers either say or presuppose about creation and, particularly, about the identity and responsibility of human creatures in relation to their creator, judge, and redeemer. At many points I can only touch on important matters and hint at implications that remain to be explored and developed further by others in every arena of life, including the fields of biblical scholarship. In that regard, I hope the book will provoke and encourage others to test and further explore the interpretation offered here.

Throughout the book I interact with a wide range of authors in wrestling with the questions raised above. I've chosen three authors in particular as primary interlocutors: N. T. Wright, Jürgen Moltmann, and Abraham Kuyper.

N. T. Wright (b. 1948) is a British biblical scholar widely known for his books and lectures as both a historian of the early Christian era and an interpreter of New Testament texts, especially the letters of Paul. Wright's importance for this book lies primarily in the way he shows how the unfolding story of Israel is the context for understanding Jesus, Israel's Messiah and Lord of the world. The destiny of God's creation, made manifest in covenants with Noah, Abraham, Israel, and David reaches its culmination, according to the New Testament, in the life, death, resurrection, ascension, and promised return of Jesus Christ. Wright repeatedly states that the biblical story refers to God as creator and thus to God's creational purposes, though he gives relatively little attention to the revelatory meaning of creaturely life and the human vocations that are part of it.

Jürgen Moltmann (b. 1926), a theologian now retired from the University of Tubingen in Germany, first became widely known for his work in developing a theology of hope. In his many volumes on Christian life and doctrine, he has emphasized the constitutive importance of hope for life in this age. In his major book on creation, he ties Christian hope to the creation order from the beginning, giving special attention to the creation's seventh day. Living in the way of Jesus Christ by faith, hope, and love orients us to God's gift of new life in the age to come, and that, in turn, should inspire our labors of love for the proper ordering of life here and now.

Abraham Kuyper (1837–1920) was the remarkable Dutch leader who worked tirelessly to educate and mobilize Christians for service to God in every earthly vocation. He was a leading theologian and churchman, yet most of his life's work exhibited his passionate belief that the Christian way of life entails more than church life. Christian faith calls for serving God in the exercise of all our responsibilities: family life and friendships, education and scholarship, politics and government, arts and sciences, commerce and industry, business and labor, the media, and every profession. Kuyper edited a newspaper, founded a university, led in the organization of the first Christian-democratic political party in Europe, and initiated a number of other culture-reforming actions. Driven by his belief in God's common grace, he urged Christians to act on the conviction that the creation belongs to God in and through Christ and that, from the beginning, the created cosmos has been destined to reveal the glory of God.

All three of these authors pay attention, in one way or another, to the meaning of divine and human governance, which has come up for some of the most heated debates and conflicts since the time of Christ to the present day. Given the fact that the biblical story deals extensively with the demands of justice, the coming of God's kingdom, Christ's lordship, and the relation of all of these to human governing responsibilities, it should come as no surprise that this subject will feature prominently in our exploration of the meaning of God's purposes for, and relation to, creation.

Acknowledgements

THE NUMBER OF PROFESSORS, authors, colleagues, friends, and family members who have contributed to the preparatory study for, and writing of, this book are far too numerous to mention. Many of them deserve more thanks than I can express in a few words, yet I want to offer special thanks to Richard Gaffin Jr., Bruce Wearne, Roy Clouser, Steve Bishop, Al Wolters, Ray Van Leeuwen, Cal Seerveld, the late John Stek, David Koyzis, Nathan Berkeley, Tyler Johnson, David Hanson, and Mary Dengler. And for their years of personal and professional encouragement, heartfelt thanks to Gordy and Priscilla Gault, Ed and Judy Henegar, Rockne and Joan McCarthy, Stanley Carlson-Thies, Bob Goudzwaard, Steve Snoey, and family members Doreen, Jeanene, Jamie, David, and John.

Introduction

LANGUAGE OF THE BIBLE

ONE OF THE FEATURES of biblical language we want to highlight at the outset is its root-edness in the experience of family life and extended kinship, eating and drinking, agri-culture and craftsmanship, rituals and animal sacrifice, buying and selling, dreams and visions, crime and punishment, warfare and governance. As a consequence, the biblical texts exhibit diverse kinds of description, dialogue, poetry, wise sayings, genealogical records, commandments, stories, prophecies, prayers, songs, and more.[1]

Gordon McConville writes, "The language of the Old Testament lends itself to the imagining of the world. This resides partly in its rootedness in the ordinary world and the basic constituents of life." When, for example, Moses "calls his hearers to 'choose life' (Deut 30:19), this life is given form in pictures of food and drink, family and household."[2] The rootedness of this language in ordinary experience is manifest in the prolific flow of similes, metaphors, and figures of speech. The Bible speaks of stars dancing and trees clapping their hands, of life's course as a journey, of a good person as one who walks upright, of God's word as a lamp to our feet and a light to our path. One lover in the Song of Songs is like a gazelle, leaping across mountains; the legs of the other are like jewels and her breasts like two fawns. A righteous ruler is a good shepherd of the people. God cares for Israel as a mother cares for her child. The bond between Israel and the Lord is like a marriage, and idolatry is adultery. The list could go on and on.

McConville explains, "The metaphorical quality of the Bible's discourse is indis-pensable to its depiction of the human. By 'metaphor,' I mean not only the figure of speech, as when Yahweh's speech is expressed as a lion roaring (Amos 1:2), but also

---

1. There is an immense literature on the interpretation (hermeneutics) of the Bible. We will not engage that literature in this book in any detail. For an introduction to the field see, for example, Bartholomew, *Introducing Biblical Hermeneutics*; Bartholomew et al., *Renewing Biblical Interpretation*; Bartholomew et al., *Canon and Biblical Interpretation*; Thiselton, *Hermeneutics*; Lundin, *Disciplin-ing Hermeneutics*; Frei, *Eclipse of Biblical Narrative*; Aageson, *Written Also*; Wright, *New Testament*, 1–145; Hays, *Reading Backwards*; and Hays, *Echoes in Gospels*.

2. McConville, *Being Human*, 89.

in a sense closer to 'typology'—that is, where events, stories, and characters undergo re-presentation in new situations and take on new meanings."[3] Terence Fretheim points to the Bible's birthing, planting, and building metaphors: God "plants Israel as a vintner would plant a vineyard and care for its growth" (Isa 5:12; Ps 80:8–9), and God lays the foundations of the earth (Isa 48:13; Ps 104:5).[4] McConville enumerates similes that characterize the human relationship to God as children of God, God's bride, God's servants, God's priests and rulers, God's treasured possession. All of these elaborate the meaning of creatures made in the image of God.[5]

Writing about the Psalms, William Brown details a host of operative images and metaphors. Two of the dominant ones are *refuge* and *pathway*. God is (or provides) a refuge for Israel. To follow the right path is to walk in tune with God on a journey of life that leads to ultimate refuge in God's presence.[6] Those two words also characterize the way humans are to treat one another—helping one another to follow the right path and offering hospitality along the way, especially to those in danger or great need. There are many other metaphors as well: God is Israel's helper who acts as king, warrior, parent, teacher, weaver, partner, judge, advocate, and healer.[7] Many of these likenesses also appear in New Testament texts: Jesus is the way, the truth, and the life, the bread and water of life, King of kings, and good shepherd.

To grasp the biblical understanding of creation, we need to relish the Bible's language in the full range of its diversity and complexity. For biblical authors, the language of poetry, simile, and metaphor was not decorative fluff that we may pass over lightly in search of logically systematized concepts that we might think are more solid and definite. Hans Boersma explains, "Metaphors are not only the best, they are the *only* way of describing the world around us. All human language is metaphorical." He quotes Sallie McFague who states even more emphatically, "Far from being an esoteric or ornamental rhetorical device superimposed on ordinary language, metaphor is ordinary language. It is the way we think." In addition, Boersma emphasizes that the "necessity of metaphorical language is given with the structure of the created order."[8] The biblical texts we will be examining speak easily and confidently of the creator and Lord in anthropomorphic terms: God's right hand overpowers the enemy; heaven is God's throne and earth his footstool. The language is revelatory because the creation

---

3. McConville, *Being Human*, 81.

4. Fretheim, *God and World*, 1–3.

5. McConville, *Being Human*, 93–94.

6. Brown, *Seeing Psalms*, 50.

7. Brown, *Seeing Psalms*, 75–79, 187–95, 211–12. Important background reading on similes, metaphors, and figures of speech include, Lakoff and Johnson, *Metaphors We Live By*; Ong, *Presence of the Word*. For detailed study of the use of metaphor and figures of speech in the Hebrew and Greek Bible, see E. W. Bullinger, *Figures of Speech*.

8. Boersma, *Violence*, 105. The McFague quotation is from her *Metaphorical Theology*, 16. Also quoted by Boersma on biblical metaphor is Gunton, *Actuality of Atonement*.

itself is revelatory of the creator, and this is especially true of the creature made in the image and likeness of God.

GOD'S CREATION WEEK

Given the Bible's language and imagery, we should not be surprised, then, to find that the opening of Genesis presents God's creation (both the "creating" and the "creatures") in the terms of a single, overarching metaphor—a seven-day week. The setting of the text is not one of our seven-day weeks at the beginning of time. In fact, as we will learn, the Genesis story presents God's seven days as the constituting order of all that exists, including our sun-and-moon days. According to Genesis 1:14–19, the greater light and the lesser light in the heavens have their identity and existence as *God's* fourth creation day. That is to say, the sun, moon, and stars are God's fourth-day creatures. In the chapters that follow, we explore the way this metaphor of a seven-day week conveys the deepest truth possible about all that exists—the entire creation from beginning to consummation, from bottom to top.

At the beginning of, and throughout, the Bible we see how ordinary experience and the rich metaphorical language that flows from it join together to present the creation in its entirety as the handiwork of God's creativity and rest—God's seven-day week. The opening of Genesis, writes McConville, "proceeds by making distinctions among the components of the world as experienced: between the heavens and the earth, between encompassing water and dry land, light and darkness, day and night, the greater and the lesser lights (sun and moon), between animal and vegetable, the 'kinds' of creatures, nonhuman and human, male and female, six days and the Sabbath. The whole world of experience is grounded here."[9] There is nothing behind, above, or outside the creation except the creator by which to account for the nature of reality. Therefore, we need to read the biblical story of God's creation week as the most profound account of what exists and why it exists.

OUTLINE IN BRIEF

In part 1, we read the opening chapters of Genesis as the story of *God's* days, not sun-and-moon-days, geological eons, or evolutionary stages. The days of God's week account for and encompass the whole of reality in the following sense: God's seven days constitute the light and darkness, waters and dry lands, sun, moon, and stars, and all the creatures that continue to generate their kind—plants, fish, fowl, animals, and humans. And that's not all; the creation story concludes with God's day of rest—the seventh day of God's creation week. The Bible's creation story is about God calling

---

9. McConville, *Being Human*, 89.

forth all creatures and all times into an interdependent marvel that culminates in God's sabbath with creation.

In part 2, we look at four characteristic patterns inherent in the seven-day order of creation. These patterns, evident in the Genesis story, have become more and more apparent with the ongoing development of creaturely life, particularly the life and history of the human generations. We name the patterns with doublets: honor and hospitality, commission toward commendation, revelation in anticipation, and covenant for community.

Then, in part 3, we explore the way God's engagement with creation in its fallen, sinful condition develops by means of judgment-redemption covenants God initiates with Noah, Abraham, Israel, and David—all of which point ahead with promises of fulfillment. We consider all of this through the lens of the New Testament, which testifies to the climax of God's covenant dealings with Israel and the nations in the life, death, resurrection, ascension, and promised return of Jesus, Israel's Messiah (the Christ). In these chapters, we focus on the way an understanding of the seven-day order of creation, with its revelatory patterns, illuminates the covenantal disclosure of reality in prophetic anticipation of the fulfillment of all things in God's (and the creation's) day of sabbath celebration.

The final four parts of the book take up topics of lively debate in biblical interpretation today. We want to show how an understanding of reality as God's seven-day week sheds new light on those subjects. Part 4 deals with the relation of the first Adam to the last Adam as Paul presents it in his letters to Roman and Corinthian believers. The next (part 5) looks at what the New Testament tells us about the *already* and the *not yet* of God's kingdom. The letter to the Colossians, for example, says to believers still living in this age, "So if you have been raised with Christ, seek the things that are above, where Christ is, seated at the right hand of God . . . For you have died, and your life is hidden with Christ in God. When Christ, who is your life, is revealed, then you also will be revealed with him in glory" (Col 3:1, 3–4). This is a classic "already/not yet" passage. It speaks of the *already* of the resurrection and ascension of Christ, in whom believers are already hidden. Their union with Christ is experienced now, however, only by faith, not yet by sight. Thus, to live by faith in Christ *now*, as the letter encourages its hearers to do, means continuing to live in anticipation of what is *not yet*, namely, the final appearing of Christ with his brothers and sisters in glory. That fulfillment will transfigure the faithful from the life of faith in this age to the resurrection life of face-to-face fellowship with God in the age to come.

Part 6 takes up the historically weighty question of the relation of God's covenant with Israel to the new covenant in Messiah Jesus. The two covenants are typically referred to as the old and the new, presented in the Old and New Testaments of the Christian Bible. Yet we want to show that the old and the new cannot be understood adequately in historically linear terms as a simple matter of before and after, or of earlier and later periods of history. The primary New Testament texts of concern to us in this part are Romans 9–11 and parts of Hebrews.

Finally, in part 7 we explore how the first six parts of the book open windows on the challenge of living faithfully in this age in service to God and neighbors in all that we do. The argument is that God calls us to follow Jesus on the pathway of life. Discipleship of that kind means much more than simply worshipping, praying, and talking about God. Following Christ Jesus, the Alpha and the Omega, entails directing all of life into the service of God in anticipation of creation's fulfillment in God's sabbath joy. To live like that, we need righteous wisdom that comes by walking with Christ by faith in the power of the Holy Spirit.

PART 1

Created Reality

1

God's Days

LET'S BEGIN OUR EXPLORATION with the first passage in the Bible, Genesis 1:1—2:4, a magnificently composed, amazingly compact portrayal of reality as God's creation.[1] It is an intricate literary masterpiece, the subtleties and complexities of which are still being explored today. Much more than a story of origins, it is "the story behind the biblical story," writes Old Testament scholar John Stek. "And more than that, it is the story behind all cosmic, terrestrial, and human history."[2]

The opening verses of Genesis present a simple, surprising, and dramatic portrayal of reality unlike any other ancient story of origins.[3] By simple I mean that the text speaks of the most familiar and obvious things that make up our world: light and darkness, earth and heavens, water and dry land, plants and trees, sun, moon

1. John Stek says that while the opening of Gen is narrative, "it is unique in that, while it moves toward climax, both conflict and tension are notably absent. In short, its literary type, as far as present knowledge goes, is without strict parallel; it is sui generis. As an account of creation it supplies for the Pentateuch what for the religions of Israel's neighbors were supplied by their mythic theogonies and cosmogonies." Stek, "What Says the Scripture?," 241.

2. Stek, "What Says the Scripture?," 242. For discussion of various textual and historical matters of dating, authorship, and the relation of the early chapters of Gen to other Near East documents, see Provan, *Discovering Genesis*, 1–58; McDowell, *Image of God*; Middleton, *Liberating Image*; Garrett, *Rethinking Genesis*; and Childs, *Myth and Reality*.

3. The seven-day week is presented in Gen with what Henri Blocher calls a masterful literary design. Gen 1:1–2:4 is a carefully composed whole: "The regular flow of thought conceals a careful construction which uses symbolic numbers: ten, three, and particularly seven. Ten times we find '*God said*' . . . Of those ten words, three concern mankind (1:26, 28, 29) and seven the rest of the creatures. The creative orders they include use the verb 'to be' ('let there be') three times for the creatures in the heavens, and seven different verbs for the world below. The verb 'to make' also appears ten times, as does the formula 'according to its/their kind.' There are three benedictions, and the verb 'create' is used at three points in the narrative, the third time thrice. Above all we read seven times the completion formula, 'and it was so' . . . seven times also the approval, 'and God saw that it was good,' and seven times a further statement is added (God names or blesses). All these heptads, or groups of seven, are independent of that of the seven days." Blocher, *In the Beginning*, 33. Richard Middleton cites even more examples of seven and multiples of seven in the Old Testament to support this point. Middleton, *Liberating Image*, 83–88.

and stars, fish and fowl, animals and humans. The story is surprising because it tells us that all of these things, and the order in which they stand in relation to one another, exist simply and wholly because God called them into existence.[4] The story is dramatic because everything created functions interdependently before the face of God in keeping with what God makes them to be and assigns them to do. The drama includes the exercise of human responsibilities: procreation along with stewardship, productive development, and governance of the earth. Moreover, it is clear that the "time" of God's creation week does not belong to the time of our days and weeks under the solar-lunar order, which God establishes as his fourth creation day. God's days constitute everything, including the sun and moon days of God's fourth day.

Genesis 1:1—2:4 is a well-known passage of scripture and accessible in many translations. We need not quote the passage here in full. The grand opening consists of a simple declaration: "In the beginning God created the heavens and the earth" (v. 1:1, TNIV). The phrase "the heavens and the earth" is an ancient Hebrew way of saying "everything."[5] Next comes a verse we'll examine in a subsequent chapter: "Now the earth was formless and empty, darkness was over the surface of the deep, and the Spirit of God was hovering over the waters" (v. 1:2, TNIV).[6] Beginning with the third verse, the text tells of God making or calling forth all creatures followed by the blessing and hallowing of the seventh day—God's rest. The creatures come forth in the following order: (1) light separated from darkness; (2) waters above separated from waters beneath; (3) dry land separated from the waters below, with vegetation growing and reproducing in the dry land; (4) the greater light, the lesser light, and the stars; (5) all water creatures and air creatures, reproducing after their kinds; (6) all animals, reproducing after their kinds, and humans blessed by God for fruitful reproduction, stewarding the earth, and serving as God's vicegerents; finally, (7) God rests. Repeated throughout the story is the phrase, "And it was so," emphasizing the effectiveness of the creator's declarations. Also repeated is the phrase, "And God saw that it was good," showing the creator to be the authoritative evaluator and ultimate judge of all that exists. Finally, an emphatic, culminating statement comes after everything has been created: "God saw everything that he had made, and indeed, it was very good" (Gen 1:31).

---

4. The emphasis on God's "calling" things into existence is not intended to overlook or submerge other verbs used in the opening of Genesis to describe God's creating and making activity. Moreover, in the rest of the Old Testament many closely related verbs are used of God's creative work, including fashioning, establishing, building up, founding, and spreading out (see particularly Isa 45:18). See Stek, "What Says the Scripture?," 207–13, 216–20. For more on God's voice and breath as "the instrument par excellence of creation," see Brown, *Seeing Psalms*, 78–82.

5. Abraham Joshua Heschel explains that in ancient Israel "there was no single word to describe what is called in Indogermanic languages 'world' or 'universe,' corresponding to the Greek *kosmos* or the Latin *mundus*. When the biblical writers intended to refer to all of creation, they spoke of 'heaven and earth' or 'earth and heaven.'" Heschel, "The Sabbath," 111.

6. We discuss Gen 1:2 in part 3, chapter 11.

Especially important in the Genesis story is the way the days are defined by their content, that is, by *what* God makes.[7] The text is not preoccupied with time but with the creatures God is making. The text does not say, "On the third day, God made this or that," as if a sequence of days already existed and the creator simply made different things on each successive day. No, the creation days are God's days and they are distinguished by *what* God makes. The phrase, "and there was evening and there was morning, the third day" comes at the *end* of each day, not at the beginning. Consequently, we should call God's fourth day the "sun-moon-and-stars" day, and when we refer to that day of divine creating, we should think of its creatures. We speak about time that way when we tell someone it is dinnertime, or bedtime, or harvest time. Each of those "times" is defined by an action or subject matter, not by a pre-determined number of minutes, hours, or days. God's seventh day does not even have an evening and morning, yet it, too, is called a day—the day when God's creation week reaches its climax. When we refer to the seventh day of creation, therefore, we should be thinking of God's rest in relation to all creatures. That is the content and action of the climactic day of the creation week.

In the chapters that follow we look at God's seven-day creation week in greater detail and consider many other passages beyond Genesis 1–2. At this point, consider just two other passages that shed light on the meaning of the seventh day, God's day of rest. In Psalm 95, the psalmist urges the people of Israel not to harden their hearts against their maker, their shepherd and king. That is what an earlier generation had done in the wilderness and God became angry with them, "declaring an oath in my anger, 'They shall never enter my rest.'" (Ps 95:11). In the Ten Commandments, as presented in Exodus, the Israelites are commanded to remember the Sabbath day (the seventh day of their week) because God rested on the seventh day of the creation week, blessing it and making it holy (Exod 20:8–11).[8] Now in Psalm 95 we hear God telling the people they will never enter God's rest due to their disobedience. The implication is that human creatures (and now specifically the children of Israel) were created to anticipate entrance into God's rest. Their disobedience and hardening of hearts against God is what brings down God's curse of "no entrance."

The word "rest" in Psalm 95 is picked up and developed further in the New Testament book of Hebrews (3:7—4:11), where the author recounts how God had held out the promise to Israel of entering "my rest." But due to their hardheartedness, God condemned an entire generation to wander in the wilderness not allowing them to enter even the earthly promised land. Later, however, according to Hebrews, God spoke to a future generation of Israel, again holding out the promise of entering "my rest." In

7. Childs writes that often in the Old Testament, the "character of the time is measured by the nature of its content," and that "the Hebrew concept of time was primarily interested in the quality of time rather than its temporal succession . . . The very fact that the Hebrew verbal system indicates qualities of action rather than tenses goes to confirm this analysis." Childs, *Myth and Reality*, 74, 76.

8. On the possible literary connection of Gen 2:1–3 to Exod 20:8–11, see Wenham, *Genesis 1–15*, 36, and Garrett, *Rethinking Genesis*, 193.

reminding readers of that history, Hebrews admonishes them not to close their ears to God's word now being spoken through Jesus or they, too, will fail to enter God's rest. The author then gives an account of what the new promise of entering God's rest means now that "Jesus, the apostle and high priest of our confession" has ascended to the right hand of majesty on high (Heb 3:1, 1:3). Yes, God's works "were finished at the foundation of the world" (4:3), and the scripture says, "God rested on the seventh day from all his works" (4:4). That wording might lead us to think that God's works and day of rest were in the past. But that is not what the author is saying. God's day of rest is not behind us, but still ahead, because the promise of entering it has been offered anew in the gospel of Jesus Christ. "So then, a sabbath rest still remains for the people of God; for those who enter God's rest also cease from their labors as God did from his. Let us therefore make every effort to enter that rest, so that no one may fall through such disobedience as theirs" (Heb 4:9–11; Ps 95:11). Here, Hebrews clearly identifies the creator's sabbath rest with the seventh day of creation, which remains open to those who do not harden their hearts against God.

Given the way we typically think about time, we should take note of the way Hebrews refers to God's day of rest using (or implying) three of our verb tenses—past, present, and future: God *did* rest from his labors (4:4); the faithful *do* "enter that rest" (Heb 4:3); and those who are still living on earth *should strive to enter* that rest, which lies in the future (4:1, 6). In other words, God's rest, the creation's seventh day, has been established. God closed it to those in Israel who closed their hearts, yet that rest remains open as the ultimate destination for those who respond with open hearts to God's word. The rest that God's people now enter or anticipate entering, writes New Testament scholar Richard Gaffin, "is none other than the rest of God at creation. Eschatological redemption-rest is not merely an analogue of God's creation-rest; the latter is not simply the model for the former. Rather, the writer knows of only one rest, 'my rest,' entered by God at creation and by believers at the consummation."[9] Built into creation, in other words, the ultimate goal of human life after all labors are completed is to enter God's rest, to join God in celebrating the creation's seventh-day fulfillment.[10] According to Gaffin, the way Hebrews draws together Gen 2:2–3 and Ps 95:11 means that God's rest was designed from the beginning for others to enter and share it. The fulfillment of life for those who hear and obey God's word, "represents nothing less than the fulfillment of the original purpose of God in creation, or more

---

9. Gaffin, "A Sabbath Rest," 39. Blocher introduces the debate about the relation of Heb 4 to Gen 1–2 in Blocher, *In the Beginning*, 56–59. Kenneth Schenck provides a contextual assessment of the meaning of rest in Heb 4 in relation to Pss 8 and 95 in Schenck, *Cosmology and Eschatology*, 51–97. See also Barrett, "Eschatology"; and Wray, *Rest as a Theological Metaphor*.

10. Oliver O'Donovan makes the point this way: "Historical fulfillment means our entry into a completeness which is already present in the universe. Our sabbath rest is, as it were, a catching up with God's." O'Donovan, *Resurrection and Moral Order*, 61–62.

accurately, the realization of his purposes of redemption is the means to the end of realizing his purposes of creation."[11]

JÜRGEN MOLTMANN'S DOUBLE SABBATH

In his major book on creation, Jürgen Moltmann gives more attention to the seven-day order of creation than have most theologians. However, his interpretation of the meaning of the seventh day is equivocal. On the one hand, he offers much that lends support to our reading of the text. Christian traditions of interpretation, he writes, have generally focused only on the six days of creation. "The 'completion' of creation through 'the seventh day' is much neglected, or even overlooked altogether."[12] According to the biblical traditions, he writes, "creation and the sabbath belong together."[13] The creator's rest "becomes at the same time the rest of his creation; and his good pleasure in his creation becomes the joy of created things themselves."[14] "We have to understand the sabbath as the consummation of creation—the completion given through the reposeful presence of the Creator in what he has created."[15] "The sabbath belongs to the fundamental structure of creation itself."[16] When Moltmann quotes Hebrews 4:9–10, he also points to Revelation 14:13, which speaks of "'the blessed dead' who 'rest from their labours, for their works follow them.'"[17]

On the other hand, in a different vein, Moltmann contends that the seventh creation day is not God's *ultimate* rest or the ultimate climax of creation. Instead, he says, the creation's sabbath will give way to, or be transcended by, a "messianic sabbath," which is "the End-time correspondence of the original sabbath of God's creation."[18] Moltmann thus reduces the original sabbath to a day within creation's time instead of recognizing it as the culmination and fulfillment of all time. He speaks of a messianic sabbath that is "both 'the eternal sabbath' and 'the new creation.'"[19] For Moltmann, there is both an original sabbath and a messianic sabbath beyond this creation.[20] "After all," he writes, "although the sabbath of creation was the seventh day for God, for the human beings who were created on the sixth day, it was the first day they experienced."[21]

11. Gaffin, "A Sabbath Rest," 39–40.
12. Moltmann, *God in Creation*, 276.
13. Moltmann, *God in Creation*, 277.
14. Moltmann, *God in Creation*, 279.
15. Moltmann, *God in Creation*, 287.
16. Moltmann, *God in Creation*, 284.
17. Moltmann, *God in Creation*, 282.
18. Moltmann, *God in Creation*, 290.
19. Moltmann, *God in Creation*, 288.
20. Moltmann, *God in Creation*, 288.
21. Moltmann, *God in Creation*, 295.

To speak in this way is quite at odds with Moltmann's earlier line of argument. If the original sabbath is simply one day in temporal experience, then it cannot be the consummation of creation in the way Moltmann first seemed to be saying it is. And it is certainly at odds with what we read in Hebrews. "Sabbath day, sabbath year and Year of Jubilee" writes Moltmann, "point in time beyond the time of history, out into the messianic time. It is only the sabbath at the end of history that will be 'a feast without end.' It is only this sabbath that will fulfil God's creation sabbath and the sabbath feast of Israel's history in the world."[22] Moltmann, as I read him, has offered an equivocal interpretation of the seventh day of creation presented in Genesis 2:1–3 and Hebrews 4.[23]

In contrast to Moltmann, I believe that the passage in Hebrews about God's seventh-day rest throws light on how we may understand the time of all seven days of God's creation week, including the first six. Look first at the language. Verbs in ancient Hebrew do not function primarily to convey past, present, and future the way English and many other languages do.[24] Hebrew, for example, can refer to God's day of rest as definite or complete and yet also, from our earthly point of view, not wholly in the past. Hebrews speaks of God's rest as definite, yet entailing a present and a future as well as a past. We might use an architectural metaphor to say that God's rest—the seventh day of creation—arches over all of the first six days of creation under the care and rule of the creator. With that image in mind, if we ask *when* the seventh day of creation is, the answer is, it is the time of God's rest and of the fulfillment of creation in God's rest. The time of God's seventh day, as Hebrews shows, is the time of the creation's culmination and fulfillment, the day without evening or morning in God's creation week that is blessed and hallowed in a special way.

Reading the whole of Genesis 1:1—2:4 in this light opens a new vista on the meaning and the time of each of God's creation days in relation to one another, as I hope to show in the chapters that follow.

---

22. Moltmann, *God in Creation*, 290.

23. Richard Bauckham offers a detailed assessment of Moltmann's idea of the relation of "creation sabbath" to "messianic sabbath," in Bauckham, "Millennium," 134–43.

24. See Waltke and O'Connor, *An Introduction*, 343–61, 455–78, 483–509. John Goldingay stresses that a noun clause like the one in Ps 90:2 ("from age to age you God") is a syntactical form that "helps Hebrew make statements that contain no time reference." Goldingay, *Old Testament Theology*, 62. See also Childs, *Myth and Reality*, 73–84.

2

Evenings and Mornings

IN THE DRAMATIC PRESENTATION of God's days of creating and resting in Genesis 1:1—2:4 there is a sentence that concludes each of the first six days: "And there was evening, and there was morning—the first [or any other] day." How are we to understand this? Let's start where the text starts, namely, with God making each new creature or group of creatures. The evening/morning phrase comes at the end, not at the beginning of each day. The focus is on *what* God creates, on what God calls into existence, not on the evening/morning phrase. Each new act of the creator makes the things that constitute that day. A seven-day week serves as the all-embracing metaphor or figure of speech to frame and organize the telling of God's creation of the world.[1] The story is not about God using an already-existing order of time, but about God creating everything, including time. These are God's days, not ours.

The evening/morning phrase appears to work the way other encompassing or entailing phrases do. We saw in Genesis 1:1, for example, that the phrase "the heavens and the earth" means *everything* God created. We use similar expressions such as "from top to bottom," or "from beginning to end," or "part and parcel" as a way of referring to a whole.[2] The evening/morning phrase works in a similar way, it appears to me. Thus, the phrase, "there was evening, and there was morning—the third day" refers to everything encompassed by God's separation of the dry land from the seas and every kind of plant and tree that grows on the land and reproduces after its kind. None of the world's countless lakes and seas is named here; none of the world's islands and continents is mentioned; none of the billions of kinds of plants and trees is identified. But the compact picture of God's third day tells us that all seas, all dry land, and

---

1. See Blocher, *In the Beginning*, 18–19, 32–34.

2. The phrase "there was evening and there was morning," is, I believe, like other encompassing phrases (called a "merism") such as "the heavens and the earth." The words in a merism "cannot be understood separately but must be taken as a unity," according to Waltke and Fredricks, *Genesis*, 59. The evening/morning phrase functions here, I suggest, as an encompassing "wrap-up" formula for each of God's first six days, referring both to the creatures of each day and to all that God has assigned them to do.

all vegetation exist and flourish by God's three commands: "let the waters," "let the dry land," and "let the earth" (1:9, 11). Dry land, water, and vegetation yielding seeds and fruit together constitute an irreducible part of God's creation and can thus be portrayed as "having their own day," which is captured in the phrase, "And there was evening and there was morning—the third day." If we ask, when or what is the *time* of God's third day of creation, the text tells us that it is the time of the waters and the dry land in their separation and of vegetation growing on the land and bearing seeds and fruit. The third day is God's time for water and dry land and vegetation; and as long as those creatures continue to exist and do what God creates them to do, the evening and morning of God's third day have not yet wrapped up that day. In a parallel fashion we can understand the time of each of God's creation days the same way. God's sixth creation day, for example, is the time of all animal and human generations, reproducing, filling the earth, and in the case of humans, subduing (governing and stewarding) the earth. The evening and morning of the sixth day also is not yet a wrap.

Since it is important not to think of God's creation days as referring to seven of our days, it is equally important that we not underestimate the figure of speech of a seven-day week as if it is simply poetic fluff that tells us nothing "substantial" about the nature of reality. God's seven-day week is presented in Genesis as the very *constitution* of reality because the creator is the originator and builder of everything in all of its diversity. Consequently, on a biblical basis there is no getting behind God's authoritative speech and action to gain a deeper, truer explanation of what constitutes reality. To imagine that we can go deeper or rise higher to explain the nature of reality by reference to some "substance" or "form" or "energy" other than (or in addition to) God is to assume that there is another foundation or starting point by which to account for things. But then, of course, we would have to ask, what is the origin of that substance, or form, or energy?

The compact story of God's seven-day week in Genesis is not a scientific hypothesis, nor is it just another ancient myth. The Latin phrase *creatio ex nihilo*—creation out of nothing—eventually came to be used by many Jews and Christians to emphasize, in contrast to many ancient myths, that the creator did not depend on some pre-existing material to create the world.[3] The creation-out-of-nothing phrase means that everything other than God exists by the will of God in dependence on God alone. There is the creator and the creator's creatures, *nothing* else. "Nothing" is not a

---

3. On the origin and development of the phrase "*creatio ex nihilo,*" see Soskice, "Creation and Glory," 172–85; and May, *Creatio Ex Nihilo.*

something.[4] There is no independent material substance or energy source from which God made things.[5]

The biblical creation story is in part an intentional challenge to the earliest creation myths dominant in Mesopotamia and Egypt. Chief among those myths was the Mesopotamian *Enuma Elish*, a story that ties the origin of the cosmos to the origin of the gods. In that story, certain intra-cosmic entities are presented as gods—sea gods, earth gods, and heavenly gods such as the sun and the moon. Yet, as Nahum Sarna points out, "The birth of the gods implies the existence of some primordial, self-contained, realm from which the gods themselves derive. The cosmos, too, is fashioned from this same element, personified in *Enuma Elish* as the carcass of Tiamat. That is to say, both the divine and the cosmic are animated by a common source."[6] In Genesis, by contrast, "creation comes about through direct divine fiat: Let there be!"[7] There is no preexisting carcass or other substance from which things are made. In fact, the *Enuma Elish* almost forces us to ask: where does the carcass of Tiamat come from?

The evening/morning phrase underlines the point about the creation's dependence on God alone. God gives every creature its distinct identity within the creation week as a whole. Nothing stands on its own as a god or self-sufficient entity. Thus, we can read the evening/morning phrase as saying that God originates and upholds each day of creatures in its entirety from start to finish and in relation to all the others in a single creation order. God opens and closes everything that pertains to the existence, identity, and interdependence of every creature. There are no independent, self-originating creatures, and there are no gods but the creator God. The text illustrates

4. Karl Barth, it seems to me, confounds evil and human finitude in a way that follows from his idea of "nothingness" as a kind of "something." "There is a whole monstrous kingdom," Barth writes, "a deep chaos of nothingness, i.e. of what the Creator has excluded and separated from the sphere of being, of what He did not will and therefore did not create, to which He gave no being, which can exist only as non-being, and which thus forms the menacing frontier of what is according to the will of God." Barth, *Church Dogmatics*, 143. Barth also writes: "In the person of Jesus Christ God has not definitively, let alone eternally, but only transiently shared the pain and death of creation. It is an act of providential care which He performs when He surrenders His own Son to the lowliness and misery of creaturely existence. He sees the hopeless peril of the created world which He has snatched from nothingness but which is still so near to nothingness." Barth, *Church Dogmatics*, 383. Barth's influence is evident in renewed attention to the meaning of "nothing" in the doctrine of *creatio ex nihilo*. See Anderson, *Christian Doctrine*, 42–53; and McFarland, *From Nothing*.

5. "It may be asked," writes Henricus Renckens, "Is matter then not also created by God? The answer is that such a question belongs to the scholastic world view, and falls outside the perspective of the author of Genesis . . . We must remain satisfied with our author's deep conviction that *everything* that exists has been brought forth by God, and that in a manner that can be compared with no kind of human activity whatever." Renckens, *Israel's Concept*, 53. See also Stek, "What Says the Scripture?," 219; Brown, *Seeing Psalms*, 178–82; and Von Rad, *Genesis*, 47.

6. Sarna, *Understanding Genesis*, 11. Richard Middleton presents a detailed discussion of Gen 1–11 as "ideology critique" of the Mesopotamian views of creation, kingship, and cultic practices in Middleton, *Liberating Image*, 185–231. See also Provan, *Seriously Dangerous Religion*, 29–31.

7. Sarna, *Understanding Genesis*, 11–12. The God of the Bible who calls Israel first of all to "have no other gods before me" and to make no idols (Exod 20:3–4) stands in unyielding opposition to all would-be gods—false gods, idols. See Halbertal and Margalit, *Idolatry*, 9–107.

this point in a subtle way with the words chosen to refer to the sun as the greater light and the moon as the lesser light. Some ancient peoples worshipped the sun and moon as gods. So the reason Genesis avoids the words "sun" and moon" is probably to undermine idolatrous worship of those heavenly bodies. The greater light and the lesser light are not gods; they are God's creatures, whom God appoints to serve the other creatures. So they are not gods but rather God-appointed fourth-day creatures.

The creation story of Genesis represents a radical break with ancient myths, according to Stek. "Here [in Genesis] was a view of God, humanity, and world so alien to that of all other peoples, so thorough and fundamental in the reorientation it demanded, that one needed, as it were, to be born into another world to understand it."[8] "The religion of Israel," writes Sarna, "is essentially non-mythological, there being no suggestion of any theo-biography . . . [The Genesis narrative] has no notion of the birth of God and no biography of God. It does not even begin with a statement about the existence of God. . . . To the Bible, God's existence is as self-evident as is life itself."[9] "For the first time in history," Sarna explains, "we have a totally new conception of cosmogony and one, strangely enough, that in its literary form has not hesitated to make use of some of the symbols of its ideologically incompatible predecessor."[10]

In ancient religious myths, furthermore, human beings are portrayed as "abject slaves and pawns in a metropolis of the gods," writes Stek. The exception is "the king, who as a man of power and the representative of the gods participates in the divine."[11] Genesis, by contrast, portrays humans as the "crown of creation and all humans alike are, while of earth, fashioned in God's image and appointed to a royal station in the creation."[12] Richard Middleton argues, "The starting point for a reading of [the Bible's] primeval history as critique of Mesopotamian ideology is the claim in Genesis 1 that God granted a royal-priestly identity as *imago Dei* to all humanity at creation."[13] This represents another "revolutionary break" with ancient mythologies, writes Sarna. "No longer is man a creature of blind forces, helplessly at the mercy of the inexorable rhythms and cycles of nature. On the contrary, he is now a being possessed of dignity, purpose, freedom and tremendous power."[14]

HUMAN IDENTITY AND RESPONSIBILITY

When the Genesis story arrives at God's sixth day of animal and human creatures, the identity of humans stands out in many ways. They are created in the very image

8. Stek, "What Says the Scripture?," 230.

9. Sarna, *Understanding Genesis*, 9–10.

10. Sarna, *Understanding Genesis*, 13.

11. Stek, "What Says the Scripture?," 231.

12. Stek, "What Says the Scripture?," 231.

13. Middleton, *Liberating Image*, 204.

14. Sarna, *Understanding Genesis*, 16.

of God for fellowship with God and for the exercise of high-level responsibilities in God's creation.[15] The forward movement of the creation story from the first day to the sixth day is dynamic, expanding in complexity with each new day of creatures. The story builds from light and darkness to an expanse between the waters above and the waters beneath, which God calls the "sky." Light and darkness are sustained when the sky is installed to separate the above from the beneath. Then, sequentially, comes the separation of the water below from dry land that produces vegetation of a seed-bearing kind, including fruits and trees. Each day of creatures depends on and serves the others, and that means God's sixth-day creatures—animals and humans—are also dependent on, and served by, all prior creatures.

To understand the Genesis portrayal of the progression and interdependence of God's days requires a distinct kind of metaphorical imagination. The progression of the days is different from the way we think of the movement of our days from a Sunday to a Saturday. If it is Tuesday for us, we know Monday is past and Wednesday has not yet arrived. We think of each day as a period of time that does not overlap the time of other days. God's creation days are different; they build on each other until all the creatures of the first six days exist and function together simultaneously. This means that the story is not about the temporal sequence of the first days of created reality but the interdependent order of God's days. The portrayal tells us about the distinct identities and interdependence of the creatures God calls into existence. And the evening/morning phrase for each day does not appear until after the actions or responsibilities of that day's creatures is described. In other words, the reproduction and governing work of the human generations are all part of the sixth creation day. If the seventh day is the day of God's rest, then the sixth day is the day of human generational unfolding and of all that human creatures are to do as God's governing stewards of the earth. The sixth day doesn't end until all that God has commanded or assigned has been completed.

Note how the story of each day directs our attention to the ongoing generation of vegetation, to the continuing service of the sun and moon to mark seasons, days and years, and to the development of the animal and human generations in dependence on one another and on all other creatures for life. When God commands the waters to "bring forth swarms of living creatures" and birds to "fly above the earth across the dome of the sky," the swarming and flying are contained within God's fifth day (Gen 1:20–23). Clearly, birds need the sky and fish need the water; the water above and the waters beneath depend on the expanse between them, and none of this continues without light and darkness. The picture here, in other words, is that of an intricate, developing, and deep ecology. Therefore, when the phrase "and there was evening and there was morning, the fifth day" wraps up God's work of that day, it does not mean the day is finished and gone, to be followed by another day that will soon be spoken

---

15. Provan also points to the progressively mounting complexity of God's creation days. Provan, *Seriously Dangerous Religion*, 28.

about in the past tense. No, the creatures and their actions of each creation day exist in simultaneous relation to all the others and all of the days exist in relation to the creator's day of rest.

The interdependence of all God's creatures comes to special focus in the creation of humans with the responsibilities God gives them. There would be no capacity of humans to govern and steward the earth if there were no land and water, no fish, birds, and animals for humans to govern and care for. And the human generations are dependent on all other creatures for their very existence. Moreover, and most important, the progression of God's creation days reaches beyond all creatures to the creator's seventh day. That is the day toward which the creation week is oriented, the day of God's rest, which has no evening or morning. The meaning of rest in this case is not that God steps away temporarily to take a break. To the contrary, the seventh day is the climax of creation, the time of God's celebration *with* all creatures. God's creation week is seven days, not six. The seventh day overarches and serves as the aim of the entire progression of the first six days.

As the text makes clear, human governing and stewarding have their meaning not just in reference to other creatures but also and above all in reference to the creator who has commissioned them with high-level responsibilities. The multifaceted responsibilities of the image of God are vast in scope and develop in ever-greater complexity over generations. By the very order of God's creation days, the unfolding human generations are to exercise all their labors in service to God in anticipation of the day when all labors are complete and God's rest becomes their rest. God's first six creation days have their evening-and-morning limits; God's seventh day has no evening-and-morning limits and is the goal or destiny of the whole creation.

KUYPER'S DAWNING INSIGHT

Abraham Kuyper eventually recognized the progression of the creation days toward a definite culmination, though he came to that recognition in a way quite different from the way we are describing. For Kuyper, as for most Reformed theologians trained in scholastic theology, the starting point of Christian thought is God's sovereignty displayed in the predestined election of some sinners to salvation from out of the sea of sinful humanity. Kuyper's theology did not begin with an exploration of the meaning of creation. Rather, he like many others started with God's sovereign grace—special grace—extended to the elect for eternal salvation. Yet that doctrinal starting point raised a question that dogged Kuyper at every turn: what is the meaning of human history and the created world as a whole (which includes all humanity and not only the elect)? Since God is the creator who upholds all things, heaping countless blessings on the entire world, the meaning of creation does not seem to be accounted for by the doctrine of electing grace.

Drawing on the insights of John Calvin and others, Kuyper gave increasing attention to the meaning of God's graciousness to all people and the whole creation—common grace in contrast to special or particular grace. That turned his attention increasingly to the meaning of creation. As a result, although Kuyper was a churchman, theologian, and pastor, he expended most of his energy on efforts to encourage Christians in the exercise of their diverse vocations—in family life, journalism, education, politics, and economic life as well as in ecclesiastical life. Yet the question of God's grace continued to challenge him: do "these two forms of grace, this *special* and this *common* grace, exist independently side-by-side or operate in connection with each other, and if so, how?"[16]

The problem with the traditional doctrine of special grace, Kuyper came to see, was that it too easily became focused on the salvation of the elect rather than on the glory of God. The focus must change; the intimate connection between God's expressions of grace must be found in God's glory, in the way the entire creation exists to reveal that glory. God's grace, he concluded, does not exist for you, the elect, "and then for the *Church* and so also for the *Body* of Christ and finally for the *Christ*. No: Christ, by whom all things exist including ourselves, is before all things."[17] All things were created by him, and in him all things hold together. Therefore, God's grace, special and common, must aim for same end: the glory of God. The Savior of the world "is also the *Creator* of the world, indeed that he could become its Savior only *because* he already was its Creator."[18]

Christians, then, must come to recognize that the whole of life in every sphere of society and not only in the church institution is to be lived to the glory of God in praise of Christ Jesus. Rethinking divine grace in relation to God's creation purposes, Kuyper saw that "the ongoing development of humanity is *contained in the plan of God*."[19] "The ages must continue not solely for the sake of the elect . . . but in the interest of developing the world itself to its consummation."[20] Kuyper was not primarily an exegete of biblical texts, and, as far as I know, he never offered a detailed interpretation of Genesis 1 and 2. He did, however, make these observations: in all God's works, there is "a precise order of succession. In the creation there is a divine order, which coheres in forms that are related with the sacred number seven."[21]

Kuyper's importance for us in this book is the attention he gave to the diverse responsibilities for which God made humans—the creatures who have been called to

---

16. From an excerpt from Kuyper's three-volume work on common grace (*De Gemeene Gratie*, 1902–1904): *Abraham Kuyper*, 165–201; 168. For an excellent study of Kuyper on this subject see Zuidema, "Common Grace."

17. Kuyper, *Abraham Kuyper*, 165–201; 169–70.

18. Kuyper, *Abraham Kuyper*, 165–201; 173.

19. Kuyper, *Abraham Kuyper*, 165–201; 175.

20. Kuyper, *Abraham Kuyper*, 177.

21. Kuyper, *Revelation of St. John*, 89.

serve God and one another throughout their sixth-day generations. God's culminating sabbath with creation entails the fulfillment of human life with all its responsibilities through all generations. God in Christ has come to reconcile and fulfill creation. From Kuyper we can learn that to understand the evenings and mornings of God's creation days in relation to God's sabbath rest, we must not think about humans in the abstract or only as sinners in need of God's redeeming grace. We must have in view actual humans in their generations with the full range of God-given responsibilities they exercise as part of God's seven-day creation purposes.

3

Architectural Wonder

THE CREATURES OF THE first six days of God's creation week do not appear and disappear one after another in a sequence like the days of our weeks. In the Genesis story, by contrast, each new day of creatures continues in existence as God adds new ones. Day builds on day. Looking at this progression from another angle we can see an architectural wonder emerging. God's work of creation is like the construction of a multi-level dwelling in which each level adds to and depends upon those that come before it. Each new "day," defined by its creatures and their assignments, nests within those that have already been created. Each created thing becomes the hospitality center for those that follow. The waters below host sea creatures. The dry land hosts vegetation, animals, and humans. The entire order of the creator's first six days serves as the palace and estate that God judges to be very good, perfectly fit for divine residence.

One feature of this architectural pattern that was noticed long ago is the way the first three days are related to the next three days. The first three portray God's work of *separation*—(1) light from darkness, (2) waters above from waters beneath, and (3) the seas from the dry land with its vegetation. The next three days tell of God *filling* the sky, the waters, and the dry land with sun, moon, stars, birds, fish, animals, and humans. In this pattern, according to Henri Blocher, there is also a correspondence of day one (light) to day four (luminaries), of day two (sky and waters) to day five (birds and fish), and of day three (dry land and vegetation) to day six (animals and humans). Furthermore, the creatures of the first three days are immobile while the creatures of the next three days are mobile.[1] This is another of the sophisticated patterns found in this remarkable text.[2] Yet while it is important to recognize the three plus three pattern

1. See Blocher, *In the Beginning*, 51; Renckens, *Israel's Concept*, 49–50; and Middleton, *Liberating Image*, 74–81.

2. Waltke and Fredricks point to the literary device of intensification or escalation evident here. "Texts commonly reflect escalating action, a sense of movement from the lesser to the greater. This is evident in the first six days in Genesis 1. These days are divided into two triads arranged by intensification. Both vegetation and humanity, symbolizing the fertility of life, were considered pinnacles of creation in the ancient Near East. The first triad ends climactically with the creation of vegetation;

as part of the complex architecture and ecological order of the creation days, it should not divert our attention from the full *seven-day* week that constitutes the whole.[3]

Stanley Jaki, drawing on Psalm 104 and other biblical passages, sees in the architecture of Genesis 1 something that was very familiar to ancient Israel. Poets such as the psalm writer described earth and heaven as a tent, a world-tent.[4] Or as Raymond Van Leeuwen says, Genesis 1–2 draws on the metaphor of a cosmic house or palace-temple.[5] The psalmist addresses God:

> You are clothed with honor and majesty,
>   wrapped in light as with a garment.
> You stretch out the heavens like a tent,
>   you set the beams of your chambers on the waters . . .
> You set the earth on its foundations,
>   so that it shall never be shaken.
> You cover it with the deep as with a garment;
>   the waters stood above the mountains (Ps 104:1–3, 5–6).

In Isaiah's words, God is the one who

> sits above the circle of the earth,
>   and its inhabitants are like grasshoppers;
> who stretches out the heavens like a curtain,
>   and spreads them like a tent to live in . . . (Isa 40:22).

Later, Isaiah announces,

> Thus says the Lord:
> Heaven is my throne
>   And the earth is my footstool,
> what is the house that you would build for me,

---

the second, the creation of humanity." *Genesis*, 36. Another part of the double triad, say Waltke and Fredricks, is this: "Each triad progresses from heaven to earth (land) and ends with the earth bringing forth. In the first triad, the land brings forth vegetation; in the second, the land brings forth animals. The number of creative acts also increases within each triad: from a single creative act (days 1 and 4) to one creative act with two aspects (days 2 and 5) to two separate creative acts (days 3 and 6)." *Genesis*, 58.

3. As Sarna explains, "The account culminates in the Sabbath, or divine cessation from creation which, to the Torah, is as much a part of the cosmic order as is the foregoing creativity." Sarna, *Understanding Genesis*, 2. Heschel speaks of Jewish rituals as an "*architecture of time* . . . The main themes of faith lie in the realm of time. We remember the day of the exodus from Egypt, the day when Israel stood at Sinai; and our Messianic hope is the expectation of a day, of the end of days." Heschel, "The Sabbath," 8.

4. Jaki, *Genesis 1*, 22–27, 279.

5. Van Leeuwen, "Cosmos, Temple," 72–77. Provan also discusses the use of a cosmic-temple metaphor and goes on to argue that the earth as a whole, and not only a limited garden area, is what the metaphor of a garden refers to in Gen 2. Provan, *Seriously Dangerous Religion*, 32–40; and Provan, *Discovering Genesis*, 57, 69–75.

and what is my resting place?
All these things my hand has made,
and so all these things are mine . . . (Isa 66:1–2).[6]

When in a dream Jacob saw a stairway resting on the earth, with its top reaching to heaven, he saw something that Isaiah's later declaration would affirm. For when Jacob awoke from his dream he said, "Surely the Lord is in this place—and I did not know it! . . . This is none other than the house of God, and this is the gate of heaven." (Gen 28:16–17). The creation is an architectural wonder. It is like a cosmic tent, an expansive royal estate where the lord of the realm dwells and in which the Lord's chief stewards—the generations of the image of God—bear immense responsibility as governors, developers, and priests.

MISUNDERSTANDING THE COSMIC TEMPLE IMAGERY

In two places in his magnum opus on the apostle Paul, N. T. Wright draws on the work of John Walton who also adopts the architectural image of a cosmic temple.[7] The ancient readers of Genesis 1–2, says Wright, would recognize that the creator's day of rest is likely a reference to the position of residence (a "base of operations") taken by the creator in the cosmic temple just constructed, from which to carry out the work of developing the creation "through the agency of his image-bearing human creatures."[8] And it won't be humans alone at work in the kingdom, Wright says later. God's "rest" on the seventh day does not mean ceasing from labor but engagement in overseeing and blessing the kingdom through the work of humans. "For God to be blessing Zion with food, its priests with salvation and its king with strength and victory, hardly sounds like the creator putting his feet up and listening to the angels playing Mozart."[9]

Wright's interpretation, however, appears to understand the progression of God's seven-day creation week as taking place at the beginning of time—as the initial set-up—which is followed by divine residence in the control room. But that picture does not square with the seven-day architecture of the creation order in Genesis. If Wright sticks with the metaphor of a week in which the creation's seventh day overarches the simultaneous unfolding of the first six days, then his idea of God's engagement from the throne room with the sixth-day human generations on the footstool might make some sense from a human point of view. However, the day of rest in the biblical framework is the seventh-day fulfillment of the entire creation constituted as the first six of God's creation days. The creation's seventh day cannot be turned into a new

6. For other passages in the Old Testament that present aspects of this understanding of creation see Boda, *Heartbeat*, 90–95.

7. Wright, *Paul and Faithfulness*, 102, 560–61; Wright's reference is to Walton, *The Lost World*, 71–85.

8. Wright, *Paul and Faithfulness*, 102.

9. Wright, *Paul and Faithfulness*, 560.

kind of workday for God. God's work of the first six days includes the responsibilities exercised by the human generations. From a sixth-day point of view not all of the human generations have run their course. But from the seventh-day point of view, God's rest is the culmination and fulfillment of the entire creation and the end of all labor for humans as well as for God.

If, therefore, Wright does not stay with the comprehensive character of the seven-day order of creation once it is understood as a cosmic temple, then the Genesis creation story begins to fall apart. Wright's deconstruction of the metaphor follows in two ways. First, he turns the seventh-day rest into a new kind of workday for God. Second, he turns God's day of rest into an earthly day in the first week of time, followed by the work of both God and humans. That erases the seventh day's identity as the day without evening or morning, the day of culminating rest, as Hebrews 4 explains. Of course Wright's work focuses primarily on Paul's letters, not on Hebrews or on Genesis 1–2, but I will try to show later, in part 4, that Paul's argument about the relation of the first Adam to the last Adam in 1 Corinthians 15:35–49 and Paul's discussion in 2 Corinthians 5:1–10 (passages that Wright interprets in detail) presuppose the same seven-day order of creation taken for granted by the author of Hebrews, the author of Genesis 1–2, the poet of Psalm 8, the language of Psalm 104, and of Isaiah 40 and 66 quoted above.

NEITHER PRIMITIVE SCIENCE NOR ANACHRONISTIC ABSTRACTIONS WILL DO

Recognizing the architectural design in the creation order presented in Genesis raises another issue. Some critics have belittled the idea of a "three-story universe," which they attribute to the biblical authors. Such an idea, they say, is out of date, manifesting mythological thinking. The three-story picture includes a dome above with sun, moon, and stars that holds back the waters above, which is the third story. Beneath that is the earth and everything on it—the second story. Under the earth is a hidden depth sometimes referred to as Sheol. Today, say the critics who look at the world from the viewpoint of modern physics, we supposedly know better than to think of the earth and its place in the cosmos in terms of a three-story tent or royal palace. Instead, we should read the creation story of Genesis and much else in the Bible as a myth. To arrive at an accurate explanation of the origin and order of the universe it is necessary to adopt a modern scientific point of view.

Many up-to-date scientists who are Christians deal with the criticism presented above by agreeing that the cosmological language of the Bible is primitive (or bad) science. However, in their view the Bible is not myth; its main purpose is to teach spiritual truth not science. Fifty years ago, for example, Paul Seely made this dual-track argument in an essay on "The Three-Storied Universe." There he examined a number of biblical texts and concluded, "The aim of the Bible is to give redemptive truth. It never intended to teach science; nor does it ever claim to be 'inerrant whenever it touches on science.'"[10] The difficulty with Seely's approach is that he implies biblical language is errant when it touches on science, but we can separate that from the Bible's "inerrant" truth about spiritual and redemptive matters.

Such an approach, it seems to me, does injustice to the Bible. To treat biblical passages such as Genesis 1–2 and Psalm 104 as if they exemplify primitive science is to adopt modern scientific criteria to evaluate them. But most of the biblical texts Seely cites have a metaphorical character drawn from everyday experience. Biblical texts also speak of God's strong arm achieving victory, of trees clapping their hands in praise, of the divine bridegroom choosing Israel as his bride. Those anthropomorphisms and figures of speech, when combined with the intensification of ordinary language about ordinary experience, do not represent primitive scientific judgments that can now be trumped by more up-to-date science. The images and language that served ancient Israelites and many other ancient peoples arose from daily experience that gave birth to countless metaphors and similes that we continue to use today. We still say the sun rises and sets; we recognize human and animal figures in celestial formations; we liken birdsong or children singing to the voices of angels; and we still *lift* our voices in joy and in anger.

Reading the Bible with this in mind, we can recognize that biblical language often has a depth of meaning with multiple allusions that must be taken on its own terms. "Heaven" or "the heavens" might indeed be used to refer to the sky above, which does appear as an awesome dome with lights in it. At the same time, the word is used to refer to where God sits, or is enthroned, far above and beyond our grasp and understanding. The language is neither science nor myth; it arises from ordinary experience that is extended and intensified through imaginative metaphors.

There is no reason whatsoever to judge that the Bible speaks authoritatively only about so-called redemptive truth. That is a misguided judgment based on assumptions that come from outside the world and texts of the Bible. Moreover, that judgment belongs to a restricted view of the Christian way of life that we rejected at the outset of this book, namely, the idea that the Bible primarily (or only) tells a sin-and-salvation story, which has little bearing on the meaning of creation and our daily lives. There are many things the Bible does not say or teach, yet it can be understood properly only in terms of its own frames of reference.

Jürgen Moltmann does something different in interpreting the relation of earth to heaven in an architectural order of below and above. Instead of working with the imagery inherent in the presentation of God's seven-day week of creation in Genesis 1–2, Moltmann takes for granted a modern problem about spatial reference that does not exist in the Bible. The theological problem he wants to resolve is how to think about God as being both *above* or outside creation and at the same time immanent *within* the creation. Theological tradition, he argues, has tended to make God's

10. Seely, "Three-Storied Universe," 22.

transcendence of the creation more important than God's immanence in creation. It thereby "puts God and the world over against one another."[11] In my judgment, however, Moltmann is struggling unnecessarily with an abstract problem of space that he brings to the text from the outside—from another frame of reference.

Let me illustrate: once when I was lecturing at a college far from where I lived, the topic of human relationships came up and I remarked that I was closer to my wife than I was to any of the students. They understood me perfectly and no one asked how that was possible, since I was standing just feet from them and yet was hundreds of miles from my wife. When I tell my children that they are in my heart, they pose no question about how that is possible, physically speaking. The Bible speaks of the creator who transcends creation, who is not a creature but rather the origin and ruler of creation. Moreover, the God who creates is also the one, biblically speaking, who is with us in any number of ways: as the bridegroom who loves his bride; as a teacher who works with her students; as a shepherd who cares for his sheep; or as a mother who nurses her child. There are no spatial contradictions or problems here in these ordinary experiences and the language we use to speak of them.

Yet because Moltmann starts by locating the relation of God to creation in "space," he must then try to overcome the contradiction of God being both "in" and "out" at the same time. His resolution of the problem is to say that both transcendence and immanence originate within God. "So if God as Creator stands over against his creation, he also stands over against himself. If the creation stands over against its Creator, God again stands over against himself. The God who is transcendent in relation to the world, and the God who is immanent in that world are one and the same God . . . [Thus] God is in himself, and yet he is at the same time outside himself. He is outside himself in his creation, and is yet at the same time in himself, in his sabbath."[12] If those sentences sound confusing, it is because Moltmann has held onto the spatial contradiction while declaring it resolved dialectically "within" God.

Notice, however, that up until the last word of the quotation—"sabbath"—the two poles Moltmann refers to are God and creation, logically distinct from one another. But with the word "sabbath" Moltmann adds something quite different in trying to overcome the spatial contradiction. He uses the language of Genesis to identify God's very close and intimate relation to creation. Whatever Moltmann's reasons for doing that, it is clear from Genesis that the creation's seventh day—God's rest—is not an abstract spatial category but belongs to the encompassing metaphor of God's creation week. That metaphor has nothing to do with the problem of transcendence and immanence in the abstract. God's day of rest is, indeed, the creation's seventh day, and that is where creatures meet God in the divinely created day of fulfillment. But God's transcendence and immanence are not at spatial odds with each other in this reality. Nonetheless, Moltmann continues to hold on to the idea of a "double world of heaven

11. Moltmann, *God in Creation*, 14.

12. Moltmann, *God in Creation*, 15.

and earth" rather than reading the full creation story on its own terms. Consequently, he cannot recognize that "heaven" is part of the creation as God's day of rest in relation to all that has been created. Instead, Moltmann says, "We call the side of creation which is open to God 'heaven.' From heaven and through heaven God acts on earth. Heaven represents the relative 'beyond' of the world, and the earth is the relative this-worldliness of heaven. In heaven creation has its relative transcendence. In the earth creation finds its relative immanence."[13]

The architectural image that comes through in Genesis 1–2, I am suggesting, reflects the experience and stories of monarchs establishing royal palaces or temples at the center of their kingdoms. The biblical author sees God as the great King above all kings, the one who creates an all-embracing seven-day wonder as his royal domain. In fact, the idea of God building the creation as his dwelling place is one of the dominant, many-sided metaphors in the Bible. The Garden of Eden, the tabernacle, the temple, the people of Israel, the body of Christ—all of these reveal something about, and point toward, the climactic, seventh-day fulfillment of them all. Every earthly expression of God dwelling with his people and the people with God serve as revelatory images of God's larger, creation-wide building project. The architectural wonder of creation is that all creatures in all their glory are made for God, for relationship with God, and for fulfillment in God's unending sabbath celebration.

13. Moltmann, *God in Creation*, 182.

4

The Human Generations

WHAT DOES IT MEAN to be human? Who are we? Who am I? Is there any purpose to life? Is there life beyond the span of our earthly days? These questions are not simply about bodily need or social circumstances, nor are they questions for scholars alone. They arise from the heart and cry out for answers. Yet by the time we begin to ask such burning questions we are already immersed in life with hopes and disappointments, with goals and doubts. None of us can start from scratch to try to find answers to such questions *before* we begin to live.[1]

From the outset of this book we have been forthright in stating our aim, which is to approach these and other questions from a biblical point of view, however preliminary and inadequate our attempt may be. And we are already well into what the Bible has to tell us about what it means to be human, male and female, in our generations. Humans are God's final sixth-day creature, made in the divine image and likeness, commissioned to serve as procreating caretakers, developers, and governors of earthly life in service to the creator whose day of rest brings the creation week to its mysterious and enticing climax. Human life throughout our unfolding generations develops in interdependent relation to all other creatures and in personal relation to the creator whose image we bear.[2] It is within that order of creation, according to the Bible, that we become aware of our deepest questions about life's meaning.

1. Today, many speak of humans having or operating with a "worldview"—an outlook on life that functions like eyeglasses through which we see everything. Wright, for example, is at pains to show that all biblical interpretation depends on various presuppositions and assumptions, including the stories and pre-commitments that shape each interpreter's worldview. There is no neutral, unbiased standpoint from which to interpret the Bible. See Wright, *New Testament*, 1–144. For more on the meaning of "worldview" see Naugle, *Worldview*; Wolters, *Creation Regained*; Walsh and Middleton, *Transforming Vision*; Heslam, *Creating a Christian Worldview*; Newbigin, *Gospel in a Pluralist Society*; Bartholomew and Goheen, *Drama of Scripture*.

2. McConville writes that "the human as 'image of God' finds deep interconnections among God, the human, and the nonhuman creation." The kind of responsibility that belongs to humans "by virtue of being 'in the image of God' does not stop with interhuman relationships but extends to the nonhuman creation, for it is to this that the command to 'have dominion' applies (1:26, 28)." McConville,

THE CREATION'S GENERATIONS

The most distinguishing organizational feature of the book of Genesis as a whole is the sequence of ten *toledoth* sections that introduce ancestor narrative epics. *Toledoth* is the Hebrew word for generations. In Genesis, the word is used within a larger phrase, "according to their *toledoth*," which means something like a genealogical account. Used in this way, says Duane Garrett, "*toledoth* is a technical term for a method of keeping family and clan records."[3] For example, in Genesis 5:1, an account of Adam's generations is introduced. Later there are the records of Noah's (10:1) and Shem's (11:10) generations. Thereafter, we learn of the generations of Abram's father Terah (11:27) and the long story leading up to the generations of Abraham's children Ishmael (25:12) and Isaac (25:19). Then come Isaac's sons Esau (36:1) and Jacob (37:2) with an account thereafter of Jacob's sons, especially of Judah and Joseph. Genesis is a book about the generations of the image of God, particularly about the generations leading to and descending from Jacob (Israel).[4]

From the account of these generations we learn, among other things, that God's covenant with Israel is not the beginning of God's work with the human generations and that God's redemption of Israel from Egypt is not the beginning of covenant history. As N. T. Wright points out, "*the promises to Abraham* directly echo the *commands to Adam*."[5] There is a clear "correlation between the placing of Adam and Eve in the garden of Eden and the promise to Abraham and his family about the land of Canaan."[6] The same can be said of God's covenant with Noah after the flood, which has the character of a creation-renewal covenant, implying the covenantal character of the creation order itself. Wright quotes Michael Fishbane who says that Genesis 9:1–9 presents Noah "as 'a new Adam', who 'presides over a restored world, a renewal of creation depicted in the terms and imagery of Gen 1:26–31.'"[7] The point is that the listing of the generations from Adam to the children of Israel is important not only as an introduction to God's covenant with Israel, but also as an introduction to God's relation to the human generations in their entirety.

Somewhat surprisingly, however, the first use of the *toledoth* phrase in Genesis 2:4a is not about human generations. The verse says, "These are the generations [*toledoth*] of the heavens and the earth when they were created." Here, the phrase does not introduce a family clan but rather everything that God creates. According to Garrett and others, we can best understand the wording as an expression of literary creativity

---

Being Human, 25, 28.

3. Garrett, *Rethinking Genesis*, 93. For more on *toledoth*, see Provan, *Discovering Genesis*, 1–6, and McDowell, *Image of God*, 28–33.

4. See Alexander, "From Adam to Judah"; and Moye, "In the Beginning."

5. Wright, *Paul and Faithfulness*, 785.

6. Wright, *Paul and Faithfulness*, 787.

7. Wright, *Paul and Faithfulness*, 787. On the creation as God's *covenant order* see Boda, *Heartbeat*, 90–103; Kline, *By Oath Consigned*, 26–27; and Provan, *Discovering Genesis*, 6–11, 108–15.

that ties the grand story of creation in Genesis 1 to the main body of Genesis that follows.[8] Garrett's insight is of considerable significance for our purposes. Although the creation story that opens the book of Genesis is an "overture,"[9] distinct from the ten generational sections that follow it, the passage 1:1—2:3 displays an important literary characteristic that is repeated often in what follows. At critical junctures throughout the book, particularly in the *toledoth* sections, a brief summary statement is followed by an elaboration of details implied by, or entailed within, the summary statement. Genesis 1:1, for example, sums up the entire story of creation in a nutshell, declaring that God created the heavens and the earth—everything.[10] That declaration is then followed by the more detailed elaboration of God's six days of creating and seventh day of rest.

In the narrative following the first verse of Genesis we learn, among other things, that God creates humans, male and female, and commissions them for their unique role in creation. Humans are the last of God's sixth-day creatures. After this narrative about the sixth day and God's pronouncement that the whole creation is "very good," God rests on the seventh day, blessing it and making it holy. The overarching narrative of God's seven-day creation week is now complete, at least in summary. Then, beginning with Genesis 2:4, the narrator draws us back inside the part of the story in Genesis 1 where God fashions the human creature. In contrast to Genesis 1:1—2:3 where the author is standing, as it were, in the presence of the creator, here in 2:4 and following, says Stek, the author "stands with his feet on the earth, in the arena of human history."[11] Very quickly, beginning with 2:7, we find ourselves reading about God making the human creature from the dust of the ground, placing that creature in a garden where animals are named and God divides the human creature into male and female.

In terms of the structure and flow of the text, in other words, the story about God making the man and the woman in Genesis 2 can be nothing other than an elaboration of what we have already been told in Genesis 1 about God creating human beings, male and female, in the divine image (1:26–30). With Genesis 2:7 and following, we are drawn into the story of the unfolding generations of humankind, *which is the generational unfolding of the final creature of God's sixth-day.*[12] Genesis 4 tells of

8. Garrett, *Rethinking Genesis*, 99.

9. Wenham, *Genesis 1–15*, 39.

10. Fretheim supports the idea that Gen 1:1 is a "summary of the chapter . . . because other genealogies (note 'generations' as descriptive of what *precedes*, 2:4a) begin with an independent sentence that provides a summary of what follows (see 5:1; 6:9; 10:1; 11:10)." Fretheim, *God and World*, 35. The first verse, according to Renckens, is "a short summary of the whole pericope." Renckens, *Israel's Concept*, 45.

11. Stek, "What Says the Scripture?," 235.

12. Thomas Keiser writes: "A review of Genesis 2 shows that it seems to presume the existence of that which was created in ch. 1. More specifically, Genesis 2 deals particularly with that which appeared on the sixth day of creation, namely, animals and humankind, plants as food, and the relationship between them. Since the structure of the Genesis 1 creation account clearly presents humankind

Adam and Eve having children, which is the story of the first couple doing what God commissioned and blessed them to do in Genesis 1:28: "Be fruitful and multiply." In Genesis 5:1, where the "list of the descendants [*toledoth*] of Adam" is given, the author again emphasizes the sixth-day identity of human creatures: "When God created humankind, he made them in the likeness of God. Male and female he created them, and he blessed them and named them 'Humankind' when they were created" (5:1–2). From Genesis 2:7 through the rest of Genesis, we find ourselves in the arena of human generational development, a narrative that can be about nothing other than the drama of the sixth-day human creatures in their relation to one another, to all other creatures and, above all, to God who orients the whole creation toward its seventh-day climax. And since humans have not yet stopped generating, you and I have our identity in the "time" of the *sixth-day* generations of humankind.[13] God's day of human and animal creatures has not yet reached completion.

Catherine McDowell explains the relation between Genesis 1 and 2 by showing that Genesis 2:4 functions as a transitional link "intended both as an introduction to the Eden story in Gen. 2:5—3:24 *and* as a summary of the creation account in Gen 1:1—2:3."[14] Genesis 2:4, she argues, functions as other *toledoth* phrases do, "as the conduit through which the focus narrows from the general to the particular: in this case, from the creation of the universe, which includes the creation of humanity . . . to the creation of humanity and their subsequent history . . ." Thus, the Eden story is "to be understood as the sequel to Gen 1:1—2:3 rather than a distinct or competing account of creation."[15] Iain Provan agrees: "The whole verse [Gen 2:4] is a carefully and coherently crafted introduction to what follows in Genesis 2, consciously picking up the language of the preceding Genesis 1." The two chapters "do not sit on the page now as two creation stories. They exist now as one entity, albeit looking at creation from slightly differing perspectives."[16]

Since it is evident to us today that human procreation continues, it follows that the human generations have not reached their end and men and women have not yet completed their sixth-day commission from God. The meaning and purpose of human life on earth has not yet reached fulfillment. The human generations continue to unfold in relation to God and interdependently with all other creatures. In the text

---

as the climax of God's work, it is no surprise that Genesis 2 takes up, in detail, that particular facet of creation. Additionally, not only does Genesis 2 take up the climax of creation as presented in the prior chapter, it features the same focus." Keiser, "Divine Plural," 144.

13. See Santmire, "Genesis Creation Narratives," 372–77.

14. McDowell, *Image of God*, 33.

15. McDowell, *Image of God*, 34.

16. Provan, *Discovering Genesis*, 60. As Stek explains, God's creating word did not call into being "an aggregate of entities" separate from one another "but components designed to function within the economy of an integrated realm," and therefore "the preserving and governing power of [God's] creation word cannot be isolated from the functioning economy of the creatures, from their 'concurrence.' The creation's economy continues to be governed by the Creator's decrees—his *creation decrees*." Stek, "What Says the Scripture?," 248.

of Genesis 1, God's word of reproductive blessing accompanies the creation of the fish, birds, and humankind (and presumably also the land animals), as Stek explains. Thus, "the self-generating creatures are preserved according to their nature by the continuing effectiveness of the once-for-all divine word of blessing."[17] With regard to humans, God's words, "Let us make" and "Be fruitful," are spoken about the "day" that finds its wrap-up in the phrase "and there was evening, and there was morning—the sixth day" (Gen 1:31). Michael Welker puts it this way: "Genesis 1 and 2 describe the entire creation as in many respects having its own activity, as being itself productive, as being itself causative. *The creature's own activity, which is itself a process of production, is not only a consequence and result of a creation that is already completed. Rather it is embedded in the process of creation and participates in that process.*"[18]

If we keep in mind everything said thus far about the architecture and the content of the creation days as presented in Genesis 1:1—2:3, we can see from our earthly point of view that God's sixth day of creation is not yet wrapped up. And since humans are unable to exercise their responsibilities and come to know themselves without light from the sun, moon, and stars, food to eat, water to drink, dry land to live on, plants and animals, and fellowship with one another and with God, then none of God's six creation days has yet been wrapped up. God's blessing sustains all of the creation days in their interdependent unfolding together. Moreover, God's celebrative rest will be fulfilled only when the actions and assignments of the creatures are complete to God's satisfaction. God's day of rest, set apart as the hallowed climax and fulfillment of all things, thus represents the day in relation to which all created things are oriented for their fulfillment.[19]

17. Stek, "What Says the Scripture?," 248–49. According to Fretheim, "Reproduction is a responsibility that human beings have in order to be the image of God they were created to be. The genealogies, so prominent in Genesis 1–11, witness to the fulfillment of this human responsibility; the genealogies may be said to speak of the spread of the image of God throughout the world." Fretheim, *God and World,* 50. With respect to ongoing reproduction as part of God's creative word, Calvin says that all fruit bearing "flows from the same word." There is no other cause for this but "that God has spoken." Calvin, *Commentary on Genesis,* 83. Blocher comments that the "frequency of the 'etymological figure,' also called the 'internal accusative': let the earth (literally) 'green with greenery' and with plants 'seeding seeds' (Gen 1:11, 12, 29); let the waters 'swarm with swarms' and let the 'winged creatures take wing' (1:20)' means that 'the instrumentality of the word follows infallibly on the word.'" Blocher, *In the Beginning,* 67. On the dynamic unfolding of human responsibilities in response to God, see McConville, *Being Human,* 24–29.

18. Welker, *Creation and Reality,* 10–11. Soskice contends, "Creation is not something that happened to the universe long ago. It is not the distant accomplishment of a distant God. *Creatio ex nihilo* [creation from nothing] underscores the belief that God imparts the being of all created things, visible and invisible. The world is graced in its createdness which is happening all the time." Soskice, "Creation and Glory," 185.

19. "There is much that philosophy could learn from the Bible," writes Heschel. "To the philosopher the idea of the good is the most exalted idea. But to the Bible the idea of the good is penultimate; it cannot exist without the holy. The good is the base, the holy is the summit. Things created in six days He considered *good,* the seventh day He made *holy.*" Heschel, "The Sabbath," 75.

Seen from the vantage point of earthly creatures, God's rest is in "heaven." God transcends—sits "above"—the creation as the one who creates all things, evaluates all things, and draws all things toward the climactic revelation of the divine glory. At the same time, the creator has bound himself to the creation as the one whose day of rest is also the creation's culmination and fulfillment. God's relation to creation in seventh-day holiness means that the entire creation exists to serve as God's hospitable host for the celebration of the divine glory. As Fretheim says, "the creation is not 'finished' *until* the seventh day. That is to say, the seventh day as a day of rest is built by God into the created order of things."[20]

THE IMAGE OF GOD, MALE AND FEMALE

McDowell observes that Genesis 1 speaks of various creatures reproducing "after their kind" or "according to its kind." With respect to humans, however, that phrase is not used. The text speaks of humans simply as God's image and likeness who are then blessed with the commission to fill the earth and subdue it. This suggests, says McDowell, that "the author was drawing a sharp distinction between humans and the other created beings." It implies that "humans were made, at some level, according to *Elohim's* [God's] *kind*, although not literally born of God."[21] This insight is supported by subsequent biblical texts that speak of humans as God's children or spouse, servants or vassals, artisans or rulers. Humans reproduce in their generations yet with an identity that is not merely "after their kind." They are revelatory of God in a uniquely relational way.[22]

Those textual distinctions are important for our understanding of the sexual differentiation of the image of God into male and female. Genesis 1:26–27 says simply that humankind is made in God's image and likeness, male and female. In Genesis 2:7–21 the human creature God makes from the dust of the ground is what Provan describes as "proto-human, because before we get to Genesis 2.22–25, we do not even have a male and a female, which together make up the image of God in Genesis 1 . . . Genesis 2.18 is explicit about this: 'It is *not good* for the man [the human] to be alone.' The creation of humanity is not yet complete."[23] Therefore, the word "human" used in Genesis 2:7 (*ha'adam*, "the creature that comes from the ground," *ha'adamah*) might best be translated as "earthling," which, according to Provan, captures the "play on *'adam* and *'adamah* in the [Hebrew]. It is only with the naming of the woman as 'Eve' in Genesis 3:20 that it becomes sensible then to go further and to translate *'adam* as a personal name, Adam."[24] The creature made in God's image is male and female

20. Fretheim, *God and World*, 61.
21. McDowell, *Image of God,* 132–33.
22. On this, see McConville, *Being Human*, 61–95.
23. Provan, *Discovering Genesis*, 68.
24. Provan, *Discovering Genesis*, 68, and further, 75–78, 89–92.

together, with all of the talents and capabilities God has given them for exercising many kinds of responsibility in the service of God.

With respect to the meaning of "the image of God," therefore, we should not look for a particular characteristic of human identity that constitutes the "image." Some, for example, have argued that the rational soul or reason is what makes humans the image of God. Others argue that it was the original righteousness prior to sinful disobedience that defined the image of God; and some say it is the male-female relationship that makes humans God's image.[25] Yet the biblical texts do not point in any of these directions. Humans, the image of God, are male and female in relation to one another; they are able to think and reason, to work and rest, to socialize and economize, to use creative imagination, to love and care for one another, and to worship God. But all of these characteristics together belong to and manifest the multigenerational creature that is, as a whole, made in God's image.

Abraham Kuyper asked whether Christians have underestimated the significance of what it means to be created in the image of God when they think only of individual persons. "Do we not come closer to the truth by saying that the bearer of the full multifaceted image of God is not the individual person but our entire human race? . . . Is it not true that, not individually but socially, the image of God can be understood in all its dimensions only if we look at what the immensely rich development of our entire race permits us to see of it?"[26] Kuyper was at his best urging Christians to develop and exercise their responsibilities in every area of life to the glory of God.[27] That is the context—the full creational context—in which the meaning of the image of God becomes manifest. Most human responsibilities involve organized efforts developed over time in families and schools, in rural communities and large cities, in the arts and the sciences, in agricultural enterprises and political communities, in business enterprises and labor unions. The distinctiveness and dignity of each person flourishes only through a variety of relationships, social organizations, and communities. Jürgen Moltmann also lays stress on the wholeness of human life in this regard. "[W]hat makes the human being God's image," says Moltmann, "is not his possession

---

25. The most influential church father, Augustine (354–430), is the source of several different interpretations of the meaning of "the image and likeness of God" in Genesis. See the fine essay by Matthew Puffer summarizing Augustine's three basic views with seven revisions of those views developed over his lifetime. Puffer, "Human Dignity," 65–82. Barth says "there is no point in asking in which of man's peculiar attributes and attitudes [the "image of God"] consists." Barth, *Church Dogmatics*, 184. Yet Barth then argues that the male-female relation is the key to understanding the image of God—"a copy and imitation of his Creator" and "at the same time a type of the history of the covenant and salvation which will take place between him and his Creator." Barth, *Church Dogmatics*, 186–87.

26. Kuyper, *Abraham Kuyper*, 165–201, 177. Compared to all other creatures, Kuyper wrote elsewhere, humans are "nobler, richer, more glorious; and especially that this higher glory consists in the more *intimate bond* and *closer relation*" they have to their creator. Kuyper, *Work of the Holy Spirit*, 219.

27. See his Stone Lectures presented at Princeton University in 1898, *Lectures on Calvinism*, in which he discusses art, science, and politics.

of any particular characteristic or other . . . ; it is his whole existence."[28] Among other things, "Likeness to God cannot be lived in isolation. It can be lived only in human community. This means that from the very outset human beings are social beings."[29]

McDowell's masterful study compares the opening of Genesis with the creation myths of Mesopotamia and ancient Egypt, and she suggests that the divine-human relationship as presented in Genesis 1 has "three major components that are intimately related to one another: kinship, kingship, and cult."[30] The intimate relation of God to humans is familial in character, which at the time of the biblical writing emphasized the relation of father to son. This comes through in Genesis 5:1–3 "where Adam begets a son, Seth, 'in his own likeness and after his image.'" Moreover, in Genesis and elsewhere, as McDowell shows, the fact that humans, metaphorically speaking, are God's son is closely related to human kingship under God. God's son is the "king ruling at God's behest as his representative." If being human entails a filial relation to God, then "being created in the image of God carries with it the responsibility to represent God and his standards in the realm of law and justice, as in Gen 9:6."[31]

Furthermore, for men and women to be God's royal son who represents God on earth contrasts with the practice in other Near Eastern kingdoms where a king places a statue or marker on the land he has conquered to represent his sovereignty over it. The biblical image and likeness of God is not a cult statue. Instead, men and women are God's living vicegerents on earth. In sum, writes McDowell, "(1) humans, unlike the other created beings, were designed to be in a filial relationship with God, (2) humans were created to rule over creation, and (3) humans rather than statues, are the 'images' who were created to dwell in the divine presence."[32]

Considering McDowell's points carefully, we cannot help but feel, when reading Genesis 1 and 2, that we are present at the opening of a grand drama. Man and woman created for procreation do more than merely perpetuate an animal species. To have the identity of the image and likeness of God is to participate in God's family, to dwell in the Lord's house, to live and walk and build with the creator of the universe, and to govern the earth as the King's prime ministers.

28. Moltmann, *God in Creation*, 221.

29. Moltmann, *God in Creation*, 222.

30. McDowell, *Image of God*, 136–37.

31. McDowell, *Image of God*, 137. McDowell's connecting of kinship and kingship echoes the major thesis of Hahn, *Kinship by Covenant*, in which he brings out the profound meaning of *kin* and *covenant* in the Bible.

32. McDowell, *Image of God*, 141. For more on the comparison of biblical kingship with patterns of other Near Eastern kings, see Kline, *Treaty of Great King*.

THRONE AND FOOTSTOOL

The oft-cited Psalm 104 expresses wonder at the mystery of God's creation in language that portrays a vast kingdom of joyful and blessed servants of the Lord.[33] The creator is the Lord Almighty, "clothed with honor and majesty," says the psalmist,

> You make springs gush forth in the valleys;
>   they flow between the hills,
> giving drink to every wild animal;
>   the wild asses quench their thirst.
> By the streams the birds of the air have their habitation;
>   they sing among the branches.
> From your lofty abode you water the mountains;
>   the earth is satisfied with the fruit of your work.
> You cause the grass to grow for the cattle,
>   and plants for people to use,
> to bring forth food from the earth,
>   and wine that gladdens the human heart,
> oil to make the face shine,
>   and bread to strengthen the human heart . . .
> O Lord, how manifold are your works!
>   In wisdom you have made them all;
>   the earth is full of your creatures . . .
> These all look to you to give them their food in due season . . . (Ps 104:10–15, 24, 27).

When Isaiah conveys God's voice saying, "Heaven is my throne and the earth is my footstool" (66:1), we see in one simple picture the integral relation of the first six days of creation to God's seventh-day glory. Throne and footstool belong together in a single throne room, in a single palace, in a creation-wide kingdom. They exist together in a single drama that has not yet reached its culmination. Seen from the standpoint of the sixth-day human generations, the creation's celebration of the final unveiling of God's kingdom-glory still lies ahead. Nevertheless, even now, through eyes of faith, we are able to anticipate that coming glory. Commenting on the testimony of the Apostle Paul, Wright says, "Paul's vision of the new creation, of the whole world flooded with God's glory at last, corresponds to the Isaianic vision in which the Temple itself is relativized by the whole creation, heaven and earth together, becoming God's 'resting place.'"[34]

Isaiah's "throne and footstool" imagery is perfectly in tune with the music of Psalm 8, which in turn echoes the dramatic overture of Genesis 1.

33. On Psalm 104 and related passages see Brown, *Seeing Psalms*, 158–62; Fretheim, *God and World*, particularly 35–36, 139–40, 217, 261–62, 280; Boda, *Heartbeat*, 89–94; and Anderson, "Introduction," 13.

34. Wright, *Paul and Faithfulness*, 561.

O Lord, our Sovereign,
   how majestic is your name in all the earth!
You have set your glory above the heavens . . .
When I look at your heavens, the work of your fingers,
   the moon and the stars that you have established;
what are human beings that you are mindful of them,
   mortals that you care for them?
Yet you have made them a little lower than God,
   and crowned them with glory and honor.
You have given them dominion over the works of your hands;
   you have put all things under their feet . . . (Ps 8:1, 3–6).[35]

God's rule as creator and Lord is the basis for the responsibilities that belong to the image of God on earth. The Lord is the one who appoints us governors and developers of the earth, putting everything under our feet. That picture of the world "put under our feet" is clearly part of the good order of creation in which humans are commissioned to steward and govern rightly to the praise of God. The portrait of the image of God as God's righteous sub-ruler on the earth—the king's plenipotentiaries—tells us that dramatic action on their part is built into the creation. Human governance, just like family life and friendship, gardening and shepherding, is part of what it means to be human and revelatory of God. According to Stek,

> At the apex of the account [of God creating humans] we find a number of especially intriguing evocations of kingly action. First, before proceeding to the creation of humankind, God announces his momentous intention to do so. Both in itself and in the language employed, this announcement recalls the scene in a royal council chamber in which a king announces his impending action to the members of his court (cf. Gen 3:22; 11:7; 1 Kgs 22:19; Isa 6:8) . . . That humanity is to be created in God's "image" and "likeness" and assigned rule over the creatures in the earth further signifies God's kingly status. No metaphor so permeates [the story following Gen 1:1—2:3] as does the political metaphor of king and kingdom. In narrative, prophecy, and psalmody, in Gospels, epistles, and Apocalypse, God's kingship and kingdom are presupposed, proclaimed, invoked, revered, and sung.[36]

35. For mention or discussion of numerous biblical passages that ground redemption in creation, see Fretheim, *God and World*; Brown, *Seeing Psalms*; and Perdue, *Wisdom and Creation*, especially 77–122.

36. Stek, "What Says the Scripture?," 233–34. See also Middleton, *Liberating Image*, 50–55, 70–74, 88. According to Waltke and Fredricks, the picture of God's throne room best explains the phrase in Gen 1:26 where God says "Let us make humankind in our image." Here, God is "addressing the angels or heavenly court (cf. 1 Kings 22:19–22; Job 1:6; 2:1; 38:7; Ps 29:1–3; 89:5–6; Isa 6:8; 40:1–6; Dan 10:12–13; Luke 2:8–14)." *Genesis*, 64. In connection with the picture of the divine court, Welker offers some valuable insights into the meaning and function of court angels and messenger angels. Welker, *Creation and Reality*, 45–59.

The creator's assessment that the creation is "very good" covers everything God has commissioned humans to do in their generations (Gen 1:26–31). Based on Genesis 1:1—2:3, therefore, we would be right to expect that after humans have completed the work God has given them to do, they will hear God's benediction, "Well done, good and faithful servants. Enter my rest."[37] The drama of God's seven-day creation, in which human governing reveals something about God's supreme governance, moves forward toward a goal, toward fulfillment.

As we know full well, the story of Adam and Eve turning away from unquestioned trust in God (the story that begins in Genesis 3) suddenly looms large.[38] Human disobedience and irresponsibility that continue into our day call into question the viability of God's creational purposes and even God's integrity. Consequently, in view of the degradation and death we have brought upon one another in defiance of our creator, how can God's assessment that everything is "very good" still be true? God has placed immense responsibility in human hands. We are so much like God that we appear to have the power to destroy the very possibility of creation reaching fulfillment in God's sabbath. The repeated phrases in the creation story, "and God saw that it was good," together with God's final word of "very good," are thus fraught with tremendous tension. How can the good creation culminate in God's glorious sabbath fulfillment if the image of God fails to be the faithful servant God created them to be?[39] According to Wright, commenting on Paul's letter to the Romans, "the tragedy of Adam is not just that he introduced sin and hence death into the world, but that humans were made to be the creator's wise agents over creation, and if they worship and serve the creature rather than the creator this purpose goes unfulfilled."[40]

At this juncture we will not explore further the mystery and tragedy of human sinfulness. We can say, however, that in the light of Genesis 1 and 2, the basic

---

37. Kuyper ventures to speculate that "sinless man would not have died . . . that as a reward for his work he would have received eternal life, i.e., being perfectly able from moment to moment to do God's will, he would always have desired and loved to do it; and for this he would have been rewarded continually with larger measures of the life and glory of God." Kuyper, *Work of Holy Spirit*, 249.

38. On the story of human disobedience in the garden and the meaning of their expulsion from it, see Provan, *Discovering Genesis*, 79–112; Provan, *Seriously Dangerous Religion*, 109–24, 134–43, 191–207; McDowell, *Image of God*, 22–42; Blocher, *In the Beginning*, 111–212.

39. In the extended biblical-theological interpretation of God's judgment and redemption of creation, Kline sheds light on the meaning of the statements in Gen 1 about God's "seeing" and "judging" that all is good. "What is in view here is the refrain: 'God saw that it was good.' Divine pronouncement, not just casual observation, is the meaning. God, judging his own works in this case, pronounced them good, so signifying that his fiat-decree had been fully executed . . . In the seventh, summarizing occurrence the pronouncement is heightened to 'very good.' Seven acts of 'seeing' by the Spirit-Creator are recorded and here, it would seem, is the ultimate source of the imagery of 'the seven eyes which are the seven Spirits of God sent forth into all the earth' (Rev 5:6) on judicial missions, the seven eyes which are seven torches of the fire burning before the Glory-throne of judgment (Rev 4:5)." Kline, *Images of Spirit*, 109–10. Fretheim also emphasizes the importance of God as "the evaluator." Fretheim, *God and World*, 40–42, 108, 163–68, 235–37.

40. Wright, *Resurrection*, 249.

and enduring patterns of human injustice against fellow humans and against other creatures find no justification in the creation order of God's seven-day week. God's creation of male and female, who are jointly the image of God, may not be read as justifying male domination of women, for example. God's mandate to humans to fill the earth and subdue it may not be read as justifying the use of other creatures in ways that endanger the ecological well-being of all creatures. The responsibility of men and women together to exercise dominion over the earth requires responsible stewardship of animals and all other creatures because they are God's creatures, not ours, and we are stewards of God's creation, not masters of our own domain.[41]

The consequences of our failure to love God and neighbors and to care for the earth have, from the beginning, driven those suffering injustice to cry out for God's mercy and for God's judgment on evildoers. How can a good God allow human depravity to continue? After Cain killed his brother, God heard Abel's blood cry out from the ground. Psalmists and prophets give voice to the sufferings of innocents. Today, so many people suffer from the horrors of crimes against humanity, starvation, constant wars and oppression, degradation of the environment, and lesser crimes and injustices everywhere. Why, O Lord, do the righteous suffer and the unrighteous get away with theft and murder?

Part of the answer to these agonizing pleas for rectification and mercy has come, and continues to come, through God's particular judgments and healings, through restraints of evildoers and protections against many kinds of destruction. Yet the darkness of our sins continues to hang over the world and to shape history and each of us in countless destructive ways. God's promises of a reordered world have not yet been fulfilled, and there are no quick, cheap answers for those suffering great harms. In the chapters ahead we will deal in greater detail with sin and evil and try to understand some of the ways in which God has responded in judgment and mercy, in curses and blessings. Everything about the seven-day creation order is at stake in this seemingly unresolvable conflict between God's good creation and the sin and degradation that disrupt it. Each of us lives at the center—in the heart—of this mystery whether we acknowledge it or not. The unfolding drama of God's relationship with the human generations continues like a marriage that manifests both sickness and health. There is light shining, but there is also heavy darkness.

The simultaneous and continuing development of the creation's first six days in relation to God's day of rest comprises the whole of reality and contextualizes all human history and the exercise of every human responsibility. Kuyper spoke of the comprehensive character of human responsibility when arguing with some of his fellow Christians whom he thought too narrowly focused on their eternal salvation. The ages of human generational unfolding, he wrote, must continue "in the interest of developing the world itself to its consummation—for as long as is needed to take the

41. See Welker, *Creation and Reality*, 64–73; Provan, *Discovering Genesis*, 75–94; Bouma-Prediger, *For Beauty*, 57–131; Middleton, *Liberating Image*, 204–7, 271–78.

world from its beginning and the earliest germination of our human life to the point where the whole process is complete and God has truly reached the final goal he had in mind for it."[42]

The exercise of human responsibilities throughout history have manifested disobedience as well as obedience, unfaithfulness as well as faithfulness, hatred as well as love, and we know these from within ourselves, not only from the lives of others. The seven days of creation establish all creaturely identities and responsibilities by which a proper understanding of each and every dimension of human and natural life is possible and in relation to which God's judgment and redemption reveal God's justice, love, and covenant faithfulness. This is the context in which human identity as the image of God comes to expression, for humans can discover who they are only in active, faithful response to the one whose image they bear, in service to the one who commissions them for service in the world, which is God's creation. This is the light in which we must come to understand the tragic darkness of human faithlessness to the creator.

42. Kuyper, *Abraham Kuyper*, 165–201, 176.

Part 2

Revelatory Patterns

5

Revelatory Patterns
Introduction

WHO AM I? WHAT does it mean to be human? If those are the central questions of each person's life, then, as we argued in part 1, the deepest and most encompassing answer, *biblically speaking*, is that we are created in the very image of God to be God's governing stewards of the earth. We are the final sixth-day creature in God's seven-day creation, made for personal fellowship and cooperation with God. The generations of the image of God thus live at the heart of God's revelatory purposes.

Yet if our identity is found in being the image of God, who then is the God we image? It would seem that only the creator can answer that question, and the beginning of that answer is God's revelatory act of making man and woman in the divine image. That brings us full circle rather quickly: in order to know ourselves we must know God, and in order to know God we must understand who we are as the image God. Yet that presents another dilemma: biblically speaking, we have no place to stand outside of our relation to the creator from which to gain a detached, start-from-scratch knowledge of ourselves and of God. The apparent dilemma begins to dissolve, however, if we accept the full biblical story. At the core of our identity we are related to God dependently and only in that relationship can we come to the knowledge of God and ourselves.

Moreover, the kind of understanding we need comes only by *doing*—doing what God has called us to do as we walk with him trustingly and faithfully. Consequently, the generations of the image of God must live patiently, trusting the self-revealing God to show us to ourselves through the course of history as we learn to follow the path of life toward God's sabbath-rest with creation. We should think of the entire creation, in other words, as a dynamic, revelatory drama, the patterns of which become evident through God's faithful engagement with all creatures, especially with humans. In the chapters ahead we want to explore four such patterns that we refer to with the following word pairs: (1) honor and hospitality, (2) commission towards commendation, (3) revelation in anticipation, and (4) covenant for community.

In exploring these revelatory patterns we are not setting out on a philosophical quest to discover laws by which we can direct our lives by rational judgment.[1] That kind of quest arose in ancient Greece and Rome and greatly influenced world history, including the history of Christianity. Later, when the unity of Western Christendom was coming undone, new ideas of natural and moral law began to guide science, philosophy, and theology, as they do to this day. The revelatory patterns we are going to explore manifest something different about the trustworthiness of the order of God's creation. The Bible speaks repeatedly of God's creation order and the obligatory bonds that hold us accountable to God. Biblical terms include covenant, statutes, promises, loving care, commands, standards, precepts, laws, and guidance. Psalm 119, for example, renders the meaning of *torah* (God's covenant bond) as God's "steadfast love" (v. 41); the "word of truth" (v. 43); "decrees" that "have been my songs wherever I make my home" (v. 54); "righteous ordinances" (v. 62); the "word" that gives hope (v. 81); a "commandment" that "makes me wiser than my enemies (v. 98); "decrees" that produce "more understanding than all my teachers" have (v. 99); and the "word" that serves as a "lamp to my feet and a light to my path" (v. 105).[2]

These are words of rightly-ordered relationships, fidelity, and enduring trust nurtured throughout the course of exercising human responsibilities in faithful response to God. Those words and phrases in Psalm 119 reveal dimensions of God's bond with creation, and indicate how humans should live in relation to God, to one another, and to other creatures. It is by living in tune with God's love and words of life that we come to know ourselves and the God whom we image. If one wants to use the words "natural law" to characterize something that holds for all creatures in their dependence on God, then it is probably best to speak of God's normative standards for creaturely life, or God's steadfast love that upholds all creatures and illumines the path of life on which we should walk. When the Bible speaks of God's ordinances and commandments for creatures, it does so in personal terms. God's faithfulness, love, statutes, and commands are not abstract rules to guide rational judgment; they are more like ligaments that hold life together. They hold us accountable and give guidance in our day-to-day responsibilities of marriage and family, education and worship, gardening and governing, animal husbandry and music-making, home construction and the building of cities. With Genesis 1 in mind, we might think of these revelatory patterns

---

1. My aim in this book is not to engage in detailed study of the history and philosophy of law. Those interested in law and statutes in biblical, Greco-Roman, medieval, and modern experience may want to consider one or more of the following volumes: Van Leeuwen, "Book of Proverbs," 17–264; Perdue, *Wisdom and Creation*; Von Rad, *Wisdom in Israel*; Clements, *One Hundred Years*, 99–117; Voegelin, *Israel and Revelation*; Brague, *Law of God*; Berman, *Law and Revolution*; Tierney, *Idea of Natural Rights*; Witte, *Law and Protestantism*; Witte, *Reformation of Rights*; Dooyeweerd, *Encyclopedia*.

2. For more on the meaning of Ps 119, see Burt, "Your Torah."

as the never-weakening reverberations of God's authoring speech, or as expressions of the never-diminishing warmth of the Word's generative breath. As the psalmist says:

> The heavens are telling the glory of God;
>   and the firmament proclaims his handiwork.
> Day to day pours forth speech,
>   and night to night declares knowledge.
> There is no speech, nor are there words;
>   their voice is not heard;
> yet their voice goes out through all the earth,
>   and their words to the end of the world (Ps 19:1–4).

Of course, as we noted in part 1 and will discuss in greater detail in part 3, our turn away from trust in God toward destruction, disoriented self-knowledge, and death means that nowhere and at no time in history have humans exhibited the unimpeachable faithfulness for which God created us. Thus, the questions of how we ought to live responsibly remain with us as long as God continues to call us to turn in repentance to follow the path of life. In that respect, the revelatory patterns of God's word function to expose human error, disobedience, and faithlessness, which is to say, every deviation from the way of life for which God has created us. God's word stands; the revelatory patterns of creation are secure; it is human rebellion against God that fails.

> The Lord exists forever;
>   your word is firmly fixed in heaven.
> Your faithfulness endures to all generations;
>   you have established the earth, and it stands fast.
> By your appointment they stand today,
>   for all things are your servants.
> If your law had not been my delight,
>   I would have perished in my misery.
> I will never forget your precepts,
>   for by them you have given me life.
> I am yours; save me,
>   for I have sought your precepts.
> The wicked lie in wait to destroy me,
>   but I consider your decrees.
> I have seen a limit to all perfection,
>   but your commandment is exceedingly broad (Ps 119:89–96).

When Hannah took Samuel, the son she thought she would never have, to serve Eli the priest, she prayed:

> My heart exults in the Lord;
>   My strength is exalted in my God . . .
> There is no Holy One like the Lord,

no one besides you;
   there is no Rock like our God . . .
He raises up the poor from the dust;
   he lifts the needy from the ash heap,
to make them sit with princes and inherit a seat of honor.
For the pillars of the earth are the Lord's,
   and on them he has set the world (1 Sam 2:1a, 2, 8).

God's wisdom, according to the Bible, is deeper than all the knowledge we can ever gain.

Surely there is a mine for silver,
   and a place for gold to be refined.
Iron is taken out of the earth,
   and copper is smelted from ore . . .
But where shall wisdom be found?
   and where is the place of understanding?
Mortals do not know the way to it,
   and it is not found in the land of the living . . .
Where then does wisdom come from?
   and where is the place of understanding?
It is hidden from the eyes of all living,
   and concealed from the birds of the air . . .
God understands the way to it,
   and he knows its place.
For he looks to the ends of the earth,
   and sees everything under the heavens . . .
And he said to humankind,
"Truly, the fear of the Lord, that is wisdom;
   and to depart from evil is understanding" (Prov 28:1–2, 12–15, 20–21, 23, 28).

"Who is wise and understanding among you?" asks the apostle James. "Show it by your good life that your works are done with gentleness born of wisdom. But if you have bitter envy and selfish ambition in your hearts, do not be boastful and false to the truth. Such wisdom does not come down from above, but is earthly, unspiritual, devilish. For where there is envy and selfish ambition, there will also be disorder and wickedness of every kind," writes James the open-eyed realist. "But the wisdom from above is first pure, then peaceable, gentle, willing to yield, full of mercy and good fruits, without a trace of partiality or hypocrisy. And a harvest of righteousness is sown in peace for those who make peace" (Jas 3:13–18).

6

Honor and Hospitality

THE FIRST PATTERN OF God's seven-day creation we want to consider is honor and hospitality. Each creature has a distinctive identity, meaning, and purpose—its God-given *honor*. And each creature provides *hospitality* for other creatures in the interdependent pattern of honor and hospitality. In the Genesis story of creation, each new day of creatures builds and depends on those that precede it. Part of the honor of every creature in its day, in other words, is the vocation of hospitality. God's blessings keep building with each new creation day on up to the final "very good"—just right. This beautifully orchestrated reality is a complex diversity of interdependent yet irreducible creatures, each with its own honor, fashioned so that all of them together serve as the hospitable hosts of God. The entire order reflects and bears witness to the greater honor and hospitality of God.

It might sound odd to speak of honor as an inherent characteristic of someone's (or something's) identity. Today we typically speak of *attributing* honor to someone, or of someone *receiving* honor. Yet, as Roger Lundin points out, the word "honor" did once express part of the identity of someone or something. We think of words such as honor and praise as "qualities that are applied to objects by the human consciousness; we honor God, or we praise our elders." But to people centuries ago, "things would have appeared exactly otherwise; for them, 'object[s] somehow emanate honor and praise, in this way performing a kind of personal role' . . . Our praise [of God, for example] is not primarily a work of creative attribution, but one of dependent participation."[1] To be recognized by, or to be in the presence of, someone with great honor is to be honored, to be drawn into that honor. To be a creature of God, especially one made in the image of God, is to reflect the honor of God and to be imbued with the spirit of divine hospitality.

---

1. Lundin, *Believing Again*, 269. Kwame Anthony Appiah recognizes that the word "honor" no longer carries much weight in contemporary writing and conversation, but he tries to show that it is key to an understanding of the revolutions that took place in overcoming slavery, dueling, and the binding of girls' feet. Appiah, *Honor Code*.

This pattern of honor and hospitality characterizes the entire creation. Irreducible light and darkness host the water above and the water beneath, which in turn become the hospitable hosts of dry land, which sustains the life of plants and trees of every kind. All of these creatures, in their increasingly complex interdependence, become the hospitality center for sun, moon, and stars, fish and fowl, animals and humans.[2] Altogether these creatures have the honor of being hospitable servants of their creator. The breadth and depth of this pattern is as inexhaustible as the creation itself, so in this chapter we can do no more than introduce its contours.

Fretheim uses the language of vocation to speak about the interdependent honor and hospitality of creatures. "All creatures have a God-given vocation within God's creation-wide purposes," he writes. For example, while both "human beings and animals are given an independent role" (Gen 1:22, 28; 2:24), they are, at the same time, "keenly dependent upon the ground (along with the trees, 2:9, 16) not only for their sustenance and livelihood but also for their very being (1:29–30; 2:5–7, 19). At the same time, the ground is dependent upon the human for its proper development (2:5, 15), as well as upon the rain (2:5). Moreover, that which is nonhuman is made dependent upon varying forms of 'dominion' exercised by the human (1:28). And both human and nonhuman creatures are caught up in the task of continuing creation (Gen 1:11–13; 2:18–25)."[3] This means, says Fretheim, that there is "*a mutuality of vocation*; both humans and nonhumans are called to a vocation on behalf of each other in the furtherance of God's purposes for the creation."[4] This interdependence of honor and hospitality is also revelatory of God's *covenant* bond with creation. Fretheim writes, "God gives human beings powers and responsibilities in a way that commits God to a certain kind of relationship with them . . . [W]hat creatures do with the gifts they have been given will *make a difference to God*."[5]

When the apostle Paul writes to the Corinthians about the identity of the generations of the first Adam (God's sixth-day human creatures), he does so in comparison with other creatures. "Not all flesh is alike, but there is one flesh for human beings, another for animals, another for birds, and another for fish. There are both heavenly bodies and earthly bodies, but the glory of the heavenly is one thing, and that of the earthly is another" (1 Cor 15:39–40). Each creature is unique with its own honor and glory, and each one reveals something of the greater splendor and honor of their maker. The psalmist expresses awe in considering the vast creation: "O Lord, how manifold are your works! In wisdom you have made them all; the earth is full of your creatures" (Ps 104:24).

The book of Job presents wonderful portraits of the honor and hospitality of diverse nonhuman creatures. Consider, for example, Job's description of the

2. See Fretheim, *God and World*, 270–73.

3. Fretheim, *God and World*, 270–71.

4. Fretheim, *God and World*, 273.

5. Fretheim, *God and World*, 272.

behemoth—perhaps the hippopotamus. "Look at Behemoth, which I made just as I made you; it eats grass like an ox . . .

> For the mountains yield food for it
> where all the wild animals play.
> Under the lotus plants it lies,
> in the covert of the reeds and in the marsh . . .
> Even if the river is turbulent, it is not frightened;
> it is confident though Jordan rushes against its mouth.
> Can one take it with hooks
> or pierce its nose with a snare (Job 40:15, 19–21, 23–24)?

Grasses, marshlands and rivers, all creatures with honor in their own right, serve as the hospitable food, dwelling place, and playground for the behemoth.[6]

Proverbs 14:31 instructs us: "Those who oppresses the poor insult their Maker, but those who are kind to the needy honor him." To exhibit the great honor of being the image of God, humans must be good stewards of one another, which excludes oppressing or showing contempt for any of them. To acknowledge the honor of God and to honor him, those created in God's image must treat one another honorably. The apostle James, writing to "the twelve tribes in the Dispersion," reminds them that they must not show favoritism to the rich and demean the poor for, if you do, "you commit sin and are convicted by the law as transgressors" (Jas 1:1; 2:9). In Mary's song of magnifying the Lord, she praises the mighty one who "has scattered the proud in the thoughts of their hearts." He has "lifted up the lowly" and "filled the hungry with good things, and sent the rich away empty" (Luke 1:51–53). To act proudly in one's own interest, failing to do right by others, is to dishonor oneself, one's neighbors, other creatures, and especially God, the maker of them all.

The fifth commandment in Exodus (20:12) instructs children to "honor your father and your mother, so that your days may be long in the land the Lord your God's is giving you." Of course, parents are to love and care for their children as gifts from God so they can grow up to become mature servants of God and neighbors, exhibiting the honor and hospitality inherent in being human. The exchange of honor and hospitality in a family, between rich and poor, with animals and all other creatures bears witness to the honor of being a member of God's family, of serving as a priest in God's creation-temple, and of holding a high post of public service in God's creation-wide kingdom. Additional examples could be multiplied almost without end; honor and hospitality stand out as part of the very fabric of life in God's seven-day week.

In many respects, this pattern shows the creation to be a complex natural and social ecosystem. The intricate unity of intertwined creatures, each with its own identity and functions, is a coherent and balanced whole, dependent on God. Human

---

6. For more on the speeches of God and Job about creation see Fretheim, *God and World*, 233–46. See also De Witt, *Caring for Creation*, 49–59.

degradation or destruction of any part of the creation, especially other humans, threatens the whole. The history of human violation of both human and nonhuman creatures is a dense and continuing travesty. There is now mounting evidence of ecological imbalances and destruction that may prove irreversible. Our responsibility to act faithfully in developing and governing the earth is the foundation for human ecological attentiveness and environmental care.[7] Of all God's creatures humans have been given the greatest honor, for they alone have received the creator's commission to exercise authority over the earth as an integral part of their relation to God.

The poet of Psalm 8 expresses amazement that God has crowned humans with so much "glory and honor." Drawing on Genesis 1, the psalmist looks to the heavens and wonders how God could be mindful of seemingly insignificant humans in so vast a universe. The psalmist's response is an elegant confession of faith: the creator has made humans just a little lower than heavenly beings yet crowned them with glory and honor, making them rulers over the works of God's hands, putting all flocks and herds, all beasts of the field, and all birds and fish under human feet—under human authority (Ps 8:3–8). And we know that the "under foot" image carries with it the responsibility to deal justly with God's treasured creatures in keeping with the honor God has given to each one. This holds true especially for the treatment of fellow humans.

Among God's many instructions to Israel as they prepared to enter the promised land were those about the appointment of judges and officials for each of the tribes and towns. The judges and officials "shall render just decisions for the people. You must not distort justice; you must not show partiality; and you must not accept bribes, for a bribe blinds the eyes of the wise and subverts the cause of those who are in the right. Justice, and only justice, you shall pursue, so that you may live and occupy the land that the Lord your God is giving you" (Deut 16:18b–20). The intricate pattern of honor and hospitality is in full view here. Humans must give honor to whom honor is due and treat one another justly because they are all created in God's image. A person placed in the high office of judge to assess the faults and crimes of others and to determine guilt or innocence must do justice and only justice. Only in that way can the people of Israel be confident of fair treatment, which is an essential ingredient of a hospitable society that recognizes the honor of God. The failure to uphold justice dishonors both the judge and the one being judged, and that is the beginning of the undoing, the dishonoring, of a community. Doing justice is one of the most important ways we manifest the honor of God who judges us all and wants to lead us into the fullness of divine hospitality.

---

7. With respect to the basis for environmental responsibility see Lee, "Creation, Ethics," 241–60; Bouma-Prediger, *For Beauty*; Nash, *Loving Nature*; Nagle, "Playing Noah," 1171–260. On some of the complexities involved in human governance of a public commons see Skillen, *Nation's Largest Landlord*, and *Federal Ecosystem Management*.

WHAT HONOR IN SUFFERING DEATH?

In Hebrews 2:5–9, the author draws Psalm 8 and Genesis 1 together in what at first glance is a surprising way. We do not yet see all things subject to human governance, writes the author, but we do see Jesus, who is "crowned with glory and honor because he suffered death." But surely, Jesus's "suffering death" does not seem like an act worthy of a crown of glory and honor. Yet it surely is, as the New Testament writers explain. Jesus stood in the place of humans who deserved death because of their disobedience, a death that would, however, seal the failure of both human governance and God's creation purposes. For Jesus to suffer death for the sins of the human generations was to give himself up to save and restore human responsibility and to make possible the reconciliation and fulfillment of all things to the glory of God. The one who tasted death for everyone is making God's sons and daughters holy and therefore is "not ashamed to call them brothers and sisters" (Heb 2:11b). He is indeed worthy of the highest honor.

Christ's suffering unto death also means that the statement in Hebrews 2:9 ("but we do see Jesus, who for a little while was made lower than the angels, now crowned with glory and honor because of the suffering of death") should not be read as saying that Jesus displaced sinful humans and is the only righteous human to be crowned with honor and glory. Rather, the message of Hebrews is that Jesus has been crowned precisely because he gave up his life to make his brothers and sisters holy. He acted as the "kinsman redeemer"[8] of his brothers and sisters to restore the covenant bond of the whole family of God, bringing "many sons and daughters" to glory. Those who are made holy by their elder brother Jesus participate in his holiness and honor, in the fulfillment of their creational vocation as the royal priesthood of God.[9] Human honor is elevated and fulfilled through our elder brother who restores the people of God to service as the hospitable hosts of God.

The crown of glory and honor for Jesus also indicates something else about the meaning of Jesus's death. Jesus, the incarnate Son of God, demonstrated through his

8. On the responsibility of a kinsman redeemer in Israel, read the story of Ruth, Naomi, and Boaz in the book of Ruth 2–4. This is directly related to the pattern of kinship obligations and relationships instituted in God's covenant with Israel. See Glanville, "The *Gēr* (Stranger)," 599–623.

9. See parallel expressions in Phil 2:8–9; Col 1:17–20; and Rev 5:6–14 about the crowning of Jesus with honor for suffering death to redeem his brothers and sisters. Wright says that in Phil 2 Christ is not being contrasted to Adam in a strictly parallel way, for "Christ's obedience is not simply the replacement of Adam's disobedience." Christ is "the solution of the problem now inherent in the first sort, namely, sin." In Wright's interpretation, "The temptation of Christ was not to snatch at a forbidden equality with God, but to cling to his rights and thereby opt out of the task allotted to him, that he should undo the results of Adam's snatching." But Jesus did not opt out of that task. And because of his faithfulness all the way to death, he has indeed been exalted to the place designed for humanity stated in Gen 1 and Ps 8. Yet there is more. In Phil 2:10–11, according to Wright, "Paul credits Jesus with a rank and honour which is not only in one sense appropriate for the true Man, the Lord of the world, but is also the rank and honour explicitly reserved, according to scripture, for Israel's God and him alone." Wright, *Climax*, 91–94.

entire life how humans are supposed to live as faithful servants of God. God creates us to give up our lives in his service. We cannot hold onto our lives; if we try to do so, we will lose them. Instead, we are supposed to lose our lives for God's sake. The life of sixth-day human beings is not the end and goal of creation; instead all creatures, including us, have been created for God and placed at God's disposal. It is God's honor to reward human faithfulness with the blessing of celebrating God's glory in seventh-day splendor. Jesus not only offered himself up as a sacrifice for sin, but exhibited by his life what it means to be human, to live faithfully, humbly, and unselfishly as servants of God.

Because humans, in the exercise of real responsibility, are so much like God, it is possible for us to disobey the creator and bring dishonor to ourselves, to the entire creation, and ultimately to God. That is the story that begins in Genesis 3 and continues to this day. In our dishonorable disobedience we become self-destructive, destructive of one another, and inhospitable toward God. The other creatures then become inhospitable to us as signaled by God's cursing of the ground, the serpent, and the man and woman after the fall into sin (Gen 3:14–19). Honor and hospitality are lost and humans stand condemned. That is the creation-disordering evil for which Christ bore God's judgment unto death. As history has unfolded, the story of the generations of humankind has been as much or more about dishonor and inhospitableness as it has been about honor and hospitality.

GOD'S HOSPITALITY AND OURS

In the face of human faithlessness and degradation, Paul takes the message of God's honor and hospitality to the Athenians on Mars Hill: "The God who made the world and everything in it, he who is Lord of heaven and earth, does not live in shrines made by human hands . . . since he himself gives to all mortals life and breath and all things" (Acts 17:24–25). "For 'In him we live and move and have our being'; as even some of your own poets have said" (17:28). In the words of Moses in Psalm 90, "Lord, you have been our dwelling place in all generations" (Ps 90:1). When Hebrews talks about the service of Moses *in* God's house, and the service of the Son *over* God's house, the passage concludes on a surprising note: "*and we are his house*, if we hold firm the confidence and the pride that belong to hope" (Heb 3:5–6; italics added). In other words, our dwelling in and with God becomes God's dwelling in and with us. God's sabbath with creation will be a mutually revelatory indwelling made possible through the death and resurrection of Jesus, the Son whom God "appointed heir of all things, through whom he also created the worlds" (Heb 1:2). It is through God's act of judgment and redemption in Christ Jesus that the honor and hospitality of creation are recovered, cleansed, made whole.

The Lord of heaven and earth governs and draws all things toward the divine honor and hospitality, and it is for the full, seventh-day unveiling of the divine glory that everything has been created, commissioned for service, and redeemed in Christ. This is the song that has been sung through the millennia by those who understand both the high honor and dignity of humankind and the greater honor and glory of God. This is the music we hear at the beginning of the letter to the Colossians: "For in him all things in heaven and on earth were created, things visible and invisible, whether thrones or dominions or rulers or powers—all things have been created through him and for him. He is before all things, and in him all things hold together . . . [H]e is the beginning, the firstborn among the dead, so that he might come to have first place in everything" (Col 1:16–18).

John the apostle, on Patmos, first hears the twenty-four elders singing:

> You are worthy, our Lord and God,
>> to receive glory and honor and power,
> for you created all things,
>> and by your will they existed and were created (Rev 4:11).

Then, in the next chapter of Revelation, the apostle hears a different song of praise:

> You are worthy to take the scroll and to open its seals,
> for you were slaughtered and by your blood you ransomed for God
>> saints from every tribe and language and people and nation;
> you have made them to be a kingdom and priests serving our God,
>> and they will reign on the earth (Rev 5:9–10).

Ultimate praise and honor is given to the God whose son and now preeminent human deserves and receives praise and honor forever and ever as the revealer of God and the image of God. He is creator, judge, and redeemer, the first and the last, the Alpha and the Omega, "who is, and who was, and who is to come, the Almighty" (Rev 1:8).

In our sin we are alienated from God and from the way of life for which we are created. We try to make ourselves the chief end of life and to hold onto ourselves instead of giving ourselves over entirely to the service of God and neighbors. But we cannot hold onto life or save ourselves, and when we try to do so we end up worshipping false gods and losing our hold on life. Despite all of this, the God of glory and honor has made manifest the depths of divine love and hospitality through the gift of his son, who has gone all the way to death to reconcile all things to God, drawing sinners to repentance and forgiving their sins.

For that reason, the regular remembrance of Christ's death among his followers by sharing the bread and wine together has the stamp of God's hospitality written all over it. Hans Boersma believes that "God's hospitality finds its climax in the celebration of the Eucharist. As the anticipation of—and indeed, the first participation in—the eschatological wedding banquet, the Eucharist suits the metaphor of hospitality better than either the preaching of the gospel or the sacrament of baptism."[10] For

10. Boersma, *Violence*, 215.

Alexander Schmemann, the blessing of the bread and the wine at the beginning of the celebration of the Eucharist in Christian worship also reminds us of the deep meaning of the creation. As we "offer to God the totality of all our lives, of ourselves, of the world in which we live," we know that "we were created as celebrants of the sacrament of life, of its transformation into life in God, communion with God. We know that real life is 'eucharist,' a movement of love and adoration toward God, the movement in which alone the meaning and the value of all that exists can be revealed and fulfilled."[11]

Even though sin and degradation continue to darken and dislocate life on earth, the righteous glory of God continues to be disclosed through the judging, reconciling, and redeeming covenants initiated by God. By the mercy of God, human honor and hospitality were exhibited through Abraham's hospitality toward the strangers (Gen 18:1–15)[12] and in the Samaritan's care for the wounded traveler (Luke 10:25–37). The principle of honor and hospitality comes to expression not only in family life but also in the responsibility of citizens to honor governing authorities (Exod 20:12; Rom 13:7; 1 Pet 2:2:17) and the responsibility of governing authorities to uphold the honor of citizens. The pattern of honor and hospitality continues to hold as a standard for the judgment of human disobedience and as a guide to right living for God's chief stewards on earth.

Christine Pohl draws attention to the richness of the biblical record that bears witness to the hospitality of God whom we image through our own hospitality. "God provides [to Israel] manna and quail daily in the wilderness for a hungry and often ungrateful people. God offers shelter in a hot and dry land, and refreshment through living water. Israel's covenant identity includes being a stranger, an alien, a tenant in God's land—both dependent on God for welcome and provision and answerable to God for its own treatment of aliens and strangers."[13] When we become inhospitable by turning from trust in God, we become deaf and blind to God's hospitality toward us. The incarnate son was not welcomed as he should have been and "experienced the vulnerability of the homeless infant, the child refugee, the adult with no place to lay his head, the despised convict."[14] Jesus nonetheless shines as the light in that darkness, as the word of truth among the deaf, revealing God's hospitable love to children, women, and men. He is the one who both "welcomes and needs welcoming," and he requires of his followers that they should both recognize their dependence on God's hospitality and offer such hospitality gratefully to their neighbors as if to him.[15]

---

11. Schmemann, *For Life*, 34.

12. See Aterbury, "Abraham's Hospitality," 359–76.

13. Pohl, *Making Room*, 16.

14. Pohl, *Making Room,* 17.

15. Pohl, *Making Room*, 17. See also Smith and Carvill, *Gift of the Stranger.* In his book, *The Hospitality of God*, Brendan Byrne offers a fruitful interpretation of Luke's Gospel as preeminently a revelation of God's hospitality.

We can summarize all of this by saying that the creation in all of its diversity exists to make known God's honor and hospitality. Everything in and about creation manifests this pattern. Every creature has a unique, irreducible place of honor, and tied to that honor is the service of hospitality toward other creatures. Faithful service to God cannot be achieved except through good governance and stewardship of all that God creates. Therefore, this pattern should become manifest in every human relationship and vocation. We cannot exhibit or enjoy the honor of being God's priests and vicegerents without serving as the hospitable hosts of the Lord of all, and we cannot be hospitable toward God without being faithful caretakers of all that belongs to God, including one another. That is possible only by the grace of God in Christ, through whom we find forgiveness of sins and restoration to the true way of life, the way of giving ourselves up in loving service to God and neighbors in all that we do.

7

Commission Towards Commendation

COMMISSIONING THE HUMAN GENERATIONS

THE SECOND REVELATORY PATTERN of the creation is closely related to the first and has to do primarily with the responsibilities God gives the sixth-day human creature made in the divine image. Even though the other creatures do not bear the kind of responsibilities humans do, they too are made for distinctive purposes and functions—their "vocations."[1] Sun, moon, and stars govern the day and the night. Plants, trees, fish, fowl, and animals bear fruit or generate offspring. All of them host humans as part of the creation's hospitable welcome and praise of God. Fretheim writes, "the testimony of Genesis 1 and many other Old Testament texts will speak, in effect, of the vocation of the nonhuman. Human and nonhuman have a commonality in that each is called to a vocation."[2] That is why the psalmist can call on all of them to worship and praise God:

> Praise the Lord! . . .
> Praise him, sun and moon;
>   praise him, all you shining stars! . . .
> Praise the Lord from the earth,
>   you sea monsters and all deeps,
> fire and hail, snow and frost,
>   stormy wind fulfilling his command!
> Mountains and all hills,
>   fruit trees and all cedars!
> Wild animals and all cattle,
>   creeping things and flying birds!
> Kings of the earth and all peoples,
>   princes and all rulers of the earth!
> Young men and women alike,
>   old and young together (Ps 148:1, 3, 7–12)!

1. See Fretheim, *God and World*, 270–71, 273, 275.
2. Fretheim, *God and World*, 275.

God has endowed the image of God, the creature of highest honor, with the greatest commission of all. What distinguishes the human vocation, writes Fretheim, is the "special responsibility to foster a world in which all receive their due as God's creatures."[3] In the course of their unfolding generations humans are to "rule over the fish of the sea and the birds of the air and over every living creature that moves on the ground" (Gen 1:28). Men and women together are to do all of this in the service of God and one another, lifting up everything in priestly love and thankful praise to God. God's royal priestly commission for humans is one to which Adam and Eve and their offspring must respond (thus, *responsibility*). Their commission, often referred to as the cultural mandate,[4] is constitutive of their identity. Humans are able to obey or to disobey the creator, but they cannot sidestep or escape the responsibility inherent in their identity and commission from God. We humans exist in a bonded relation to the one who has made us and called us to a very wide range of responsibilities. Furthermore, this sixth-day calling is backed by God's blessing: "God said, 'See, I have given you every plant yielding seed that is upon the face of all the earth, and every tree with seed in its fruit; you shall have them for food'" (Gen 1:29).[5]

With the unfolding of the human generations and the historical development of their talents and capabilities, their response to God's commission diversifies into a vast array of responsibilities. Humans name the animals, begin to tend the garden, bear children, and in the course of their generational unfolding discover more and more ways to develop the creation and their own talents in exercising royal and priestly responsibilities. Humans make music, invent tools, nurture friendships, engage in commerce, and govern clans, cities, and nations. All of these and many more require the kind of cooperation and organization that can be achieved only through mutual honor and hospitality, only by recognizing and commending the talents and services of one another, and only by jointly governing and caring for other creatures.

In one of his books on biblical hermeneutics, Craig Bartholomew emphasizes the importance of listening attentively to God as an act of courtesy and hospitality befitting the image of God. Humans cannot respond as faithful stewards to God's commission without listening attentively to, and acting as hospitable recipients of, God's word.[6] Surely this also means responding with courtesy and hospitality to what

---

3. Fretheim, *God and World*, 275.

4. Gregory Beale proposes that the cultural mandate should be understood as God calling priest-kings to extend the garden. Beale, "Garden Temple," 3–50. Iain Provan emphasizes that the garden metaphor comes to the fore in Gen 2 and refers to the whole earth. "Put succinctly, the creation narrative of Genesis 1 is retold in Genesis 2, this time through the metaphor of the garden rather than the temple. Indeed, if the garden is not the whole earth, it is unclear how the whole earth is supposed to be populated and governed by human beings in line with Genesis 1:28." Provan, *Seriously Dangerous Religion*, 34.

5. For a somewhat different understanding of the relation between "commission" and "blessing" see Stek, "What Says the Scripture?," 256–58.

6. Bartholomew, *Introducing Biblical Hermeneutics*, 17–47.

God reveals through creation, including fellow human creatures. The seemingly innumerable responsibilities we now exercise with and for one another and other creatures require wisdom and expertise that come only from listening, discipleship, and apprenticeship. To respond to God's calling we must learn to distinguish the identities, characteristics, and functions of different creatures. To reach maturity as good stewards we need to start as humble apprentices, learning from those who are wise and mature in centuries-old arts of music-making, medical care, child raising, animal husbandry, tilling the earth and harvesting its produce, engineering, exploration of the macrocosm and innumerable microcosms, speaking and writing, economic development, public governance, and more.

In a book with an intriguing title, *The World Beyond Your Head*, Matthew Crawford criticizes the modern quest for human autonomy and freedom that leads people to act as if the meaning of life can be found only or primarily by seeking to satisfy self-generated preferences. The ideal of freedom from that point of view means being unencumbered by demands and rules that come from outside one's self. It means living as if what matters most is doing one's own thing ("doing it my way," getting what I want). Instead, says Crawford, we need to submit to the disciplines of apprenticeship. We will never really be free unless we develop the talents and responsibilities that allow us to engage with the world beyond our heads. We won't be free to engage at a high level of playing the organ, designing clothing and machines, judging cases in a court of law, preparing food, or advancing scientific research unless we relinquish the myth of autonomy. We must help to develop and promote "*ecologies of attention.*" The perception of a skilled practitioner, says Crawford, "is 'tuned' to the features of the environment that are pertinent to effective action."[7] The paradox of the autonomy ideal is that it "seems to work against the development and flourishing of any rich ecology of attention—the sort in which minds may become powerful and achieve genuine independence."[8] Crawford's project "is to reclaim the real, as against representations. That is why the central term of approbation in these pages is not 'freedom' but 'agency.'"[9]

What Crawford is getting at with the word "agency," it seems to me, is human "responsibility," which requires attentive listening above all to God and to the reality of God's ordered creation, a reality we did not create and in which we are not the only creature. Moreover, in this world God's word and purposes establish the ground on which we are able to stand, speak, and act with purpose. Operating as if that is not true, believing that we are, or can become, completely autonomous is to go directly against the grain of reality. For we are *not* gods and our maturity and independence depend on "ecologies of attention" necessary for the proper exercise of our commission as God's servants. In discussing Genesis 2:15–17, where God tells Adam and Eve

7. Crawford, *World Beyond Your Head*, 23–24.

8. Crawford, *World Beyond Your Head*, 25.

9. Crawford, *World Beyond Your Head*, 27.

they may not eat from the tree of the knowledge of good and evil, Fretheim comments that "for all the creative power God entrusts to human beings, the human relationship to God provides an indispensable matrix for the proper exercise of that power." Humans are to recognize that their "creativity is derivative" and they "are not freed from all limitations in its exercise or from God's good intentions for creaturely life."[10]

The considerable time and effort that Kuyper devoted to the development of human responsibility in different areas of life reflects the kind of attentiveness to creation that we are talking about. In defending the importance of art, for example, in addition to science, politics, business, and higher education, he wrote that "art is no fringe that is attached to the garment, and no amusement that is added to life, but a most serious power in our present existence, and therefore its principal variations must maintain, in their artistic expression, a close relation to the principal variations of our entire life." Since all of life is bound up in our relation to God, "would it not be both a degradation and an underestimation of art [to treat it as] independent of the deepest root which all human life has in God?"[11] Along the same line, Moltmann reminds us that the Hebrew word for "spirit" (*ruach*) used in Genesis 1:2—"hovering over the waters"—is the word for wind or breath and it suggests a vibrating, quivering movement. Therefore, when we think of the creation originating through God's word, he writes, we might do better to imagine the sound of music, the "*song of creation*"—"something like a *cosmic liturgy* and *music of the spheres*."[12] No wonder the gifts of making music and listening attentively are so important.

The fact that artistic ability and capacity "can have room in human nature, we owe to our creation after the image of God,"[13] writes Kuyper, who made a similar argument about education on the occasion of founding and opening the Free University of Amsterdam in 1880. In his address at that time, he urged Christians to recognize the importance of the university as a distinct sphere of human responsibility that requires its own development for the service of God. Since academic vocations have a distinct character and aim, the university should be independent of the governance of both church and state. Yet all vocations exist to fulfill our one human calling to serve God through the development of the creation in service to God and neighbors. If you ask me, he said, whether we want this distinct sphere of development "not only for theology but for all the disciplines, and if you can scarcely control a smile when someone scoffs at 'Christian medicine' and 'Christian logic,' then listen to our reply to that objection. Do you think," he asked rhetorically, "that we would confess God's

10. Fretheim, *God and World*, 59.

11. Kuyper, *Lectures on Calvinism*, 151. In the realm of the visual arts alone, sometimes extending into theatre and music, two of the most comprehensive, international resources of Christians at work today are, *Image: Journal of Arts and Religion* (https://imagejournal.org) and *Artway* (www.artway.eu). See also Begbie, *A Peculiar Orthodoxy*; and Edgar, *Created and Creating*.

12. Moltmann, *Way of Jesus Christ*, 288–89.

13. Kuyper, *Lectures on Calvinism*, 156.

revelation . . . as the starting point of our efforts and draw upon this source only as theologians, scorning it as artists, jurists, and students of letters?"[14]

THE DOXOLOGICAL COMMENDATION

Having said this much about our commission from God to procreate and to develop and govern the earth, we may legitimately ask about the goal of that commission. God's calling to humans is *not* one of work without end. It is not a command to keep going day after day, generation after generation, with no end in view, no rest, no hope of completing any tasks or celebrating worthy achievements. Kuyper put it this way with a rhetorical question: "Personally, we cannot imagine . . . that the carpenter should do nothing century after century but saw and plane his wood or that the sailor would drift, age upon age, from port to port . . . Could all that was or still is have had no other destiny than mere continuation?"[15] No, the biblical answer is that our human labors anticipate completion and the celebration of work well done. The creation reaches its climax not with the process of work, as honorable as that is, but with its completion and reward through Christ Jesus as part of the fulfillment of the entire creation in God's day of rest. That is the day when all creatures celebrate the glory of God. It is the climactic day of divine satisfaction, when God commends faithful stewards for their faithful labors (Heb 4:9–10; 11:39–40). The seventh day, not the sixth day, is the one that has no evening or morning.

The promise to enter God's rest, articulated in Hebrews 4, is, among other things, the promise of the completion of our labors in the joy of reward. To be sure, due to our falling away from trust in God, there can be no human entrance into God's rest except through Jesus, yet the rest into which the faithful may anticipate entry is the creation's seventh day. Schenck shows that the promise of rest for the people of God, who are Christ's brothers and sisters, is closely related to the promises of their entrance into the land of promise, into the city that Abraham was looking for, and into their perfection or fulfillment. "In Hebrews, something is perfected when it has attained its appropriate status within the purposes of God . . . [P]erfection is the attainment of God's intended destiny and is thus to reach true rest and finality."[16] Pulling those elements together, Schenck says that "most of the language of promise in the epistle" is about the attainment of final perfection, of glory and honor, and of victory over death in God's day of rest.[17] This, of course, is the language of ultimate fulfillment, of rest with God in sabbath joy, which comes following the full extent of our earthly lives and labors in this age as we exercise our responsibilities in multiple spheres of life.

---

14. Kuyper, *Abraham Kuyper*, 461–90; 487.

15. Kuyper, *Abraham Kuyper*, 441–60; 455.

16. Schenck, *Cosmology and Eschatology*, 71.

17. Schenck, *Cosmology and Eschatology*, 73.

For their earthly journey, God called Israel to exercise habitual practices of rest that anticipated in a revelatory way the ultimate completion of all earthly labors in God's rest. Israel was told to work only six days and to enjoy the blessing of rest every seventh day (Exod 20:8–11). Every seventh day provides time to offer thank offerings to God with the fruits of human labors and for everyone, including servants, to enjoy a day of rest. Every seventh year is to be a sabbath year during which the land, the animals, and everyone dwelling in Israel are to enjoy an entire year of rest and celebration (Lev 25:1–7). And after seven of those sabbath years, an additional year of jubilee is to be observed as a culminating commendation of faithfulness, including release from debts and bondage (Lev 25:8–55).[18] All of these sabbath celebrations point beyond this age to the ultimate reward and jubilee of God's sabbath with creation.

Humans are commissioned for rewarding, goal-oriented work, for the development and expression of all their gifts and talents that make it possible for everyone to participate in the ongoing expansion and refinement of vocations that disclose diverse dimensions of the glory of God. At the same time, no human effort gets started or continues without hope of completion and commendation. At the end of the day, at the end of the week, at the end of our lives, we long to hear the words, "Well done, good and faithful servant." We are made for work that leads to the commendation of work well done. We yearn to hear, see, and taste the fruits of our labors that include words of congratulation from fellow workers, praise from a spouse, words of thanks from students to teachers, the return of love from one's child or parent. After the skilled artists and craftsmen who created Israel's tabernacle had finished their work, "Moses inspected the work and saw that they had done just as the Lord had commanded. So Moses blessed them" (Exod 39:43). Just as the tabernacle revealed something of the greater glory of God's ultimate dwelling place with the people, so the blessing of Moses on those who built the tabernacle was a foretaste of God's ultimate sabbath blessing of all faithful servants of God throughout this age.

The parable of the talents told by Jesus in Matthew 25:14–30 conveys this same message. The kingdom of God is like a man going on a journey, who calls his servants and entrusts his property to them. The man—the owner—gives five talents of money to one servant, two talents to another, and one to another, "to each according to his ability." Each servant is thus placed in a high position of stewardship with great responsibility. The story has deep roots that go all the way back to Genesis 1:26–30. What is the expectation of the owner and the servants? When the master returns to see the results of the servants' hard work, both owner and stewards anticipate reward for their investment and productivity. Indeed, the words of commendation from the master to the first two servants upon his return are exactly that. He sees that they have accomplished what they were asked to do and says to each of them, "Well done, good and trustworthy slave; you have been trustworthy in a few things, I will put you in charge of many things; enter into the joy of your master" (Matt 25:21). But to the

---

18. On the year of jubilee, see Ollenburger, "Jubilee," 208–34.

servant who did not follow through with his commission the owner had only words of reproof and condemnation. The original commission, we see, is oriented toward a goal. Fruitfulness in one's stewardly vocations anticipates the master's joy and blessing of work well done. Finally, that blessing will be the welcome into the never-ending joy of our creator and redeemer.

There is an important continuity between God's commission and commendation in this sabbath pattern that mirrors the continuity between this age and the coming age, between all that transpires in God's six creation days, including the labors of the human generations, and God's seventh-day rest. Interpreting Paul's first letter to the Corinthians, Wright says that the argument of 1 Cor 6:12–20 "depends on Paul's belief that what is done with the present body matters precisely because it is to be raised. The continuity between the present body and the future resurrection body is what gives weight to the present ethical imperative," which is that we should live with the awareness that our bodies are members of the Messiah.[19] Earlier in that letter, Paul states emphatically that God's final judgment of sin does not obliterate the continuity between this age and the coming age. "Nowhere else [outside 1 Cor 3] do we have such a strong sense of the continuity, across the moment of fiery judgment, between the work done in the present and the new world that the creator god intends to make. Well-built houses, says Paul, will last; they will, in other words, be part of the coming world the creator intends."[20]

I would rephrase Wright's statements slightly to say that that the continuity assumed by Paul is the continuity between this age, in which we are exercising our sixth-day responsibilities, and the coming age of the creation's fulfillment in God's seventh-day rest. The age to come is not a "new world" in the sense of a second creation that God "intends to make" but rather the fulfillment of *this* creation cleansed of sin and death and fulfilled in God's rest through Christ Jesus. This is where the picture of "well-built houses that last" fits into the trajectory of continuity that Wright is describing. To be sure, the coming resurrection age will manifest such a magnificent transfiguration of God's first six creation days that several New Testament writers, including Paul, often use the language of "new creation" and of "all things made new." But, of course, if everything is going to be entirely new and different, in the sense that the entire original creation is discarded, then there would be no continuity whatever between the "first" and "second" creations. There would be totally new creatures in the second because the generations of humankind in this creation would have no place in it. That would also mean no relation whatever between the Alpha and the Omega, between the Son of God through whom all things have been created and the resurrected incarnate Son, Jesus Christ, who makes a new creation. Yet that is not the way Paul speaks in 1 Corinthians 15 about those from the generations of the first Adam who are resurrected in Christ, the new Adam, for life in the age to come.

19. Wright, *Resurrection*, 289.
20. Wright, *Resurrection*, 285.

I find the same potential ambiguity about continuity and discontinuity in Jürgen Moltmann. He speaks of the "new creation" as beginning "with the raising of Christ from the dead, for the new creation is the world of the resurrection of the dead. Just as Israel's sabbath turns our gaze back to God's works in creation and to our own human week-day work, the Christian feast of the resurrection looks forward into the future of a new creation."[21] This way of speaking seems to disconnect the original creation from the new creation to which Moltmann refers. Yet that contrast doesn't square with another of his statements about Genesis 1: "The Creator will arrive at his rest when the whole creation becomes his temple, into which his glory can enter and dwell," which is "the eschatological image in the Revelation of John too (Rev 21)."[22] It seems to me that either the resurrected, incarnate Christ and those raised with him are of the human generations of this age (the sixth-day generations), transfigured through resurrection into God's one and only sabbath rest, or, if they are not, then the discontinuity between God's past creation and the new creation seems to be total.

Biblical references to a "new creation" and "all things made new" are ways of speaking about the creation cleansed of sin and death and humans transfigured through resurrection in Christ into the joy of the age to come—the creation's fulfillment in the seventh-day presence of God. The images Paul uses in 2 Corinthians 5:1–4 are helpful here to get at the continuity and discontinuity. At present, we live in an earthly tent and are clothed with earthly clothing, Paul writes, but through faith in Christ we are anticipating an eternal house in heaven, not built by human hands. That will mean putting on new clothes and entering a new kind of dwelling. The same people made for life in this age will be raised through the second Adam to a new mode of resurrection existence, the seventh-day fulfillment with God. We now live by faith, but then we will see face-to-face (2 Cor 5:7). Wright's interpretation of the continuity that extends from this age, "across the moment of fiery judgment," to the coming age is why Paul writes that we must "make it our aim to please him," whether we are at home in this body or away from it.[23] "For all of us must appear before the judgment seat of Christ, so that each may receive recompense for what has been done in the body [of this age], whether good or evil" (2 Cor 5:10). In other words, our faithful labor now, in Christ, anticipates fulfillment and reward in the age to come—God's sabbath rest. The earthly commission orients humans toward God's ultimate and final commendation.

We must also remember that God's climactic benediction will not consist merely of words and an awards ceremony at a celebrative banquet. God's commendatory blessing will be part of the fulfillment of the entire creation. We should anticipate it in the ways the Bible urges us to anticipate it: as the consummation of the long-anticipated marriage between Christ and his bride; a great family reunion; an ongoing banquet of unimaginable bounty; the establishment of God's just kingdom in which

21. Moltmann, *God in Creation*, 295.
22. Moltmann, *Way of Jesus Christ*, 302.
23. Wright, *Resurrection*, 285.

all of its citizens will rule with Christ; and the celebration by all God's children of their inheritance as joint-heirs with their elder brother Jesus, the Lord of all.

THREATENED BY SIN AND DEATH

What we know from history and our own experience tells us that humans have not followed the path of the first two servants in Matthew 25 but instead that of the third. The creator's vocation for the generations of humankind with our built-in hope for fruitful labor and congratulatory benediction has been corrupted because we—royal, priestly stewards—have not acted faithfully to carry out our commission. Faithlessness is why God drove Adam and Eve from the hospitable garden and punished them for their disobedience. Human irresponsibility, dishonor, and inhospitableness have brought upon us condemnation and retribution for our wickedness instead of blessings. Human loss, emptiness, and death are exactly fitting "rewards" for willful blindness and deafness toward God. The outcome of irresponsibility is fruitlessness, degradation and death, not fulfillment and reward in joyous celebration (see Lev 26:14–39; Deut 8:1–20). The consequences, as told at the end of the parable in Matthew 25 about the master's rebuke of the unfaithful servant, are this: throw that worthless slave "into the outer darkness, where there will be weeping and gnashing of teeth" (Matt 25:30).

With God's justifiable condemnation of sinners, the question of the creation's destiny pushes to the forefront of our concern. How can God take joy in creation and open the door to seventh-day blessings for the human generations whose commission has gone unfulfilled? The Bible tells us that the drama of human history continues to unfold only because of God's merciful patience, triumph over sin, and reconciling love. Yet redemption comes only with the judgment of that which violates God's creation purposes.[24] That is the reality of Christ's incarnate mission. The Son of God becomes one of us in the full scope of our humanity. He offers himself as the sacrificial lamb to bear God's judgment of sin—the sins of the world. He comes as kinsman redeemer to restore repentant brothers and sisters to the life and responsibilities God has given them. Christ Jesus, the one truly faithful human servant, the one through whom the human vocation is fulfilled, leads the way, drawing brothers and sisters with him into earthly faithfulness and on into God's sabbath fulfillment of all things in commendation of work well done.

Due to the tension between our sin and God's mercy that upholds the good order of creation, the unfolding of history up to the present moment continues to manifest an antithetical struggle between obedience and disobedience, between faithful stewardship and faithless neglect, between joy and broken-heartedness, between hope and despair, between enrichment and degradation, between expectation of reward and dreaded fear of punishment and death. In all arenas of life we see the evidence of

24. See Fretheim on the Old Testament's witness to God's acts of judgment. Fretheim, *God and World*, 157–81.

God's blessing and cursing, which will continue until all is fulfilled. One thing that the biblical story makes clear is that God *is* bringing the creation to its culmination through Israel's Messiah, Jesus. No matter how great the mystery of human actions and God's actions, it is God's benedictory promise of sabbath rest for the people of God that is the climactic blessing humans have been created for and that they long to see and hear.

By faith, Isaiah caught a glimpse of that final benediction when he saw the glory of the Lord appear over Israel.

> Nations shall come to your light,
>> and kings to the brightness of your dawn . . .
> Foreigners shall build up your walls,
>> and their kings shall minister to you; . . .
> Your sun shall no more go down,
>> or your moon withdraw itself;
> for the Lord will be your everlasting light,
>> and your days of mourning shall be ended.
> Your people shall all be righteous;
>> they shall possess the land forever" (Isa 60:3, 10, 20–21).

That vision of the climactic jubilee of Israel and the whole creation is the same one that the author of the letter to the Hebrews speaks about in regard to Abraham's life-long journey: by faith, Abraham "looked forward to the city that has foundations, whose architect and builder is God" (Heb 11:10). The announcement of that coming glory continues to go out to all the earth, calling sinners to repentance, forgiveness, and renewal through Messiah Jesus, who is at work by the Spirit even now, shaping each of the building blocks that will compose the new Jerusalem, the house of God. The creation order is seven days, not six, and the entirety of our lives in every sphere of earthly responsibility should bear witness to the God we image and to the Son of God who has been revealed as preeminent in all things. The creation's pattern of commission towards commendation has not been lost or discarded. It is confirmed and fulfilled in Jesus Christ.

8

Revelation in Anticipation

BY OUR VERY IDENTITY as the image of God we reveal something of the creator. Yet it is not only humans that are revelatory in that sense. Paul says, "Ever since the creation of the world his eternal power and divine nature, invisible though they are, have been understood and seen through the things he has made" (Rom 1:20). This comes through in many of the Psalms. Fretheim points to the Bible's frequent use of "nature metaphors" about God. "For example, God is light, water, rock, fire, wind, as well as a few animals, such as the eagle . . . God's righteousness is like the mountains (Ps 36:6) or God's faithfulness is like the fixed orders of creation (Jer 31:35–36)." If "rock and eagle and other natural metaphors for God are in some ways descriptive of God, then they reflect in their very existence, in their being what they are, the reality which is God."[1]

The creation and its creaturely relationships tell us a great deal about God in relation to creation. That is particularly true of God's relationship to humans: the generations of the image of God are God's ruling stewards on earth. The children of Israel are God's children. God's covenant with Israel is likened to a marriage bond (Isa 54:4–8; Hos 2–4), and Paul speaks about marriage as a mystery that is revelatory of the love between Christ and his bride (Eph 5:22–33).[2] God tends Israel as a shepherd tends his sheep. God is like a vineyard keeper who prunes and cares for the vines. There are countless passages that speak of our governmental, judicial, and public administrative responsibilities revealing something of God, the governor, judge, leader, king, and legislator of the creation kingdom.

---

1. Fretheim, *God and World*, 56–57. McConville makes the same point. "Natural imagery is the stock-in-trade of the biblical poets"; "The metaphorical quality of the Bible's discourse is indispensable to its depiction of the human"; "Both particularity and metaphor are deeply embedded in the Old Testament literature and its capacity for meaning." McConville, *Being Human*, 90, 81, 84.

2. "The erotic language in Hosea, and also Jeremiah (2:2–3), lends credibility to the interpretation of the Song of Songs in which human love is taken as a metaphor of the love of God." McConville, *Being Human*, 94. On the Song of Songs, see Falk, *Song of Songs*; Bloch and Bloch, *Song of Songs*; Seerveld, *Greatest Song*. See also Kline, *Images of Spirit*, 50–56, 94–96; and Schmemann, *For Life*, 84.

It is the meaningfulness of created reality that makes all such likenesses possible. Genesis 1:26–27 is emphatic that humans are like God in that they image the creator. As sixth-day creatures, embraced by the hospitality of all other creatures, humans are to experience their identity—the meaning of their lives—as revealers of the God with whom they can walk and talk throughout their faith-led journey on earth. Human life represents a disclosure of meaning that comes to expression in the rich diversity of responsibilities and institutions developed throughout history. That which is revelatory in God's relations with humans is dynamic, not static, mounting up in anticipation of the fullness of that meaning still to be unveiled.[3]

The discernment of the creation's revelatory character emerges in the course of human experience and is expressed through multiple similes, metaphors, and figures of speech as well as in art, architecture, and liturgies of worship and life.[4] God's seven days of creation are likened to a human week in such a way that God's days are understood to be the original, the foundation of all creatures, including the time of our earthly days and weeks. Every creature depends on and refers to other creatures in a dynamic display of the glory of God. Likeness follows likeness, metaphor builds on metaphor because of the revelatory character of creation.[5] Humans are not sheep, but a shepherd's intimate knowledge and care for sheep leads to the insight that humans are like sheep in relation to the good shepherd. Likewise, those in certain offices of responsibility, such as parents, teachers, priests, or governing authorities, can be thought of as shepherds of those they care for, lead, or govern.[6]

Take another example: a house, temple, or palace that serves as one of the prevalent images of God's covenantal purposes. After God liberates Israel from Egypt, the Israelites are told to construct a portable tabernacle that will represent God's intimate

3. Following the lead of Calvin, who described history as the "theater of God's glory," Michael Horton characterizes the revelatory character of creation history as a drama. This accords with the argument of others that the relation of God to the generations of humankind is disclosed through an extended story, a metanarrative, or grand drama. To recognize the revelatory character of human life in this age as that which anticipates its full disclosure in God's sabbath rest supports the presumption that, despite human sin, God sustains the unfolding of creation as a revelatory drama. Horton, *Covenant and Eschatology*, 184–85, 9–12, 99–120. See also Skillen, "Reengaging Figural Interpretation," 181–203.

4. On the relation of art, architecture, work, worship, liturgy, and community, with a focus on late medieval and earthly modern Italian culture, see Skillen, *Putting Art (Back)*.

5. T.A. Perry comments that the extraordinary power of comparisons in the Hebrew Bible, such as, for example, comparing a person's demise to the undoing of creation itself, or comparing youth to the morning of life, is grounded in the principle of analogy. "Such understandings are in fact so embedded in our ordinary language as to appear simply descriptive rather than metaphorical extensions." Perry, *God's Twilight Zone*, 130. Northrop Frye writes, "We clearly have to consider the possibility that metaphor is, not an incidental ornament of Biblical language, but one of its controlling modes of thought." *Great Code*, 54, and further, 53–77, 139–68. For more on how metaphors and similes are embedded in our thinking and speaking, see Lakoff and Johnson, *Metaphors We Live By*. For more on metaphors, similes, and figures of speech in the Bible see, Paul, "Metaphor and Exegesis," 387–402; and Brown, *Seeing Psalms*.

6. See, for example, Golding, "Imagery of Shepherding," 18–28.

dwelling with them as they travel through the wilderness. Generations later, God allows Solomon to build a permanent temple in the promised land that will serve the same purpose. Both tabernacle and temple were constructed to reflect, microcosmically, God's rightly ordered creation and dwelling place with humans. Meredith Kline explains that God's presence with Israel in the tabernacle and temple represented "a cosmic royal residence or temple." The two buildings served as a "microcosmic house of God."[7] Then, as the dynamic unfolding of the human generations continued, it became ever more clear that the tabernacle, the temple, and the promised land itself were not the final dwelling place of God with the chosen people. All those representative dwelling places pointed beyond themselves to something more, to the Sabbath fulfillment of the entire creation when the faithful will dwell with God and God with them face-to-face and forever (see Exod 24–31, 39–40; 1 Kgs 5–8; Pss 93, 99; Isa 66:1–2; 1 Cor 3:16–17; 2 Cor 6:16; 1 Pet 2:4–10; Heb 3:1–6; Rev 21:1–5, 22–27).[8] God's promise for the final city speaks of a splendor beyond anything yet known:

> Afflicted city, lashed by storms and not comforted,
>   I will rebuild you with stones of turquoise,
>   your foundations with lapis lazuli.
>   I will make your battlements of rubies,
>   your gates of sparkling jewels,
>   and all your walls of precious stones (Isa 54:11–12, TNIV).

Consider another example of the revelatory character of the creation's relation to God. Humans need wisdom to carry out their commission of service to God through care for one another and stewardly development of the earth. Wisdom itself is revelatory of the all-wise God. Wisdom, according to Proverbs, is like the pearl of great price. The fruit of wisdom "is better than gold, even fine gold" and its yield is better than "choice silver" (Prov 8:19). Wisdom is that by which "kings reign, and rulers decree what is just" (Prov 8:15). Wisdom, according to Wright, "is required if humans are to be truly human, taking that place over creation which, outlined in Genesis 2.15–20, is then spelt out in more detail throughout Proverbs. Humans are to be the vice-regents over God's creation, and are therefore to take the place within the divine economy that in Proverbs 8.22ff is given to Wisdom herself."[9] Those who exhibit wisdom manifest

---

7. Kline, *Images of Spirit*, 35–37.

8. Wright comments that Jews saw the temple as symbolic of God's promise that heaven and earth would ultimately come together. "The original creation was good and is to be redeemed, and is indeed to be flooded with the divine presence and power 'as the waters cover the sea.' The original creation was a kind of temple, with heaven and earth held together; conversely, the wilderness tabernacle and then Solomon's temple were seen as microcosmic, the 'little world' in which heaven and earth came together dangerously but powerfully, *anticipating the day when heaven and earth would be one forever.*" Wright, "Responding to Exile," 321–22.

9. Wright, *Climax*, 113. For more on the revelatory character of wisdom and its role in human responsibility in creation see Seerveld, *Biblical Studies*; Perdue, *Wisdom and Creation*; Van Leeuwen, "Proverbs"; Witherington, *Jesus the Sage*.

a likeness to God's mediator of creation, lady wisdom. Wisdom is like a lamp that illumines the right path for doing the creative work God has called us to do on our way to fulfillment. A wise ruler exhibits a likeness to God, the ruler of all things.

Turning away from full trust in God is to fall away from the path of wisdom, to stumble in the dark in the snares and brambles of foolishness that produce confusion, degradation, and a deathward spiral. The wisdom neglected by fools turns against them, exposing their foolishness, which follows inevitably as a consequence of distrusting God and forsaking divine wisdom.

> The lips of the righteous feed many,
>> but fools die for lack of sense (Prov 10:21).

> A fool finds pleasure in evil conduct,
>> but a man of understanding delights in wisdom (Prov 10:23).

> Doing wrong is like sport to a fool,
>> but wise conduct is pleasure to a person of understanding (Prov 12:15).

> Truthful lips endure forever,
>> but a lying tongue lasts only a moment (Prov 12:19).[10]

When God elects Israel, Wright explains, the redeeming purpose "entails restoration of human wisdom. God chooses Israel to be the particular place where this Wisdom dwells, establishing her as the creator's true humanity; and, where we find messianic expectation cherished in Judaism, we find it as the focal point of the aspiration of the nation as a whole. Solomon, David's son, is at the same time the model of the coming great king and the model of the truly wise man. The categories fit neatly together: Israel's vocation to be the true humanity, indwelt by the divine Wisdom, is focused on one man, her representative king, who in Psalm 89.27 is described as Yahweh's 'firstborn.'"[11]

The biblical story of the revelatory drama of wisdom reaches its high point with the incarnation, death, and resurrection of Jesus. The great poetic hymn of Colossians

10. According to Perry, the biblical theme of wisdom in relation to justice manifests "a particular twist" when it comes to foolish and evil persons. "Especially in the form of the retribution meted out to the wicked, [justice] is viewed as a fact of life, as a perfectly natural, predictable, almost fatalistic structure of reality. There is never a doubt that such a state of things derives from God, of course, but the stress in on the pre-existent universal moral mechanism rather than on providence and God's explicit imposition of justice. By contrast, in many passages in the Torah punishment is directly meted out by God. Psalm 1 replies that both are operative, but with distinct roles: it is the Lord Himself that rewards or cares for the righteous, whereas the wicked, being left to their own devices, self-destruct or perish from their own movement and without any outside intervention." Perry, *God's Twilight Zone*, 114–15.

11. Wright, *Climax*, 113. The relation of the king to wisdom is closely related to the king as representative lover of God's law. For more on this, see Grant, *King as Exemplar*, 213–33. Wisdom in Israel is closely related to the idea (image) of the right pathway, which is "practically coextensive" with torah, as Brown explains. Brown, *Seeing Psalms*, 34–36. For more on the revelatory character of wisdom see Fretheim, *God and World*, 199–247.

1:15–20, according to Wright, is in part a poem in praise of Jesus as the embodiment of wisdom. The poem envisions "God's purpose in creation as being to sum up all things in the man Jesus." Yet we should not abandon the passage's reference to the one "who, though not yet a human being . . . was God's agent in the creation of the world, and thus perfectly fitted to *become* human and so to take the leading role in the unfolding drama of God's purposes for recreating the world. In becoming, under God, the predestined human lord of the world, he has taken his rightful place, since from the beginning he was the Father's agent, as the true Wisdom of God, in the work of creation."[12] Human wisdom, restored and exhibited in Jesus Christ, is revelatory of divine wisdom because all things, including humans, have been created in and through him in the first place.

ANTICIPATORY

I am using the word "anticipatory" in a way that captures something more than expectation, or watchful waiting. Think, for example, of a building under construction. After we see that the foundation has been laid, we might say, subjectively, that we are looking forward to seeing the completed building. We "anticipate" seeing something in the future that is not yet there. But we could also say that the first stage of construction is anticipatory of the completed building in the sense that what is anticipatory—the foundation—is also constitutive of what is yet to be completed. In other words, what is now manifest is not simply a pointer to something still to come but is also part of what is not yet complete. The building's foundation is a constitutive part that is anticipatory of the completed whole of which it is and will continue to be a part. This is how I want to explain the creation's pattern of "revelatory and anticipatory," or "revelation in anticipation."

Understanding the creation as revelatory of God means that we must relinquish the assumption that God's transcendence implies an obscure unknowability and total otherness. To the contrary, the Bible takes for granted that the creator spoke the creation into existence to reveal the divine glory. God creates not to obscure the divine but to reveal it. The Son of God becomes fully human to make God known. The question then is not whether the creation makes God known but how and toward what end it does so. The fact that we have been created to live by faith in this age and that our sinfulness leads us into darkness means that we do not yet see the divine glory in its fullness, but that does not discount the revelatory character of what is created. Moreover, the unfolding generations of humankind—creatures of God's sixth day— are not the end of God's revelatory intentions. And that is why the word "anticipatory" requires our special attention.

---

12. Wright, *Climax*, 115–16.

Everything God is now revealing in and through created reality is pregnant with more that is still to be revealed. God's revelation in and through created reality, including our human generations, is not yet the full and climactic revelation of the mystery God is making known. The seventh-day climax of creation in transformative glory will take us beyond the limits of what is being disclosed in the first six creation days in a culminating way. Our lives in this age, therefore, are "revelatory in anticipation." The pattern of "revelatory in anticipation" takes us directly to the major metaphor in the Bible about the house God is building. The building blocks of the completed house are being shaped and fitted out now, throughout this age. The blocks that constitute the completed house (Heb 3:6) are now being polished and integrated. The building is going up. Thus, what is *revelatory* now is *constitutively anticipatory* of the completed house that will be revealed in all its glory as the dwelling place of God.

Speaking from our vantage point as sixth-day creatures, we can say that the revelatory character of the creation's first six days has a built-in eschatological orientation—oriented toward the culminating revelation of the mystery of God in the creation's seventh day. Every loving marriage now reveals something of the bond of love that unites Christ with his bride, yet the full meaning of marriage will be disclosed only in the ultimate celebration of that climactic union. Every act and institutionalization of justice through our earthly lawmaking and adjudicatory actions is a constitutive, revelatory anticipation of God's completed kingdom of justice and righteousness. This means that the yet-to-be-revealed completion of God's creation purposes is a drawing and compelling force (proleptically) in our present experience.

In his discussion of 1 Corinthians 5–6, Wright says that Paul, with Daniel 7 in mind, urges Christians to live in the present in accord with their vision and hope of the future. "Learn to think in terms of the world that is to be . . . and of the people you will be within it, and then you will see clearly who you must be in the present time."[13] I would add that we can turn that statement around. Right now, as we live by faith, hope, and love in this age, we should concentrate on being the people God has made us to be, trusting that God's fashioning, shaping, and disciplining of us in Christ Jesus will make us fit for the day of final revelation in God's presence (see Eph 6:10–20; Phil 2:12–16; 1 Thess 5:12–24; Heb 5:11–14, 10:23–25).

Nothing that is positively constructive in human experience throughout the history of our sixth-day generations will be lost. Instead, by the grace of God in Christ, the final revelation of God's glory will make manifest the full meaning of all that God has been revealing throughout this age in anticipation of the great day of fulfilling joy. Just as each day of creation does not end when God calls the next day into existence, but instead finds part of its honor in the hospitality it provides, so too the seventh-day revelation of the glory of God will not set aside the first six days, but will draw all that is good into fulfillment through Jesus Christ to the praise of God forever and ever.

13. Wright, *Resurrection*, 288.

It seems to me, therefore, that this is part of what Jesus conveys through many of his parables. A small mustard seed anticipates constitutively the bush that grows to be as large as a tree. Yeast mixed into a large amount of flour works its way through the dough (Matt 31–33). At present, many do not see the revelatory character of the seed or the yeast but it continues to work its way to the grown tree and the full loaf of bread. Not everyone in Israel understood the revelatory character of God's promised seed to Abraham that would become a great family tree in which many birds would come to perch. Not everyone in Israel recognized that their regular sabbath rests and years of jubilee were anticipatory constituents of the climactic fulfillment of all things in God's sabbath rest. Few people in Jesus's time recognized in him the seed and the yeast at work in revelatory anticipation of the kingdom of heaven. By the power of the Spirit, the revelatory reality of God at work with creation can be discerned through eyes of faith, and every teacher of God's covenant faithfulness who is instructed about the kingdom of heaven will be like "the owner of a house who brings out of his storeroom new treasures as well as old" (Matt 13:52). Jesus came not to do away with the law, not to discard Israel, not to do away with what is created, but to fulfill them all. All things made new, when finally made manifest in kingdom glory, will include revelatory treasures of old.

KUYPER'S DILEMMA

Abraham Kuyper had a strong sense of the revelatory and anticipatory character of creation in its movement toward the culminating disclosure of God's glory. He stated emphatically "that the ongoing development of humanity is contained in the plan of God . . . Scripture speaks of the 'consummation of the ages' [Matt 13:39–40], a term that does not mean the centuries will terminate at some point but that they are directed toward a final goal and that everything contained in those centuries is linked to that final goal." The link is not always apparent now, however, for "God does not reveal all at once what he alone can show us."[14]   The development of human responsibilities through the course of history, Kuyper argued, has been, and continues to be, possible because humans are social (generational) creatures. "From this viewpoint the highly ramified development of humanity acquires a significance of its own, an independent goal, a reason for being aside from the issue of salvation. If it has pleased God to mirror the richness of his image in the social multiplicity and fullness of our human race, and if he himself has deposited the nuclei of that development in human nature, then the brilliance of his image has to appear."[15]

This is the point, however, where I believe Kuyper's understanding of different goals for common grace (supporting human development now) and special grace (saving the elect for eternity) keeps him from grasping how the revelatory creation

14. Kuyper, *Abraham Kuyper*, 165–201, 175–76.

15. Kuyper, *Abraham Kuyper*, 165–201, 178.

(including human labors) is to be *fulfilled* in God's day of rest through the reconciling and saving work of Christ. According to Kuyper, "Holy Scripture repeatedly tells us of the intertwinement of the life of special grace with that of common grace but simultaneously discloses that the point at which the two come together is not Christ's birth in Bethlehem but his eternal existence as the *Eternal Word*."[16] Yet what does Kuyper understand to be the relation between the eternal Word and the incarnate Word? Do they remain distinct insofar as the goals of common grace and special grace remain distinct, or do they come together again in Christ's reconciling fulfillment of creation in the creation's seventh day? I cannot find an unambiguous answer to this question in Kuyper's writing.[17]

Kuyper's reading of the Bible pushes him at points toward the dissolution of that duality even as he holds on to it as his unquestioned point of departure. With respect to the convergence of the two graces, Kuyper says that Jesus is "first the original Mediator of creation and after that also the Mediator of redemption to make possible the enforcement and fulfillment of the decree of creation and everything entailed in it." That is why "the work of redemption accomplished by special grace cannot stand isolated from the life of the world. The two, proceeding as they do from a single decree and from the self-same person in the triune Godhead, are and remain basically one." Common grace, therefore, "must have a formative impact on special grace and vice versa. All separation of the two must be vigorously opposed."[18]

At the same time, however, Kuyper apparently believes that the two graces operate together only in this age, which for him is the world of God's creatures. The separation, which he says "must be vigorously opposed," is specifically the separation of "our life in the world and our life in the church"; the realm of religion and the realm of civil life; the church and the state. His intention, it appears, is to associate "church life and religion" in this age with special grace while connecting the world outside the church, including civil life and the state, with common grace.[19] Seeing it this way appears to drive Kuyper in the direction of disconnecting creation through the Word from the redemption of creation through the incarnate Word at the end of this age when the creation has reached its temporal goal. While God is redeeming the elect in this age, he seems to be saying, they should be busy with the same creaturely work that engages nonbelievers, because God's common grace upholds all of them together. Yet common grace upholds life only in this age.

Is it not true, however, that the eternal Word who became the incarnate redeemer is the one through whom all things are created and hang together? Is he not the one who stated upon resurrection that all authority in heaven and on earth belongs to

16. Kuyper, *Abraham Kuyper*, 165–201, 183.

17. On the tension and ambiguity in Kuyper's understanding of common and special grace, see Zuidema, "Common Grace."

18. Kuyper, *Abraham Kuyper*, 165–201, 185.

19. Kuyper, *Abraham Kuyper*, 165–201, 185–86.

him? And is it not true that this word of God who is one with us in our humanity, died, was raised, and is now seated at the right hand of majesty on high? Whatever one might conclude about the Bible's teaching about the final separation of the wheat and the tares, the elect and the non-elect, surely there can be no question about the relation of Christ to the whole creation from its beginning to its fulfillment. Yet it seems that Kuyper started with the distinction between two graces as fundamental in the Bible's teaching, instead of starting with God's seven-day creation order. Consequently, when he correctly points out that John's Gospel "begins not with the Mediator of redemption but with the Mediator of creation," he interprets this by saying that John "starts out from the position of 'common grace' and from there arrives at the position of 'special grace.'"[20] In other words, Kuyper's base distinction between two kinds of grace seems to exclude the reconciling fulfillment *of* creation through Christ in the Sabbath rest of God. Kuyper's distinction between graces, I believe, cuts off the possibility of recognizing that what is revelatory of God in this age is constitutive of what will be the creation's fulfillment in the final revelation of God's glory.

If my assessment is correct, then we may hypothesize that Kuyper wants to keep the closest connection between God's common grace and special grace in this world, but he thereby leaves unaddressed the question of the culminating fulfillment of creation (this world) through Christ in the age to come. Or perhaps we can say more definitely that Kuyper disconnects the new creation from the old creation to such an extent that we are left to assume that with Christ's second coming, the final judgment, and the resurrection of the dead, common grace will end and only special grace will remain. But if that is true, then what can we learn from it about the revelatory and anticipatory character of creaturely life?

THAT WHICH IS REVELATORY
IS CONSTITUTIVELY ANTICIPATORY

In contrast to Kuyper, I do not believe the Bible's starting point is with God's decrees of election and reprobation, leading to the distinction between common grace and special grace. Instead, it seems to me, the biblical starting point is with the full reality of God's seven-day creation week, entailing as it does both this age and the age to come. God's unmerited favor, which comes to full disclosure in Christ Jesus, upholds all creatures and continues to do so even after humans have turned from trust in God. God's separation of wheat and tares, of sheep and goats, of the faithful from the faithless does not predetermine the order of creation nor does it frustrate the course of Christ's reconciling work, through judgment and redemption, of all things to the glory of God in the creation's seventh day. Each day of creation has its own honor and hospitality. Each creature has its commission that opens toward commendation. All

20. Kuyper, *Abraham Kuyper*, 165–201, 183.

creatures reveal something of God because they are constituted in their very identity to be revelatory in anticipation of the fulfilled creation. The days of plants, trees, fish, fowl, animals, and humans unfold together through their generations and are commissioned to fulfill the assignments and responsibilities God has given them. Sixth-day human creatures—God's image, male and female—are elaborately and intimately revelatory of God through our exercise of real responsibilities as royal priests in communion with God through faith. The final disclosure of the meaning of every dimension of God's creation becomes possible only when all assignments and commissions of the first six days have been fulfilled. This means that the fullness of what is yet to be made manifest has a proleptic (drawing and driving) influence in the present. That which is "not yet" functions as a compelling force in the here and now. Insofar as our experience is in part revelatory of what it anticipates, it means that the climax of God's sabbath glory through Jesus Christ is at work even now, by the power of the Spirit, encouraging, drawing, and shaping us through hope, faith, and love.

Jesus Christ, our elder brother, is already raised from the dead and seated at the right hand of majesty on high, and it is in him, *through faith*, that we have already died and been raised to new life. It is union with Christ that makes this possible. Thus, Paul urges the Philippians to "work out your salvation with fear and trembling, for it is God who is at work in you, enabling you both to will and to work for his good pleasure" (Phil 2:12b–13). To the Romans Paul writes, it is the Spirit himself "bearing witness with our spirit that we are children of God," for the whole creation waits in eager expectation for the children of God to be revealed. Not only other creatures, "but we ourselves, who have the first fruits of the Spirit, groan inwardly while we wait for adoption, the redemption of our bodies. For in hope we were saved. Now hope that is seen is not hope. For who hopes for what is seen? But if we hope for what we do not see, we wait for it with patience" (Rom 8:16, 19, 23–24). When John on Patmos has a vision of believers suffering under great tribulation, he hears a voice from heaven say, "'Write this: Blessed are the dead who from now on die in the Lord.' 'Yes,' says the Spirit, 'they will rest from their labor, for their deeds follow them'" (Rev 14:13).

Paul explains to Corinthian believers that from now on, because of faith-union with the risen Christ, "we regard no one from a human point of view; even though we once knew Christ from a human point of view, we know him no longer in that way" (2 Cor 5:16). By "human point of view" Paul means the viewpoint of the sixth-day human generations. Since the resurrected Christ is now ascended, we should henceforth regard him from that point of view, the viewpoint of the life-giving Spirit of seventh-day fulfillment. That means we should also regard one another from that point of view because we are united with him by faith through the Spirit. Paul's point is that through eyes of faith we can now see and begin to experience that fulfillment. "So if anyone is in Christ, there is a new creation: everything old has passed away; see, everything has become new!" (2 Cor 5:17). This is true *already* by faith even though we continue to live in this age and carry forward the message of Christ's reconciling work until he comes again.

Understanding the proleptic power of hope has been central to Jürgen Moltmann's understanding of Christian faith from early in his career. In one of his first books, *Theology of Hope*, he writes, "Jesus is recognized in the Easter appearances as what he really *was*. That is the ground of faith's 'historical' remembrance of the life and work, claims and sufferings of Jesus of Nazareth. But the messianic titles, in which this identity of Jesus in cross and resurrection is claimed and described, all anticipate at the same time the not yet apparent future of the risen Lord. This means that the Easter appearances and revelations of the risen Lord are manifestly understood as foretaste and promise of his still future glory and lordship."[21]

That statement comes very close to Paul's explanation that we should no longer regard Christ from a human point of view. In a later book Moltmann writes, "The feast [of the Eucharist] itself is celebrated in expectation of the parousia [the coming of the Lord]. That is why the cry 'maranatha' [come Lord Jesus] probably has its origin in the celebration of the Lord's Supper. The congregation begs the Christ who is present in the Spirit of God for the coming of his kingdom. The fellowship of the eucharistic feast is therefore understood as a gift given in advance, and as an anticipatory presentation of the great banquet of the nations at which all human beings will be satisfied."[22]

To use Paul's language in his first letter to the Corinthians (15:42–54), the life that we live by faith in the earthly body (as sixth-day creatures) is "perishable" (expendable), but when in Christ we are raised from the dead, we will be reconstituted as spiritual bodies (seventh-day creatures) that are imperishable, immortal. We will no longer live by faith and hope but by sight, face-to-face. God's ultimate blessing (commendation) of the completed household of faith will be the eucharistic gift of union with Christ, who, as redeemer, bridegroom, elder brother, friend, shepherd, high priest, and King, will draw our sixth-day labors, honors, and hospitality into the seventh-day presence of God's glory when we will hear God say, "Well done good and faithful servants."

All of this is why the motivating hope of the coming of God's kingdom empowers our labors for the Lord here and now. As Moltmann puts it, Paul's hope for the final appearance of the Lord (Phil 3:20–21) "is not a flight from the world . . . not a matter of mere 'waiting,' guarding oneself, and holding fast to the faith. It goes far beyond that, reaching out to the active shaping of life. It is life in anticipation of the coming One, life in 'expectant creativity.' People do not live merely from traditions. They live from expectations too."[23] Wright makes the same point when commenting on Paul's letter to the Philippians regarding the transition from life now to the new creation. Paul insists, "the body will be transformed, not abandoned." And because

21. Moltmann, *Theology of Hope*, 84–85.
22. Moltmann, *Way of Jesus Christ*, 338–39.
23. Moltmann, *Way of Jesus Christ*, 340.

of that continuity, Christians should not be focused on "waiting for a different life altogether but on 'standing firm in the Lord' (4.1)."[24] All the more as we see the day of the Lord approaching, we should be working to spur one another on to love and good deeds (Heb 10:24–25).

24. Wright, *Resurrection*, 230–31.

9

Covenant for Community

A FOURTH CONSTITUTIVE PATTERN of the creation drama intertwines the first three. God's fundamental covenant is the seven-day creation, which manifests the creator's bond with all creatures. Within the covenantal order of creation, God established the covenants with which we are most familiar from reading the Bible, those with Noah, Abraham, Isaac, Jacob, the children of Israel, and Messiah Jesus. The latter, according to Hebrews, is the ground and fulfillment of them all (Heb 1:1–4, 8:1–6, 9:23–24).[1] God's judgment-redemption covenant in Christ Jesus makes known that through him God created all things in the first place (John 1:1–3; Col 1:16–17; Heb 1:1–2). Thus, all of God's covenants with the human generations have their ground in God's bond with creation, which is upheld through the Son from its foundation (Alpha) on through to the Son's incarnation, death, resurrection, and ascension to the right hand of majesty on high as Lord of all (Omega).[2]

God's covenant with creation is not a contract between two independent parties. God establishes the terms of the covenant as well as all the creatures that are part of it. The covenant of creation is a unilateral covenant, established entirely from one side—the creator's. The generations of the image of God are thus, by their very nature, covenant-bound creatures constituted for a unique relationship with God and other creatures. Men and women do not start in a neutral position from which to decide to enter or not enter into relationship with God. By their very identity they are already bound to God whom they image. Moreover, humans are constituted from the start with responsibility both for one another and for other creatures as part of their

1. For a thorough introduction to the types of historical covenants (kinship, treaty, and grant), see Hahn, *Kinship by Covenant*.

2. Although Hahn does not discuss the creation order as the original *covenant* bond established by God, he does say that God's covenant with Noah (Gen 6:18) indicates a covenant undergoing renewal rather than a covenant being initiated. "The covenant that undergoes renewal can be traced back to creation." Hahn, *Kinship by Covenant*, 95. In his note on this statement, Hahn cites a number of sources that deal in greater depth with the idea of the covenant of creation and the Noachian covenant as a creation-renewal covenant (388).

relationship to God. The creation covenant also reveals that God has made commitments to the creation that include its seventh-day culmination in God's sabbath rest. Thus, God has set in motion a divine-human drama of multi-generational partnership that can be called a covenant of community for community. That is to say, God creates man and woman whose generations develop into a vast community of partners for God in this age. And all of that generational unfolding and exercise of royal-priestly responsibilities keeps building toward the seventh-day fulfillment of the covenant community with God.

God's covenant with creation is, therefore, the ground of the judgment-redemption covenants God made with Abraham and his line through Isaac and Jacob. Consider, for example, the book of Leviticus, which is preeminently about God's presence with Israel in the tabernacle and its priestly services. Thank offerings and sin offerings regularly offered to God as part of the covenant bond reach their high point every year on the Day of Atonement when the high priest enters the holy of holies and sprinkles blood on the ark of the covenant. Highlighting the significance of that annual act, Nehemia Polen explains, is the contact of blood with the ark. The contact of "the fluid of life itself, with the precise center point of the structure of sacred space erected within the Israelite encampment, intimates contact with God Himself whose Presence hovers over the ark cover and who alone can effect atonement and restore the tabernacle and the cosmos to their state of original purity."[3] The aim of the tabernacle and all that relates to it, writes Polen, is to domesticate the Sinai theophany (Exod 19–20) and to serve as "a symbolic return to Eden, indeed to the pristine state of the world at Creation. As Moshe Weinfeld once put it, the completion of the tabernacle is parallel to the completion of the universe in Genesis."[4]

Polen puts emphasis on the tabernacle ceremony as a rite of purification of Israel and a symbolic return to pristine Eden. The tabernacle "is to domesticate the Sinai theophany" and serve as "a symbolic return to Eden." However, if we add to that interpretation some of what the prophets said, we discover something more. More than representing a return to Eden, the tabernacle, and later the temple, were anticipatory revelations of creation's *fulfillment* through the covenant with Israel. Later in Israel's history, Isaiah even denounced the "meaningless offerings" and "appointed feasts" of Israel, telling them to stop, because they were continuing in their sin and thus making a mockery of the ceremonies (Isa 1:10–17).[5] In the end, according to Isaiah, it will be evident to Israel and all nations as it was to Solomon (1 Kgs 8:27) and as God declares, "heaven is my throne and the earth is my footstool" (Isa 66:1). Jeremiah, prophesying Judah's exile in Babylon and the destruction of the temple, spoke repeatedly of Israel's continuing uncleanliness. In declaring the word of the Lord, Jeremiah does not speak of a real or symbolic return to Eden but of a new covenant that will go beyond the old

3. Polen, "Leviticus and Hebrews," 221–22.

4. Polen, "Leviticus and Hebrews," 216.

5. See the insightful essay by Duff, "Blood of Goats," 765–83.

one. "'This is the covenant I will make with the house of Israel after that time,' declares the Lord. 'I will put my law in their minds and write it on their hearts. I will be their God, and they will be my people'" (Jer 31:33). Jeremiah does indeed hear the Lord swearing an oath on the endurance of creation (31:35–37), but the promise in his oath was of a new Jerusalem, not a return to Eden—the promise of creation fulfilled, not of Eden restored.

COVENANTS OLD AND NEW

God's creational purpose from the beginning has been to reveal the divine glory to and with humans who are to manifest, through their covenant faithfulness in this age, the faithfulness of God in building that community. If, with the help of the Letter to the Hebrews, we take Polen's interpretation of the tabernacle as "domesticating the Sinai theophany," and translate it into a vision of creation fulfilled, we can see, by faith, the ultimate goal of the Sinai revelation. Israel's gathering at Sinai and their veiled experience of God's presence in the tabernacle were anticipatory revelations in this climactic gathering of the faithful of all ages around Mount Zion in face-to-face fellowship with God. "You have not come to something that can be touched, a blazing fire, and darkness, and gloom, and a tempest, and the sound of a trumpet, and a voice whose words made the hearers beg that not another word be spoken to them." Instead, writes the author of Hebrews, "you have come to Mount Zion and to the city of the living God, the heavenly Jerusalem, and to innumerable angels in festal gathering, and to the assembly of the firstborn who are enrolled in heaven, and to God the judge of all, and to the spirits of the righteous made perfect, and to Jesus, the mediator of a new covenant, and to the sprinkled blood that speaks a better word than the blood of Abel" (Heb 12:18, 22–24).

God's seven days of creation are ordered as a covenant for community, the community God is building throughout this age on the way toward its fulfillment in God's sabbath glory. In this age, the human generations play a part in the construction of that community through faithful, loving service to God and neighbors in the exercise of all their responsibilities. In the age of resurrected life still to come, the community of saints of all ages will join together, through Jesus Christ, in the celebration of God's glory, in which their own purified glory and that of all creatures will be unveiled. The meaning of human life, in other words, is being disclosed through two different modes and times of existence. Life in this age for the sixth-day image of God—the generations of the first Adam—has its covenant relation to God *through faith*, not yet by sight. In this earthly mode of existence, human communion with God points by way of revelatory anticipation to the second mode of communal existence in the last Adam, Jesus Christ, the life-giving Spirit of seventh-day fulfillment. In that never-ending year of jubilee the covenanted community will be fully manifest as the new Jerusalem, house of God, body of Christ, bride of the bridegroom, brothers and sisters of their elder brother, joint heirs with the Lord, and citizen-governors under the King of kings.

Very much in tune with the patterns of honor and hospitality, commission toward commendation, and revelation in anticipation, the pattern of covenant for community becomes manifest through human history in accord with all of God's promises, blessings, and covenant faithfulness. Central to the creation's revelatory unfolding are God's covenants of judgment and redemption with Noah, Abraham, Isaac, Jacob, and the children of Israel. The covenants of community in this age thereby point ahead to, and are empowered by, their still-to-be-experienced fulfillment in the heavenly Jerusalem through God's new covenant in Messiah Jesus.[6]

CREATION AND COVENANT IN BARTH'S INTERPRETATION

Karl Barth's understanding of "creation" and "covenant" misses something of importance here, in my judgment. He argues that "creation is the formal presupposition of the covenant in which God fulfills the will of His free love . . . Creation is one long preparation . . . for what God will intend and do with it in the history of the covenant. Its nature is simply its equipment for grace. Its creatureliness is pure promise, expectation and prophecy of that which in His grace . . . God plans for man and will not delay to accomplish for his benefit."[7] There is nothing here, however, to suggest the covenantal character of creation at its root, nothing about the creation revealing God's free love from the start. For Barth, God's covenant with humans follows on creation or comes on top of creation; creation is a platform for, or formal presupposition of, God's covenant love for humans. Consequently, Barth does not recognize the seventh day of creation as its built-in covenantal destiny from the foundation.

Barth's interpretation of the revelation of Jesus Christ depends on his understanding of creation and covenant. He recognizes that God's free love for humans moves toward an eschatological goal of communion. Yet Barth's argument flows from his conviction that God's free love is unbounded, unencumbered by any creational bonds or obligations. God's covenant bond does not begin with creation but with the free inbreaking of God's love from outside or above it. "In this way," Barth explains, "creation is the road to the covenant, its external power and external basis, because for its fulfillment the latter [the covenant] depends wholly on the fact that the creature is in no position to act alone as the partner of God, that it is thrown back wholly and utterly on the care and intercession of God Himself."[8]

6. According to Witherington, the apostle Paul "speaks of Christians on earth as already being part of a heavenly commonwealth or community (see Phil 3:19–20; Gal 4:25–27). It was precisely this that Jesus sought . . . It is not just any movement of gathering and awakening, but the *eschatological* gathering of God's people. The central content of Jesus' preaching after all, was that with his appearance the time was fulfilled." Witherington, *Jesus, Paul*, 81, 85.

7. Barth, *Church Dogmatics*, 230–31.

8. Barth, *Church Dogmatics*, 231.

The implication of Barth's argument seems to be that if we were to recognize the creation, and particularly human beings, as having any obligations or responsibilities prior to God's gracious action in free love, then humans would be in a position to "act alone as the partner of God." If that were the case, then apparently God's love would not be (could not be?) freely initiated. However, hasn't God created in such a way as to make all creatures wholly and utterly dependent on him such that humans have never been in a position to act alone as God's partner? Have they not been utterly dependent creatures from the beginning? Yet, at the same time, is it not also the case that God creates humans to be the kind of partners who are capable of acting with real responsibility, capable even of acting in sinful disobedience against God, without that implying that they are actually independent of God in any way?

"What we now see," writes Barth, "is that the covenant is the internal basis of creation," and consists in the fact that "the wisdom and omnipotence of God the Creator was not just any wisdom and omnipotence but that of His free love . . . What God created when He created the world and man was not just any place, but that which was foreordained for the establishment and the history of the covenant, not just any subject, but that which was to become God's partner in this history, i.e., the nature which God in His grace willed to address and accept and the man predestined for His service."[9] After the creation of humans, Barth is saying, God established a covenant of grace with them because they had been predestined for such a partnership with God. And this means, "the covenant whose history had still to commence was the covenant which, as the goal appointed for creation and the creature, made creation necessary and possible, and determined and limited the creature."[10] In other words, there was a predetermined necessity built into creation to receive God's covenant, and therefore, human creatures, are "determined and limited" by that necessity. This is the route Barth takes to relate Jesus Christ to the creation. The creation, as predetermined preparation for the covenant, "is itself already a unique sign of the covenant and a true sacrament; not Jesus Christ as the goal, but Jesus Christ as the beginning (the beginning just because He is the goal) of creation."[11]

Does Barth in this way finally recognize that God's relation to creation in Christ is a covenant bond? Yes and no. No, in that God's covenant of grace with human creatures is logically subsequent to creation, distinct from creation, a free act of love that is not bound by creation. But yes, in the sense that while Jesus is the goal of creation as the expression of God's free-loving covenant of grace, he is, thereby, the beginning of creation as its predetermined covenant goal. Creation is not covenantal, and the covenant is not creational; but by a twist of logic Barth contends that the subsequent covenant of grace in Christ is the prior cause of the creation's necessary reception of the covenant. Therefore, Christ is the beginning of creation only because he is its

9. Barth, *Church Dogmatics*, 231.
10. Barth, *Church Dogmatics*, 231.
11. Barth, *Church Dogmatics*, 231–32.

predetermined goal. Nevertheless, Christ, as the "beginning," is *not* the beginning of a creation bound to God in covenant love. Creation may be predestined to experience God's free love in Christ, but creation does not exhibit that love and is only a preparation for that covenant. In Barth, it seems to me, there is no recognition of a covenantal bond of God through the Son with creation from its foundation that would yield revelatory anticipations of the creation's fulfillment.

In contrast to Barth, the interpretation we have been developing is that creation is a seven-day covenant bond with God from its foundation, through and through. The New Testament proclaims that through God's revelation in Jesus Christ, the Son (and Word) of God who became fully human as Jesus, is the one through whom all things were made. God freely loves the creation from its foundation. Within that creation drama, the revelation of God's love for sinners reaches its culmination in Jesus, the incarnate Son who has borne God's judgment against sin and is reconciling the creation to God. That response of God to sinners reveals an extension and a deepening of the same free love of God. God's judgment-redemption covenants presuppose God's covenant with creation. God has loved the creation from its foundation, oriented as it is toward God's sabbath rest. God's sacrificial love for sinners revealed in Christ is not the beginning of God's free love toward humans, nor does it create the Sabbath rest of God into which Christ's entrance opens the way for repentant and restored brothers and sisters to follow in his train.

In the power of the Holy Spirit it is indeed now possible to interpret history from the perspective of God's climactic covenant in Christ Jesus. By faith we can understand how God has kept covenant with the creation in response to human sin, which violates the covenant bond and calls God's own righteousness and faithfulness into question. God is not the one who breaks troth with creation but the one who continues to sustain it even as divine wrath falls upon human faithlessness and injustice. God's dealings with humankind through the judgment-redemption covenants with Noah, Abraham, and Israel reaffirm God's promise to fulfill creation by washing it clean of all unrighteousness. God never breaks troth with creation even though humans throughout their generations have broken troth with God. The terms of God's commissioning of human creatures have not been changed or discarded due to sin but are brought to fulfillment in and through the sacrifice of Jesus and his resurrection as the last Adam.[12]

---

12. Hahn's interpretation of the Old Testament covenants is illuminated by his close reading of Gal 3–4 and Heb 1–9. With regard to Heb 1–2, he concludes that the language of kinship is central and that "the structure of kinship relationships is part of the creation's order, rooted in God's original plan for humanity (2:8–9; cf. Ps 8:4–6) which unfolds in the patriarchal period, culminating in God's sworn blessing to 'Abraham and his descendants' (Heb 2:16; cf. Gen 22:16–18; Heb 6:13–17). The content of this blessing is, in its essence, the restoration of the original, creational familial (specifically, filial) relationship between God and his people, with all its privileges (e.g., priesthood and kingship)." Hahn, *Kinship by Covenant*, 325.

THE BOND OF THE BODY OF CHRIST

Commenting on 1 Corinthians 11–14, Wright explains that the theme of the covenanted community as a body "comes into its own in chapter 12 with one of Paul's greatest metaphors . . . What the creator god has accomplished in and through Jesus is the renewal of the human race, that for which humankind was made in the first place. What better image, then, to use for its corporate life than that of a human body, with limbs and organs working as they were meant to do."[13] As we noted earlier, the choruses of heavenly praise for the exalted Christ arise not only for the reason that he gave up his life blood to purchase (redeem) those cut off from God in their sin (Rev 5:9–10), but also, and first of all, because he "created all things." He is worshipped by those who "cast their crowns before the throne," singing, "You are worthy, our Lord and God, to receive glory and honor and power, *for you created all things*, and by your will they existed and were created" (Rev 4:10–11, italics added). The sacrificial savior redeems and sets right the creation, which he has upheld covenantally from the beginning. The bond is so close that the divine-human relationship can be described as a marriage and, with the revelation of Christ, as his body.

Since the creation manifests a covenant bond with the creator from beginning to end, through judgment and redemption, and on to its seventh-day fulfillment, it is obvious that the bond between God and the image of God is constituted in order to realize a divine-human community of immeasurable richness and breadth that includes the good fruits of all human relationships and labors as well as the vast grandeur of all other creatures. The sixth day of God's creation is bound together with all other days, entailing the human obligation to steward the wider world of God's honorable and hospitable design in service to God. The multi-generational image of God, male and female, thus lives and serves as the chief steward of God's kingdom in anticipation of God's benediction to Christ Jesus—his body, his bride, his brothers and sisters, and his joint heirs. That is the day without evening or morning when God draws the faithful of all ages, through Christ's life, death, resurrection, and ascension, into the fully realized community of face-to-face fellowship and mutual indwelling with God.

From all of this, it is abundantly clear that human participation in the fulfilled community God is creating is possible only through God's reconciling covenant in Christ Jesus. The covenantal *incorporation* of descendants of the first Adam into the resurrection life of the last Adam is possible only because the one through whom all things are created is the one who became fully human with us, taking to himself our responsibilities and our failures. His death and resurrection become ours now through faith by the working of the Spirit, in anticipation of completed incorporation in the final resurrection. That is why Paul encourages the faithful alive in this age to realize that "your life is hidden with Christ in God. When Christ who is your life is revealed, then you also will be revealed with him in glory" (Col 3:3–4). That is why

13. Wright, *Resurrection*, 295.

Hebrews warns believers not to harden their hearts, as covenant breakers in Israel did in the wilderness, so that they may enter God's rest (Heb 3:7—4:11). David Hay explains that the author of Hebrews speaks of the suffering of Jesus as once-for-all, yet speaks in past, present, and future tenses of Jesus's ascension to the right hand of majesty on high (the heavenly "session"). Jesus has entered God's rest, and believers "seeing" him there by faith are to run their earthly race as Jesus did, looking ahead to the joy of entering God's rest.[14] God's covenant for community *began* before our time, *is* presently incorporating believers into it, and *will be* fully revealed when time is fulfilled.

CONCLUSION

In the chapters of part 2, we have considered four revelatory patterns of God's creation, each of which plays a part in the unfolding drama of God's relation to the human generations and the whole creation. God's relation to us is made manifest in creation-wide developments that include the particular dramas of our friendships and families, talents and occupations, tribes and nations, cultures and civilizations. The Genesis story, which is affirmed or presupposed throughout Scripture, paints the picture of reality in its entirety as God's creation. Creatures made in the image of God receive a unique commission to govern and develop creation in loving partnership with God through a revelatory, multigenerational drama. The fact that each honorable creature is constituted for hospitality raises the dramatic question: where does all this hospitality lead? The fact that each creature receives its assignment or commission raises the pressing question: when and how will human creatures fulfill their commission and receive their commendation? The fact that each creature is revelatory raises the urgent question: what do all the incomplete revelations point toward? Will we ever see the fulfillment of God's purposes anticipated by all the covenantal revelations to date?

Genesis 1–2 portrays reality through a highly compact picture-story that locates the drama of the divine-human community in the context of God's six days of creating and seventh-day rest. What is clear from all of this is that there is no dualism between this world and another world. As Michael Horton writes, "Against Plato's irrepressible 'two worlds,' accentuated again in Kant, appears Paul's 'two ages.' . . . Instead of the 'true world' of eternal perfection versus the 'apparent world' of temporal change we find 'this present age' and 'the age to come.'"[15] To say it slightly differently, the seven-day covenant of creation that reveals the glory of God is oriented from its foundation toward its climax in the age to come. There is no way for any human to stand outside

---

14. Hay, *Glory*, 88–89.

15. Horton, *Covenant and Eschatology*, 32. Horton has no qualms about speaking here of an "eschatological dualism," but since the word "dualism" suggests an opposition or tension, I think it would be better to speak of a "duality" of ages, or, even better, of the important distinction between the sixth and seventh days of God's creation order.

the creation of which we are a part to describe, analyze, or tell this story. The seven days of creation can be understood, imagined, and portrayed, therefore, only through trusting communion with God as we exercise the responsibilities given to us.

The language of the creation story is not foreign to human experience and imagination, and God's successive judgment-redemption covenants have revealed more and more of creation's meaning. To question the validity of this story as the truth about reality requires a standpoint within a different story from which to call biblical revelation into question. Yet if reality is what Genesis and the whole Bible says it is, then there is no other standpoint available, and every attempt to account for reality from other standpoints will prove to be inadequate at best and misguided at worst. If, indeed, we are the sixth-day image of God, participants in a covenant-for-community drama of seven days that is constituted by patterns of honor and hospitality, commission towards commendation, and revelatory anticipation, then the only way to live meaningfully and to come to know God and ourselves fully is to live in faith-led communion with the one whose self-disclosing drama embraces us from beginning to consummation.

PART 3

The Covenantal Disclosure of Reality

10

A Developing Drama

THE COVENANT BOND OF HEAVEN AND EARTH

JACOB, THE SON OF Isaac and grandson of Abraham, was traveling from Beersheba to Haran. When evening came, he stopped for the night and slept on the ground. While sleeping, he had a dream in which he saw a "stairway resting on the earth, with its top reaching to heaven, and the angels of God were ascending and descending on it. There above it stood the Lord, and he said: 'I am the Lord, the God of your father Abraham and the God of Isaac'" (Gen 28:12–13a, TNIV). The Lord extended to Jacob the same promise he had made to Abraham and Isaac: "I will give you and your descendants the land on which you are lying. Your descendants will be like the dust of the earth, and you will spread out to the west and to the east, to the north and to the south. All peoples on earth will be blessed through you and your offspring" (28:13b–14, TNIV). When Jacob awoke, he was afraid. "How awesome is this place! This is none other than the house of God; this is the gate of heaven" (18:17, TNIV). In the dream, Jacob caught a glimpse of the bond between heaven and earth. He was awed by the glory of the Lord's throne room and the stairway ascending to it. He was convinced that he was in the very house of God.

In the story of Jacob's dream, he is identified as a son in the line of Abraham and Isaac. There is no direct mention of his being in the line of the sixth-day human generations, though God's promise that through him and his offspring "all peoples on earth will be blessed" makes that connection. Also in this passage, when Jacob sees the stairway to heaven, no reference is made to the seventh day of creation, though Jacob's professed belief that he was standing at the gate of heaven, in the house of God, makes that connection. The passage we discussed in earlier chapters—Hebrews 4:3–11—is explicit about the seventh day of creation being God's day of rest and God's promise that the faithful will enter that rest. That clue in Hebrews, I believe, gives us reason to look again at the nature of God's bond with the human generations, because Abraham, Isaac, and Jacob do follow in the line of the sixth-day generations of humankind, and God's unique covenant with them is related to the heavenly (seventh-day) glory that Jacob witnessed in his dream.

Jacob's dream revealed, on the one hand, God addressing him from above, from the throne room or inner sanctum of the divine glory, which is not the realm of Jacob's ordinary, day-to-day life on earth. When he awakens, he can only bless the spot on which he slept, using the stone on which his head had rested to memorialize the place, which he calls "Beth-el"—the house of God.[1] The connection between earth and heaven is intimate even if heaven is glimpsed only in a God-given dream. On the other hand, the Lord's words to Jacob are about the future of this age. Jacob hears not only about the promises God made to Abraham and Isaac but also about what was yet to come in human history as a consequence of God's covenant promises to him. The human generations, whom God addresses in a new way through the family of Abraham, will continue to unfold far into the future. And that generational unfolding continues today under the canopy of creation's heaven, from where God communicates with men and women about a goal that transcends the experience of earthlings yet is intimately related to human history.

The dreams, the visions, and the voice of the Lord covenanting with a particular earthly family for the sake of all peoples will be repeated in different ways in the course of history, reaching its culmination in the coming of Jesus. Jesus makes the connection clear when he begins calling disciples to follow him. He says to Nathaniel (who by faith recognized him as the King of Israel), "Very truly, I tell you, you will see heaven opened and the angels of God ascending and descending upon the Son of Man" (John 1:51). Not only does that promise hark back to the Lord's revelation to Jacob, it also draws God's long, covenantal drama with humankind to a culminating focus on the lordship of this Messiah Jesus through whom all peoples and nations would be blessed.[2]

By beginning this chapter with the story of Jacob's dream, we have entered the Bible's record of divinely initiated judgment-redemption covenants. God's revelation to Jacob points ahead to a creation-wide message and purpose. The Lord chooses Jacob (later Israel) for a purpose that is still to be realized, beginning with the land of promise for his innumerable descendants not yet born, and God's blessing of all nations on earth. What Jacob saw in his dream corresponded to what he heard—the worldwide reach of God's covenant promises connecting heaven and earth, God's

---

1. Later on, God spoke again to Jacob in a dream about Bethel: "I am the God of Bethel, where you anointed a pillar and where you made a vow to me" (Gen 31:13). Still later, God told Jacob and his family to go to Bethel to settle and build an altar to the Lord in remembrance of God's appearance to him there (Gen 35:1–7).

2. "From the perspective of the Christian canon," writes Hahn, "the fulfillment of both the Davidic covenant (an eternal heir on David's throne) and the Abrahamic covenant oath of the Aqedah (blessing to all the nations) must await the New Covenant established in Christ. The Gospel of Matthew introduces Jesus Christ specifically as the 'Son of Abraham' and the 'Son of David,' that is, the one who will fulfill the covenant oaths to both these patriarchs," Hahn, *Kinship By Covenant*, 122.

kingdom and human governance, the seventh day of God's rest, and the first six days of anticipatory revelation.

Our aim in the chapters of part 3 is not to rehearse the history and details of the biblical covenants. Thankfully, there are many fine studies to which the reader can turn for all or part of that history.[3] Our aim is to introduce the argument that covenant history is central to God's mounting disclosure of the meaning of created reality. God's unfolding covenant drama with creation reaches its denouement, according to the New Testament, in the incarnation, death, resurrection, and ascension of the Son of God, Messiah Jesus. Yet Israel's ascended Messiah, the Lord of creation, has not yet completed all that is entailed in the promised fulfillment of God's kingdom. Between the time of Christ's ascension and his promised return, his Spirit is at work in this age, continuing to woo a bride into Christ's embrace; creating a worldwide family of God; guiding stewards in their creation-care; cutting and polishing the human stones that will compose the final Beth-el; and establishing a company of royal officials to serve Christ the King as governors of God's vast domain. The culmination of the divine-human drama will come with Christ's return, the resurrection of the dead, the last judgment, and the celebration of God's glory in the seventh-day rest of new Jerusalem, when God's will is done on earth as it is in heaven and the joy of all creatures is full to overflowing.

A MULTIGENERATIONAL DRAMA

The first time the word "covenant" (*berit*) is used in the Bible is with God's call to Noah to build an ark in anticipation of the flood-judgment of corrupt and violent humankind (Gen 6:18). As Hahn points out, however, the way the word is used in that text suggests that it has the character of a creation-renewal covenant.[4] The connection is confirmed with the language of the covenant God makes with Noah and his family after they leave the ark, language that echoes Genesis 1:26–30. The words of covenant blessing are for human procreation, for dominion over the earth, and for food to eat, along with the statement that God's covenant is with every living creature on earth. Although the word "covenant" is not used in Genesis 1, we can recognize that by "creating the world God committed himself to it,"[5] as William Dumbrell says. On

3. Hahn distinguishes the biblical covenants of kinship, suzerainty treaty, and kingship in *Kinship by Covenant*. Other valuable studies of the biblical covenants include, Wright, *Mission of God*; Williamson, *Sealed With an Oath*; Miller, *Way of the Lord*; Miller, "Divine Command/Divine Law"; Horton, *Covenant and Eschatology*; Wright, *New Testament*; Wright, *Climax*; Dumbrell, *Covenant and Creation*; Hillers, *Covenant*; Kline, *By Oath Consigned*; and Kline, *Treaty of Great King*.

4. Hahn, *Kinship by Covenant*, 95. There is debate about how broadly the word "covenant" should be used and whether it may be used to characterize the creation order. John Stek wants a restricted use, arguing that the word "covenant" should not be asked to bear the weight that should be borne by the word "kingdom." Stek, "'Covenant' Overload." See also the response to Stek by Bartholomew, "Covenant and Creation."

5. Dumbrell, "Covenant with Noah," 7. Others who recognize in the Noachian covenant a

that basis, the Noachian covenant is a creation-reaffirming and -renewal covenant. In other words, all of God's judgment-redemption covenants, beginning with Noah and continuing through Abraham, Israel, and David, build on one another in expanding ways to uphold and carry forward the creation purposes to which God has pledged covenantal troth. In that sense, consequently, the historical covenants can be considered creation-renewal covenants that build on one another toward the fulfillment of creation through God's new covenant in Jesus Christ.

According to John Goldingay, God's covenant established with Israel after delivering them from bondage in Egypt also entailed the renewal of creation. "The story of deliverance thus begins with a report of creation blessing, of how 'the Israelites became fruitful and prolific and numerous and strong—very much so—and the land became full of them' (Exod 1:7). The comment systematically interweaves notes from Genesis 1–11 and Genesis 12–50. The people's life is working out in keeping with the intention and pattern of events at the Beginning. Its deliverance will match up with this creation purpose of blessing."[6] God redeems Israel from Egypt to send them on to the promised land. God has a mission for them and the covenant at Sinai sets them on a path of renewed life and hope on earth in expectation of the ultimate revelation of the kingdom of God.[7]

The ongoing development of covenantal revelation will include new disclosures as well as reminders of what has already been made known about God and God's purposes for Israel and the nations. Early in Moses's leadership of Israel, when Pharaoh was placing ever-increasing burdens on the enslaved people, Moses complained to God for having failed to rescue them. The Lord responded with forward-looking promises that continued to demand faith and patience on Israel's part and assured them of deliverance. God also told Moses something new: "'I am the Lord. I appeared to Abraham, Isaac and Jacob as God Almighty [*El-Shaddai*], but by my name 'The Lord' [*Yahweh*] I did not make myself known to them' . . . Say therefore to the Israelites, 'I am the Lord [*Yahweh*], and I will free you from the burdens of the Egyptians and deliver you from slavery to them . . . I will bring you into the land that I swore to give to Abraham, Isaac and Jacob; I will give it to you for a possession. I am the Lord'" (Exod 6:2–3, 6, 8).

Words old and new: God Almighty reiterates the promises to Abraham and by revealing the new name "Yahweh" gives added reason for Israel to trust the Lord to do for them in the future what he is promising. This revelation also builds on what God told Moses at the burning bush when Moses asked how he should respond when the

---

creation-renewal covenant include: Spykman, *Reformational Theology*; Robertson, *Christ and Covenants*.

6. Goldingay, *Old Testament Theology*, 290. See also Fretheim, *God and World*, 109–11.

7. The covenantal mission of Jesus, enacted through his obedience to God and proclaimed by his apostles, builds on and fulfills this long history of promise and anticipation of the kingdom of God. See Goheen, *Light to Nations*; and on the "narrative" of the mission as Luke unfolds it, see Tannehill, *Narrative Unity*.

people ask him, what is the name of the God who sent you? "God said to Moses, 'I am who I am.' He said further, 'Thus you shall say to the Israelites, "I AM has sent me to you"'" (Exod 3:14).

Throughout God's dealings with Israel, as the Bible tells the story, the remembrance of past revelations and the reception of new disclosures build on the praise of El-Shaddai, Yahweh, and other names of God. In the verses of choral response of Psalm 136, for example, where each verse ends with "for his steadfast love endures forever," we hear words of praise for God's continuing and developing promises through generations. This psalm of remembrance begins with thanks for the Lord's goodness and majesty, and continues with praise of God for making heaven and earth, the waters, and the greater and lesser lights. It moves on to thanksgiving for God's liberation of Israel from Egypt and for guiding them into the land of promise and defeating their enemies. Finally, the psalm concludes with praise for the one who "gives food to all flesh," admonishing the faithful, "O give thanks to the God of heaven, for his steadfast love endures forever." The pattern here is repeated again and again in the Bible. It is the pattern of remembering God's covenant faithfulness, which has revealed so much already—even while new promises point ahead to what is yet to come.[8]

In this connection, Mark Boda draws attention to Nehemiah, chapter 9, one of the weightiest of the rehearsal-and-anticipation passages in the Old Testament.[9] Nehemiah was a leader in Israel's history long after Jacob, long after God led Israel out of Egypt into the promised land, and at the end of Judah's long exile in Babylon. After the Persians defeated the Babylonians, in the first year of King Cyrus, God moved Cyrus to authorize the rebuilding of the temple in Jerusalem and to allow captives from Judah and Benjamin to return to their land. After the reconstruction in Jerusalem had begun, Ezra and Nehemiah returned to Jerusalem where Nehemiah became the governor and led the rebuilding project. After the city wall was completed, all the people assembled to celebrate, and in doing so they were inspired to listen to Ezra, a scribe and teacher of the law, read the whole book of the law God gave to Israel through Moses. The celebration and praise of God was powerful and it moved the people to confess their sins and the sins of their fathers that led to God's judgment of the separated kingdoms of Israel and Judah.

Boda emphasizes the way Nehemiah 9 summarizes God's long history of faithfulness with Israel. The passage is too long to quote in full, but excerpts can suggest its sweep. With Levites leading the celebration, the people are told, "Stand up and bless the Lord your God from everlasting to everlasting. Blessed be your glorious name, which is exalted above all blessing and praise . . . You are the Lord, you alone, you have made heaven, the heavens of heavens, and all their host, the earth and all that is on it, the seas and all that is in them. To all of them you give life, and the host of heaven

8. Some other passages that exhibit all or part of this pattern include Pss 68, 78, 105, 106, 132, 135, 145; Dan 9:1–19; Acts 7, 13:13–41.

9. Boda, *Heartbeat*, 80–87.

worships you" (Neh 9:5b–6). Then the prayerful address recalls God's covenant with Abraham, Israel's slavery in Egypt, the giving of the covenant at Sinai, entrance into the promised land, and then the exile. Throughout, there are remembrances of Israel's covenant failures, confession of sin, and praise for God's faithfulness. "You are the Lord, the God who chose Abram and brought him out of the Ur of the Chaldeans and gave him the name Abraham; and you found his heart faithful before you, and made with him a covenant . . . [Y]ou have fulfilled your promise, for you are righteous" (Neh 9:7–8).

"And you saw the distress of our ancestors in Egypt . . . You performed signs and wonders against Pharaoh . . . You made a name for yourself, which remains to this day" (9:9–10).

"You came down also upon Mount Sinai, and spoke with them from heaven, and gave them right ordinances and true laws, good statutes and commandments, and you made known your holy sabbath to them and gave them commandments and statutes and a law through your servant Moses" (9:13–14).

"But they and our ancestors acted presumptuously and stiffened their necks and did not obey your commandments; they refused to obey, and were not mindful of the wonders you performed among them . . . But you are a God ready to forgive, gracious and merciful, slow to anger and abounding in steadfast love, and you did not forsake them" (9:16–17).

"And you gave them kingdoms and peoples, and allotted to them every corner, so they took possession of the land . . . You multiplied their descendants like the stars of heaven, and brought them into the land that you had told their ancestors to enter and possess" (9:22, 24).

"Nevertheless they were disobedient and rebelled against you and cast your law behind their backs and killed your prophets, who had warned them in order to turn them back to you, and they committed great blasphemies. Therefore you gave them into the hands of their enemies, who made them suffer. Then in the time of their suffering they cried out to you and you heard them from heaven, and according to your great mercies you gave them saviors who saved them from the hands of their enemies. But after they had rest, they again did evil before you, and you abandoned them to the hands of their enemies . . . " (9:26–28).

"Now therefore, our God—the great and mighty and awesome God, keeping covenant and steadfast love—do not treat lightly all the hardship that has come upon us, upon our kings, our officials, our priests, our prophets, our ancestors, and all your people, since the time of the kings of Assyria until today. You have been just in all that has come upon us, for you have dealt faithfully and we have acted wickedly . . . " (9:32–33).

The drama from which the biblical narrative arises and to which it attests is the development of human history in relation to God. From the viewpoint of earthlings like us, the disclosure of God's purposes for creation has emerged and continues to build gradually over many generations. God's bond with creation has been, and continues to be, developed with creatures made "very good," who are now degraded and faithless covenant-breakers. Yet God in his patience and mercy continues to uphold the creation with its corrupted human generations for purposes we do not fully understand. God's steadfast love for Israel and the nations does not put an end to the mystery but only deepens it. All human understanding, even after generations of God's judgments and revealing mercy, remains limited; wisdom and insight come from living within our creaturely limits as faithful, humble, thankful stewards of all that God has called us to be and to do. Yet even those who confess their sins and call on God, as the returning exiles under Nehemiah and Ezra did, will not fathom the mystery in this age. As M. C. Smit puts it, "Whatever the angle of our approach to God, we encounter the mystery. Equally, whatever the angle of our approach to historical reality, we encounter the mystery; for God stands in such close relation to his world that as long as there is mystery in God there will be mystery in earthly existence."[10] The creation is by its very nature revelatory of the creator, and therefore it will always draw us into the mystery of God's unfolding revelation that is beyond our grasp.

THE MYSTERY OF LIFE AND THE COVENANT TESTIMONY

In the Scriptures, written and collected by the children of Israel and the followers of Jesus, we are made conscious that the mystery God is unveiling is through the divine-human drama of creation. The limits of creaturely life do not point away from, or hide God. They do not interfere with our attempts to know God and ourselves. Rather, the creatures of God's first six days exist as both participants in and witnesses to the unfolding revelation of the mystery. We see this in Jacob's dream, and it comes through in all the Scripture. What we read in the Bible about God and the human generations is conveyed in language that typically draws on creational metaphors, pictures, and descriptions that are perfectly apt for God's revelatory purposes. We read of heavenly bodies following their courses like humans running a race; of plants and other creatures generating seeds, fruits, and offspring, and sometimes dancing or clapping their hands; of humans being compared to ants, foxes, sheep, goats, angels, and God; and of God the Almighty, the Lord, acting from within the mysterious depths of his royal domain as king, judge, accountant, bridegroom, vineyard keeper, eagle, lion, nurse, mother, and father. All of these portrayals are integral to the character of the covenants, which keep on disclosing aspects of the meaning of God's engagement with us and with the whole creation. Listen, for example, to the beginning of Psalm 95:

> O come, let us sing to the Lord;
> > let us make a joyful noise to the Rock of our salvation! . . .
> For the Lord is a great God,

10. Smit, "Divine Mystery in History," 233.

> and a great King above all gods.
> In his hand are the depths of the earth;
>   the heights of the mountains are his also.
> The sea is his, for he made it,
>   and the dry land, which his hands have formed (Ps 95:1, 3–5).

Again from the psalter, listen to these words from Psalm 102, which is the prayer of an afflicted man who speaks from within the *house* of God's creation days, some of which the Lord wears like clothes:

> But you, O Lord, are enthroned forever;
>   your name endures to all generations . . .
> Let this be recorded for a generation to come,
>   so that a people yet unborn may praise the Lord:
> that he looked down from his holy height,
>   from heaven the Lord looked at the earth,
> to hear the groans of the prisoners,
>   to set free those who were doomed to die; . . .
> He has broken my strength in midcourse;
>   he has shortened my days.
> "O my God," I say, "do not take me away at the midpoint of my life,
>   you whose years endure throughout all generations."
> Long ago you laid the foundations of the earth,
>   and the heavens are the work of your hands.
> They will perish, but you endure;
>   they will all wear out like a garment.
> You change them like clothing, and they pass away;
>   but you are the same, and your years have no end.
> The children of your servants shall live secure;
>   their offspring shall be established in your presence (Ps 102:12, 19–20, 23–28).

The Lord God is enthroned forever in his heavenly sanctuary even as the human generations continue their development along with all other creatures of the first six creation days. The psalmist writes for sons and daughters not yet born, telling them in advance to praise the Lord who is always there acting, calling, drawing from above. The covenant-making Lord is the creator of the earth and the heavens, the whole of which is at his disposal to be changed like clothing. Nevertheless, like Moses (Ps 90:16–17), this psalmist believes that the mystery of the Lord's years will never end and that "the children of your servants shall live secure" in the Lord's presence, fulfilled in God's rest.

The great oration of God to Job offers a wealth of descriptive pictures, reminding readers of the identity, the boundaries, and the mystery of God's creation covenant. God asks Job,

Where were you when I laid the foundation of the earth?
  Tell me, if you have understanding.
Who determined its measurements—surely you know!
  Or who stretched the line upon it?
On what were its bases sunk,
  or who laid its cornerstone
when the morning stars sang together
  and all the heavenly beings shouted for joy? (Job 38:4–7) . . .
Who has let the wild ass go free?
  Who has loosed the bonds of the swift ass,
to which I have given the steppe for his home,
  the salt land for its dwelling place (Job 39:5–6)? . . .
Is it by your wisdom that the hawk soars,
  and spreads its wings toward the south?
Is it by your command that the eagle mounts up
  and makes its nest on high? (39:26–27)

What is God like? How can we understand him? How can we understand ourselves? For Amos, God is like a judge in a courtroom, like a vineyard keeper, a repairer of tents, a warrior, a roaring lion, a shepherd, and a devouring fire. Let's join Amos in the cosmic courtroom and listen to God's charge against Israel and against us:

Ah, you that turn justice to wormwood,
  and bring righteousness to the ground! . . .
They hate the one who reproves in the gate,
  and they abhor the one who speaks the truth.
Therefore because you trample on the poor
  and take from them levies of grain,
you have built houses of hewn stone,
  but you shall not live in them;
you have planted pleasant vineyards,
  but you shall not drink their wine.
For I know how many are your transgressions,
  and how great are your sins—
you who afflict the righteous,
   who take a bribe,
  and push aside the needy in the gate.
Therefore the prudent will keep silent in such a time;
  for it is an evil time.
Seek good and not evil,
  that you may live;
and so the Lord, the God of hosts, will be with you,
  just as you have said.
Hate evil and love good,

and establish justice in the gate;
It may be that the Lord, the God of hosts, will be gracious
to the remnant of Joseph (Amos 5:7, 10–15).

Faithless Israelites seem to forget that they live in God's world, in God's vineyard, in God's house, all on God's terms and by his grace, subject to the blessings and curses handed down by the righteous judge in God's courtroom.[11] Learning to do justice, to love mercy, to walk humbly with God—that is what it means to be truly human, to speak and work, to love and dance as the image of God.

What God discloses through the covenantal unfolding of creation is not suddenly and completely accomplished in a single human generation. The mystery is too great. God did not reveal everything about his purposes for creation in the Garden of Eden, or in Jacob's dream, or in the exodus from Egypt, or to Moses on Sinai, or through the words of Israel's prophets, or in Israel's return from exile to Jerusalem. Even with the arrival of the long expected Messiah Jesus—"the radiance of God's glory and the exact representation of his being" (Heb 1:3, TNIV)—not everything has yet been disclosed through his birth, life, death, resurrection, and ascension. The human generations continue to unfold, and more and more of the mystery of God's covenant promises are being illumined by the power of God's Spirit, inspiring the faithful to intensified expectations of the arrival of the day of the Lord. God has commissioned us with responsibilities that have not yet been completed even though God's day of rest has already been opened to creaturely fulfillment through Christ's ascension to the throne on high. We live at the foot of the stairway to heaven, at the foot of Sinai, at the foot of the cross, surrounded by a great cloud of witnesses with whom we are joined together worshipping God in anticipation of the final unveiling of God's sabbath with creation.

---

11. Fretheim provides some wonderful commentary on the revelatory character of creation throughout the Old Testament. With regard to Amos in particular, Fretheim says, "Amos's recurrent use of references to the natural order and the linkage he draws to human words and deeds cannot be reduced to poetic imagery. This language is 'not just hyperbole. Rather, the prophets employ numerous cosmic metaphors to underscore the significance of the historical events that occasion their oracles.' The word *metaphor* is appropriate here, providing one does not deny continuity between language and reality, recognizing the yes as well as the no in all metaphoric language. The natural order is *actually* affected by human behaviors; social order and cosmic order are in fact deeply interrelated." Fretheim, *God and World*, 171.

11

The Spirit Hovering

RETURN WITH ME TO Genesis 1:2. In the light of God's later covenantal revelations, Meredith Kline explains, Genesis 1 locates the creation in the presence of the "theophanic [God-revealing] Glory." This is the glory with which Jacob will be confronted in his dream and the awesome glory that will make Israel tremble at Sinai (Exod 19:16–19).[1] According to Kline, Genesis 1:2b says that at the beginning, when there was only an "unbounded deep-and-darkness . . . 'The Spirit of God was hovering over the face of the waters.'" The verb translated "hovering" is used at only one other place in the Pentateuch, Deuteronomy 32:11. There it likens God to "an eagle hovering protectively over its young, spreading out its wings to support them," leading Israel through "the waste howling wilderness" (Deut 32:10) on the way to Canaan. In Exodus 19:4 another verb is used, similarly describing God "as bearing Israel on eagles' wings."[2]

Kline speaks of theophany during the exodus and wilderness wanderings as God's "Glory-Presence," a mode of appearance that is cloaked or screened for the disclosure of divine mystery in this age. God appeared in a pillar of cloud by day and a pillar of fire by night. The "Glory-cloud" performed both an overshadowing function and a guiding function. In passages like Ezekiel 1:24 and 10:5, as well as in other ancient Near Eastern records, says Kline, divine glory is "depicted by a winged disk, which represented the canopy of heaven with associated phenomena like (storm)-clouds."[3] When God allows prophetic vision to penetrate "the thick darkness, the cloud is seen to be alive with cherubim and seraphim. The sound of its coming is, in the prophetic idiom, the sound of their wings."[4] The fact that, in both Genesis 1:2b and

---

1. Kline, *Images of Spirit*, 13.

2. Kline, *Images of Spirit*, 13–14. Brown's study of the Psalms yields the insight that "the most vividly iconic image associated with refuge and divine protection is that of God's 'wings.'" Brown, *Seeing Psalms*, 20. "The most detailed elaboration of the wing metaphor," says Brown, "is found in Psalm 91." Brown, *Seeing Psalms*, 21.

3. Kline, *Images of Spirit*, 14.

4. Kline, *Images of Spirit*, 14.

Deuteronomy 32:10, the verb "hovering" is used in relation to an "unbounded deep-and-darkness" (in the first) and a "waste howling wilderness" (in the second), suggests that the intention of the text is to liken "God's presence as Israel's divine aegis in the wilderness" to "God's presence over creation."[5] We can go even further, according to Kline, and see in the exodus story a reenactment of the creation drama with the pillars of cloud and fire being like the Spirit of God who brings light into darkness, divides the waters, and makes "dry land appear in the midst of the deep," leading on to "the Sabbath in the holy paradise land."[6]

The conclusion Kline reaches about Genesis 1:2b is that we should interpret the hovering "Spirit of God" as a "designation for the theophanic Glory-cloud."[7] It refers to more than the Spirit of God alone; it is a picture of the divine court with all its heavenly hosts. "When the inner reality veiled within the theophanic cloud is revealed, we behold God in his heaven. The world of the Glory theophany is a dimensional realm normally invisible to man, where God reveals his presence as the King of glory enthroned in the midst of myriads of heavenly beings."[8] This is what Jacob saw in his dream of the stairway to heaven with angels ascending and descending and the Lord above. It is, I would argue, the divine throne room toward which the entire creation is oriented.

"God's theophanic glory," Kline continues, "is the glory of royal majesty. At the center of the heavens within the veil of the Glory-cloud is found a throne; the Glory is pre-eminently the place of God's enthronement. It is, therefore, a royal palace site of the divine council and court of judgment."[9] Kline emphasizes that the various dimensions of theophany have to do with God's purposes for creation from the very beginning and we now know from the apostle John's visions on Patmos that the risen Christ is the creation's Alpha as well as its Omega. As the Son of God is the mediator of creation so the Spirit of God hovers over and guides it, playing a special role in God's covenants from the beginning.

For Jürgen Moltmann, the sound of the Spirit's "vibrating, quivering, moving and exciting" breath suggests music as much as Eagle's wings. In hearing the verses that follow Genesis 1:2, says Moltmann, we should think of the "*song of creation*. The word [of God] names, differentiates and appraises. But the breath is the same in all the words, and binds the words together. So the Creator differentiates his creatures through his creative Word and joins them through his Spirit, who is the sustainer of all his words. In the quickening breath and through the form-giving word, the Creator sings out his creatures in the sounds and rhythms in which he has his joy and his

---

5. Kline, *Images of Spirit*, 14.

6. Kline, *Images of Spirit*, 14–15.

7. Kline, *Images of Spirit*, 15. Cf. Johnson Lim, "Explication of an Exegetical Enigma in Genesis 1:1–3," 301–14.

8. Kline, *Images of Spirit*, 17.

9. Kline, *Images of Spirit*, 17–18.

good pleasure. That is why there is something like *a cosmic liturgy* and *music of the spheres.*"[10]

TABERNACLE, PROMISED LAND, AND TEMPLE

The Lord's Glory-cloud, which guided Israel through wilderness wanderings, led to ongoing disclosures of the divine presence. When the Lord instructed Moses to build a mobile tabernacle in which to meet the people (Exod 25–31), the meaning of creation as the house of God (Bethel) was reiterated. The tabernacle, like the pillars of cloud and fire, was the place of God's meeting with the people both in judgment and in blessing during the time that Israel was on the move toward the promised land. Fretheim explains:

> Verbal and thematic links between the accounts of creation and tabernacle (Exod 25–31; 35–40) have long been noted. Jon D. Levenson puts it well: "the function of these correspondences is to underscore the depiction of the sanctuary as a world, that is, an ordered, supportive, and obedient environment, and the depiction of the world as a sanctuary, that is, a place in which the reign of God is visible and unchallenged, and his holiness is palpable, unthreatened, and pervasive." In other terms, the tabernacle is a microcosm of creation (cf. Pss 11:4; 78:69; Isa 66:1–2); it is the world order as God intended, writ small in Israel.[11]

Fretheim goes on to explain, "The moving of the spirit of God in Gen 1:2 is paralleled by the spirit-filled Bezalel and other craftsmen who build the tabernacle (31:1–11). The same living, breathing spirit that grounds the creation of the world is engaged in the completion of this worship world for Israel. Their intricate craftsmanship mirrors God's own work (and the work of participating creatures)."[12] As Exodus makes clear, the Spirit of God filled Bezalel "with ability, intelligence, and knowledge in every kind of craft, to devise artistic designs, to work in gold, silver and bronze, in cutting stones for setting, and in carving wood, in every kind of craft" (Exod 31:3–5). Later, the immobile temple, which God allowed Solomon to build in the promised land, represented the settled rest into which God had invited Israel to dwell with him (1 Kgs 6–8).[13]

---

10. Moltmann, *Way of Jesus Christ*, 288–89.

11. Fretheim, *God and World*, 128. Richard Moye also shows how the narrative in Exodus about the completion and consecration of the tabernacle repeats the terms of the creation account: Moye, "In the Beginning," 596–97.

12. Fetheim, *God and World*, 129.

13. For more on tabernacle and temple, see Wright, *Mission of God*, 333–40, 494–98, 523–30; Dumbrell, *Search for Order*, 47–49; 67–71; 105–8; 238–39; Beale, "Garden Temple," 3–50; Friedman, "Tabernacle in Temple," 241–48; Barker, *Great High Priest*; Westfall, "Messianic Themes of Temple," 210–29.

As we know from the ongoing story of Israel and the mounting disclosure of God's purposes, the tabernacle, the promised land, and the temple all point beyond themselves to something even more permanent and glorious—to the fulfillment of creation in God's seventh-day rest when God dwells with the people and the people with God. Long before the tabernacle and temple were constructed, Jacob saw in his dream what Isaiah would later hear from the Lord: "Heaven is my throne and the earth is my footstool" (Isa 66:1). The author of Hebrews tells us that Abraham (and by implication the children of Israel) "stayed for a time in the land he had been promised, as in a foreign land . . . For he looked forward to the city that has foundations, whose architect and builder is God" (Heb 11:9–10). With the incarnation of the Son of God, Jesus *tabernacles* among us on earth, identifying with us fully and providing atonement for sin (John 1:14, 29). And through the ministry of the Spirit, God continues even now to draw followers of the way toward the royal palace of God where Christ sits enthroned. As Hebrews says, "we are his house if we hold firm the confidence and the pride that belong to hope" (Heb 3:6). The Lord dwelling with us and we with him is nothing less than life in the presence of the unveiled glory of God.

Israel's exodus from Egypt, wandering in the desert, and looking ahead to entrance into the land of promise, was guided by the hovering Spirit. Their way of life was to be a pathway of justice, mercy, forgiveness, and reconciliation, all of which were to image and disclose God's covenant love.[14] Fretheim puts it this way: "God's presence in the tabernacle is a statement about God's intended presence in the entire world. The glory manifest there is to stream out into the larger world. The shining of Moses' face in the wake of the experience of the divine glory (Exod 34:29–35) is to become characteristic of Israel as a whole, radiating out into the larger world of those glorious effects of God's dwelling among Israel. As a kingdom of priests (19:5–6), they have a role of mediating this vision and purpose of God to the entire cosmos."[15]

The prophet Ezekiel had visions of God's redemption of Israel and the creation (e.g. Ezek 33:23–33) and heard God's voice and saw the glory of the Lord entering the temple. By the hand of the Lord and the power of the Spirit, he was shown a valley of dry bones rising up to live (Ezek 37:1–14). He saw trees, plants, and living creatures flourishing on both banks of a river with fruit trees whose leaves never wither and whose fruit never fails to grow (Ezek 43:1–10; 47:1–12; see Rev 22:1–2). He glimpsed nothing less than the creation's fulfillment in God's vast yet intimate kingdom of shalom.

Similar visions and words from God were given to other prophets. Isaiah heard God calling, "Ho, everyone who thirsts, come to the waters; and you who have no money, come, buy and eat!" (Isa 55:1). God proclaims that his word "shall not return

---

14. What God was doing with Israel, writes Fretheim, was revealing something that would keep growing into the grand reclamation and fulfillment of the entire creation. Fretheim, *God and World*, 131.

15. Fretheim, *God and World*, 131.

to me empty, but it will accomplish that which I purpose, and succeed in the thing for which I sent it" (Isa 55:11). The voice and breath of the creator will not be withdrawn until God's judging and redeeming work is finished and the whole creation honors and celebrates the glory of the Lord. God promises Israel,

> For you shall go out in joy and be led back in peace;
> the mountains and hills before you shall burst into song,
>   and all the trees of the field shall clap their hands.
> Instead of the thorn shall come up the cypress;
>   instead of the brier shall come up the myrtle;
> and it shall be to the Lord for a memorial,
>   for an everlasting sign that shall not be cut off (Isa 55:12–13).

The apostle John on Patmos is lifted up in the Spirit to see and hear more of what Isaiah and Ezekiel saw and heard: trees that bear their fruit in all seasons, wealth and plenty available without price (Rev 21:9—22:5). These prophetic glimpses of a new heaven and new earth have nothing to do with the idea that God will destroy the present creation in order to try his hand at another one. "New heavens and new earth" are what we will see when God's will is finally done on earth as it is in heaven, when the creation is redeemed, healed, and fulfilled, and dry bones are resurrected to new life. "New" means judged, atoned for, reconciled, cleansed, and fulfilled to God's sabbath satisfaction. God's original approval of creation—"God saw everything that he had made, and indeed, it was very good" (Gen 1:31)—has been confirmed and sealed in the work of Jesus Christ, the beloved son whom God raised from the dead to be "the last Adam . . . a life-giving spirit" (1 Cor 15:45).

The hovering Spirit of God at the beginning of the creation story signals the Alpha of God's creative disclosure through the Word (John 1:1–4); the Omega of God's self-revelation comes with the fulfillment of creation (Rev 1:17; Col 1:18–20). The biblical story moves from glory to glory, from a beginning to a climax in the self-disclosure of God. Throughout the unfolding of God's creation days, including that of the sixth-day human generations, there is a built-in orientation of all things toward the seventh-day climax. Colin Gunton explains it this way: if creation is oriented toward an end, then "what we call redemption is not a new end, but the achievement of the original purpose of creation. It only takes the form of redemption—of a 'buying back'—because of sin and evil. That does not detract, however, from the basic claim that it is prior. What is realised in the incarnate involvement of the Son in time and space is the redirection of the creation to its original destiny, a destiny that was from the beginning in Christ, for all creation is through and to the Son."[16]

All of earthly life, therefore, is a journey of anticipatory revelation that is building toward the unveiling of God's glory. What God is revealing now in the course of human history can only be partial in the experiences of daily life, through prophetic visions,

---

16. Gunton, *Christ and Creation*, 94.

and from words of the Lord under the Spirit's hovering protection and guidance.[17] Water and clouds, fire and tempest, vineyards and flocks, marriages and families, music and crafting arts, seedtime and harvest, education and government—these are the active human media of the Spirit-guided revelation of God's covenant faithfulness. Fretheim points to Psalm 148 in which heavenly, human, and nonhuman languages flow together. That is to say, "only as all creatures of God together join in the chorus of praise do the elements of the natural order or human beings witness to God as they ought to." This, says Fretheim, "brings the discussion back to the truth in the eschatological interpretation of these materials; in the new heaven and earth (and the totality of this language ought not to be lost), nature's praise of God will have a clarity and a perfection unknown this side of the eschaton."[18]

BIBLICAL TESTIMONY AS COVENANT CANON

God communicates in this age through the whole of creation by dramatic events and in a still, small voice, with the tender care of mother for child and through the just judgments of an elder in the gate, by pillars of cloud and fire, at sabbath services and in priestly oblations, by a shepherd's watchfulness and prophetic testimony, in penance and thanksgiving, and climactically in the flesh and blood of Jesus Christ, crucified, buried, and raised to seventh-day glory as the shepherd of a people who hear his voice and follow. The incarnate life of the Son of God was historical reality, yet it was more than historical, for it opened history and all creation to fulfillment in the seventh-day glory-presence of God. As a consequence of Christ's ascension to the right hand of the Father, the Spirit of God has been dispatched from that heavenly communion of righteousness and love to blow across the world and into the enclaves of every heart and nation in judgment and mercy, driving all things and all of history toward the day of the Lord (John 16:5–16; Acts 2:1–39; 1 Cor 12:1–11; Rev 1–4).

What we have outlined above about the Spirit's hovering over and guiding creation through blessing and judgment emphasizes God's intimate involvement with creation from beginning to end. This is the Bible's narrative trajectory, its progression of covenantal disclosures of God's relation to creation. Clearly, then, it is the Bible we are trusting as *canon*—the rule for faith and practice by the power of the Holy Spirit—as our written guide through the drama of this age.[19] Speaking about life in

17. The multi-generational identity of the image of God means that it takes time for God's revelatory relationship with human creatures to reach full disclosure. God's sixth-day time for the human generations is constitutive of their identity, not a hindrance or confinement that keeps them from knowing or reaching God. In Gunton's words, "our being in time is not a defect of being, but part of its goodness . . . It is an implication of the patient wisdom of God that not only does he will a world that is very good in its temporality, but that he also continues to act in and toward it in a way appropriate to its structure." Gunton, *Father, Son*, 136, 141.

18. Fretheim, *God and World*, 265.

19. It is not part of our purpose here to discuss the formation of the biblical canon and different

this world as a Spirit-led drama in which God is intimately and mysteriously engaged may sound strange to many. On the one hand, it may sound strange because most westerners, and many others beside, assume that God is not an actor at all in "secular" economic, social, political, and recreational life. Some allow that a clockmaker god might have gotten things started, but now the world runs on its own by natural laws and human ingenuity. On the other hand, God's active engagement with creation may sound strange to many because even those who want to take the Bible seriously often treat it too narrowly as a book about salvation for life after death, or about religion and theology, or about spiritual meditation and ethical motivation, not as the book of life about God's relation to the whole of created reality.

There is yet another reason we have difficulty appreciating the Bible for what it is. While its accounts and history, its poetry and wisdom, its prophecies and letters flow from God's engagement with the human generations, the Bible's grand narrative overarches human history as witness to an origin and culmination that transcend the experience and knowledge of sixth-day humans. The Bible is a multi-generational collection of covenant texts that cohere as evidence of, and witness to, the God-directed, forward-moving drama in which the Bible's authors, and we ourselves, participate as responsible actors. The Bible speaks from and to life in the real world, from and to experience beyond its covers; it is not like a novel or play whose drama is contained within book covers or on stage.[20] At the same time, the world of our ordinary experience is filled with mystery beyond our fathoming. The biblical story, on its own terms, in other words, is about a creation-wide drama that is open toward a not-yet-completed history in a not-yet-fulfilled creation that includes our generation today.[21]

The Bible, to be sure, is not the kind of book that covers or tracks every human practice in an encyclopedic fashion. But we may not, for that reason, approach it as a narrowly spiritual or theological text concerned only with "salvation history." The biblical texts are about the meaning of the entire creation and the whole of human life in its generations, set in the course of the mounting disclosure of God's self-revealing purposes. The Bible speaks of humans marrying and raising children, tilling the ground and shepherding animals, making tents and composing music, forging tools

---

ways of understanding the canon and its authority. In general, I am in sympathy with the canonical approach of Brevard S. Childs and others influenced by him. See, for example, the essays and excellent bibliographies in Bartholomew et al., *Canon and Biblical Interpretation*, particularly the chapter by Christopher Seitz that introduces Childs's work and provides an overview of the canonical approach: "Canonical Approach and Theological Interpretation," 58–110, and the chapter by Christopher Wright, "Response to Gordon McConville," 282–90; (McConville's essay, in the same volume, to which Wright is responding is "Old Testament Laws and Canonical Intentionality," 259–81). See also Wright, *Last Word*; and Kline, *Structure of Biblical Authority*.

20. Writing on the way Hebrews speaks of the word of God, or of God speaking, Schenck says "In a pre-modern interpretative paradigm, the interpreter does not view a story in the text as story *in* a text, but as a window on history—the same history in which the interpreter is a part." Schenck, "God Has Spoken," 323.

21. See Skillen, "Reengaging Figural Interpretation," 181–203.

and building cities, governing and judging, shop-keeping and trading, going to war and making peace.

The Bible, as we have it, is a compilation of many kinds of texts, some of which depended on oral traditions, some of them reaching back before any words were ever carved into stone or scratched onto scrolls.[22] We can only marvel then at the mystery of how a real-life drama tied primarily to a specially chosen people—Israel—has been carried forward over countless generations in a coherent way that encompasses the origin, development, and destiny of the whole world. The biblical texts convey a story that only God can tell. Our big questions about who we are and why we exist, of where we come from and toward what end we are destined, are all addressed in the Bible within the framework of the creation's seven-day order in which every dimension of human life finds its meaning in relation to the self-revealing creator, judge, and redeemer of all things. The culmination of that disclosure, as the Bible makes clear, is not something that will be achieved by human design and effort; it is, and will be, the gift of God, something God brings to pass through Christ Jesus by the power of the hovering and guiding Spirit.

---

22. The ancient world was an oral culture, writes Schenck, so we must remember "that we are deal-ing with 'oral writings,' despite the fact that New Testament authors refer to the Scriptures as writings. With regard to Hebrews, the oral orientation of its author is obvious . . . While God spoke the Law through angels, while he spoke the Prophets and various Writings through the prophets, God spoke most definitely through a Son beyond any scriptural text, even if the scriptural texts bore witness to the Son." Schenck, "God Has Spoken," 335.

12

Faith*ful*ness or Faith*less*ness in the Covenant Bond

FROM BEGINNING TO END, God holds the creation in an embrace so strong it will never be broken. That bond is more than simply a commitment by the creator to the goodness and fruitfulness of the creatures. It is a bond of love originating with God and drawing all things to himself. Listen to the lovers' dialogue in the Song of Songs:

> Set me as a seal over your heart,
>   as a seal upon your arm;
> for love is strong as death,
>   passion fierce as the grave.
> Its flashes are flashes of fire,
>   a raging flame.
> Many waters cannot quench love,
>   neither can floods drown it.
> If one offered for love all the wealth of one's house,
>   it would be utterly scorned (Song 8:6–7).

The apostle Paul puts it this way: "For I am convinced that neither death, nor life, nor angels, nor rulers, nor things present, nor things to come, nor powers, nor height, nor depth, nor anything else in all creation, will be able to separate us from the love of God in Christ Jesus our Lord" (Rom 8:38–39).

God's love for creation is demonstrated in many ways, as the Bible makes clear, likening it to a marriage bond, a father-son relationship, and the love of mother for child. The Lord is also the shepherd of Israel, a guide through the wilderness, a defender of justice for the poor, and the unfailing promise keeper. Those diverse biblical texts are built primarily around the several *covenants* that God established with particular human representatives: Noah, Abraham, Israel, and David, culminating in the new covenant in Messiah Jesus anticipated by Jeremiah (Jer 31:23–34) and other prophets.

The commitments God makes are clearly articulated and the obligations that bind humans within the covenants are stated with equal clarity, summarized most succinctly in Jesus's response to the Pharisees: "'You shall love the Lord your God with all your heart, and with all your soul, and with all your mind.' This is the greatest and the first commandment. And a second is like it: 'You shall love your neighbor as yourself.' On these two commandments hang all the law and the prophets" (Matt 22:37–40). However, what we know from history and from within ourselves is a persistent failure to love God with all our hearts and our neighbors as ourselves.

Responses to God with love and trust are essential to the healthy development of human and nonhuman life. God's creatures all have a purpose or calling in their ecological interdependence and in their utter dependence on God. Insects pollinate plants and trees, which bear fruit and multiply, supplying other creatures with food and much more. Fish, fowl, animals, and humans all function in their distinctive ways: eating, resting, reproducing, and doing their work. Humans, like all creatures, have their inviolable identity, honor, and commission in the dynamic unfolding of God's creation, including the distinctive capacity to exercise *responsibility*—to act with initiative in working with their creator in the development of creation.

In direct contrast to covenant-keeping love and trust, unloving and untrusting responses run counter to God's creation purposes. They arise in *antithesis* to the great commandments. God has created humans with the ability to turn a deaf ear to God, to distrust their creator, to try to go their own way in disregard of God. While love and trust of God open the way to fruitfulness, understanding, wisdom, and the deepening of relationships with God and neighbors, movement in the opposite direction brings on foolishness, injury to others, and death, perpetuated through the diverse cultures of human history

The early church father Augustine (354–430 AD) concluded that humans were created good with the ability to sin or not to sin. After Adam fell into sin, however, humans have continued in unrighteousness from generation to generation and are now unable *not* to sin, said Augustine. The Bible makes clear that were it not for God's mercy and grace, which uphold the creation, there would be no goodness or righteousness on earth, and no hope of entrance into the city of God. God remains faithful to the covenants, which accounts for whatever love and trust we do see, even when humans break troth with God.

THE ANTITHESIS HAS NO GROUND OF ITS OWN ON WHICH TO STAND

Throughout history, the opposition between covenant-keeping and covenant-breaking has manifested a strong antithetical character. God's good creation and historical covenants might be called God's *thesis*, God's solid word of life and righteousness that constitutes and upholds all things. Human faithlessness in turning away from full trust in God is a rebellion, an attempt from within the creation order to act *antithetically* to God's thesis. However, God's thesis and the rebellious antithesis are not parallel opposites; the rebellion can take place only within, not outside, the bounds of creation and human creatureliness. The creator decides what will exist and on what terms it will exist. The creator is the one who judges between the legitimacy of covenant-keeping and the illegitimacy of covenant-breaking.

The dynamic tension between trust and distrust, between faithfulness and faithlessness is made starkly clear in God's covenant with Israel. When the redeemer Lord was preparing Israel for entrance into the promised land, he reiterated the terms of the covenant grounded in the promises to Abraham and Isaac. God admonished the Israelites to choose the path of life and to reject the path that leads to destruction.

> You shall put these words of mine in your heart and soul, and you shall bind them as a sign on your hand, and fix them as an emblem on your forehead. Teach them to your children, talking about them when you are at home and when you are away, when you lie down and when you rise . . . See, I have set before you today life and prosperity, death and adversity. If you obey the commandments of the Lord your God that I am commanding you today, by loving the Lord your God, walking in his ways, and observing his commandments, decrees, and ordinances; then you shall live and become numerous, and the Lord your God will bless you in the land that you are entering to possess. But if your heart turns away and you do not hear, but are led astray to bow down to other gods and serve them, I declare to you that you shall perish; you shall not live long in the land that you are crossing the Jordan to enter and possess (Deut 11:18–19; 30:15–18).

God's aim in calling for covenant faithfulness and purity of life in Israel was not only for Israel's sake but for the sake of the whole world. A pure and righteous Israel was to shine like a light in the world, exposing the foolishness of unbelief and ungodliness among the nations. Israel was to exemplify the good way of life, walking faithfully with the Lord who made covenant with them. All of the covenant codes of purity recorded in Leviticus, for example, make this clear, and God's later judgments on Israel and Judah for their failure to be God's faithful witnesses tell the same story.

Israel's history and the history of humanity bear testimony to God's covenant faith*ful*ness and to human faith*less*ness. Long before the covenant with Israel, the Bible tells of God's dismissal of Adam and Eve from the garden following their disobedience, of God's flood judgment of humankind from which only Noah and his family were saved, and of countless other instances of God's blessings and curses. Furthermore, the biblical story shows that this antithesis extends beyond the realm of sixth-day human responsibilities. That is why Paul tells the followers of Christ in Ephesus they need to "put on the whole armor of God" in order to "stand against the wiles of the devil." For in the final analysis, "our struggle is not against enemies of blood and flesh, but against the rulers, against the authorities, against the cosmic powers of this present darkness, against the spiritual forces of evil in the heavenly places" (Eph 6:11–12). God's drama with creation, which encompasses more than life on earth, culminates in the climactic battle portrayed in the book of Revelation between the rider on a white horse whose name is Faithful and True and the great beast with its armies composed of the kings of the earth. Ultimately, the beast is defeated; the devil is thrown into the lake of fire, and finally, the Holy City, New Jerusalem, comes down from heaven to fill the earth forever (Rev 19:11–21; 22:6).

According to Augustine, humans continue to be motivated by two opposing loves, drawn by competing spiritual powers. Those who by God's grace give themselves over to the love of Christ move toward the city of God. Those who persist in lives of self-love are moving toward the earthly city's destruction and death. Neither of these cities has yet been realized in its fullness; they are the ultimate destinations toward which hearts are set and lives directed. Consequently, the deepest root of conflict, darkness, and destruction throughout this age is the antithetical movement against the love of God. Yet life, even in its opposition to God, is only possible on the basis of God's love and sustaining mercy. It is only the love of God at the foundation of creation and inscribed in every earthly covenant that can overcome the deathward momentum of self-love and redirect repentant sinners to the faithful giver of life who opens the way to the city of God, the New Jerusalem.[1]

In the next two chapters we will look more closely at the relation between God's blessing of faithfulness and curse of unfaithfulness stipulated in the covenant bond. At this point we want to highlight just two things: first, the dynamic unfolding of the human generations takes place entirely within God's covenant order of creation, which we referred to above as God's founding *thesis*. At the same time, God has created humans with the ability to exercise real responsibilities and has called them to give creative shape to countless aspects of life in the unfolding of history. This means that the human generations do not stand—and never did stand—on neutral ground. Our lives do not begin in a position of unencumbered self-sufficiency from which we decide whether to choose God or the devil, good deeds or evil deeds. By our very nature, created in God's image, we exist from the start in complete dependence on God within the seven-day covenant bond of God's faithfulness. Our identity is that of God's royal stewards, God's servants, made for cooperation with God in the development of creation. Thus, from within that order of life, the only way to live is by maintaining trust in God; otherwise we die by turning from God in distrust. Every attempt to try to follow the second path is a fool's errand, a step into darkness, for it means trying to live a lie, in opposition to reality. The *antithesis* does not arise from a source independent of God's creation; humans do not create their ability to act responsibly or irresponsibly. Those created in the image of God have an identity and a range of responsibilities

---

1. Augustine's primary articulation of this argument is in his *City of God*.

of such magnitude that they are able to imagine they are autonomous. But even in trying to live that lie they remain entirely dependent on God's love for creation, the creator's *thesis of life* for them.

The second point is that faithful and unfaithful responses to God touch everything that human's do. The bond between God and creation embraces human life in its entirety, in every dimension. Sin against God and our neighbors is not simply a personal matter, involving a few one-on-one relationships and narrowly conceived moral issues. Sin is not confined within the interior of each person's heart or even within human society. To the contrary, from the inner heart to the outer extremities of personal, corporate, cultural, and civilizational life, to try to live by self-love in distrust of God develops and perpetuates personal habits, institutional patterns, and cultural contours that degrade or destroy what is good. Human degradation inevitably extends outward to ecological destruction in violation of the responsibility to exercise priestly stewardship of the earth. We can see evidence of the tension between good and evil, between covenant-keeping and covenant-breaking in our conduct of business and commerce, politics and governance, family life and schooling, the arts and the sciences, and, yes, in churches and seminaries.[2] When Jesus spoke of himself as a vine and his followers as the branches, he said, "Those who abide in me and I in them bear much fruit, because apart from me you can do nothing. Whoever does not abide in me is thrown away like a branch that withers; such branches are gathered, thrown into the fire, and burned" (John 15:5–6). One is either alive in the grace of God, bearing fruit in all of life, or one becomes a dead branch.

Paul told the Thessalonians, "test everything; hold fast to what is good; abstain from every form of evil" (1 Thess 5:21–22). Solid food that only mature believers are able to eat, says Hebrews, is "for those whose faculties have been trained by practice to distinguish good from evil" (Heb 5:14). Maturity, in other words, comes with constant training in the practice of righteousness. "By justice a king gives stability to the land, but one who makes heavy exactions ruins it," says the proverb (Prov 29:4; cf. 1 Kgs 3:9; Amos 5:14–15). "Those who oppresses the poor insult their Maker, but those who are kind to the needy honor him" (Prov 14:31). There is no suggestion in these and countless other biblical passages that faithfulness and faithlessness are only a matter of the heart, or of a person's attitude and feelings. The whole of life is at stake. That is why Paul says, "Test everything"—in every vocation, in every relationship and responsibility.

2. Working to confront the antithesis in all areas of life was central to the vision and work of Abraham Kuyper. The reason the political party he led was named the "Antirevolutionary Party" was because he wanted its constructive (thetical) contributions to appear in stark contrast to the works inspired by the spirit of the French Revolution with its cry of "neither God nor master." See Kuyper's speech at the 1891 party's convention titled "Maranatha," in Kuyper, *Abraham Kuyper*, 205–29.

KUYPER, WRIGHT, AND HAHN

The contribution of Abraham Kuyper shines brightly at this point. He not only urged Christians to recognize and understand the antithesis, he also worked to help them practice covenant faithfulness in education, politics, business, labor relations, journalism, and more. With regard to the antithesis at work in creation, Kuyper follows in the line of Paul's words to the Ephesians about putting on the whole armor of God to stand against the devil's schemes. "Were it possible to pull aside the curtain that hides the world of spirits from our view," wrote Kuyper, then "I am convinced a conflict so intense, so volcanic, so sweeping in its reach would present itself to our mind's eye that the bitterest war ever waged on earth would look, by comparison, like child's play. The collision of forces that really matter is occurring not here but up there, above us. In our struggles here below we experience only the after-shocks of that massive collision."[3] The collision to which Kuyper referred originates with spiritual forces challenging God and culminates in their destruction through the death and resurrection of Christ. The armor Paul wants us to put on (Eph 6:10–18) is not only for the protection of our inner spirit or religious conscience but also for the protection and empowerment of every vocation we have on earth, because the collision above touches everything on earth.

Kuyper writes in one of his treatises that Christians must not try to operate by means of "two distinct circles of thought: in the very circumscribed circle of your soul's salvation on the one hand, and in the spacious, life-encompassing sphere of the world on the other."[4] The people God is calling to life in Christ are created in God's image and commissioned to exhibit that honor in all they do. It is in every dimension of life that "the brilliance of [God's] image has to appear." Only after the potential of human life has been fully developed will the full glory of God's image be disclosed. The realization of that glory is not first of all "for the sake of humanity but for God. The supreme Artisan and Architect will want all that has gone into his design to be realized and stand before him in a splendid edifice. God will take delight in that high human development."[5] This is why Christ's life, death, and resurrection challenge every kind of opposition to God's loving embrace of creation. "Jesus Christ," says Kuyper, "did not come into the divine plan from without as a strange element enlisted as a result of our fall. Rather, the Son of God with the Father and the Holy Spirit himself determines the plan of the world . . . [He] is first the original Mediator of creation and after that also the Mediator of redemption to make possible the enforcement and fulfillment of the decree of creation and everything entailed in it."[6] This is the vision that took hold of Kuyper and led him throughout his life to address through word and deed the tasks

---

3. Kuyper, *Abraham Kuyper*, 87–124; 88.

4. Kuyper, *Abraham Kuyper*, 165–201; 172.

5. Kuyper, *Abraham Kuyper*, 165–201; 178.

6. Kuyper, *Abraham Kuyper*, 165–201; 185.

of government and citizenship,[7] business and labor,[8] schooling and journalism,[9] the sciences and the arts,[10] as well as the institutional church.[11]

There are two other authors we should consider at this juncture, both of whom have given detailed attention to the covenantal disclosure of creation: Wright, one of our primary interlocutors, and Scott Hahn, whose book, *Kinship by Covenant*,[12] offers an intriguing thesis with many creative insights.

Wright's understanding of the Bible, which he articulates primarily through his interpretation of Paul's letters, is covenantal in character.[13] Jesus Christ, Wright argues, is the Messiah of Israel in fulfillment of God's covenant promises to Abraham, promises that reach back to the very purpose of creation. God's creational purposes have been darkened and threatened by the antithetical faithlessness of Adam, yet those purposes have been reaffirmed through the covenants with Noah, Abraham, and Israel, foreshadowing the ultimate fulfillment of all things in the death and resurrection of Messiah Jesus. Wright explains that even though "Paul does not refer to the tree of life in Genesis 3, his controlling narrative is constantly pointing to the way in which the creator finally brings his human, image-bearing creatures, and indeed the entire cosmos, through the impasse of the fall, of the thorns and thistles and the whirling, flashing sword, to taste at last the gift of life in all its fullness, a new bodily life in a new world where the rule of heaven is brought at last to earth."[14]

According to Wright, at the time of Jesus (late in the period of second-temple Judaism), the Jews worshipped one God as creator whose response to evil came to focus in the covenant election of Israel to be God's chosen nation—a light to all nations. The

---

7. See for example Kuyper's *Our Program,* which reflects the developing engagement of the Antirevolutionary political party in the Netherlands in the late nineteenth and early twentieth centuries.

8. Kuyper, *Abraham Kuyper,* 231–54; Kuyper, *Problem of Poverty.*

9. Most of what Kuyper did and said on the matter of schooling, especially in his organizing efforts and work in parliament, is reported or written in Dutch, but one can catch the drift of his views in his speeches and essays included in *Abraham Kuyper,* particularly "Evolution," 403–40, "Common Grace," 441–60, and "Sphere Sovereignty," 461–90. For the most detailed treatment of Kuyper's work on education, see the doctoral dissertation by Naylor, "Abraham Kuyper and Emergence."

10. See Kuyper, *Lectures on Calvinism,* 110–70. For an insightful interpretation of Kuyper on these subjects see Heslam, *Creating a Christian Worldview,* 167–223. Note particularly his discussion of the significant difference between Kuyper's approach to the sciences and his approach to the arts with respect to the operative influence of the antithesis.

11. Kuyper, *Lectures on Calvinism,* 9–77; Kuyper, *Abraham Kuyper,* 19–44 and 65–85, respectively. See further, Heslam, *Creating a Christian Worldview,* 113–41, and Bratt, *Abraham Kuyper,* 149–93.

12. Hahn, *Kinship by Covenant.*

13. Wright's covenantal interpretation of the Bible has been evident from at least the time of his study of key New Testament passages in *Climax.*

14. Wright, *Resurrection,* 373. Commenting on the first four chapters of 1 Cor, Wright says, "Paul believes that with the resurrection of the Messiah the new world has already begun; that the Spirit comes from that future into the present, to shape, prepare and enable people and churches for that future; and the work done in the power of the Spirit in the present will therefore last into the future." Wright, *Resurrection,* 285.

apostles and earliest Christians, says Wright, reshaped this view in the light of their witness to the life, death, and resurrection of Jesus and the subsequent outpouring of God's Spirit at Pentecost. Jesus, they professed, has now been "shown to be Israel's representative Messiah, and his death and resurrection is the proleptic achievement of Israel's restoration *and hence* of the world's restoration."[15] According to Wright, Paul's mention in Romans 8 of the glory and honor of humans (as portrayed in Ps 8) is set in contrast to the existing condition of sinful humanity, and thus the redemption of sinners in Christ goes hand in hand with the restoration of creation. "When human beings are raised from the dead [in Christ] . . . having been delivered from death itself and from the sin which brings it about (8.10), then creation will itself be set free to be truly itself at last under the rule of the redeemed 'children of God' (8.21)."[16] Creation will be fulfilled; only the antithetical rebellion within creation will be destroyed.

According to Wright, God's covenants have dealt with sin in order to fulfill creation. The link between Adam and Noah, Abraham, and Israel "is thus not only *resumptive*, getting the human project back on track after the fall, the curse and the exile from the garden. It is also *redemptive*. God acts to undo the fateful sin in the garden."[17] The covenant in Christ is not only the last to be revealed, historically speaking, but is also the culminating, climactic covenant that fulfills the promises of every preceding covenant for all eternity. The new covenant has now been sealed through Christ's death, resurrection, and ascension, but the completion of everything that is now assured has not yet come to pass in its fullness. That will occur with the return of Christ, the final judgment, the resurrection of the dead, and the revelation of God's glory in his sabbath with creation.

Scott Hahn takes a different, though not incompatible, approach to the interpretation of the biblical covenants. After briefly examining several Old Testament covenants and explaining their distinctive types (kinship, treaty, and grant), he then turns to the New Testament texts of Luke-Acts, Galatians, and Hebrews. "Luke, Paul, and the author of Hebrews," writes Hahn, "followed the example of Israel's prophets—notably Ezekiel (cf. Ezek 20:1–44)—by interpreting Israel's scriptural history in light of the significance, sequence, and interrelationships of the divine covenants. They understood the meaning of the life, death, and resurrection of Jesus Christ primarily within this covenantal-historical matrix."[18]

The distinctive way Hahn interprets the "significance, sequence, and interrelationships" of those covenants is worth summarizing here. His argument is that all the biblical covenants have at their base a *kinship* character. That is to say, within the

---

15. Wright, *Resurrection*, 581–82.

16. Wright, *Paul and Faithfulness*, 1092. Very close to Wright's reading of Psalm 8 in the light of Romans 8 is Schenck's reading of Psalm 8 in the light of Hebrews 2:5–11: *Cosmology and Eschatology*, 51–60.

17. Wright, *Paul and Faithfulness*, 788.

18. Hahn, *Kinship by Covenant*, 332.

paternalistic cultural patterns of those ancient times, the bond of father to firstborn son (entailing primogeniture) was fundamental to all social relations and obligations, not only to the laws of inheritance. The role of the father included priestly and royal responsibilities that were passed down to the firstborn son. The biblical covenants reflect this pattern, writes Hahn, though they are lifted above the human-to-human level to the divine-human level. According to Hahn, the "privilege of royal priestly primogeniture was God's *original intent* for both Adam (i.e. mankind) and the people of Israel. Adam, the firstborn Son of God (cf. Luke 3:38), was given the royal role of universal dominion (Gen 1:28) and the priestly duty to guard and tend the primordial garden sanctuary of Eden (Gen 2:15)." Similarly, "God claimed Israel as his 'firstborn son' (Exod 4:22–23) and promised him (them): 'You shall be to me a *royal priesthood*, a holy nation' (Exod 19:6)." Due to their faithlessness and disobedience, however, "both Adam and Israel lost these privileges."[19]

God's covenant with Israel, Hahn argues, presents a contrast to the preceding covenant with Abram/Abraham. God instituted the Abrahamic covenant in three episodes.[20] In the first, after Abram met and was blessed by Melchizedek, God called him and promised countless offspring. Abram believed God and that was credited to him as righteousness (Gen 15). In the second episode, God changed Abram's name to Abraham and again promised to make him the father of many nations. God also promised a land for Abraham's offspring that would be "an everlasting possession." And with that pledge God instituted the covenant sign of circumcision and again promised that Abraham and Sarah would have a son (Gen 17). Finally, in the third episode (Gen 22), after the seemingly impossible birth of Isaac to Abraham and Sarah, God tested Abraham to the limits, asking him to offer up this firstborn son of the promise as a sacrifice to God. When Abraham went forward in full trust of God to sacrifice Isaac, God stopped him at the last moment and praised his faith, which demonstrated his righteousness. At that point God swore a significant oath: "By myself I have sworn, says the Lord: Because you have done this, and have not withheld your son, your only son, I will indeed bless you, and I will make your offspring as numerous as the stars of heaven and as the sand that is on the seashore. And your offspring shall possess the gate of their enemies, and by your offspring shall all the nations of the earth gain blessing for themselves, because you have obeyed my voice" (Gen 22:15–18).

The covenant that God established with Abraham by that self-obligating oath meant God's promises to Abraham were *unconditionally* assured of fulfillment. Hahn draws a contrast here between Abraham and Adam, both of whom were called by God to be the father of nations. Abraham exhibited faithfulness through his continued trust in God; Adam had not done that. Similarly, Hahn draws a contrast between God's covenant with Israel and the subsequent covenant with David.[21] Israel had been

19. Hahn, *Kinship by Covenant*, 279.

20. Hahn, *Kinship by Covenant*, 101–35

21. On the Davidic covenant and its relation to the others, see Hahn, *Kinship by Covenant*,

adopted as God's son but did not keep faith with God as demonstrated in their making and worshipping the golden calf at the time God was giving Moses the covenant-words of life for them (Exod 32). But unlike Israel, who failed to keep trust with God and fell under the curses of the law, David, like Abraham, received God's promise (in an *unconditional*, self-obligating oath) to establish his royal throne forever. "Your house and your kingdom shall be made sure forever before me; your throne shall be established forever" (2 Sam 7:16).

Hahn details many intricacies of this covenant history, yet the primary line of his argument is that God's original covenant with Adam was one of royal priestly sonship, which was forfeited through sin. Through God's covenant with Abraham, the promise of a firstborn son through whom all nations would be blessed was renewed, and God's self-obligating oath assured the fulfillment of that promise. The people of Israel as a whole were the heirs of God's promise of a son to Abraham. That fruitful son became the people of Israel, God's firstborn nation, a kingdom of priests, through whom all nations would be blessed. But Israel forfeited the blessings of that sonship and suffered the covenant's curses because of their sin. Nevertheless, in keeping with God's promise to Abraham God elected a new son, David, from within Israel, and promised unconditionally to establish David's throne forever (2 Sam 7:1—8:29).

What the New Testament shows, says Hahn, is that God's new covenant in Christ fulfills the Abrahamic and Davidic covenants of unconditional promise. This firstborn Son of God takes on our flesh and suffers the curse of death to which all the children of Adam and Israel are subject. In doing so, Christ serves both as the high priest after the order of Melchizedek and as the sacrificial lamb, which was foreshadowed by the ram that God gave to Abraham to take the place of Isaac. Christ is also the promised king who inherits the Davidic kingdom with its covenant promises of never-ending rule over all nations. God's covenant with Abraham thus sets the conditions for the covenant with Israel, not vice versa, as Paul explains in Galatians. The nation of royal priests called to life from death in Christ will be the extended family of God—the brothers and sisters of Christ who is God's firstborn Son—embracing the faithful of all God's covenants with Adam, Noah, Abraham, Israel, and David.[22]

The covenantal disclosure of reality, as the work of Wright, Hahn, and others demonstrates, is a forward-moving, accumulating build-up of covenant promises and their fulfillment. The movement is from simplicity to complexity, from clans and nations to the worldwide kingdom of God, from a garden to the new Jerusalem. This dynamic of the ever-expanding revelation of God with, to, and through the human generations keeps intensifying in anticipation of the culminating fulfillment of all that has been, and is being revealed. To underestimate or to miss the intensification of this mounting covenantal disclosure is to miss the revelatory and anticipatory character

---

176–213.

22. See Hahn's summary of his study of Heb 1–9 and his concluding theological reflections on the book as a whole in Hahn, *Kinship by Covenant*, 321–38.

of God's purposes for and with creation. God's covenantal drama with creation is the context in which to understand how the blessings and curses of God's covenants cut to the core of our being.

13

Blessings and Curses I

WHO TALKS ABOUT JUDGMENT and condemnation these days? Isn't the gospel the good news of Christ's love and forgiveness? The Old Testament God may have delivered harsh judgments, but surely the message of the New Testament is God's kindness, mercy, and love. Is it even "politically correct" to talk about sin in today's culture? After all, what right does anyone have to speak of others as sinful or immoral? That would be judgmental, wouldn't it? Instead, many say, let's focus on overcoming mistakes, finding therapies for those who may harm others or themselves, and making progress through education to achieve more happiness for more people. Today, Christians should be sharing the good news of Christ's love—God's blessings—and not talking of divine condemnation and curses.

But is it true that the gospel message is forgiveness without judgment, mercy without justice, love that overlooks sin? No, it is a misunderstanding of the gospel to focus on part of the truth in a way that obscures the larger truth of God's relation to human creatures. Jesus told his disciples and the crowds not to be afraid of those who could kill them but instead to "fear him who, after he has killed, has authority to cast into hell" (Luke 12:4–5). In another setting he said, "Do not think that I have come to bring peace to the earth; I have not come to bring peace, but a sword" (Matt 10:34). Paul, writing to Jews and gentiles in Rome, told them "the wrath of God is revealed from heaven against all ungodliness and wickedness of those who by their wickedness suppress the truth" (Rom 1:18). Don't think you are in a position to judge others, Paul continued, for everyone is a sinner. In judging others you condemn yourselves, because God is the ultimate judge. When you show contempt for the true judge because of "your hard and impenitent heart you are storing up wrath for yourself on the day of wrath, when God's righteous judgment will be revealed. For he will repay according to each one's deeds" (Rom 2:5–6; see also 14:9–12).

Those few words from Jesus and Paul are not odd statements picked out as proof texts. The same message appears throughout the New Testament and not only in the Old. The good news of forgiveness and new life is not proclaimed apart from condemnation of sin and warnings of judgment to believers and unbelievers alike. If we are to understand the drama of the covenantal disclosure of reality, we may not abstract expressions of God's love and kindness from the full context of God's relation to the whole creation in which divine faithfulness as well as human responsibility have their meaning.

God created us to exercise immense responsibility on earth. We are accountable to God, as part of the very meaning of our identity as God's image. Yet it is clear from history and our own experience that the human generations have been irresponsible, unloving, and unjust in countless ways. The apostle Paul warned young Timothy, a minister of the gospel of Christ, to pay attention to the degrading darkness that was still present even after the revelation of Christ Jesus. There will be terrible times in the last days, Paul wrote. "For people will be lovers of themselves, lovers of money, boasters, arrogant, abusive, disobedient to their parents, ungrateful, unholy, inhuman, implacable, slanderers, profligates, brutes, haters of good, treacherous, reckless, swollen with conceit, lovers of pleasure rather than lovers of God, holding to the outward form of godliness but denying its power. Avoid them!" (2 Tim 3:1–5).

In our day, we witness the same things within ourselves and from others: deceitfulness, disregard of neighbors, racial hatred and discrimination, sexual abuse, ruthless acts of violence, even by governments, and economic practices and systems that give advantage to the few and disadvantage to the many—to mention only a few of today's hatreds and degradations. The list is long. Our sins are many. If a just and righteous God condemns such ungodliness yet continues to be patient, slow to anger, and merciful toward us, then surely there must be some basis for it that does not ignore or discount sin and suffering. But when will the tension be released? When will the scales of justice finally be balanced? When and how will God reconcile all things by righteous judgment and complete the cleansing that will make possible the reconciliation of all things to the glory of God?

Our aim in this chapter and the next is to try to understand God's longsuffering mercy that goes hand-in-hand with the condemnation of unrighteousness and warnings of final judgment.[1] How are we to understand and respond to God's blessings and curses? Throughout the Bible, the "blessings and curses" are stated and restated in different ways. Listen to God's words in Leviticus to Israel, the people God chose and embraced with loving kindness.

Blessings:

---

1. In this chapter, and the next, we do not try to deal with every topic that theologians usually organize under categories of sin, judgment, substitutionary atonement, justification, forgiveness, reconciliation, final judgment, and so forth. Rather, we want to learn how human disobedience and God's response to it illuminate the meaning of God's seven-day creation covenant. For discussion of some of these doctrines and their disputes, see, for example, Boersma, *Violence*; Wright, *Justification*; Wright, *Evil and Justice* Provan, *Seriously Dangerous Religion*; Hahn, *Kinship by Covenant*; Gathercole, *Defending Substitution*; Green and Baker, *Recovering Scandal*; Wright, *An Eye for an Eye*.

> If you follow my statutes and keep my commandments and observe them
> faithfully, I will give you your rains in their season, and the land shall yield
> its produce, and the trees of the field shall yield their fruit . . . And I will
> grant peace in the land, and you shall lie down, and no one shall make you
> afraid . . . I will look with favor upon you and make you fruitful and multiply
> you; and I will maintain my covenant with you . . . I will place my dwelling in
> your midst, and I shall not abhor you. And I will walk among you, and will be
> your God, and you shall be my people (Lev 26:3–12).

Curses:

> But if you will not obey me, and do not observe all these commandments, if
> you spurn my statutes, and abhor my ordinances, so that you will not observe
> all my commandments, and you break my covenant, I in turn will do this to
> you: I will bring terror on you; consumption and fever that waste the eyes and
> cause life to pine away. You shall sow your seed in vain, for your enemies shall
> eat it . . . And if in spite of this you will not obey me, I will continue to punish
> you sevenfold for your sins. I will break your proud glory, and I will make
> your sky like iron and your earth like copper . . . I will bring the sword against
> you, executing vengeance for the covenant; and if you withdraw within your
> cities, I will send pestilence among you, and you shall be delivered into enemy
> hands . . . And you I will scatter among the nations, and I will unsheathe the
> sword against you; your land shall be a desolation, and your cities a waste (Lev
> 26:14–33).

Promised mercy:

> But if [the people of Israel] confess their iniquity and the iniquity of their
> ancestors . . . ; if then their uncircumcised heart is humbled and they make
> amends for their iniquity, then will I remember my covenant with Jacob; I will
> remember also my covenant with Isaac and also my covenant with Abraham,
> and I will remember the land. For the land shall be deserted by them, and
> enjoy its sabbath years by lying desolate without them, while they shall make
> amends for their iniquity . . . but I will remember in their favor the covenant
> with their ancestors whom I brought out of the land of Egypt in the sight of the
> nations, to be their God: I am the Lord (Lev 26:40–45).

Later, after Joshua led Israel into the promised land, he admonished them to serve
God in faithfulness, and they pledged to do so. Yet knowing their history to that point,
he warned, "You cannot serve the Lord, for he is a holy God. He is a jealous God; he
will not forgive your transgressions or your sins. If you forsake the Lord and serve
foreign gods, then he will turn and do you harm, and consume you, after having done
you good" (Josh 24:19–20).

THE MYSTERY OF JUDGMENT AND MERCY

God's condemnation and judgment of unrighteousness arises from the covenant bond with creation and not only from God's covenants with the children of Israel. God's "very good" creation, rightly ordered, makes no room for unrighteousness; justice cannot walk hand-in-hand with injustice; keeping covenant with God is incompatible with turning away from God. At the same time, it is also clear from both the biblical story and our own experience that sinful degradation and alienation from God are not the only things shaping human history. There is more to the story than human disobedience and God's condemnation of it.

Genesis tells us that when God placed humans—earthlings—in the garden, they were told they could eat from all the trees of the garden *except* "the tree of the knowledge of good and evil" (Gen 2:16–17). If they ate from the forbidden tree, they would surely die. Beginning with Genesis 3, we read about the man and woman doing the very thing God told them not to do. They heed the serpent's suggestion, which directly challenges God's command that they not eat from the tree of the knowledge of good and evil. As a result, their eyes are opened, but not in the way they desired or expected. André LaCocque explains that what they saw when their eyes were opened was a distortion of reality, the opposite of the *good* world as God created it. They saw their own nakedness and were afraid. Furthermore, LaCocque continues,

> [F]ar from mastering creation, as the humans thought they would, they are incapable of distinguishing what is good for them; their alleged "clear-sightedness" is myopia . . . Yes, now they *know* something they did not know—that they are naked, in the proper and figurative sense . . . They are self-centered, incapable from now on of true communication. Their senses created for reaching out have become superfluous. Adam and Eve are now the "foolish and senseless people" of Jeremiah 5:21, "they have eyes but see not; they have ears but hear not." They have lost the relation of communion with God that allowed them to see as he sees, to share in his vision/interpretation (cf. Psalm 7:10; Job 34:21). Something that has lost its reference to God is indeed senseless and disgruntling.[2]

The confusion that besets Adam and Eve arises from the *disorientation* that led them to heed the serpent in the first place, an act that violated their identity, position, and responsibility in creation. The image of God is created for communion with God and for the exercise of responsible authority over, not submission to, other creatures. Yet the man and the woman submitted themselves to the serpent, thus turning away from the trusting, life-giving fellowship with God.[3] Separation from God had begun, yet the promise that they would die was delayed. God penalized them severely, but not with immediate death.

2. LaCocque, "Cracks in the Wall," 19.
3. LaCocque, "Cracks in the Wall," 12–13.

God exposes Adam and Eve in their sin, curses the serpent (though not by dialogue with it),[4] and delivers harsh punishments that continue to be borne by subsequent generations. Then, in order to make sure the man and woman do not eat from the tree of life, God banishes them from the garden and posts cherubim and a flaming sword to keep them from reentering it. Just as God evaluated all creatures in the beginning as "very good" (Gen 1:31), so now God evaluates and condemns human disobedience. The creatures God makes are good, but their response to God is not good. God's curses express God's anger, which, as Iain Provan explains, "is never arbitrary; it is always directed at what is evil." And as we see in the human drama, which develops from that point on, God's anger continues to manifest a passion for justice, including "justice for those who are oppressed by others."[5]

As told in Genesis 4 and following, Adam and Eve have children, and the generations of the sixth-day image of God continue to unfold. God has not destroyed the creation that is now darkened and degraded by human disobedience. Cain murders Abel, so despite God's patience and mercy, evil continues to gain ground. Consequently, God continues to enact judgments, including death, on sinners. At the same time, all that is dark and destructive has not utterly destroyed what is good. God continues to uphold creation, restrain sin, and hold out promises of forgiveness to those who repent of their iniquities. God promises the renewal and fulfillment of creation with cleansing from all unrighteousness.

The continuing antagonism between good and evil, light and darkness, stands out in the apostle John's announcement of the good news of Emmanuel—of God coming to dwell with us (John 1:1–18). The one through whom all things are created, writes John, is the light of life, and that light is now shining in darkness, "but the darkness has not understood it." Even though everything and everyone is made through this word of God, "the world did not know him" (John 1:10). Moreover, it is not only those outside of Israel who fail to welcome the light of the world. The very people God claims as his own do not welcome him. "He came to what was his own, and his own people did not accept him" (John 1:11). This was true of many in Israel and has been true since the coming of Jesus among many who profess belief in God. In many places in the New Testament, as well as the Old, God's prophets and ministers warn of judgment that falls on the faithless. Don't harden your hearts, the author of Hebrews pleads with his readers (Heb. 3:12; 4:11–13), warning them, it is "impossible to restore again to repentance those who have once been enlightened, and have tasted the heavenly gift, and have shared in the Holy Spirit, and have tasted the goodness of the word of God and the powers of the age to come, and then have fallen away, since on their own they are crucifying again the Son of God and are holding him up to contempt" (Heb 6:4–6).

---

4. LaCocque, "Cracks in the Wall," 14.

5. Provan, *Seriously Dangerous Religion*, 68.

Human disobedience, as the Bible shows, leads to falling away from trust in the true God and turning instead to idols and false gods. God's anger at idolatry manifests itself in jealousy and vengeance, says Provan.[6] God has no tolerance for false gods, as the Ten Commandments make clear. "You shall not make for yourself an idol, whether in the form of anything that is in heaven above, or that is on the earth beneath, or that is in the water under the earth. You shall not bow down to them or worship them; for I the Lord your God am a jealous God, punishing children for the iniquity of parents, to the third and fourth generation of those who reject me, but showing steadfast love to the thousandth generation of those who love me and keep my commandments" (Exod 20:4–6).

In the Bible, idolatry is often likened to a violation of the most intimate human relationship, that of marriage (see for example, Hos 2–3; Eph 5:28–33; Rev 21:1–2). Moshe Halbertal and Avishai Margalit emphasize how closely the prophets of Israel connect idolatry with sexual relationships. "Where Hosea describes idolatry as prostitution, Ezekiel portrays it as nymphomania," and Jeremiah "compares the relationship between God and Israel to the relationship between husband and wife," violated by faithlessness.[7] In these cases, it is the revelatory character of the creature made in the image God that allows us to understand covenant-breaking for what it is. God's anger and jealousy are those of a jilted lover, the spouse who is pierced to the core by the faithlessness of the beloved. From that point of view, Israel's obligation "to worship one God stems from the fact that God in Heaven chose Israel on earth as his wife, and so according to the norms of marital life idolatry was forbidden for Israel."[8] Humans have spurned God's love and separated themselves from it. God is justifiably angry and jealous because of their violation of the marriage covenant.

Because of God's jealous anger, the unrighteous have every reason to fear God's vengeance. They—we—*should* be afraid! At the same time, and for equally good reason, God's vengeance against evildoers is the very thing innocent people plead for; they want God to avenge their enemies—the ones who are maltreating and oppressing them. One hears the cry again and again in the Psalms and the prophets.

> O Lord, you God of vengeance,
>   you God of vengeance shine forth!
> Rise up, O judge of the earth;
>   Give to the proud what they deserve!
> O Lord, how long shall the wicked,
>   how long shall the wicked exult? (Ps 94:1–3; see also Ps 74; Job 10:2–3)

6. Provan, *Seriously Dangerous Religion*, 68–72.

7. Halbertal and Margalit, *Idolatry*, 19.

8. Halbertal and Margalit, *Idolatry*, 22. For an overview of idolatry in the Bible, see Wright, *Mission of God*, 136–88.

Brown shows from the Psalms how "God's coming" is associated with divine judgment. Psalm 98 "depicts YHWH as 'coming to judge the earth . . . with righteousness,
and the peoples with equity' (v. 9). Judgment rendered is justice established, and God's
'coming' marks the eve of its execution . . . God comes to save and to judge, to deliver
and to preserve, as well as to indwell and reign. In a world of struggle and injustice,
God's 'coming' is the *necessary* complement to God's 'reigning,' for it affirms that all is
not yet right with the world."[9]

THE PROMISE TO ABRAHAM

In the darkest of times, God determined to destroy human life on earth, saving only
Noah and his family from the flood-judgment. Then, with rainbow mercy and hope,
God established a creation-renewal covenant with Noah and his offspring. In Genesis
12 and following we read of the multi-generational line from Noah's son Shem[10] to
Abram whom God calls out of Haran (Gen 12) to become the bearer of a new promise
that builds on God's commissions and promises to Noah and to Adam.[11] God covenants with Abram (renaming him Abraham) and promises that through his seed all
nations on earth will be blessed. Abraham's trusting response to God is accounted to
him as righteousness, so once again we encounter the mystery of a righteous person
chosen from among the nations. God's covenant with Abraham, which is extended
by generational lineage to Isaac and Jacob (Israel), has all nations in view, not only
Abraham and his seed, because God intends through Abraham's seed to bless *all nations*. How can it be, we ask, that God will bless all nations, sinful as they continue to
be, through this one righteous man who also continues in the line of Adam and Noah?

God's covenant with Isaac's son, Jacob, and his children (Israel) expands further
what God is disclosing in the increasingly diversified and complex covenant with
creation. If Abraham was a chosen son, as Noah and Adam were, Israel is the chosen
family (to become a nation) to serve as a light to all families and nations. Israel is to
be God's exhibit to the world of what a righteous people should be. That is the meaning and purpose of the covenant with which God binds Israel to himself. Moreover,
taking into account the ingrained sinful habits of the people of Israel, the covenant
stipulates a diversified range of practices that will demonstrate God's mercy by calling
the Israelites to repentance. Sin offerings and guilt offerings are instituted in further

---

9. Brown, *Seeing Psalms*, 44–45. See also Glasson, "Theophany and Parousia," 259–70.

10. Hahn discusses the hypothesis that Shem should be identified as the one whom the Letter
to the Hebrews refers to as Melchizedek. Shem is "the only righteous firstborn son in all of Genesis,"
a status that "foreshadows Israel's vocation and mission among the nations, contrasting sharply and
ironically with the scattered builders of Babel in Genesis 11." Hahn, *Kinship by Covenant*, 98; 97–100,
297–304.

11. See Wright, *Paul and Faithfulness*, 787; the book from which Wright quotes on this subject is
Fishbane, *Biblical Interpretation*, 372–73. See also Hahn, *Kinship by Covenant*, 95.

disclosure of God's blessings and curses of the creatures God has entrusted with such weighty responsibilities on earth.

As diverse responsibilities are developing through the human generations, the expansion of unrighteousness becomes possible. Governing officials, whether law-makers, judges, or executives, for example, are supposed to execute justice, not take bribes or act to benefit themselves over others. Yet listen to the psalmist, whose voice we can also hear in the words of countless prophets in Israel and Judah:

> Do you indeed decree what is right, you gods?
> Do you judge people fairly?
> No, in your hearts you devise wrongs,
> your hands deal out violence on earth.
> The wicked go astray from the womb;
> they err from their birth, speaking lies . . .
> O God, break the teeth in their mouths;
> tear out the fangs of the young lions, O Lord! (Ps 58:1–3, 6)

God's gifts and promises of restored life, justice, faithfulness, and enduring love have continued to restrain sinful degradations as well as the full force of divine condemnation throughout this age. Yet the injustice of judges, the corruption of business executives, the failures of educators, and the evil deeds of thieves, rapists, and murders will not continue forever. Lord, have mercy upon us, we pray. Lord, defeat the enemies that are destroying us. What is at stake is not only the destiny of Israel but the destiny of the whole world. For without the fulfillment of creation there will be no culminating celebration of God's glory.[12]

The apostle John, on the island of Patmos, saw a vision of the coming of the Lord in final judgment, recorded in the memorable imagery of the "great winepress of the wrath of God" (Rev 14:19). As the final judgment of God draws closer, an angel pro-claims the gospel to every nation, tribe, language and people, saying in a loud voice, "Fear God and give him glory, for the hour of his judgment has come" (Rev 14:7). Later, another angel comes out of the temple in heaven with a sharp sickle and is told to use the sickle to gather the clusters of grapes that are ripe for judgment and throw them "into the great winepress of the wrath of God" (Rev 14:17–20). The destruction of unrighteousness must be completed, because when the Lord dwells with his people, there will be no more tears. "Death will be no more; mourning and crying and pain

---

12. LaCocque comments, "Even [God's] judgment over, and his condemnation of, his people is to be seen from the perspective of God's personal commitment. For the judgment is here not just forensic, it is always close to the lament, 'O my people, what have I done to you? In what have I wearied you? Answer me!' (Micah 6:3 NRSV). It is indeed highly paradoxical when exilic Prophets, Ezekiel in the first place, claim that the people will know 'that I am Yhwh' when submitted to God's fury (Ezekiel 6:12–14; 12:15f; 24:24). Ezekiel 23:49, for instance, shows that the Name does not convey only salva-tion (as in Exodus) but also judgment and condemnation; not only life but also death." And yet, writes LaCocque, "The people's death remains penultimate, Israel shall rise from the dead (cf. Ezekiel 37)." LaCocque, "Revelation of Revelations," 323.

will be no more, for the first things have passed away" (Rev 21:4). There will be no place in the new order for "the cowardly, the faithless, the polluted, the murderers, the fornicators, the sorcerers, the idolaters, and all liars," for "their place will be in the lake that burns with fire and sulfur, which is the second death" (Rev 21:8).

Who can stand against such judgment? Who can stand against God? Since all have sinned and continue to fall short of the glory of God, will God's mercy finally reach its limits so that everyone is lost? It is evident throughout the Bible that God's anger, jealousy, and vengeance spring from love for the creation and especially for humans created to be God's wife, children, friends, coworkers, and royal stewards. How, then, will the faithful Father be able to continue loving the children who do not return his love? What will the King do with royal stewards who are committing treason? How will the faithful husband deal with his faithless wife?

14

Blessings and Curses II

BLOOD SACRIFICE

THE COVENANTS AROUND WHICH most of the Old Testament revolves entailed the sacrifice of animals for various occasions, all related to the worship and service of God. Some of the sacrifices sealed human-to-human covenants, some were offered as sin or guilt offerings. All of them demonstrated through ritual ceremony that life belongs to God. As the letter to the Hebrews explains,

> Hence not even the first covenant was inaugurated without blood. For when every commandment had been told by Moses in accordance with the law, he took the blood of calves and goats, with water and scarlet wool and hyssop, and sprinkled both the scroll itself and all the people, saying, "This is the blood of the covenant that God has ordained for you." And in the same way he sprinkled with the blood both the tent [tabernacle] and all the vessels used in worship. Indeed, under the law almost everything is purified with blood, and without the shedding of blood there is no forgiveness of sins (Heb 9:18–22).

Of course, the participation of the children of Israel in these ceremonies was to express their trust in the Lord who gives and takes life. However, to the extent that the people offered sacrifices without commensurate obedience and wholehearted trust in God, they became hypocrites. Out of anger with such brazen affront, God told Israel to stop bringing meaningless offerings: "I do not delight in the blood of bulls, or of lambs, or of goats" (Isa 1:11). "Wash yourselves; make yourselves clean; remove the evil of your doings from before my eyes; cease to do evil, learn to do good; seek justice, rescue the oppressed, defend the orphan, plead for the widow" (Isa 16–17).[1] The sacrifice of animal blood represented the blood of those who were offering the sacrifices.

---

1. Several other passages on God's rejection of sacrifices that are offered in disregard of covenant obligations include: 1 Sam 15:22–31; Ps 40:6–8; Hos 8:11–14; Amos 5; Mic 6:6–8. Ps 119 presents many exemplary professions of covenant faithfulness pleasing to God.

Knowing that the children of Israel were sinners, God had built into the covenant the rituals by which Israel could regularly acknowledge their sins and receive God's forgiveness.[2] When the guilt offering or sin offering was offered in atonement for sin, it served not only to express repentance and thanksgiving for God's forgiveness but also to recommit sinners to serve God faithfully. For that reason, to offer sacrifices without heartfelt repentance while living in violation of covenant obligations was to mock God. The Lord would have none of it and called Israel to quit sinning and to demonstrate contrite hearts through deeds of obedience required by the covenant.

The apostle Paul was at pains to explain that God's covenant with Israel, which included sin offerings, could not by itself produce sinless creatures. Just as righteous Noah and Abraham still carried in them the sin of Adam, so Israel followed in that line. The Mosaic covenant was not at fault for Israel's iniquities; it was the fault of the sinners who kept violating the bountiful covenant. God had drawn Abraham, Isaac, and Jacob (Israel) into a bond with the one who initiates covenants, forgives sins, accredits righteousness, and restores life. In response to God's gracious initiative, Abraham and his offspring were to put their full trust in the Lord and follow him. Through such trust they would come to understand what the covenant rituals and sacrifices represented. And since Abraham had put his faith in God long before the law was given to Israel, it was his trust in God that was credited to him as righteousness (Rom 4:1–12; Gen 15:6). It was not as if God decided to overlook Abraham's sin or to disregard standards of righteousness in making covenant with him. Rather, it was that Abraham trusted the Lord, who asked him to offer up his son Isaac as a sacrifice and Abraham obeyed (Gen 22:1–18).

According to the Gospels, when Jesus celebrated the Passover with his disciples and told them to eat the bread and drink the wine, he said, "for this is my blood of the covenant, which is poured out for many for the forgiveness of sins" (Matt 26:28; see also Mark 14:24 and Luke 22:20). Jesus was putting himself and his own lifeblood in the place of the sacrificial animals of Israel's covenant. Margaret Barker explains that if we are to understand the new covenant in Christ, we need to see it in relation to the creation order, the temple (and tabernacle) in Israel, and Christ's atoning sacrifice. In Israel, the temple represented (stood as a microcosm of) the creation, and offenses committed by the people polluted not only them but also the land and the whole creation. "The damage was restored by ritual in the temple. 'Life', i.e. blood, was applied to the damaged parts and the impurity was absorbed, 'borne' by the priest who performed the *kpr* [atonement]. It was the ritual of restoration and healing."[3] This is the background for understanding Christ's atonement for sin, writes Barker. "The whole point of the argument in the Epistle to the Hebrews is that it was Jesus the high

---

2. Some key passages on animal sacrifices and the ceremonies in the tabernacle and the temple, include Exod 25–30; Lev 1:1–17, 4:1—6:13, 16:1–34, 17:8–14; Num 15:22–31; 1 Kgs 6:1–38, 8:62–66; 2 Chr 7:1–22, 29:1–36.

3. Barker, *Great High Priest*, 49.

priest who took his own blood into the heavenly sanctuary and thereby became the mediator of a new covenant (Heb 9.11–15)."[4] This is the background for answering the question of what the understanding of atonement was that gave rise to the Christian claims about cosmic reconciliation, which some interpreters have argued came from pagan sources.[5] There was no pagan influx into Christian faith and practice at this point, says Barker; the New Testament is entirely dependent on the atonement ritual in Israel.[6]

Jesus is revealed as the one faithful, righteous human, who gave up his life in faithfulness to God, going all the way to shedding his blood on the cross for the sins of the world. Jesus is God's gift of righteousness.[7] In Jesus, the Son of God tabernacled among us, died on the cross, and rose from the dead to sit at the right hand of majesty on high. In him, sins are forgiven, all covenants are fulfilled, and the seven-day order of creation is reaffirmed and assured of fulfillment. Jesus has entered the holy place of God's rest, the age of creation's consummation.

THE CURSE OF DEATH AND
THE BLESSING OF RESURRECTION LIFE

The death that Jesus suffered for sinners is God's promised curse for sin, the curse that cuts us off from fellowship with God and denies entrance into the promised land of seventh-day life with God. The curse of death is not that of passing away from our present (sixth-day) mode of existence; rather, the curse and sting of death is separation from the righteous one in whom alone the blessings of life in this age and the coming age are poured out. If through faith we are buried and raised with Christ, then we need not fear passing from earthly life, for if in Christ we die, then in him we will be raised. Paul explains this to the Corinthians with the metaphor of a seed. Earthly life, our present mode of existence, is like a seed that is planted and then generates a living plant. We will be sown as a natural body but raised as a spiritual body (1 Cor 15:37–44). Paul is not saying here that a material body will die while an immaterial soul will not die. He is saying that our earthly mode of life—our embodied life in this

---

4. Barker, *Great High Priest*, 54.

5. Barker, *Great High Priest*, 54.

6. This, says Barker, "would explain the cosmic unity described in Ephesians 1.10: 'to unite all things in him, things in heaven and things on earth . . .' and in Colossians 1.17–20: 'In him all things hold together, . . . through him to reconcile to himself all things whether on earth or in heaven . . .' It would explain Matthew's use of the Servant text 'he took our infirmities and bore our diseases' in the context of healing miracles (Matt 8:17). It would explain why a sermon in Acts refers to Jesus as the Righteous One and the Servant but also as the Author of life (Acts 3.13–15). It would explain all the new life and new creation imagery in the New Testament. Above all it would explain the so-called kenotic hymn in Philippians 2.6–11; the self-emptying of the Servant would have been the symbolic life-giving, when the blood, the life, was poured out by the high priest on the Day of Atonement to heal and restore the creation." Barker, *Great High Priest*, 54–55.

7. For an interpretation of Jesus as God's righteousness see Hays, *Echoes in Paul*, 46–57.

age—will be planted, and in Christ, the life-giving Spirit, we will be raised to a new kind of embodied life—a spiritual (seventh-day) body.

In offering himself as a sacrifice for the sins of the world, Jesus took on to himself the curse of separation from God. "My God, my God, why have you forsaken me?" (Ps 22:1). Yet that curse and separation are not the end of the story. God did not leave Jesus in the grave but raised him to triumph over death. The life to which he was raised is that of seventh-day glory seated at the right hand of majesty on high. God did not resuscitate him for the continuation of his earthly life. His kingdom, he told Pilate, is not from this world in the line of every other historical kingdom. Rather, the kingdom given him by his Father in heaven is rule over all things. As he told his disciples when commissioning them for their subsequent earthly service, "All authority in heaven and on earth has been given to me" (Matt 28:18). The death and resurrection of Jesus are not only to expiate sin but also to restore life all the way to its fulfillment and the fulfillment of the entire seven-day creation.[8]

Just as God declared the creation to be "very good," so also the covenant (the law) that God established with Israel was very good. However, as the Bible testifies, it was not Israel's attempt to live by the law that gives life now and guarantees life beyond this age. God is the giver and restorer of life. God's covenants with Noah, Abraham, Israel, and David did not turn sinful humans into sinless humans. Commenting on the apostle Paul's account of God's covenantal disclosures, Wright explains, "The crucifixion and resurrection of Israel's Messiah teaches Paul something new. *Israel itself is 'in Adam.'*"[9] It is the blood sacrifice of Jesus, the one man who is without sin, that opens the way to the renewal of earthly life now and the assurance of resurrection life with God in the age to come. The transforming reality of Christ's resurrection takes hold of us now by faith, renewing our minds and hearts, disciplining us for faithfulness in all earthly vocations, warning us against falling away, and inspiring us with the hope of fulfillment in the age to come.

What God is revealing in and through Christ is precisely the new covenant anticipated by the prophet Jeremiah, as Hebrews explains. The new covenant is not like the covenant that God made with Israel when he brought them out of Egypt. That covenant was sound and revelatory of God's mercy and love, but it, too, pointed beyond itself to the covenant that brings all earthly covenants to fulfillment. As Hebrews restates God's word through Jeremiah,

> This is the covenant that I will make with the house of Israel
> after those days, says the Lord.

---

8. There is a long history of doctrinal argument in the church about the curse of death and how death in this age is related to "eternal" death and judgment. It is not our aim here to go into the arguments but rather to show how an understanding of the seven-day order of creation provides a different frame of reference for understanding them. For a brief introduction to the arguments from the time of the early church fathers to the present, see Moltmann, *Coming of God*, 85–93.

9. Wright, *Paul Debate*, 63.

I will put my laws in their minds,
  and write them on their hearts.
and I will be their God,
  and they shall be my people.
And they shall not teach one another
  or say to each other, 'Know the Lord,'
for they shall all know me,
  from the least of them to the greatest.
For I will be merciful to their iniquities,
  and I will remember their sins no more (Heb 8:10–12; see Jer 31:31–34).

From a priestly point of view, the blood sacrifice of the new covenant in Jesus is quite different from the sacrifices of the old covenant. As Hebrews puts it, Jesus did not enter an earthly tabernacle time after time, but entered the more perfect tabernacle of the very presence of God. Jesus "entered once for all into the Holy Place, not with the blood of goats and calves, but with his own blood, thus obtaining eternal redemption. For if the blood of goats and bulls, with the sprinkling of the ashes of a heifer, sanctifies those who have been defiled so that their flesh is purified, how much more will the blood of Christ, who through the eternal Spirit offered himself without blemish to God, purify our conscience from dead works to worship the living God!" (Heb 9:11–14)

The Spirit of God is initiating the renewal of hearts in this age, as we learn from God's blessing of Abraham, Moses, and all the faithful, guiding us along the path of life, urging us to "hold firm the confidence and the pride that belong to hope" (Heb 3:6). As long as it is still today we must keep on learning the heart-renewing habits of repentance in order to practice obedience to the Savior of sinners and Lord of the world, for we continue to be responsible to God and to one another for our thoughts and deeds in all relationships and institutional responsibilities. The covenantal disclosures that have been building up in anticipation of the revelation of Christ have made clear the meaning of righteousness and how unrighteousness debases and destroys. The life, death, and resurrection of Christ reveals what all past covenants were pointing toward, namely, the judgment of sin, the restoration of righteousness, and the reconciling fulfillment of God's creation purposes.

MOLTMANN AND CHRIST'S ATONEMENT

In Jürgen Moltmann's discussion of the sufferings of Christ, it seems to me he misses something important about God's condemnation and judgment of sin. He writes about Christ suffering the conflicts and contradictions of the world, and redeeming the world for resurrection life.[10] Quoting Romans 4:25, *"Christ 'was put to death for our trespasses and raised for our justification,'"* Moltmann writes, "the meaning and

10. Moltmann, *Way of Jesus Christ*, 170–81.

purpose of [Christ's] suffering is our liberation from the power of sin and the burden of our guilt." That purpose, he writes, has as its goal: our justification by faith; Christ's lordship over the dead and the living; the conquest of death and a new creation; and the glorification of God through a redeemed world.[11] Yet the covenantal significance of our responsibility and accountability for "trespasses" does not come up for consideration here. Moltmann understands from Paul that "Christ died the accursed death on the cross," and was raised and justified to redeem "from the curse of the law those who are his" (Gal 3:13). He says this shows that Christ thereby "surmounts" the divine torah in justifying the unjust and those who suffer under injustice.[12] For Moltmann, the law's curse against covenant-breaking is apparently surmounted by the gospel of Christ. But what does he mean by "surmount"?

Moltmann's interpretation of Paul at this juncture is illuminated by his stated objection to the traditional Christian teaching that Christ offered an "expiatory sacrifice" (atonement) for sin by taking "our sins and God's judgment on himself." That teaching, he states, is backward looking. The traditional understanding of reconciliation "presupposed an unscathed world which was destroyed by human sin, and which reconciliation restores." Reconciliation in that sense, he says, is merely a negation of a negation. That older idea of atonement as the means of salvation "can be applied to Christ's death, but not to his resurrection," for it cuts "Christ's death off from his resurrection, so as to relate that death to the restoration of a covenant with God which is the premise of the idea."[13]

But where in Scripture does Moltmann find the idea that Christ's atonement for sin looks backward to the recovery of an unscathed creation without a forward look to the resurrection? Instead of showing how Paul and other New Testament writers actually articulate the connection between Christ's sacrificial death and resurrection, or offering his own way to connect the two, Moltmann appears to let the dichotomy stand between an atoning sacrifice and a redemptive resurrection and then shifts toward an interpretation of Christ's resurrection apart from an "expiatory sacrifice" for sin. His reasoning seems to be that if an expiatory atonement washes away sin, then it accomplishes only a return to an undefiled creation that never had a transcendent (seventh-day) destiny. Despite all that Moltmann has said about the importance of creation's sabbath, he does not seem to recognize in this context that from its foundation the creation has been oriented to God's seventh-day rest.

In his book on creation,[14] Moltmann distinguishes "creation in the beginning" (*creatio originalis*) from the "continuing creation" (*creatio continua*), and from the "new creation" (*creatio nova*), in a way that to some degree disassociates the original and continuing creation from the new creation. That sheds light on his argument

11. Moltmann, *Way of Jesus Christ*, 182–83.

12. Moltmann, *Way of Jesus Christ*, 184.

13. Moltmann, *Way of Jesus Christ*, 187–88.

14. Moltmann, *God in Creation*, 206–14.

about the backward-looking meaning of the atonement. "Paul," he writes, "understood the righteousness of God as God's creative acts in and for those who are threatened by absolute death because they have come under 'the power of sin', which is contrary to God." Moltmann's use of the passive voice here in speaking of humans coming "under 'the power of sin'" plays down, if not discounts, human responsibility for sin and alienation from God. Moltmann does come closer to recognizing human responsibility when he characterizes "sin" as "the condition in which a person closes himself off from the source of life, from God."[15] Closing oneself off from God, says Moltmann, can be caused by "hybris (sic), or depression, or 'the God complex', or because of a refusal to accept what human existence is about." Those errors, he says, lead to "the self-destruction of the regenerating energies of life, and thus to death." However, all of the references in Moltmann's language here are to offenses a person commits against oneself, not offenses against God in violation of the covenant bond of life. By the word "sin," Moltmann means "missing the mark of being" in the deep sense that leads to "absolute death," which is deeper than, and the source of, "infringing the laws of life."[16] But what is the relation between "missing the mark of being" and turning against God in distrust and disobedience?

Moltmann's discussion of salvation focuses on release from the sufferings of this present time rather than on release of irresponsible, rebellious men and women from the penalty of death for having caused that alienation from God. "Through *the forgiveness of sins*," writes Moltmann, "the gospel breaks through the compulsive acts of sinners which are the enemies of life, cutting sinners loose from sin, and creating the possibility of 'conversion', a turn to life. Through *the justification of sinners*, the gospel brings men and women who are closed in upon themselves into the open love of God."[17] But how does the gospel break through in this way and release sinners from the power of sin and create the possibility of a turn to life and the open love of God? Is any penalty paid for sin? On what basis does God justify (accredit righteousness to) sinful humanity? In Moltmann's discussion I do not find clarity on the relation between Christ's atonement for sin and our release "from the power of sin" through God's accrediting of Christ's righteousness to us. Nor do I see how our "turn to life" is related to Christ's resurrection from the dead.

COVENANT FAITHFULNESS AND ATONEMENT FOR SIN

Biblically speaking, as I understand the texts, Christ's sacrificial death for our sins is intimately related to the covenant character of creation and therefore to the fulfillment of God's creation purposes. There is, of course, much more to salvation in Christ than the propitiation of sins. Salvation entails the restoration of righteousness, the renewal

15. Moltmann, *Way of Jesus Christ*, 184.

16. Moltmann, *Way of Jesus Christ*, 184–85.

17. Moltmann, *Way of Jesus Christ*, 185.

of life and human responsibility in this age, and the resurrection of the dead in Christ for everlasting life with God. Yet it is hard to imagine, on biblical terms, how God's merciful blessings, which entail the restoration of righteousness and the fulfillment of all things, can achieve forgiveness of sins and reconciliation with God apart from an acceptable sacrifice for sin. Whether we are considering life under the old covenant or under the new, right living in tune with God's revealed will is at the heart of the great love commandments and central to righteousness. "My little children, I am writing these things to you so that you may not sin," writes John. "But if anyone does sin, we have an advocate with the Father, Jesus Christ the righteous; and he is the atoning sacrifice for our sins, and not for ours only but also for the sins of the whole world. Now by this we may be sure that we know him, if we obey his commandments" (1 John 2:1–3).

If, through faith in Christ, believers are credited with Christ's righteousness, then it follows that we should live *in him* by the power of the Spirit in accord with God's will. What sense would it mean to go on sinning? Paul asks. God's grace has not been given in order to make room for sin to flourish but to do away with sin. That is what our baptism into Christ's death means. Paul tells the Roman Christians, "How can we who died to sin go on living in it? Do you not know that all of us who have been baptized into Christ Jesus were baptized into his death? Therefore we have been buried with him by baptism into death, so that, just as Christ was raised from the dead by the glory of the Father, so we too might walk in newness of life" (Rom 6:1–4). Paul continues, "For if we have been united with him in a death like his, we will certainly be united with him in a resurrection like his. We know that our old self was crucified with him so that the body of sin might be destroyed, and we might no longer be enslaved to sin. For whoever has died is freed from sin" (Rom 6:5–7).

Paul writes to the Romans, "if Christ is in you, though the body is dead because of sin, the Spirit is life because of righteousness. If the Spirit of him who raised Jesus from the dead dwells in you, he who raised Christ from the dead will give life to your mortal bodies also through his Spirit that dwells in you" (Rom 8:10–11). This, it seems to me, identifies our earthly life (mortal body) as dead because of sin. Yet we are alive through faith in Christ because of his Spirit living in us. And because God raised Christ from the dead, Christ's Spirit that lives in us now through faith will give life to our mortal bodies. Therefore, Christ who represents us and sheds his blood for us does not die alone so that we won't have to die, but rather takes into his death all who are incorporated into him. Therefore, those who die in Christ are assured of being raised with him. That is why we need not fear death; the Spirit of God that lives in us now will give life to our mortal bodies, which will be transfigured into resurrection bodies.[18]

God has not overlooked or discounted covenant-breaking but has dealt with it at its root by incorporating sinners into Christ's blood sacrifice and resurrection. All

18. On this subject compare Hooker, *From Adam to Christ*, 26–41.

the earthly blood sacrifices God ever instituted for Israel pointed toward, and derived their effective power from, God's forgiving mercy achieved through the atoning death of Christ Jesus. But the judgment of sin in Christ's death was not the end of the matter or the goal of God's response to sin. God's goal has always been more than to destroy sin. God wills to cleanse and reconcile the whole creation to himself—he raised Jesus from the dead in order to fulfill it. Sin's curse that separates us from God has been dealt with in him. Death is buried, and life in him both now and in the age to come abounds.

This is why the urgent call goes out to everyone: *repent and believe the gospel!* Turn around and do what is right by the power of the Savior who alone can forgive sins and reconcile us with God. Today is the day of salvation, of human accountability, of human responsibility to accept God's gifts of salvation, forgiveness of sin, and the good news of resurrection life through the righteousness of Christ.

Before his death and resurrection, Jesus announced the coming of the kingdom of God and the urgency of repentance. "Repent, for the kingdom of heaven is near," he proclaimed, as he went about forgiving sins and "healing every disease and sickness among the people" (Matt 4:17, 23; 9:2; Luke 5:17–26). After his resurrection from the dead and before his ascension, Jesus spent forty days instructing his disciples about "the kingdom of God" (Acts 1:1–3). There are countless blessings now for those who respond to the call of John the Baptist and of Jesus to repent and welcome the arrival of the Messiah. Yet the blessings experienced now, which instill faith, are but a foretaste of what is to come when the kingdom of God is revealed in its fullness.

Wright explains in his exposition of Galatians 3:10–14 that "the death of Jesus finally exhausts the curse which stood over the covenant people, so that the blessing of Abraham might after all come upon the Gentiles. And the demarcating mark of this new covenant family, of Gentiles and Jews together, is of course precisely faith: the faith which was Abraham's faith at the beginning." This is nothing less than "covenant theology," says Wright, which is characteristic of Paul's whole worldview.[19] The fulfillment of God's covenant promises is now sealed in Messiah Jesus. The people of God in Paul's proclamation, according to Wright, are those alive "in the Messiah," through whom "they became a single family, whose one and only badge of membership was *pistis* [faith], their faithful allegiance to the one God of Israel who had revealed himself as the God who raised Jesus from the dead and appointed him as Lord of the whole world."[20]

Being alive in Christ now through faith does not mean that the faithful will avoid departing from life in this age. Life in Christ does not mean being able to hold onto our "earthly tent" forever. Through faith in Christ we need not fear that passing, for in the risen Christ "we have a building from God, a house not made with hands, eternal in the heavens" (2 Cor 5:1). Between now and the death of our mortal bodies, Christ

19. Wright, *Climax*, 156.
20. Wright, *Paul Debate*, 91.

assures us of comfort, encouragement, and sustaining love from the indwelling Spirit. In that hope, our earthly lives can open to the rich meaning and purpose of earthly life—our sixth-day commission to serve God and neighbors in developing and caring for one another and other creatures, all in revelatory anticipation of the fulfillment of all things in resurrection glory.

To live truly is to live by faith in the resurrected Christ in every dimension of earthly responsibility. By the very order of creation, there is an integral connection between life in this age and life in the coming age. Nowhere else does Paul emphasize this continuity more strongly, says Wright, than in 1 Corinthians 3:12–15. The life of faith now is a life of storing up treasures in heaven, of building for eternity, of working toward the fulfillment of God's kingdom. We live in "an eschatological narrative, a story which runs from the present age to the age to come," and "the work done in the power of the Spirit in the present will therefore last into the future."[21]

Trusting God in all things also means relinquishing every attempt to save ourselves and learning instead to give ourselves up freely in service to others for Christ's sake so that our lives will bear testimony to God and to the revelatory goodness of the creation upheld by God's righteousness in Christ (Luke 9:23–25; Gal 2:20, 6:14). For as Paul says, "For to me, living is Christ and dying is gain" (Phil 1:21). "I want to know Christ and the power of his resurrection and the sharing of his sufferings by becoming like him in his death, if somehow I may attain to the resurrection from the dead" (Phil 3:10–11). Life in our sixth-day generations is, by the very order of creation, oriented beyond itself toward God's sabbath rest. Life in this age, in our sixth-day mode of existence is precisely what God created us for, but it cannot be held onto. It is to be spent, given up, in the confidence that everything we do that is trustworthy and in tune with God's redemption of creation in Christ will find its way into the kingdom of God. Stand firm brothers and sisters, writes Paul. "Let nothing move you. Always give yourselves fully to the work of the Lord, because you know that your labor in the Lord is not in vain" (1 Cor 15:58). Walking with our elder brother now by faith means that life in this age takes on its true meaning as we mature in our royal-priestly service to God and neighbors. Although we do not yet see everything on earth made subject to humankind, we may live and die now with confidence, thankfulness, and joy *because we see Jesus*, in and through whom all things are being reconciled and fulfilled.

---

21. Wright, *Resurrection*, 285.

15

The Kingdom of God

THE KING AS EXEMPLAR

IN THIS BOOK IT is not possible to write about everything in human experience and how it exemplifies God's covenantal disclosure of reality. In this chapter, we enter one arena of human responsibility that has a long reach through the Bible and throughout history, namely, human governance and its revelatory relation to God's governance. God's royal priestly commission of humans to serve as governing stewards of the earth has been of major importance from the beginning. That commission entails many kinds of responsibilities, and with the unfolding of the human generations those responsibilities have differentiated into countless vocations of family life, schooling, agriculture, sciences and technologies, medical arts, music and other arts, to mention only a few. One of those differentiated responsibilities is what today we know as civic life and the governing of political communities, distinct from familial, academic, artistic, business, and ecclesiastical responsibilities.[1]

In the Bible we read of tribal governance, elders in the gate, judges, and monarchs, which reveal something about God as lawgiver, adjudicator, supreme ruler, and more.[2] Prior to the institution of monarchy in Israel, the people lived under judges in tribal units of the children of Israel. Moses was God's commissioned leader of Israel at the time of the exodus from Egypt, and his responsibility combined the roles of governor, chief prophet, and leading judge under God's covenant rule of Israel. Under Moses and Aaron, other offices of government and priestly authority were established, including, for example, an extensive hierarchy of judges under Moses (see Exod 18:7–26 and Deut 16:18–20).

---

1. The argument that citizenship and governance in political communities belong to humans by their created nature is developed in Skillen, *Good of Politics*.

2. On kingship and other forms of government in the ancient world, see Finer, *History of Government 1*.

Our point of departure for the following discussion is a careful study by Jamie Grant, *The King as Exemplar: The Function of Deuteronomy's Kingship Law in the Shaping of the Book of Psalms.*[3] Grant approaches the book of Psalms as a purposefully organized unity rather than as an ad hoc collection. In reading the book this way, Grant highlights the importance of several psalms in particular: 1, 2, 18–21, 118 and 119. Those psalms, he demonstrates, are strategically placed *kingship* and *torah* (covenant law) psalms,[4] which send major signals about the aim and character of the book as a whole.[5] The Book of Psalms, which draws together poetry, music, and liturgy from many generations of Israel's communal existence, begins with an emphatic introduction provided by Psalms 1 and 2—torah and kingship psalms.

"Psalm 1 celebrates the rule of the torah in the life of the believer," Grant explains, and "Psalm 2 celebrates the rule and reign of Yahweh and his anointed over all the kings and rulers of the nations of the earth."[6] The placement of a torah psalm with a kingship psalm right at the beginning is no accident, according to Grant. It signals one of the central purposes of the book, which is to show that God's people are to follow the way of life marked out for them by the law of the covenant and that the king must do the same thing because his office also exists under God's covenant with Israel. The king's calling (vocation, commission) is to be a servant ruler of the people in keeping with the covenant. In fact, the king, as the image of God in that role, is to be the exemplar of faithfulness, representing God's faithfulness to Israel. In that way, a faithful, covenant-keeping king and people will reflect and represent their covenant-keeping God who is the ultimate King, the epitome and source of faithfulness and righteousness in all and over all. In practicing covenant faithfulness, the king and people will come to know themselves truly as God's royal representatives on earth, called out (made holy) to be a light to the world by *exhibiting the truth of justice* as God's righteous nation—a faithful covenant *community.*[7]

---

3. Grant, *King as Exemplar.* A more abstract and conflicted interpretation of kingship in Israel is Jacques Ellul's reading of 2 Kgs in *Politics of God.* There are many books and essays on the subject of God's kingship and kingdom, including classics such as Bright's *Kingdom of God* and Ridderbos's *Coming of Kingdom,* and more recent volumes such as Schreiner's *King in His Beauty,* and Brettler, *God is King.*

4. Grant explains the difficulty of using the English word "law" for the Hebrew "torah" particularly when interpreting the psalms. The word "torah" has a broader meaning, including that of "instruction" that God gives as a guide for life. Torah has also come to stand for the books of the covenant that include law/instruction and more. Grant, *King as Exemplar,* 255–62. The use of the word in Pss 1, 19, and 119, says Grant, does not carry with it any "explanation of what this 'torah' actually is, making it difficult to pinpoint precisely the referent of this term." Grant, *King as Exemplar,* 257. For more on this matter, see Burt, "Your Torah."

5. For more on the organization and purpose of the final form of the Book of Psalms, see Grant, *King as Exemplar,* 9.

6. Grant, *King as Exemplar,* 10. Brown says much the same thing in *Seeing Psalms,* 17, 34–35, 187–91. See also Tigay, "Divine Creation," 246–51.

7. Walter Brueggemann comes at the relationship between kingship and torah in a different way but reaches much the same conclusion as Grant. Kingship in Israel, writes Brueggemann, "emerges

This relationship between God and Israel under monarchy is articulated clearly in Jeremiah's declaration of Yahweh's word to Judah's king Shallum, son of the righteous king Josiah, at a time when God was about to allow the Babylonians to conquer what remained of Israel. God condemns Shallum: "Woe to him who builds his house by unrighteousness, and his upper rooms by injustice, who makes his neighbors work for nothing, and does not give them their wages" (Jer 22:13). That is *not* what makes one a king, God tells Israel through Jeremiah. A true exemplar was Shallum's father, Josiah, the king who was satisfied to have food and drink, and who did what was right and just, defending "the cause of the poor and needy" (Jer 22:15–16). Then comes God's punch line: "*Is not this to know me?* says the Lord" (22:16b, italics mine). In other words, for a king to *know* God he must act justly and humbly in his office in covenant obedience to Yahweh, who rules both the king and the people. For the people to properly *know* God by living in covenant faithfulness, they and their king must exemplify God's faithfulness in the way the king governs them and the way they respond to God. King and people must *do* justice and *live* justly in order to know God truly. Following the way of the Lord is true knowing, and knowing the truth comes from living faithfully within the covenant bond that God has established with Israel. Grant makes the point this way:

> Why is Israel's king *not* to be characterised by weapons, women and wealth? . . . First, the sole source of the king's power is to come, not from these external factors, but rather from absolute trust in Yahweh himself; and, secondly, the king is not to exalt himself over his brethren, over the covenant community . . . The limitations on the power of the king seem to be fundamentally based in the concept of covenant—the king is to be entirely dependent upon Yahweh's promise and he is to be equal in status with all Israelites as he and they are under the same covenant.[8]

Yet Grant is saying more than simply that the Psalter is organized to highlight the integral relationship of torah and kingship. His wider argument is that particular psalms and the order of the book of Psalms as a whole represent a "conversation"[9] between Psalms and the book of Deuteronomy, particularly the "kingship law" of Deuteronomy 17:14–20, a passage we quote here in full.

---

as a mode of Yahweh's relatedness. Kingship is Israel's odd assertion that Yahweh's way toward Israel is visible in human agency, a human agency that is deeply subject to the conditionality of the historical process . . . Thus kingship as mediator is to be understood (a) as congruent with the kingship of Yahweh; and (b) as somehow situated between the high royal ideology and the reservation and qualification of the Torah traditions springing from the Mosaic covenant." Brueggemann, *Theology of Old Testament*, 610–11. See also Brettler, *God is King*.

8. Grant, *King as Exemplar*, 202.

9. The idea of textual interaction as a "conversation" comes from Patrick Miller, "Deuteronomy and Psalms," 3–18, cited in Grant, *King as Exemplar*, 29. Grant writes in greater detail about the kingship law of Deuteronomy at 192–202 and 221–22.

When you have come into the land that the Lord your God is giving you, and have taken possession of it and settled in it, and you say, "I will set a king over me, like all the nations that are around us," you may indeed set over you a king whom the Lord your God will choose. One of your own community you may set as king over you; you are not permitted to put a foreigner over you, who is not of your own community. Even so, he must not acquire many horses for himself, or return the people to Egypt in order to acquire more horses, since the Lord has said to you, "You must never return that way again." And he must not acquire many wives for himself, or else his heart will turn away; also silver and gold he must not acquire in great quantity for himself. When he has taken the throne of his kingdom he shall have a copy of this law written for him in the presence of the levitical priests. It shall remain with him and he shall read in it all the days of his life, so that he may learn to fear the Lord his God, dili-gently observing all the words of this law and these statutes, neither exalting himself above other members of the community nor turning aside from the commandment, either to the right or to the left, so that he and his descendants may reign long over his kingdom in Israel.

In this passage, we see many aspects of the way the king and the people are to live in relation to God and to one another including: (1) the humility that should character-ize the king; (2) the king's equal standing alongside the Levites, who have their own God-given responsibilities and from whom the king is to receive a copy of the law; (3) the common bond of king with "his brothers"; (4) the special identity of Israel, who must not become subject to a foreign king or return to Egypt and its ways; and (5) God's supreme authority exercised through the law of the covenant and the one who should choose Israel's king. This is a highly unusual text, says Grant. "The Law of the King is, without question, quite an extraordinary document in its context within the ancient Near East [ANE]. Whilst Israel was not the only ANE society to provide written advice for rulers, we find no other ancient texts which seek to limit the power of the king in this way."[10]

IS MONARCHY GOD'S PREFERRED FORM OF GOVERNMENT?

One question that has long been raised about the monarchy in Israel is whether it was even legitimate for Israel to have a king in the first place. In 1 Samuel we read the story about the people of Israel demanding a king. Samuel is displeased by this, but God says to him, "Listen to the voice of the people in all that they say to you; for they have not rejected you, but they have rejected me from being king over them. Just as they have done to me, from the day I brought them up out of Egypt to this day, forsaking

---

10. Grant, *King as Exemplar*, 192. Quoting Gary Knoppers and Gordon McConville, Grant con-tinues, "'The king as presented here differs enormously from that of the usual ancient Near Eastern concept of the king as the chief executive in all aspects of the nation's life.'" 192–93. See also Berman, *Created Equal*.

me and serving other gods, so also they are doing to you. Now then, listen to their voice; only—you shall solemnly warn them, and show them the ways of the king who shall reign over them" (1 Sam 8:7–9). Samuel goes on to warn the people of the wrongs that a king will commit but they won't listen to him. Finally God says to Samuel, "Listen to their voice and set a king over them" (1 Sam 8:22). Some readers believe this text shows that God granted Israel a king only grudgingly, perhaps as judgment for the hardness of their hearts. Some read the story as teaching that God stands opposed to monarchy in principle and prefers a theocracy or perhaps a priestocracy, or an aristocracy, or a constitutional democracy.[11] Some even read the passage to say that all human forms of government are suspect since they are vehicles for the denial of God's sovereignty.

However, if we read Samuel's words in the light of Psalms and Deuteronomy, something quite different comes into view. God's disappointment with Israel is not because of their attraction to kingship compared to some other form(s) of human government, but because of their failure to recognize and follow Yahweh as the true and ultimate King who rules over them. Yahweh had made covenant with Israel and led them out of Egypt into the promised land. What human king could have done that? If Israel had been committed to authentic faith-communion with God in keeping with the covenant, they would have seen that their unity as a people is constituted and upheld by God's rule.

Partly in response to Israel's falling away from full trust in God, God allows them to have a king. But that allowance is not the grudging grant of a faulty institution that violates the creation order and human responsibility to God. Instead, it is an allowance that can open the way to a further, historically differentiated disclosure of the creation's meaning in relation to God. Through kingship, *on God's terms*, Israel might learn to know God their king even more clearly as the supreme ruler over all and themselves as his royal representatives. In other words, since God is their ultimate ruler, a humble and just human ruler can manifest something of God's kingship in a way that is parallel to the way parents reflect God's parenting care, or the way spousal love images the love between the divine bridegroom and his wife, or the way the shepherding of sheep can be likened to God's shepherding of Israel. That is why Deuteronomy's kingship law tells Israel the kind of king God wants them to choose. That is why the kingship psalms can be so eloquent about the king as a revelatory image of the divine King.[12]

11. In late medieval and early modern England and the European Low Countries, scholars examined the Old Testament to find support for a republican form of government in opposition to monarchy. They abstracted this passage from Deuteronomy and other biblical texts to make their case. On that development and how it influenced Europe and eventually the United States, see Nelson, *Hebrew Republic*.

12. Moshe Halbertal and Stephen Holmes, in their book *The Beginning of Politics*, present an insightful interpretation of 1 and 2 Sam, focusing on the kingships of Saul and David. They offer brilliant insights into political practices and calculations of kings doing the things Samuel warned the

Furthermore, the clear evidence from Deuteronomy and Psalms (and Jeremiah 22 and Job 29) is that the revelatory meaning of kingship (and other forms of governance) is not to be found in the practice of *dominance* by some people over others in the negative sense of that term, but rather in the kind of *servanthood*—public service—that is appropriate to the office and authority of government. Grant, quoting Patrick Miller, gets at this through Psalms 18 and 19 where Miller "observes that, 'the term "servant," according to the book in general, but more particularly in this collection, is to be associated with two figures, the ruler and the torah lover, *two figures who here merge into one.'* [Miller] goes on to propose that, 'the collection in Psalms 15–24 may be seen as defining proper kingship at the beginning of the Psalter. Obedience to torah and trust in Yahweh's guidance and deliverance are the way of Israel and the way of kingship.'"[13] This is also surely part of the point Jesus makes to his disciples at the Last Supper when he contrasts gentile rulers, who lord it over their people, with his own mode of servant leadership that characterizes divine rule over all (Luke 22:24–30).

We also need to keep in mind that monarchy is not presented in the Bible as an ideal *form* by which all other forms of government are to be compared and assessed. What comes through instead is the *norm* of justice, the call to do justice, rather than a particular *form* of government. When Jeremiah conveys God's judgment against Judah's king Shallum, it is not for the reason that Shallum was a king rather than a republican president but because Shallum built his palace by unrighteousness and treated the workers unjustly. He violated norms of justice in governing (Jer 22:11–13). The king and people of a political community that is ordered justly can function as one of the revelatory communities of the human generations because it is one exhibit of the meaning and identity of the image of God in relation to God.

The point of this limited exploration of kingship is to emphasize again that Israel, called by God's covenant into a God-honoring way of life, is God's *creation-renewal people*. They are to be God's creation-redeeming exemplar of how the sixth-day human generations should live as faithful servants of God and of one another. Israel's judges, scribes, and poets did not invent monarchy out of the blue as a construct of their self-serving ambitions. Political community is creationally rooted and realized through historically formative development and differentiation as part of the covenantal disclosure of reality. Monarchy is one form of government for a political community and it can be exercised justly or unjustly. Many monarchies and other types of government are distorted because of human disobedience, but through the kingship law of Deuteronomy and various psalms and prophets, God's torah-normativity for

---

people against when they asked for a king. But Halbertal and Holmes do not look closely enough at the normative meaning of government and politics that is celebrated in a number of the psalms and Deuteronomy and that serves as the standard by which the prophets recognize and condemn injustice.

13. Grant, *King as Exemplar*, 176. On the king as servant see also Goldingay, *Old Testament Theology*, 425–28, 818–24.

kingship and all governance is made clear. In them, we can see God's ongoing disclosure of the creation-order pattern that includes the human commission to royal service, which points beyond itself as anticipatory revelation of the fulfillment of God's kingship in the Messiah. The Lord tells Moses to tell the people, "Now therefore, if you obey my voice and keep my covenant, you shall be my treasured possession out of all the peoples. Indeed, the whole earth is mine, but you shall be for me a priestly kingdom and a holy nation" (Exod 19:5–6). Just as the Levites fill an office of service that is supposed to demonstrate what it means for Israel to be the renewed priests of creation, so Israel as a kingdom of priests is supposed to demonstrate to the world what all humans should be, namely, servant-priests of God.

RETRIBUTIVE JUSTICE AS FURTHER DISCLOSURE

As is evident today and historically, a government and a governed community, like all other human communities and responsibilities, can be distorted and destructive through sinful disobedience, leading to all the associated evils God warned Israel about through Samuel and later through Jeremiah (see 1 Kgs 12:1–24). What the psalms make clear in relation to Deuteronomy is that Israel's kingship can be revelatory of God in a limited way that is revelatory of God's kingdom, which is being disclosed through history and will be unveiled in its fullness in God's seventh-day glory. The meaning of the anticipatory revelation of just governance and citizenship shines through in God's blessing of faithful keepers of torah. At the same time, the binding character of the covenant is also revealed in acts of retributive justice when God's curses fall on king and people for their failure to keep the covenant and act justly. When the Lord blessed the work of King Solomon in building the temple by consecrating it and putting his name on it forever (1 Kgs 9:3), he also warned Solomon that if he or his children were to turn aside from God, and fail to "keep my commandments and my statutes that I have set before you, but go and serve other gods and worship them, then I will cut Israel off from the land that I have given them; and the house that I have consecrated for my name I will cast out of my sight; and Israel will become a proverb and a taunt among all peoples" (1 Kgs 9:6–7). God's blessings and curses are two edges of the same sword that confirm and enforce the truth and rightness of God's covenant in the course of the generational history of Israel and humankind.

We learn from all of this not only that political community and public governance are a legitimate part of our human identity as God's image, but also that retributive justice—punitive and corrective justice—becomes part of that governing responsibility in response to theft, murder, fraud, and other malicious maltreatments of neighbors. Many Christians believe that God established government only because of sin and that if humans had not sinned there would have been no need for government. But we have just seen in the Bible that governance for a constructive purpose is presented as part of our identity as the image of God. We are, by creation, made to be royal stewards of God, the King. What God ordains because of sin is an added duty of human governments, namely, to restrain evil and punish those who commit injustice. This is for the sake of upholding a sound political community. Human governance does not come into existence because of sin; rather the responsibility of governments to exercise retributive justice arises in response to sins of public injustice.[14]

The added duty for governments to exercise retributive justice is one of the ways God's intended partnership with humans is exhibited. Yet it is also clear that the human exercise of retributive justice must be limited by the restraints God sets for it. Human governments are not given authority to pass final judgment on the totality of human and nonhuman life. As an illustration of limits on the exercise of retributive justice, consider the restrictions that developed in regard to vengeance taking. In a number of passages in the Old Testament, we read of the practice of revenge or honor killing by one family or tribe that suffers murder or dishonor at the hands of another family or tribe. Vengeance taking was a formal matter of redressing grievances by the standard of an eye for an eye, a tooth for a tooth. It was operative in many places where smaller social units were not bound under a higher authority within an operative legal system. It has continued to the present day in some parts of the world and was evident in the practice of dueling in the American colonies and early history of the United States. Absent a higher rule of law, however, it is evident that the back-and-forth of vengeance taking might continue without end if no mutually recognized resolution is reached.[15]

When Israel entered the promised land, the Lord told them to establish cities of refuge from among the cities that were set aside for the Levite priests (see Num 35:1–30; Josh 20:1–9). Persons who killed or were believed to have killed someone could flee to a city of refuge for protection from an avenger until a proper judicial review and judgment could be made in accordance with the law of the covenant to determine the guilt or innocence of the person. We can see this as a stage in the early development of the rule of law over Israel that restricted vengeance taking and shed new light on the nature and limits of retributive justice to be carried out by governing authorities.

By the time Paul was writing to believers in Rome, in the context of both Jewish and Roman legal systems, he tells his readers that those in the Christian community should relinquish all vengeance taking against a neighbor. "Bless those who persecute you, bless and do not curse them . . . Beloved, never avenge yourselves, but leave room for the wrath of God; for it is written, 'Vengeance is mine, I will repay, says the Lord'" (Rom 12:14, 19). Then, in the following chapter, Paul explains that God has

---

14. The argument that government is given by God because of sin goes back to Augustine. See Skillen, *Good of Politics*, 50–62; Marshall, *God and Constitution*, 37–63; O'Donovan, *Ways of Judgment*, 101–24; Boersma, *Violence*, 235–61; and Brueggemann, *Theology of Old Testament*, 735–42.

15. See the discussion of this practice in Israel, even in the time of David, in Halbertal and Holmes, *Beginning of Politics*, 118–27.

appointed government ministers to exercise precisely the responsibility of revenge (or avenging) that Paul refers to as God's responsibility. So it is clear that God recognizes official ministers of justice on earth as having authority to exercise some of the avenging responsibility that is not to be exercised by those without such an office (Rom 13:1–5). By clarifying the distinct and limited responsibility of government to exercise retributive justice under law, it became possible for public criminal justice systems to break cycles of vengeance in which private parties would otherwise be engaged. Moreover, just as God had commanded Israel that children are to honor their parents, so Paul admonishes believers to honor the governing authorities as God's servants and to give respect and pay taxes to them. In this way, the further differentiation of government's responsibility to control the use of force under law was advanced over vengeance taking.

In all cases, it is clear from the Bible that God alone has authority to exercise final judgment and that the complete elimination of sin and evil will be accomplished by God alone (see Matt 13:24–30, 36–43). God has given human governments some responsibilities of retributive justice, but not all. "Vengeance is mine, I will repay, says the Lord." The picture Paul presents of God's victory over evil is that of putting sin and death under Christ's feet in judgment (1 Cor 15:22–28). John's extended portrayal of the final great battle between God and sinful Babylon in the book of Revelation is an apocalyptic vision (Rev 15–19). The rider on a white horse named Faithful and True judges and makes war against all the opponents of God. "From his mouth comes a sharp sword with which to strike down the nations, and he will rule them with a rod of iron; he will tread the wine press of the fury of the wrath of God the Almighty. On his robe and on his thigh he has a name inscribed, 'King of kings and Lord of lords'" (Rev 19:11–16).

CHRIST THE KING

In the New Testament, Jesus Christ is revealed as the faithful human servant-king, the heir and son of David, who leads the people by the unexpected route of giving up his life on the cross in service to them, to save them. God then exalts him to the throne on high as the divine-human Lord of all, with his people following in his train into the fulfillment of God's kingdom. Jesus Christ has become the life-giving second Adam who redeems and fulfills the true meaning of human governance under God. Through Christ, God reveals the way of life for human discipleship that will be transfigured into resurrected servant-rule with Christ.[16] When God has completed the reconciliation

16. Wright explains that the reordering of the world that Paul describes in 1 Cor 15:23–28 represents Paul's "extended exposition of Psalm 8.7, where the key verb ('God has *put all things in order under his feet*') is repeated and exploited to build a theology of new creation as the fulfilment of the intention for the old. Within this, he has woven the theme of kingship, of messianic rule, from Psalm 110 and Daniel, in order to emphasize that the future bodily resurrection of all the Messiah's people is guaranteed because Jesus fulfils the roles through which, according to the promises, the world is

of all things through Christ, then the oil of God's sabbath blessing will pour down on the heads of all who belong to his faithful Son: well done, good and faithful servants; enter your reward.

Paul's words in Philippians 2 and 1 Corinthians 15 follow closely on the meaning of the king as exemplar in Deuteronomy and Psalms. In the oft-quoted hymn of Phil 2:5–11 about Jesus not holding on to equality with God, but emptying himself to become a human servant and die on the cross, we see that God's response to Jesus's faithfulness is to exalt the faithful Son to the highest place, giving him the monarchical name above every name,

> so that at the name of Jesus every knee should bend,
> in heaven and on earth and under the earth,
> and every tongue should confess that Jesus Christ is Lord,
> to the glory of God the Father (Phil 2:10–11).[17]

In his first letter to the Corinthians, Paul writes in the following way about the culminating revelation of the reign of Christ: "Then comes the end, when he hands over the kingdom to God the Father, after he has destroyed every ruler and every authority and power. For he must reign until he has put all his enemies under his feet. The last enemy to be destroyed is death. For 'God has put all things in subjection under his feet.' But when it says, 'All things are put in subjection,' it is plain that this does not include the one who put all things in subjection under him. When all things are subjected to him, then the Son himself will also be subjected to the one who put all things in subjection under him, so that God may be all in all" (1 Cor 15: 24–28).[18]

Wright interprets Philippians 2 as saying that because of Christ's resurrection and ascension to "the highest place" with "a name above every name" (Phil 2:9), our citizenship on earth is thereby related to our citizenship in heaven because we are in Christ who is working in and through us to do God's will (Phil 2:13). Our future resurrection "thus provides and undergirds the present status, *the present political stance*, and the present ethical life of Christians" (italics added).[19] Yet it is surpris-

---

to be brought under the saving rule of its creator God. The focal point of this saving kingdom is the defeat and abolition of death itself (verse 26)." Wright, *Resurrection*, 335. See also Dumbrell, *Search for Order*, 72–73.

17. For more on this passage, see Wright, *Climax*, 84.

18. Cummins explains that Paul's testimony here is closely related to his explanation of what it means for believers to be *"in* Christ. In the ancient world, not least in Israel, the people were represented by and saw their identity and destiny as being bound up with that of their king." This was part of "Jewish messianic expectations concerning a Davidic Messiah/Son of God figure," and the apostle Paul "intends to convey precisely this kind of relationship between Christ and his people." In other words, Paul shows that Jesus took on the human responsibility of just governance of the earth under God, and he shows his disciples (brothers and sisters) what that means, moving from servanthood in Christ to being joined to Christ's resurrection as King of kings, yet still subject to God as servants. Cummins, "Divine Life," 200.

19. Wright, *Resurrection*, 235.

ing that having said this, and having also emphasized that our earthly bodies will be transformed into resurrection bodies, Wright says nothing more about the meaning of the exercise of our earthly governing responsibility as part of our identity as God's image redeemed in Christ Jesus. According to Wright, our responsibility, exercised in anticipation of our future resurrection, undergirds our "present political stance," but he does not comment on how the exercise of just governance and citizenship in this age can be revelatory in anticipation of God's fulfilled kingdom.[20] He sees continuity between this age and the coming age, but he does not give attention to the unfolding covenantal disclosure of created reality as revelatory of God in the multiple dimensions of human responsibility.

Kuyper is also unclear or equivocal about how Christ's kingship is related to human political responsibility in this age. Due to his continued struggle with the relation of "common grace" to "special grace," he variously asserts a basic contrast between Christ's kingship and God's authorization of human government. At the same time, he insists that Christians should recognize and honor Christ's claim of authority over every square inch of life on earth.[21] Kuyper wants to see the entire creation come to fulfillment in God's glory through Christ's mediatorial priesthood and kingship, while also believing that earthly government is but a temporary means of God's common grace to restrain sin and punish evildoers in this age. Thus, in many respects, Kuyper remains rooted in the Augustinian belief that God established government because of sin rather than as part of the creational responsibility of the image of God from the beginning.

Moltmann's lack of attention to the relation of Christ's kingship to earthly politics is not unlike the weaknesses in Wright's and Kuyper's approaches. Despite the importance he attaches to *hope* and its inspirational power for the way we should live now, his discussion of the relation between humans and God tells us little about the revelatory character of the diverse responsibilities humans exercise in this age. In the concluding pages of his book on eschatology, Moltmann refers to "interactions between divine and human activity." Yet his focus is almost exclusively on God's glorification in Jesus, "the Messiah who sanctifies God's name and does God's will and thereby brings God's kingdom."[22] When Moltmann relates this to our joyful response to Christ's resurrection, and what it might mean for our "participation in the divine life," he emphasizes that our participation is not only about joy and hope for "life in

---

20. Wright, *Resurrection*, 225–41. This is also the case in Wright's other publications as I've discovered, though I may have missed something in his vast corpus.

21. The equivocation and even dualism in Kuyper on this subject is evident in his lecture on politics in *Lectures on Calvinism*, 78–109, and in his three-volume, 1911–12 publication, Pro Rege, on the kingship of Christ. The first two volumes of the latter work have just been published in English translation as *Pro Rege: Living Under Christ's Kingship*.

22. Moltmann, *Coming of God*, 334.

'the world beyond', 'life after death'; it is an awakening, a rebirth, already here and now, and the endowment of earthly life with new vital energies."[23]

Yet what does Moltmann believe the awakening, rebirth, and endowment of new vital energies means for our earthly lives, including our earthly political life? He concludes with comments about the anticipated feast with God that will come with the culmination of redemption, saying, "In the feast of eternal joy all created beings and the whole community of God's creation are destined to sing their hymns and songs of praise."[24] Yet what fruits of their labors will humans bring to the banquet? How should we be singing songs of praise now? What will we offer up, in Christ, as priestly thank offerings? When God blesses the redeemed of the Lord, saying "Well done, good and faithful servants," what acts or patterns of faithfulness in earthly labors, including civic and governing responsibilities, will Christ the King be commending them for?

In contrast to Wright, Kuyper, and Moltmann, I believe the eschatological feast with God will take place as the *fulfillment* of this creation, the one and only seven-day creation of God. Therefore, the creation's climax in God's day of rest has everything to do with the responsibilities of God's sixth-day servants throughout their generations. The climactic celebration of the glory of the Lord in the new Jerusalem, where Christ is enthroned, will include thank offerings lifted up by all the saints from their faithful labors in every arena of responsibility in this age. The feast will celebrate, among other things, the fulfillment of just governance in Christ, in which king and people are joined together in one worldwide kingdom of righteousness to the praise of God (Ps 45:6–7; Isa 1:21–26; Ezek 37:15–28).[25] The banquet hall will pulse with joy in hearing God's commendatory blessing of the faithful for all their labors in this age, offered up to God in and through their faithful brother and Lord of all, Jesus Christ.

The seventh-day climax of creation—God's sabbath rest fulfilled—will reveal not only the fulfillment of Christ's kingship in the kingdom of God but also the glorious marriage of Christ and his bride and the ingathering of the entire family of God—all the brothers and sisters of Christ. The good shepherd will gather in all the sheep that have heard his voice.[26] In that culmination, the completed construction of the house of God will be unveiled with every faithful "building stone" firmly in place (1 Pet 2:4–5; Heb 3:6). God's day of rest will also reveal the promised economy of plenty in which joint heirs with Christ share in all the riches of his kingdom (Rom 8:17; Rev 21:18–21, 24–27; Isa 60:1–14). All of the offices of human stewardship on earth, including those of public governance, will be fulfilled in Christ in praise of God and

---

23. Moltmann, *Coming of God*, 337.

24. Moltmann, *Coming of God*, 338.

25. In this regard, see Trotter's reading of Psalm 45 as a coronation psalm, "Genre and Setting." In his careful analysis of the structure of Psalm 103, Stek helps to bring out the psalm's combination of familial and monarchical imagery in "Psalm 103."

26. See Golding, "Imagery of Shepherding."

the fulfillment of God's covenanted community.[27] John's vision on Patmos presented in Revelation sums it up this way:

> Then the angel showed me the river of the water of life, bright as crystal, flowing from the throne of God and of the Lamb through the middle of the street of the city. On either side of the river is the tree of life with its twelve kinds of fruit, producing its fruit each month; and the leaves of the tree are for the healing of the nations. Nothing accursed will be found there any more. But the throne of God and of the Lamb will be in it, and his servants will worship him; they will see his face, and his name will be on their foreheads. And there will be no more night; they need no light of lamp or sun, for the Lord God will be their light, and they will reign for ever and ever (Rev 22:1–5).

27. The revelatory character of the image of God in all vocations is at the root of typological and figural interpretation of the Bible. See Hays, *Reading Backwards*, and Skillen, "Reengaging Figural Interpretation."

PART 4

First Adam, Last Adam

16

The Consummation of Creation

"FOR PAUL," ACCORDING TO N. T. Wright, "the resurrection of Jesus of Nazareth is the heart of the gospel (not to the exclusion of the cross, of course, but not least as the event which gives the cross its meaning); it is the object of faith, the ground of justification, the basis for obedient Christian living, the motivation for unity, and not least, the challenge to the principalities and powers."[1] Paul's identification of Messiah Jesus as the last Adam is the consequence of Christ's resurrection from the dead. In the next chapter, we will look in detail at 1 Corinthians 15:35–54 where Paul compares the last Adam to the first Adam. There are other passages of scripture that use different terms to speak about Christ's resurrection into a new mode of human life with God, the resurrection mode of life. Both Paul's teaching and that of other apostles illumines both the continuity and the discontinuity between life in this age and life in the age to come, between earthly life and resurrection life, between the life of the generations of the first Adam and the life of those resurrected in the last Adam.

Consider the following New Testament passages: the first is the story of Jesus's resurrection found in the Gospels of Mark and Luke. The morning after the Sabbath, following the death and burial of Jesus, three women—Mary Magdalene, Mary the mother of James, and Salome—"bought spices, so that they might go to anoint him," but when they get to the tomb he is not there. A young man "dressed in a white robe" sitting at the tomb says to them, "Do not be alarmed . . . He has been raised; he is not here . . . [H]e is going ahead of you to Galilee; there you will see him, just as he told you" (Mark 16:1–7). The women go to the tomb to anoint a dead body, the body of a man whose lineage could be traced back through Israel and Abraham to the first Adam (Luke 3:38). But the body they wanted to anoint is not there. Jesus is risen and plans to meet them in Galilee, "just as he told you." In other words, the same Lord Jesus, who died and would later meet them in Galilee (continuity), died to the life of this age and rose to a new kind of life (discontinuity) about which he told them and

---

1. Wright, *Resurrection*, 266.

soon would tell them again. Later on, the risen Jesus would meet with more than five hundred of those who followed him prior to his death (continuity) and would assure them of life to come and of his return from glory to meet them in a new way (discontinuity). See Luke 24:1–53, Acts 1:1–11, and 1 Cor 15:1–8.

The second passage is in Paul's second letter to the Corinthians. Paul is explaining the kind of ministry he and other followers of Christ have in this age as a result of Christ's resurrection from the dead. Paul says of Christ: "he died for all, so that those who live might live no longer for themselves, but for him who died and was raised for them. From now on, therefore, we regard no one from a human point of view; even though we once knew Christ from a human point of view, we know him no longer in that way" (2 Cor 5:15–16). At one point, according to Paul, when Jesus lived on earth, his followers regarded him from the perspective of life in this age, the age of the generations of the first Adam. But now, through eyes of faith opened by Christ's resurrection, his followers are to regard him from the perspective of his resurrected life in the new age now coming. Paul adds that this is also the perspective from which believers should now regard one another. Yes, we are still living on earth, but since by faith we understand that we have been buried and raised with Christ, we should now regard one another from the perspective of Christ's resurrected life, that is from the perspective of the last Adam in whom we are joined. The same people (continuity), namely, Jesus and his followers, can be regarded from two different points of view (discontinuity), and it is important now to adopt the perspective opened to us by Christ's resurrection and ascension in order to understand both him and those who are in him.[2]

Finally, consider the vision of the new creation that John sees on the island of Patmos, a vision of the fulfillment of the kingdom of God. In John's vision, Jesus Christ appears not only as the Omega but also as the Alpha of all things (Rev 1:8; 22:13). The heavenly hosts praise him not only because he purchased humans with his blood (5:9), but also because he created all things (4:11). In his vision of the culmination of God's kingdom, John sees a new *earth* and not only a new heaven. The revelation of God's glory through Jesus Christ begins, therefore, at the beginning of all things and culminates with the risen Christ in heavenly glory. The book of Revelation is, through and through, a vision of *creation fulfilled, not of creation abandoned.* John's vision of a *new* creation is not the vision of a *second* creation, with God starting over again after

---

2. The distinction Paul is describing here is, in my view, also the basis of Paul's defense of his ministry in the third chapter of 2 Cor. Paul is responding to critics who apparently question his authority and want to see letters of recommendation. But Paul says to his readers, "You yourselves are our letter" (2 Cor 3:2–3). He is not starting a new organization for this age, but proclaiming the good news of the new covenant God has inaugurated in Christ, the life-giving Spirit, who is bringing this age to fulfillment in the age to come. God in Christ has commissioned Paul with authority to serve as a minister of the gospel, "not of letter but of spirit; for the letter kills, but the Spirit gives life" (2 Cor 3:6). It is not ink on paper that will confirm Paul's competency, but the Spirit writing on their hearts and equipping them to be living letters of the glory of the Lord. For an extended interpretation of 2 Cor 3, see Hays, *Echoes in Paul,* 122–53.

destroying the first creation. Instead, what John sees is the judgment, cleansing, and reconciliation of the one and only creation to which God has bound himself from its foundation to its seventh-day fulfillment.

To be sure, as the biblical writers anticipate, the features of our present human experience will be transformed so significantly through Christ's glorious triumph (discontinuity) that John can describe what he sees as "a new heaven and a new earth, for the first heaven and the first earth had passed away" (Rev 21:1). He sees that the *new* Jerusalem needs no sun or moon because the lamb is its lamp and there is no night there (Rev 21:23, 25). At the same time, John says that "the kings of the earth will bring their glory into [the new Jerusalem]" and the "glory and honor of the nations" will be brought into it (Rev 21:24, 26). God's voice from the throne proclaims, "See, the home of God is among mortals. He will dwell with them; they will be his peoples, and God himself will be with them" (Rev 21:3). God's people to whom John is writing are the very ones whom Christ is redeeming from among the generations of the first Adam, drawing them into the creation's sabbath fulfillment. Christ's promise to his betrothed—to the faithful in *this* age—is that he is "coming soon" (Rev 22:7, 12, 17, 20). Dwelling with God in resurrection life will be the magnificent wedding gift Christ gives to his bride (Rev 21:2; 22:12, 14, 17). The new heavens and the new earth will see Christ ruling, together with all who belong to him, in fulfillment of the generational commission of priestly governance that God has given the image of God, male and female. The King of kings and Lord of lords will offer up to God the entire creation, fully reconciled and justly ordered, and God's glory will fill all things full in the creation's consummation (see also Heb 2:5–11; 1 Cor 15:20–23; Phil 2:5–11; Isa 60–62).

CONTINUITIES AND DISCONTINUITIES

What we find in the New Testament is actually two kinds of discontinuity that must not be confused. One kind is that between created life in this age and the fulfillment of creaturely life in the age to come. The other kind is that between death and new life, between slavery to sin and freedom in restored righteousness. The contrast in the first discontinuity is rooted in the continuity of the seven-day order of creation: humans experience it as the contrast between their sixth-day mode of life on earth and the resurrection mode of life in God's seventh-day rest. The contrast in the second kind of discontinuity is due to sinfulness and God's judgment of it. Humans in this case are God's good creatures who have become sinners, but faithless disobedience brings death not life. Life fulfilled has no continuity whatever with sin and death.

The element of continuity in both cases is due to the fact that there is only one creation and only one God of creation. The difference between the two kinds of discontinuity is that one belongs to the creation order and the other does not. The difference between sixth-day creaturely life and seventh-day creaturely life is inherent in God's creation. On the other hand, sinful disobedience violates—is antithetical to—life in the good creation and will have no part in creation's fulfillment. There is no continuity between death and life. Humans must be *redeemed from* sin and death and reconciled with God in order to find fulfillment in the creation's consummation. When the resurrected Christ puts an end to sin and death, he will not put an end to the creation, but rather will lead the cleansed and reconciled creation to its consummation in the glory of God.

Interpreters of the New Testament differ about whether to place the accent on the continuity or the discontinuity in various passages, and much depends on whether they focus on the difference between this age and the age to come, or on the antithesis between sin and salvation. According to Leonhard Goppelt, John's vision of the new creation and the resurrected Christ represents the climax of the New Testament's Adam-Christ typology in which Adam is understood to be a type of Christ.[3] However, Goppelt points primarily to Paul's contrast in Romans 5 and other passages that emphasize the difference between Adam the sinner and Christ the redeemer. The definitive exposition of this typology, writes Goppelt, is found in Romans 5:12–21. In verse 5:14, we read that Adam was "a pattern [a type] of the one to come."[4] "Through Christ," says Goppelt, "those who believe in him are freed from the association with corruption that began with the first Adam and they are created anew in the image of the second Adam."[5] The typological relation of Adam to Christ, as Goppelt sees it, appears in the fact that "Christ, as the first fruit of the new creation, steps into the center and forms new creatures . . . Whoever is in Christ is a new creation" (2 Cor 5:17; Gal 6:15).[6] This is eschatological language, says Goppelt, because Paul is not referring to "the restoration of man to the condition in which he was created," but is speaking of "a new creation that will come about through Christ and be lived through Christ."[7] Goppelt thus emphasizes the discontinuity between the first Adam and the last Adam, identifying the first with sin and corruption, and the second with new life and a new creation. The only similarity appears to be that both Adam and Christ are sources or originators of heirs—the first, Adam's descendants caught in sin and death, the second, Adam's brothers and sisters elevated to the eternal life of the new creation.

---

3. Goppelt contends that the Adam-Christ typology can be found not only in Paul's epistles but also throughout the New Testament. Luke, for example, saw the importance of tracing the genealogy of Jesus all the way back to Adam, not just to David or Abraham, in order to set up the contrast. Mark's Gospel works with the same typology, writes Goppelt, when referring to Jesus's temptation in the wilderness: "The first man fell in the temptation, and in his fall he drew all men after him. Christ, however, overcame the temptation . . . Jesus reopens the Paradise closed by the first man." In contrast to Israel (God's chosen people who like Adam also fell into sin), Jesus exhibits the obedience expected by God and therefore becomes "the firstborn of the new people of God." Goppelt, *Typos*, 97–100.

4. Goppelt, *Typos*, 129. See also Wright, *Climax*, 35–40.

5. Goppelt, *Typos*, 130–31.

6. Goppelt, *Typos*, 131.

7. Goppelt, *Typos*, 132.

However, what continuity is there between Adam, God's good creature, and Christ the redeemer of creation if the accent is placed so fully on the discontinuity between corrupt humans and the righteous Christ? The discontinuity Goppelt sees shows little or no relation between God's good creation and the new creation. Does that mean the generations of the sinful first Adam will be discarded when God makes new creatures in Christ? Moreover, what about the resurrected Christ? Is he not also one of us, a human creature of this age, the *incarnate* Son of God, who was raised to new life? If all things have been created in and through the Son of God and all things hang together in him, then is there not a significant continuity between the Son of God, who is the mediator of creation, and Christ Jesus, the mediator of the new creation?

Wright also accents the discontinuity we've just noted in Goppelt in his interpretation of Romans 5:15–21 (and its close parallel in 1 Cor 15:20–28), yet he also recognizes considerable continuity. There is an important difference (discontinuity), to be sure, between the first Adam and the second, as Wright explains, insofar as "Christ did not begin where Adam began. He had to begin where Adam ended, that is, by taking on to himself not merely a clean slate, not merely even the single sin of Adam, but the whole entail of that sin, working its way out in the 'many sins' of Adam's descendants, and arriving at the judgment spoken of in [Rom] 1.32; 2.1–16; and 3.19–20."[8] Through Christ's obedience unto death, "Adam's sin and its effects are thus undone, and God's original intention for humanity is thus restored in the Age to Come, which has already begun with the work of Jesus Christ" (Rom 5:21).[9] Sin is a disruption deserving of death that threatens God's original intention for humanity. Christ's redeeming work is not only to destroy death but also to overcome it so that God's creation may be fulfilled.

Elsewhere Wright comments that 1 Corinthians 15:20–28 is "all about new creation as the fulfillment and redemption of the old." Paul is "thinking his way through a theology of creation and of humankind," quoting or referring indirectly to Genesis 1:26–28, 3:17–19, and Psalm 8.[10] Paul's climactic point, according to Wright, is that "the failure of humankind ('Adam') to be the creator's wise, image-bearing steward over creation has not led the creator to rewrite the vocation, but rather to send the Messiah as the truly human being. The purpose is that in his renewed, resurrected human life he can be and do, for humankind and all creation, what neither humankind nor creation could do for themselves."[11]

---

8. Wright, *Climax*, 37.

9. Wright, *Climax*, 39.

10. Wright, *Resurrection*, 334.

11. Wright, *Resurrection*, 334. At another point, Wright connects the phrase "new creation" primarily with "renewed creation." Throughout Paul's letters, says Wright, he is telling the story of "creation and new creation. A consistently Jewish thinker, Paul never imagines that creation is evil. It is the good creation of the good God, and to be enjoyed as such. But, in line with much apocalyptic thought, Paul believes that God is planning to renew creation, to bring it out of its present state of decay and

Yet Wright is not always clear about the connection between the creation and the new creation, between this age and the coming age. In Romans 8, for example, he highlights the "glory" that the resurrected people of God will enjoy, including their share in the Messiah's "kingly reign."[12] Such glory, says Wright, is in part a synonym for "resurrection" because the risen body "will no longer be subject to decay and death. But those who are raised will also enjoy 'glory' in the sense of new responsibilities within the new creation."[13] Although Wright quotes the verses in Romans 8 about creation waiting eagerly for the sons of God to be revealed and for its liberation from its bondage to decay (Rom 8:19, 21), he reads them as speaking of liberation from the old creation and entrance into the new creation. He fails to make the distinction between the good creation, on the one hand, and its bondage to sin, on the other. Yet, is not Romans 8 about the expectation of the liberation of God's one and only creation so it can participate in the glory of God? And isn't the glory that humans will enjoy in their resurrection life the fulfillment, at a new level, of the creaturely glory for which God created them? Is it not the case that the glory of the resurrected Christ entails the fulfillment of the glory of earthlings with all their responsibilities and not only the glory that will come with new heavenly responsibilities?

A similar ambiguity comes through in Moltmann's discussion of this creation and the new creation. Although Moltmann does not deal with Paul's contrast of the first Adam and the last Adam, he does engage the matter that concerns us here. In a summary of Calvinist theology's view of this world being "transfigured" through Christ's resurrection, Moltmann expresses the belief that the transfiguration will reveal "a continuity between *the grace of Christ* experienced in history and *the glory of Christ* expected in the consummation. In individual believers too there are seeds of eternal life, which will there grow up to their fullness." For the Calvinists, in contrast to earlier Lutheranism, says Moltmann, the present world will not be entirely annihilated but transformed "out of transience into eternity."[14] In his criticism of Calvinism, Moltmann argues that the idea of "transformation" does not "penetrate deeply enough." "If the new creation," he writes, "is to be an imperishable and eternal creation, it must be new not only over against the world of sin and death, but over against the first temporal creation too. The substantial conditions of creaturely existence itself

---

death and into the new world, where it would find its true fulfillment." Wright, "Yet the Sun," 63–64. Here, however, we must ask, what does Wright mean by saying that God will bring the *renewed* creation "into the new world?" Does "new world" mean the same thing as "renewed creation"? Or does Wright mean to say that the renewed creation is lifted into (relocated in) another world different from the first one? Is the "new world" then a second creation of God, or the fulfillment of the first and only creation? Wright's language seems to me to be ambiguous.

12. Wright, *Resurrection*, 257.

13. Wright, *Resurrection*, 257–58.

14. Moltmann, *Coming of God*, 271.

must be changed."[15] Moltmann here sounds like he is placing the accent heavily if not entirely on discontinuity between this creation and a new creation.

In his book on creation, however, Moltmann shows greater appreciation for continuity. Because of Christ's death and resurrection, heaven opens itself for the earth, he writes. The risen one is Lord of the earth as well as of heaven. If "heaven is pushed out of the doctrine of creation, it becomes difficult to go on interpreting the earth as God's creation at all."[16] In his book on Jesus Christ, Moltmann is even more emphatic about the continuity of heaven and earth. "The creation psalms tell us that creation-in-the-beginning was already understood as 'God's temple.' Heaven and earth are his home, the home in which he desires to dwell and arrive at his rest. And in designating the cause and basis of creation, this also names its purpose and end: God's endless sabbath."[17] Nevertheless, we must keep in mind that Moltmann makes a significant distinction between (1) creation in the beginning, (2) the continuing creation, and (3) the new creation.[18] So the continuity he sees between earth and heaven in the original creation does not necessarily mean that he sees continuity between "creation in the beginning" and the "new creation."

CONCLUSION

In the preceding chapters we have argued that the Bible, from the opening chapters of Genesis onward, explicitly portrays, or implicitly presupposes, the seven-day creation order in which the sixth-day human generations are called to exercise highly important God-given responsibilities as royal stewards and chief priests of the creator-King. The generations of the first Adam, consequently, are not first of all sinners but rather, creatures made in the image of God with a crucial role to play in revealing God's glory. God sustains the creation with its human responsibilities while condemning sin in a way that does not pit a new heavens and new earth over against God's original purposes for the creation. Rather, God's condemnation of sin is directed to the human *corruption* of creation, and that antithesis is overcome through Christ's death and resurrection.

It seems to me, therefore, that recognition of the sabbath-oriented order of creation makes it possible to dispel the ambiguities we have found in Goppelt, Wright, and Moltmann with regard to the relation of the creation to its fulfillment ("new" creation). The deathward direction taken by human disobedience is certainly antithetical to God's purposes for creation. Thus, Paul's emphatic contrast between the man by whom death entered the world and the man through whom reconciled life comes, is of great importance. Nevertheless, as we will see even more clearly in the next two

15. Moltmann, *Coming of God*, 272.

16. Moltmann, *God in Creation*, 172–73.

17. Moltmann, *Way of Jesus Christ*, 290.

18. Moltmann, *God in Creation*, 206–14.

chapters, there is a deeper kind of continuity and discontinuity indicated in the New Testament that needs to be recognized as the basis for understanding the discontinuity between the sin of the first Adam and the redeeming grace of the second Adam.

17

First Corinthians 15:35–57

TWO MODES OF HUMAN EXISTENCE

Paul offers a distinctive argument about the first Adam and the last Adam in the latter part of 1 Corinthians 15 that is different from his argument in 15:20–26. Although he does not use the language of the seven days of creation here, I want to show how his argument presupposes Genesis 1–2 and the seven-day order of creation articulated there. Richard Gaffin explains that in the later passage "Adam is introduced not as fallen, as a sinner, as he is in Romans 5 as well as earlier in this chapter [1 Cor 15:21–22]. Rather, he is in view as created, as he was before the fall, as unfallen creature made in God's image. In its full scope, then, the contrast in verse 45 is between Adam as he was by virtue [of] creation and Christ as he is by virtue of resurrection." In fact, says Gaffin, in 1 Cor 15:44b Paul is "arguing *from* the pre-resurrection body *to* the resurrection body. He is no longer simply contrasting them."[1] Paul is reasoning "directly from the psychical body [of the first Adam] to the spiritual body [of the last Adam]. The former is made the condition for the latter; the latter is postulated on the basis of the former."[2]

Beginning with 1 Corinthians 15:35, where Paul entertains the questions, "How are the dead raised?" and "With what kind of body will they come?," he refers to two kinds of bodies or modes of human existence in God's creation. The metaphor Paul turns to is that of a seed planted in the ground that eventually emerges as a plant. The seed and the mature plant represent different kinds of "bodies" (vv. 37–38), says Paul, who then stretches and shifts the metaphor to emphasize the differences among God's creatures: "Not all flesh is alike, but there is one flesh for human beings, another for

---

1. Gaffin, "Last Adam," 199.

2. Gaffin, *Resurrection and Redemption*, 79. Christianity owes much to Augustine for its understanding of the image of God and the relation of the first Adam to the last Adam. According to Matthew Puffer, there were three main stages in the development of Augustine's views, which have influenced subsequent interpretations of 1 Cor 15 and other biblical passages ever since. See Puffer, "Human Dignity," 65–82.

animals, another for birds, and another for fish. There are both heavenly bodies and earthly bodies, but the glory of the heavenly is one thing, and that of the earthly is another" (vv. 39–40). Paul starts by speaking of bodies, then shifts to different kinds of flesh, and then returns to different kinds of bodies, yet it is clear all along that he is talking about different creatures of God's first six creation days, each of which has its own identity, character, and honor as God's good creature ("very good," as Genesis 1:31 puts it).[3] Wright summarizes it this way: "Objects on earth do not shine as do the sun, moon and stars; but they still have their own proper 'glory.' Here 'glory' seems to mean 'honour', 'reputation', 'proper dignity.'"[4]

A few verses later, Paul brings back his agricultural metaphor in speaking about the kind of human body that is "sown" like a seed in death but "raised" to life as a different kind of body (1 Cor 15:42–49). Yet while Paul continues with this organic metaphor, he pushes beyond it in saying that the "raised" body is not something that emerges organically from the seed but is something that comes from another source altogether. Moreover, when he speaks of the seed dying before the plant can emerge, he recognizes the seed as a good thing. He is not suggesting that the seed is something sinful or evil. The seed and the plant are different kinds of good "bodies" or modes of creaturely existence. The contrast Paul then draws between different modes of human existence is between "a natural body" and "a spiritual body." By "natural," he does not mean sinful, and by "spiritual," he does not mean something immaterial or without a body. Paul's interest, says Gaffin, "is to show that from the beginning, prior to the fall, a higher or different kind of body than the body of Adam, the psychical body, is in view. Adam, by virtue of creation (not because of sin), anticipates and points to another, higher form of somatic existence."[5] The second or higher mode of bodily existence is not an afterthought that God comes up with in response to the first Adam's disobedience. Both the "natural" and the "spiritual" are good, creaturely modes of existence, yet they are different kinds of life, each with its own splendor.[6]

3. See Wright, *Resurrection*, 341–42.

4. Wright, *Resurrection*, 345. Wright here picks up on what we have described as the pattern of "honor and hospitality" in the creation order, with every creature having its own special dignity, honor, or glory.

5. Gaffin, *Resurrection and Redemption*, 82. Given Paul's implied reference to Genesis 2:7 in 1 Cor 15:45, Gaffin offers this summary of the Pauline passage: "(a) Adam is in view as created and unfallen and, as such, contrasted with Christ, the last Adam, as resurrected. (b) The Adam of Genesis 2:7, as the 'first' anticipates a 'last.' The original creation has in view a consummation." Gaffin, "Last Adam," 198. Gaffin goes on to add, "The *imago Dei* in which Adam was created . . . is eschatologically oriented . . . [I]n this sense eschatology is prior to soteriology." Gaffin, "Last Adam," 202–3. Cf. Wright, *Resurrection*, 353.

6. Jon Levenson argues that in the Hebrew Bible (the Old Testament), the prophets believed that the resurrection mode of life would entail a different kind of human existence and not simply the recovery of life as we now know it or the extraction of the soul into an eternal beyond. "To 'be radiant like the bright expanse of sky' (Dan 12:3) is (if the pun may be pardoned) light years away from having to reinhabit one's old body for all eternity. This is worth noting because scholars often present the issue as if the only alternatives are immortality of the soul, on the one hand, and resurrection of the body,

As Gaffin explains, Paul's words translated "natural" and "spiritual" do not stand for something "physical" over against something "immaterial," or for what is "natural" over against what is "supernatural." The word "natural" translates the Greek word "*psychikon*" derived from "*psyche*," which really means a "living soul" or "person" in the sense of Genesis 2:7, where we are told God took soil and breathed into it and the composite whole was a "living soul"—the human person. In other words, a "living soul" was not breathed into a ball of mud. Soul or "psyche" does not refer to an immaterial part of the human person (in contrast to the body) but rather to the whole, living person in this age. "Spiritual" refers to the new kind, or new mode, of bodily, soulish existence (in its entirety) into which the risen Christ has entered and into which those raised with him will also enter.[7]

"Earthly humanity," according to Wright, "is like Adam's body, heavenly humanity like Christ's body, and believers, who presently share the one, will at last share the other."[8] According to Paul, "Just as we have borne the image of the man of dust [Adam's image continued on through his descendants], we will also bear the image of the man of heaven," (v. 49). Wright explains, "the verb used for 'bear' (*phoreo*) is often used for the wearing of clothes; as in Ephesians and Colossians we found the language of putting off the set of clothes belonging to the former humanity, and putting on those belonging to the new one, so here, and as we shall see in 2 Corinthians 5, Paul speaks of present and future in terms of 'wearing' one model of human existence or the other one."[9] John Currie makes much the same point in commenting on the passage in 2 Corinthians 5: "Why did the vision of putting off this temporary earthly dwelling and putting on the eternal heavenly dwelling embolden [Paul] and why should it embolden us?" Currie answers this way: Paul "knew that the resurrection body is the realization of the very thing we were created for. The vision of future bodily resurrection is so empowering because it is not only the final remedy for sin but the realization of that for which we were created but which sin corrupted."[10]

The full context of the passage in 1 Corinthians 15:35–49 shows clearly that Paul is distinguishing two modes of human existence, two kinds of "body." As Gaffin explains, Paul's contrast is "even broader than that of whole persons. There are two different orders or kinds of existence in view, not simply the different persons of Adam and Christ. "A living body," says Gaffin, "is not an abstraction; it does not exist in a vacuum. It necessarily implies a context; it is an index of an environment or 'world.'"[11]

---

on the other. Doing so is to neglect the key fact that resurrection was thought to yield a transformed and perfect form of bodily existence and thus a state of being both like and unlike any we can know in the flesh." Levenson, *Resurrection,* 189.

7. Gaffin, "Last Adam," 200.

8. Wright, *Climax,* 32.

9. Wright, *Resurrection,* 356.

10. Currie, "Preaching by Faith," 557.

11. Gaffin, "Last Adam," 203.

This is apparent from the way Paul moves directly from the contrast of soul and spirit to the contrast of earth (or earthly) and heaven (or heavenly) in 1 Corinthians 15:45–49. "The perspective from which Paul views the believer's resurrection, then, is nothing less than cosmic."[12] What Paul is presupposing, I would argue, is nothing less than the seven-day order of creation in which the generations of the sixth-day Adam are like seeds planted that become the resurrected company of the last Adam, the life-giving Spirit. Humans are alive now as "natural," sixth-day creatures in the full environment or world of God's six creation days, which are oriented from the beginning toward God's day of rest. The risen Christ, and those raised with him, will live a seventh-day mode of existence, which is the fulfillment of the whole creation in God's sabbath rest.

The "natural body," Paul contends, is the kind of life God has given the generations of the first Adam (the sixth-day generations of the image of God). "The first man was from the earth," referring to Adam as God created him, not to Adam as sinner. The "second [or last] man," by contrast, "is from heaven" (v. 47). "'The first man, Adam, became a living being'; the last Adam became a life-giving spirit" (v. 45), and through him, natural humans are changed into the new or second mode of bodily existence. According to Wright, "Paul looks all the way back to the creation of humans in the divine image in Genesis 1.26–8, and all the way on to the ultimate future, when all those 'in the Messiah' . . . will be 'conformed to the image of the son of God, so that he might be the firstborn of a large family.'"[13] The generations of the first Adam live now as natural (sixth-day) bodies, not as spiritual or heavenly (seventh-day) bodies. Jesus, the incarnate Son of God, is therefore also a natural man in the line of Adam's generations, for he was born of a woman who was herself born in the line of Adam's generations. But Jesus Christ is now the resurrected man who has ascended to his father, the first human to enter the new mode of human existence. In that capacity he is the last Adam who is drawing together the faithful from all generations into the new and final mode of human existence when God dwells with us face-to-face.[14]

12. Gaffin, *Resurrection and Redemption*, 83.

13. Wright, *Resurrection*, 356.

14. There is nothing in the 1 Cor 15 passage to suggest that the first Adam was not related to God from the beginning as the image of God. The incarnation of the Son of God is not what makes men and women "real humans," as Karl Barth seems to suggest; in fact, the incarnation presupposes human existence as the mode of existence the Son took on. We now know from further revelation that the Son of God who became incarnate in Jesus is the one through whom all things were created, so in that sense he is prior—the foundation of creation, including the generations of the first Adam. Barth's account of human creatures is not, in my view, compatible with Paul's presentation of two modes of human existence. Barth (in *Church Dogmatics*) asserts the distinction between "phenomenal man" and "real man." "The ontological determination of humanity," he writes, "is grounded in the fact that one man among all others is the man Jesus." Only in relation to Jesus can we get beyond mere "phenomenal man." Jesus is the one creature with whom we deal directly with the being of God. "He is the creaturely being in whose existence God's act of deliverance has taken place for all other men." Jesus as deliverer and savior is the real man and thus prior to human creatures in relation to God. In Barth's frame of thought, therefore, deliverance and redemption in Jesus come prior to human creatures related to God. So, the biblical drama of the unfolding creation and the revelatory covenants,

A COVENANTAL MODE OF EXISTENCE AND DISCOURSE

Paul's entire discussion of the earthly mode of existence and the heavenly mode of existence represents *covenantal* thinking through and through. Adam stands for the human generations (in their entirety) whom God constituted as sixth-day stewards in the creation's seven-day covenant bond with God. Likewise, Christ stands for, or represents, the redeemed brothers and sisters who are being reconciled through him for entrance into the creation's seventh-day family. Adam and Christ in 1 Corinthians 15, says Gaffin, are thus "representatives, corporate persons, heads within a contemplated solidarity, respectively, for all who are 'in' them."[15] In 1 Corinthians 15:45–49, "Adam and Christ are in view as they exemplify and are instances, respectively, of the pre-resurrection bodies (of all human beings) and the resurrection bodies of believers."[16]

It is important to remember that while Paul's attention is focused on the relation of the first Adam to the last Adam, the historical development that has led him and the other apostles to understand this is the revelation of Jesus as the Christ, the Messiah of Israel. Hans Boersma explains it this way: "There is a profound awareness among New Testament scholars today that Jesus came as the representative of Israel—the embodiment of the New Israel—and that as such he came as the culmination of a particular historical journey of fellowship (and the lack thereof) between Yahweh and the Abrahamic nation. To be sure, behind the Israelite history lies the story of all humanity. Jesus is not just the New Israel; he is also (and ultimately) the Second Adam."[17] In other words, Paul saw, with eyes of faith, that the Messiah of Israel is the fulfillment not only of Israel but of humankind, God's sixth-day human generations. That is the basis for the use of covenantal language not only about Israel and the Messiah but also about humankind and the last Adam.

Now, return with me to the text of 1 Corinthians 15. "As was the man of dust" says Paul, "so are those who are of the dust; and as is the man from heaven, so also are those who are of heaven" (v. 48). To be a human creature in the line of the first Adam is to have one kind of existence in covenant with God by virtue of the very order of creation. Yet the splendor and honor of that sixth-day existence cannot inherit the kingdom of God (v. 50). The glory of the first Adam is not the same as the honor and glory of the second Adam—the splendor of the "spiritual body." Due to our sin, we certainly deserve the judgment of God, the curses of the covenant, and exclusion from seventh-day dwelling with God. It is only through Christ's faithfulness as faithful

---

which lead to the later historical incarnation of the word of God, do not factor into Barth's ontological anthropology, and the two modes of human existence, as Paul presents them, do not come into view either. Nor is Barth's dialectical theology controlled by the radical significance of Jesus as the incarnate *human* in the line of the first Adam suffering death and being raised to become the life-giving Spirit of the new mode of human existence as last Adam.

15. Gaffin, "Last Adam," 195.

16. Gaffin, "Last Adam," 195.

17. Boersma, *Violence*, 171.

human servant that the covenant of seventh-day promise is opened through his death and resurrection to those who are *in him*. That is why Paul can talk about the transformation of humans into the heavenly or seventh-day mode of existence. "Just as we have borne the image of the man of dust, we will also bear the image of the man of heaven" (v. 49).

Paul, in other words, assumes that the change from one mode of existence to the other involves significant continuity for creatures who are changed from the natural to the spiritual, because he says of himself and of the Corinthian believers, *we* who are now like the first Adam will be like the last Adam. This is different from the contrast between sin and salvation. There can be no continuity between sinfulness and righteousness. Thus, God's covenant in Christ is a creation-renewal and creation-fulfillment covenant that deals with sin in a way that does not destroy the good creation order, which entails two modes of human existence. The two bodies or modes of covenantal existence (earthly or sixth-day; heavenly or seventh-day) are different, but both modes are intended for humans.[18]

When Paul speaks of the natural body, he is speaking of the generations of the first Adam. However, even apart from sin, that mode of existence is not, and cannot by itself become, a heavenly, spiritual, or seventh-day mode of existence. Entrance into God's sabbath rest is the creator's gift, a gift that entails a new mode of existence that the children of the first Adam cannot generate by themselves in this age, even if they were without sin. The mode of existence that experiences no evening or morning and is not perishable is a mode of existence to which we have access only by the creator's design. Because of our sin, access to the imperishable mode of life comes only through the faithful and righteous "last Adam," the "life-giving Spirit." That climactic mode of existence, it seems clear, is identical with what the author of Hebrews identifies as God's sabbath rest, the seventh day of creation. Gaffin refers to the two modes of existence—the natural and the spiritual—as two eras or eons, which (as I am interpreting the passage) correspond to (1) this age, the life of the sixth-day human generations in relation to all other creatures, and (2) the age to come, the fulfillment of human life and the whole creation in God's seventh-day glory.[19]

To distinguish these two modes of human existence and to identify them with the sixth and seventh days of God's creation is not to overlook the fact that for Paul, new life in Christ begins to be experienced in this age, *through faith* by the Spirit, while believers are still living as natural sixth-day persons. Living now by the power of the Spirit is possible because of our identity through faith with the risen Christ. Much of the confusion throughout history about when and how the new life in Christ begins

18. Wright, *Resurrection*, 356.

19. The two modes of existence, writes Gaffin, comprehend two eras of life. "As the era of the first Adam, the psychical order [natural, this-worldly, sixth-dayish] is the preeschatological aeon, the incomplete, transitory, and provisional world-age. As the era of the last Adam, the pneumatic order [spiritual, seventh-dayish] is the eschatological aeon, the complete, definitive, and final world-age." Gaffin, *Resurrection and Redemption*, 83.

comes from overlooking the fact that *faith* (whether placed in the true God or to false gods) is constitutive of our earthly mode of existence in contrast to the seventh-day mode of existence. Paul and the author of the Letter to the Hebrews make this clear in many ways. The entire history of the church in this age is a history of living by faith in the true God in anticipation of the fulfillment to come. The fullness of the resurrection mode of existence in Christ cannot be brought down to earth but can be experienced and anticipated now only by faith through the indwelling Spirit of God.

To read Paul's words to the Corinthian Christians about the first Adam and the last Adam should remind us of the distinctive responsibility we have in this age. The image of God, male and female, is God's sixth-day steward, royal official, and high priest of God's kingdom, and we have been created for precisely this kind of faith-guided, bodily existence now, in this age. The generations of the first Adam bear a multi-generational responsibility to develop (gain dominion over) the earth and to love one another in cooperatively developing the full range of human talents and relationships that reveal something of the God whom we image and are to glorify. In the second Adam's reconciling redemption of creation, we are restored to life again, to the very life God has given to the sixth-day stewards of creation in anticipation of the day when all human labors are fulfilled to the glory of God. That fulfillment and that glorification are now assured through God's faithful servant, the incarnate and risen Son of God. Precisely as sons and daughters of the first Adam, called to life in the last Adam, we should be able to recognize that everything about human life, from marriage and family to horticulture and animal husbandry, from education to engineering, from business and commerce to public lawmaking, is what we are now to be offering up to God through Christ with thanksgiving until all things are filled full and God is all in all.

After Paul's magnificent closing shout for joy in 1 Corinthians 15:57—"But thanks be to God, who gives us the victory through our Lord Jesus Christ"—he concludes by making this point: "Therefore, my beloved, be steadfast, immovable, always excelling in the work of the Lord, because you know that in the Lord your labor is not in vain" (v. 58). Joined by faith with Christ, we can already behold the true glory of what it means to be human: the honor and hospitality of spending ourselves freely in the service of the one who made us and loves us and commissioned us for such significant responsibility as servants of God. The fruits of our faithfulness in every responsibility are being gathered up through Christ's sacrificial death and resurrection into the creation's fulfillment in God's rest. The people of God in Christ are none other than the children of the first Adam who are being forgiven, reconciled, and renewed in faith-union with the last Adam, Jesus Christ. When Christ returns, faith will be transformed into sight and earthly bodies will be transfigured into resurrection bodies.

18

Perishability and Weakness of the First Adam

IF 1 CORINTHIANS 15:35–49 describes two different modes of *good* creaturely existence, namely, that of the first Adam and that of the last Adam, there appears, nonetheless, to be a significant challenge to that interpretation from three verses within the passage. In vv. 42–44 Paul describes the contrasting modes of existence as follows: "What is sown is perishable, what is raised is imperishable. It is sown in dishonor, it is raised in glory. It is sown in weakness, it is raised in power. It is sown a physical body, it is raised a spiritual body. If there is a physical body, there is also a spiritual body." Many interpreters have identified these contrasts with those in Romans 5:12–19 and 1 Corinthians 15:21–23, namely, the contrast between Adam as the source of sin (or being sowed because of sin) and Christ as the one who brings redemption from sin and resurrection life. If that identification is correct, then we must in some way qualify or reinterpret vv. 35–49.

Richard Gaffin, on whom we have depended for some of our interpretation in the last chapter, offers just such a qualification. He believes that Paul interrupts the flow of his argument in vv. 35–49 at vv. 42–44a, where he reverts to his earlier contrast between the first Adam who brings death and the last Adam who brings life. As Gaffin sees it, the predicates "perishable," "dishonor," and "weakness" are not characteristics of Adam the good creature, but are "brought about by the fall, a result of the curse brought upon the creation by human sin (e.g. Rom 5:12ff.; 1 Cor 15:21–22)."[1] It seems to me, however, that Gaffin has simply asserted this to be the case because of what Paul says in the other passages. In doing that, however, he creates a difficulty for his interpretation of the fourth contrasting pair of words in v. 44a: the "physical (or natural) body" and the "spiritual body."

Paul contrasts the natural body and the spiritual body in both 15:44a and 15:44b. In v. 44a the natural body is sown and then raised a spiritual body; in v. 44b the wording is, "if there is a physical [or natural] body, there is also a spiritual body." Gaffin has no doubt that the sowing of the natural body in 44a is a function of the body's

---

1. Gaffin, "Last Adam," 199.

death due to sin, while in 44b he believes the natural body refers to the good mode of life of the first Adam.[2] In another publication, Gaffin states it this way: "It will not do, while recognizing that the creation body is in view in verse 44b, to extend to it the depreciatory predicates of verses 42–44a. Paul teaches too plainly elsewhere (Rom 5:12ff.) that these things result not from Adam's creation but from his disobedience."[3] How odd, however, to imagine that Paul shifts from one contrast to the other within the same verse when the passage as a whole is all about the contrast of two modes of good human life. Why assume that the words "perishability, dishonor, and weakness," in vv. 42–44a are "depreciatory" in the sense of referring to sin-corrupted humanity rather than referring to the "natural" (sixth-day) human creature?

Let's assume for a moment that Gaffin is mistaken and that Paul in vv. 42–44a is continuing without interruption his line of argument that runs from v. 35 to v. 49, and probably all the way to v. 57. Look again at the contrasting word pairs in vv. 42–44: perishable/imperishable, dishonor/glory, weakness/power, and natural/spiritual. Note that the pairings of perishable/imperishable and natural/spiritual are the very ones Paul uses in vv. 45–49, which contrast the first Adam that God made good "from the dust of the earth" with the last Adam who is "from heaven." The natural body is like a good seed that is sown (vv. 35–38), and it is "perishable" by its very nature. It comes first and is made for planting, as a seed is planted. It is not like the imperishable body of the last Adam..

Now, if the words "natural" and "perishable" in the first and last word pairs of vv. 42–44 are perfectly fit for Paul's argument about the first Adam as God's good sixth-day creature, is it possible that the same can be said about the words "dishonor" and "weakness" in the other two word pairs? If so, we can read Paul to be saying that the body of the first Adam's generations has a glory that is nonetheless perishable. For the sixth-day image of God was created to be like a good seed to be sown and not like something made to last forever. That is also why the natural mode of existence appears less glorious in comparison with the imperishable mode of life of the last Adam.

In that light, we can then understand the words "weakness" and "dishonor" in the same way. Clearly, when compared with the "power" of the resurrection mode of life, the natural mode of life appears "weak." The natural does not have the strength to endure forever, and thus when it perishes, its relative weakness is evident. Recognizing the sinful condition of the generations of the first Adam is not necessary in this context to account for the relative weakness of what is made to be perishable. The mode of life of the first Adam is limited in ways that contrast so significantly with that of the power of the last Adam's mode of life that the first now appears very weak indeed. The same can be said of the "dishonor" in which the natural body is sown. Paul says in v. 40, the glory of the earthly body is different from the glory of the heavenly body. The contrast is so great that when the two are compared, the glory of the one that is sown

2. Gaffin, "Last Adam," 201.

3. Gaffin, *Resurrection and Redemption*, 81.

appears strikingly inglorious, even dishonorable, in contrast to the one that is raised. Again, it is not necessary to appeal to the subsequent sinful condition of the human generations in order to account for the "dishonor" of which Paul is speaking here.

This interpretation of the contrasting word pairings in vv. 40–44 is supported, I believe, by what Paul writes in 2 Corinthians 3:7–11. There, he compares the glory of the Mosaic covenant with the glory of the new covenant in Christ, and after the covenant in Christ appears, says Paul, the glory of the first covenant has no glory at all. The ministry of Moses came with such glory that the Israelites could not even look at Moses's face, and if that was true, says Paul, how much greater will the glory of the ministry of the Spirit be? "Now if the ministry of death, chiseled in letters on stone tablets came in glory so that the people of Israel could not gaze at Moses' face because of the glory of his face, a glory now set aside, how much more will the ministry of the Spirit come in glory? For if there was glory in the ministry of condemnation, much more does the ministry of justification abound in glory! Indeed, what once had glory has lost its glory because of the greater glory; for if what was set aside came through glory, much more has the permanent come in glory!" (2 Cor 3:7–11). It could not be more clear that Paul recognizes two different kinds of glory: that of the first covenant and that of the final covenant. Both are glorious, but when the final one comes, the first one looks positively inglorious by comparison. This comparison, which emphasizes the "surpassing glory" of the new covenant, makes the same point I believe Paul is making in 1 Corinthians 15:42–49.

If we read vv. 42–44 this way, then all of the words used to describe the body that is sown—perishable, dishonor, weakness, and natural—can be understood to refer to the first Adam's good mode of creaturely life and not to deformities resulting from his sin. Altogether, Paul's descriptions here can be understood as corollaries of his statement that "flesh and blood cannot inherit the kingdom of God" (v. 50). This is not because flesh and blood are sinful by nature but because flesh and blood are characteristics of the generations of the first Adam as God created them.

Wright recognizes the contrast in 1 Corinthians 15:45–49 between two good modes of human existence when he writes, "'The first man's sort of humanity is from the earth, the second's is a gift from heaven' . . . Earthly humanity is like Adam's body, heavenly humanity like Christ's resurrection body, and believers, who presently share the one, will at the last share the other."[4] In another place, Wright says, "The fundamental leap of imagination that Paul is asking the puzzled Corinthians to make is to a body which cannot and will not decay or die: something permanent, established, not transient or temporary."[5] According to Philippians 3:20–21, in Wright's judgment,

---

4. Wright, *Climax*, 31–32. If this understanding is correct, says Wright, "Adam and Christ as individuals are not the main subjects of discussion, but a buttress to the anthropological assertions of [1 Cor 15] vv. 42–44, 46–47 . . . The sense in which he [Christ] is the prototype for resurrection existence is not brought out until the conclusion in vv. 48–49, where again the point being made is not Christological but anthropological." Wright, *Climax*, 32.

5. Wright, *Resurrection*, 347.

"the new body will have both a status . . . and a capability of which the present body knows nothing. The sense . . . is of human beings becoming what they were made to be, attaining at last their proper *doxa* [glory] instead of the shameful, dishonouring status and character they presently know."[6] The words "shameful" and "dishonouring" that Paul uses here to characterize the present human condition are drawn from a Greek word variously translated "our humiliation," "humble bodies," and "lowly bodies." Surely, however, there is no shame in being the kind of sixth-day creature God made us to be—lowly and humble servants of God to be sure, yet commissioned to govern the earth. If there is any "dishonor" in this, it shows up only in contrast to the body of Christ's glory, the imperishable resurrection mode of life opened through him.

Wright confirms our interpretation of 1 Corinthians 15:35–49 at another point when he turns to the passage in 1 Corinthians 15:24–28, which clearly contrasts Adam, the one through whom sin entered the world, with Christ, through whom imperishable life comes. According to Wright, Paul, "in a manner quite unusual for him, makes Psalm 8 the basis of a detailed exposition [1 Cor 15:24–28] in which the theme of subjection 'under the feet' is explored and worked out in relation to the final events culminating in the subjection of even the Messiah to the one God." This is because Paul also has in mind Genesis 1–3. "God's plan, to rule his world through obedient humanity, has come true in the Messiah, Jesus," Wright explains. "That which was purposed in Genesis 1 and 2, the wise rule of creation by the obedient human beings, was lost in Genesis 3, when human rebellion jeopardized the divine intention, and the ground brought forth thorns and thistles. The Messiah, however, has now been installed as the one through whom God is doing what he intended to do, first through humanity and then through Israel."[7] The incarnate Son of God is restoring the human vocation in fulfillment of God's original aim to "put everything under their feet" (Gen 1:26–28 and Ps 8:5–6).

ALL THINGS UNDER THEIR FEET

If we draw together the threads of the foregoing discussion, we can see how the relation between the first Adam and the last Adam is illuminated by the two different meanings of "under their feet" or "under his feet." The first Adam, representing sixth-day humanity, is created to be God's chief steward, high priest, and royal authority on earth; the first Adam's generations are commissioned to fill the earth and develop it to the glory of God. God placed everything under human feet for the good purpose of revealing something of the supreme lordship of the God they serve (Gen 1:28; Ps 8:4–8; Isa 66:1–2). That humble service aims for a higher end, for a greater glory in the final revelation of the kingdom of God. From the beginning, all the responsibilities of

6. Wright, *Resurrection*, 347.

7. Wright, *Climax*, 29.

the generations of the first Adam have pointed beyond themselves in a revelatory and anticipatory manner to the culminating celebration of God's glory. God's first six days of creatures, including the life of the human generations, were never intended to be the end of creaturely meaning. God's final commendation of faithful human service is to come as a gift of entrance into God's rest through the life of the last Adam (Heb 4:4–11). In that fulfillment, the positive meaning of God placing the earth under human feet will become evident. To recognize the creaturely goodness of the first Adam and of Abraham and Israel, who looked ahead to the "city with foundations, whose architect and builder is God" (Heb. 11:10), is to begin to understand the meaning of perishable human life in this age moving toward imperishable life in the age to come.

It is also clear from Scripture, however, that because of human disobedience, the exercise of responsible governance under God has taken a deathward direction, alienating us from God, from one another, and from other creatures, cutting off hope of the final blessing of entering God's rest. Consequently, God's judgment confronts our unrighteousness. Curses instead of blessings fall upon faithless humankind. Continuing in Adam's sin, we have failed to keep covenant with God. Thus, as the unfolding disclosure of God's covenant faithfulness makes clear, sin and death must be dealt with if human responsibility to govern the earth is to be exercised properly all the way to its completion. The good news that has come as light into this darkened world is that the incarnate Son's faithfulness, even to death, and his resurrection from the dead have put all things under his feet both for judgment of sin and for the restoration of creation. The majestic picture Paul presents in 1 Corinthians 15:24–28 makes this clear. The constructive and culminating goal will be reached when the victorious Christ "hands over the kingdom to God the Father, after he has destroyed every ruler and every authority and power. For he must reign until he has put all his enemies under his feet. The last enemy to be destroyed is death. For God 'has put all things in subjection under his feet'" (1 Cor 15:24–26). Of course, says Paul, "all things" does not include "the one who put all things in subjection under him," because "the Son himself will also be subjected to the one who put all things in subjection under him, so that God may be all in all" (15:27–28).

We can see from Paul's testimony that Christ's acts of earthly dominion in destroying sin had, as their wider purpose, the reconciliation and fulfillment of creation, including the fulfillment of human governance in Christ, under God. The faithfulness of Christ Jesus did indeed include the defeat of God's enemies including death—putting them all under his feet as victorious conqueror. Yet what Christ submitted to God, so that God would be all in all, was not just the defeat of enemies. His victory achieved the cleansing and reconciliation of all things so that the creation's true meaning and purpose would be realized and lifted up to God in praise. In Christ, we witness the true and faithful man of the sixth-day generations who becomes the last Adam—the life-giving spirit of seventh-day life.

WE WILL ALL BE CHANGED

There is yet another important and related point to make about Paul's argument in 1 Corinthians 15. The mystery of the resurrection, Paul writes, is that "we will all be changed, in a moment, in the twinkling of an eye, at the last trumpet. For the trumpet will sound, and the dead will be raised imperishable, and we will be changed" (vv. 51b-52). How does Paul describe the change? He uses the language he will use later in 2 Corinthians 5. "For this perishable body must put on imperishability, and this mortal body must put on immortality" (1 Cor 15:53). The metaphor of changed clothing only works if the two parts in the contrast are compatible in a two-stage fashion, that is, if it is fitting for the perishable to put on the imperishable. It would not make sense to say that the sinful puts on imperishability. Sin and death must be eliminated, washed away, and sinners must be forgiven, made right with God, and cleansed from sin. That is the issue Paul is dealing with in Romans 5 and the first part of 1 Corinthians 15. In the last part of 1 Corinthians 15 and in 2 Corinthians 5, however, it is the good seed that is sown in order to become a living plant; it is the good, earthly mode of life that puts on imperishable clothing. It is a glorious transfiguration, to be sure, when the sixth-day mode of mortal life puts on the seventh-day mode of immortal life. But as we already know from what Paul has written in 1 Corinthians 15:35–49, the creator has made humans for two modes of existence, and it is only with the arrival of the surpassing glory of the last Adam that the glory of the first Adam's mode of life dims by comparison.

According to Paul, as I read him, the resurrection of Christ is the reason why the perishability of our earthy mode of existence holds no fear for us, because perishing—departing from our present, natural, sixth-day mode of existence—does not mean that death has gained a victory over us (1 Cor 15:50–57). Death's sting that causes fear is sin, but in Christ, our sins are forgiven. The sting of death comes because of sin, which destroys life and separates us from God and closes off access to God's gift of resurrection life. The fault or problem at present is sin, *not* the impermanence or perishability of our earthly mode of life in this age. Because of God's forgiveness of sin through the sacrificial death and resurrection of Christ, the perishing of our mortal existence is swallowed up in Christ's victory and we are clothed with immortality.

Paul Minear explains that Paul uses a total of seven word-pair contrasts in 1 Corinthians 15 to speak of the transition from the natural body to the spiritual body, from flesh and blood to God's kingdom, and so forth. "In none of the seven does the act of sowing coincide with the moment of death or with the disposition of a corpse; rather it connotes the entire span of earthly life, from birth to death." Consequently, Minear continues, "the mortality of the first Adam is free of morbid or psychotic obsession with death; it views the physical body positively, as a form of God's sowing in spite of its perishability." "For Paul," according to Minear, "the time of sowing covered the whole existence of the believers, including the time of their 'falling asleep'; similarly, the time of resurrection covered the whole work of Christ 'in our mortal flesh,' beginning with the baptism into his death and including an ultimate transformation. From first to last the confidence was firm: 'What is sown is perishable, what is raised in imperishable'" (1 Cor 15:42).[8]

The entire passage of 1 Corinthians 15:35–50 is, I believe, built on the contrast between two modes of good creaturely existence rather than on the contrast between death due to sin and redemption through the last Adam. From a typological or figural point of view, we may consider Jesus Christ to be the antitype of the first Adam (the type), because the first Adam stood at the beginning of the sixth-day generations of humankind and Christ stands at the head (as elder brother, spouse, friend, lord) of seventh-day humankind. God created the generations of the first Adam for a very good "sowing" purpose that anticipates the imperishability of God's sabbath with creation. Christ Jesus, the last Adam, who was born into the generations of the first Adam, is the first to be raised to seventh-day life for the good purpose of bringing human life to its fulfillment in God's day of rest.

In sum, the relation between the two dimensions of the first Adam/last Adam typology articulated by Paul can be put this way: in 1 Corinthians 15:35–57 the first Adam—the sixth-day earthling—was created good and stands in contrast to the last Adam—the seventh-day life-giver from heaven. In Romans 5:12–19 and 1 Corinthians 15:20–24, by contrast, the "first human" is the Adam through whom sin entered the world and is distinguished from the "second human," Jesus Christ, who ushers in redemption and creation's fulfillment. These two contrasting sets cannot be isolated from one another because there is no human being in the present mode of existence who is without sin, and there is no sinner in need of redemption who is not, in the first place, made in the image of God as a good creature. What Paul does in the entirety of 1 Corinthians 15 is to explain the meaning of Christ's resurrection, which sheds a bright light on the relation of the first Adam to the last Adam in God's seven-day creation.

8. Minear, *Christians and New Creation,* 74, 73.

19

Firstborn Over All Creation

UP TO THIS POINT in part 4, we have focused on Jesus Christ as the last Adam in relation to the first Adam. Now, in conclusion, we consider another closely related biblical identification of Jesus Christ.

In Colossians 1:15 and 1:17, Paul refers to Christ as the "image of the invisible God," the "firstborn of all creation," and the one who is "before all things."[1] Similar to the identification of Jesus Christ as the Alpha of all things in John's vision on Patmos (Rev 1:8), Paul identifies Christ with the beginning and not only with the end of all things. In some sense then, Christ, the last Adam, is before the first Adam and the entire creation. Here in Colossians, writes Herman Ridderbos, Paul appears to have "denoted the divine glory of Christ both in his pre-existence and in his exaltation with a qualification ["image of God"] that also held for the first Adam, although, of course, in another sense [than] appropriate to the first Adam."[2]

"Whereas in 1 Corinthians 15 and Romans 5 Christ is the second or last Adam, who follows after the first in the order of redemptive history," writes Ridderbos, "in Colossians 1:15 as the Firstborn, the Image of God, etc., he is antecedent to the first, and in this respect the first Adam cannot be regarded as his 'type.'"[3] In order to understand Jesus Christ, therefore, we need to understand the sense in which, from one point of view, he is the culminating antitype of the first Adam, while also, from

1. We are presuming Pauline authorship of Colossians, as many scholars do, though there is disagreement about that.

2. Ridderbos, *Paul*, 72. This passage in Colossians, like 2 Cor 4:4, writes Ridderbos, is "directly reminiscent of the creation story." The whole of the hymn in Col 1:15 "speaks of creation. The expression Image of God is here clearly rooted in Genesis 1:27. This is further corroborated by the fact that Christ is here likewise called the Beginning (*arche*) and the Firstborn (*prototokos*; 1:15, 18), and is set forth as World Ruler, an idea to be met with as well in the late Jewish Adam-theology. The conclusion is: 'We have before us [in Col 1], therefore, a christological interpretation of Genesis 1.'" Ridderbos, *Paul*, 71.

3. Ridderbos, *Paul*, 84.

another point of view, he is the image of God who is foundational for the first Adam and the whole creation.

At certain points, says Ridderbos, when Paul refers to Christ as the "firstborn within a large family" (Rom 8:29) or "firstborn from among the dead" (Col 1:18), he is speaking of Christ's resurrection, which places him first in rank and dignity among humans in leading "many brothers" into resurrection glory. At another point, however, as in Colossians 1:15, Paul speaks about Christ as the "firstborn of all creation" immediately after referring to him as the image of God. This, says Ridderbos, is an allusion to the first Adam but in a way that subordinates the first Adam to Christ, Christ being the preeminent image of God through whom and for whom all things (including Adam) were created (Col 1:16–17). What happens in Colossians 1:15 is that Paul applies the categories that are used in describing Christ's significance as the last Adam (image, firstborn) to his position in first things—at the foundation of creation.[4]

After Paul met Jesus on the road to Damascus, he was enabled—by faith, through the power of the Spirit—to understand Jesus Christ in this way. Humans have their identity as the image of God in and through the Son of God who is the preeminent image of God from all eternity. The glory of the first Adam is a reflection of the glory of that preeminent image of God. Hebrews puts it similarly: the Son of God through whom God made the universe "is the reflection of God's glory and the exact imprint of his very being" (Heb 1:3). "Thus Christ's exaltation as the second Adam," says Ridderbos, "refers back to the beginning of all things, makes him known as the one who from the very outset, in a much more glorious sense than the first Adam, was the Image of God and the Firstborn of every creature."[5]

N. T. Wright's comments on this passage emphasize its connection with the biblical wisdom tradition, particularly the extended presentation of wisdom as having been with God in the beginning (Prov 8). Christ is now likened to the personification of God's wisdom in Proverbs through whom creation is established.[6] Wright's comments also connect the revelation of Christ with the covenantal tradition of Abraham through Israel that anticipates a Messiah, whom Paul and the other apostles announce

---

4. Ridderbos, *Paul*, 81–82.

5. Ridderbos, *Paul*, 85. As Ridderbos sees it, 1 Cor 15:45–49 assumes "the closest relationship" between Christ as the "heavenly" image to "the image of the first man." "The 'image' that Christ represents and which he gives to his own is thus very clearly thought of here as parallel to the image of the first man and to that which he communicated to his descendants. In this context such passages as Ephesians 4:24 and Colossians 3:10 also come to stand in a clearer light. On the basis of all these materials it is difficult to deny that the absolute use of the Image of God as a qualification of Christ must be connected with what is said in Genesis 1ff. of the first Adam. In the nature of the case Christ is not herewith put on a level with the first Adam. The glory of the second Adam is incomparably greater than that of the first. But it must certainly be ascertained that Christ's divine power and glory, already in his pre-existence, are defined in categories that have been derived from his significance as the second Adam." Ridderbos, *Paul*, 73.

6. Wright, *Climax*, 99–119.

as having arrived in Jesus. Citing the earlier work of C. F. Burney,[7] Wright summarizes four results from Burney's careful examination of the passage:

> (a) that the poem of Colossians 1:15–20 was conceived as a whole, within the framework of Jewish monotheistic celebration of creation and election, (b) that it was intended to evoke a well-established tradition in which Genesis 1.1 and Proverbs 8.22 were read as mutually explanatory, (c) that it was therefore intended to evoke the figure of "Wisdom" as the means of creation and as the key to the election of God's people, and (d) that it was intended to apply all that might be said about Wisdom . . . to Jesus himself, no mere hypothetical hypostasis but a human figure, an "image of God" of recent memory.[8]

This passage brings together many facets of Paul's understanding of Christ Jesus as Son of God, firstborn over all creation, the image of God incarnate, firstborn from the dead, eschatological Lord of all, and the one through whom we praise and thank God for our creation and redemption.[9]

When Ridderbos turns to discuss the last Adam's preeminence in resurrection glory, however, he seems to lose the close connection indicated earlier between the origin of creation and its fulfillment. "The new creation that has broken through with Christ's resurrection," Ridderbos says, "takes the place of the first creation."[10] This language can be misleading if we read the phrase "takes the place of" to mean displaces, dispenses with, or pushes aside. That does not appear to be what Paul is saying. There is for Paul continuity between the "we" who bear the likeness of the first Adam and "we" who bear the likeness of the last Adam. There is continuity between the one through whom all things were created and the one who took on flesh and became the firstborn from the dead to redeem and fulfill creation. In the Colossians passage, Paul's praise of Christ concludes with the exclamation that in Christ God is reconciling "to himself all things, whether on earth or in heaven, by making peace through the blood of his cross" (Col 1:20). Everything created is being reconciled, not displaced. Therefore, the new creation that breaks through in Christ's resurrection does not *take the place of* the first creation but rather brings the whole creation to its reconciled fulfillment in God's seventh-day rest. To be sure, the glory of the resurrected last Adam is superior to the glory of the first Adam, and the resurrection mode of existence far

7. Burney, "Christ as APXH," 160–77.

8. Wright, "Poetry and Theology," 113.

9. Paul's reinterpretation of Judaism, says Wright, is a "christological monotheism which is most obviously *creational*, affirming the goodness of the original creation and announcing the dawn of its renewal. It is also *eschatological* monotheism, in the inaugurated sense that Jesus, as the divine Wisdom, is in himself the God of Israel . . . [And it is] also *cultic* monotheism. The aim of it all is that the Colossians will learn how to *give thanks* to God the father for all he has done (1.12). Thanksgiving is, in fact, a major theme of the whole letter. And this thanksgiving is the exact correlate of creational and covenantal monotheism, the appropriate response of God's people to their creator, rescuer and lord. It is what the Psalms are all about." Wright, *Paul and Faithfulness*, 676.

10. Ridderbos, *Paul*, 85–86.

surpasses the present earthly mode of existence. But in accord with 1 Corinthians 15, this means that the glory of the last Adam characterizes the creation's seventh-day glory into which, by his death and resurrection, Christ is drawing the faithful of all ages into the fulfillment of all things.[11]

This is the context in which we can best understand the statement in Colossians 1, "that he might come to have first place in everything" (v. 18). The passage is all-encompassing, reaching from beginning to end, from lowest to highest, nothing excluded. The unfathomable mystery now being revealed is that Jesus Christ is the divine mediator of the creation (Alpha); the supreme revealer of God (the supreme image) through whom the sixth-day image of God is created; the first human whom God commends and blesses for his faithful service; the first human raised from the dead to become the seventh-day giver of life; and the one who reconciles everything to God in fulfillment (Omega) of the creation to God's satisfaction and glory.

Ridderbos has it right, it seems to me, when he writes that Paul's identification of Christ as both the "Firstborn of every creature" and "as the last Adam" is not a joining of two incompatible interpretations of Genesis 1–3. Rather, he says, we have here "Paul's vision of the all-encompassing significance of the salvation that has appeared in Christ."[12] Or to say it somewhat differently, Paul's vision of the extensive glory of the Alpha and the Omega leads him to speak of Christ in terms of every facet of his supremacy. Paul saw the beginning from the end, or perhaps better said, Paul was given a vision of the full disclosure of God's creation—from beginning to end—summed up in the revelation of Jesus Christ. In a word, says Ridderbos, Paul nowhere abstracts Christ's "Sonship and his Redeemership" from the all-encompassing story.[13] A longer quotation from Ridderbos is worthy of inclusion here:

> Starting from the risen Christ as second man or last Adam (1 Cor 15), and from his glory as Image of God (2 Cor 4), Paul regards the whole of the divine Sonship from this point of view. There is in all this something highly characteristic of Paul's "Christology." Without any doubt Christ is for him the Son of God, not only in virtue of his revelation, but from before the foundation of the world, God, to be blessed forever. But as such he is from before the foundation of the world and to all eternity God-for-us. It is not the Godhood of Christ

---

11. According to Wright, "Though Paul does not refer to the tree of life in Genesis 3, his controlling narrative is constantly pointing to the way in which the creator finally brings his human, image-bearing creatures, and indeed the entire cosmos, through the impasse of the fall, of the thorns and thistles and the whirling, flashing sword, to taste at last the gift of life in all its fullness, a new bodily life in a new world where the rule of heaven is brought at last to earth." Wright, *Resurrection*, 371.

12. Ridderbos, *Paul*, 85.

13. Ridderbos, *Paul*, 77. David B. Garner offers more on the meaning of *sonship* in relation to the comparison of the first and second Adams in "The First and Last Son," 255–79. Moltmann makes much the same point as Ridderbos about the way Paul refers to Christ: "Since it is through Christ that the new, true creation begins, Christ must already be the mystery of creation in the beginning. The earlier is understood in the light of the later, and the beginning is comprehended in the light of the consummation." Moltmann, *God in Creation*, 226.

in itself, but that he is God and God's Son for us which is the content and foundation even of the most profound of his christological pronouncements. He is God, who became man and was to become man. He is called Image of God as the one who was predestined to become man, and as the Firstborn of many brethren to make others share in this image (Rom 8:29; 1 Cor 15:49; 2 Cor 3:18). He is the Son of God, who was sent (Rom 8:3; Gal 4:4), who was not spared by God (Rom 8:32), who was born of the seed of David (Rom 1:3), who died (Rom 5:10), who by his resurrection was declared to be the Son of God in power (Rom 1:4).[14]

Exalting in the grand revelatory work of God that reaches from the beginning to the end of all things, Paul locates himself and the Colossian believers in the story this way: "For he has rescued us from the dominion of darkness and brought us into the Kingdom of the Son he loves, in whom we have redemption, the forgiveness of sins" (Col 1:13–14). The "us" and "we" of whom Paul speaks are descendants of the first Adam, created in the image of God as revelatory of the Son of God who has, in the flesh, become our redeemer. Children of the first Adam, locked into the darkness of their disobedience discover in Christ the forgiveness of sins and release from their bondage. Through faith in Christ they come to know that their redemption has been achieved by the humble, self-giving Son of God, Son of man, who went all the way to death on the cross as a sacrifice for their sins. Through his resurrection into the new life of God's fulfilled kingdom, Christ is recognized as the first fruits of the resurrection harvest that will include all who are his. Redemption and the forgiveness of sins in Christ means the restoration of right relation to God, to neighbors, and to all creatures so that Christ's followers may learn the habits of repentance and again serve God in faithfulness throughout their earthly lives, looking ahead as they do to the fulfillment of their labors in the imperishable kingdom to come where they will offer up never-ending praise of God through Christ Jesus.

SUMMING UP

What Paul proclaimed, and the apostle John saw and heard on Patmos, is the inauguration and the fulfillment of creation in Jesus Christ, the firstborn image of God and the last Adam. The reality of redemption and consummation in Christ is conveyed to us even now by the power of the Spirit who incorporates us, through faith, into Christ's death and resurrection. In Christ's new life, our lives in this age are to be redirected along paths of faithfulness until we join him and all the saints in the new mode of life secured through Christ's resurrection. This is what Paul anticipated when he spoke of the hope believers have as "the creation waits with eager longing for the revealing of the children of God." (Rom 8:19). This is what Hebrews refers to as the

14. Ridderbos, *Paul*, 77.

Sabbath rest "for the people of God; for those who enter God's rest also cease from their labors as God did from his" (4:9–10).

The sixth-day glory of the generations of the first Adam comes to light through their stewardly management and just governance of the earth, as well as their hospitable love of God and of one another. We exist as the image of God by virtue of God's creating work through the Son of God, the preeminent image of God. The generations of the first Adam are the only creatures made for the exercise of royal priestly responsibility under God. Despite Moltmann's ambiguity about the relation of "creation in the beginning" to "continuing creation" and "new creation," the following profession of his faith is apt here:

> Just as creation is creation for the sabbath, so human beings are created as the image of God for the divine glory. They themselves are God's glory in the world—*Gloria Dei est homo*, as Irenaeus said. In glorifying God, the creatures created to be the image of God themselves arrive at the fulfilment of what they are intended to be . . . [H]uman beings are the last to be created before the sabbath, and are created for that. They are priestly by nature, and stand before God on behalf of the earth, and before the earth on behalf of God. As God's earthly image, they reflect the Creator's glory. They are not merely commissioned by God; they are also the mode of his appearance in his creation. The messianic calling of human beings to be "conformed"—like in form—to Jesus the Messiah brings them into the eschatological history of the new creation: from calling to justification, from justification to sanctification, from sanctification to glorification. Just as the coming glory of God lights up the face of the raised Messiah, so believers, filled with the Spirit, even here, and even now, also reflect the glory of God "with unveiled face." A strong eschatological drive pervades the messianic present. What is here only perceived in fragmentary form, through a mirror "in a saying hard to interpret," will then be seen "face to face" (1 Cor 13.12). Even for those who are "God's children now" it still "does not yet appear what we shall be. But we know that when he appears we shall be like him, for we shall see him as he is" (1 John 3.2).[15]

The relationship between humans and God is revelatory—revelatory as a love communion, a family, a marriage, a fellowship of friends, a school of disciples, a kingdom of priests, and a community of citizen-rulers. Everything that belongs to the sixth-day identity and responsibility of humans *reveals* in part something of the firstborn over all creation and also something of the last Adam in seventh-day glory. The completed divine-human dwelling place of the age to come, whose cornerstone is Jesus Christ, will be composed of all the living stones and fabrics of faithful men, women, and children alive in Christ (Heb 3:6; 1 Pet 2:4–5).[16]

15. Moltmann, *God in Creation*, 228.

16. Meredith Kline puts it this way: "Man as created was already crowned with glory and honor, for made in the likeness of the enthroned Glory, a little lower than the angels of the divine council,

Here again we must emphasize that the "new creation" is not a second cosmos or a disconnected heaven that God invents in reaction to Adam's desecration of the first creation. There is only one creation held together in Christ Jesus, who is preeminent in all things from beginning to end, the Alpha and the Omega, the revealer of the glory of God. The "new creation" is the Bible's language for creation fulfilled in God's seventh-day rest. And we now know, through faith, that Jesus Christ is preeminent in all things—from the foundation of creation to its culmination and completion in God's glorious kingdom.

---

man was invested with official authority to exercise dominion as priest-king in God's earthly courts. Yet, the glory of man's royal functioning would be progressive as he increasingly fulfilled his historical task of subduing the earth, his ultimate attainment of functional glory awaiting the eschatological glorification of his whole nature after the image of the radiant Glory-Spirit." Kline, *Images of Spirit*, 31.

PART 5

Already and Not Yet

20

An Apparent Paradox of Time

A CONTRADICTION IN TERMS?

CLOSELY RELATED TO THE revelation of Jesus Christ as the last Adam is the dynamic tension between the "already" and the "not yet" of the coming of God's kingdom. According to the apostle Paul, the last Adam is the life-giving Spirit of God's imperishable kingdom—creation reconciled and fulfilled in resurrection glory (1 Cor 15:45–54). Christ is risen, the first among the generations of the first Adam to be raised from death to the new mode of resurrection life—immortal life in the presence of God glorified. Through his death and resurrection, Christ is drawing the whole company of God's people, from all ages, into that new mode of resurrection life (1 Cor 15:20–23). Since Jesus Christ is now seated at the right hand of the Father, God's purposes for the seven-day revelation of the kingdom are sealed (Eph 1:15–23). Considered from the standpoint of Christ's death, resurrection, and ascension, therefore, God's kingdom is *already* at hand: the chief cornerstone has been set in place. The King of the kingdom has been revealed and now holds sway over all things in heaven and on earth (Matt 28:18). Fulfillment of the royal, priestly stewardship and rule of the image of God is assured in Jesus Christ.

However, from the standpoint of the ongoing life of the human generations, the kingdom of God has *not yet* been fully realized. Earthly work remains to be done in this age by the living and those yet unborn; God has not yet brought to a close the exercise of sixth-day human responsibilities. Moreover, evil principalities and powers still contend against the King and his royal stewards; Jesus Christ has not yet revealed the final subjection of all God's enemies to himself (Rom 6:1–14; 1 Cor 15:24–26; Eph 4:17–32).[1] We continue to await Christ's return and our own resurrection. We live

---

1. With reference to the apocalyptic vision of judgment in the book of Revelation, Carl Braaten points to the *already* of Jesus' victory over the Beast. "Jesus, the one who was slain by the Dragon and the Beast, who has been exalted to heaven, who now sits at the right hand of the Father, holds the whole world in his hands. This is the victory that supports our faith. The rule of God has already begun." Though Braaten does not emphasize the *not yet* of the apocalyptic imagination, it is implicit in his recognition that our vision of the victorious Christ is *by faith*, and our faith is "on account of

now by faith and in the hope of the full revelation of creation's redemption and fulfillment (Rom 8:18–25). The resurrection of the dead by which the faithful are gathered into face-to-face fellowship with God has *already* begun in Jesus Christ, for he is the firstfruits of the single resurrection harvest, but the harvest is *not yet* complete (1 Cor 15:20–23). We must continue to pray and to work everyday for God's will to be done on earth as it is in heaven.

Herman Ridderbos writes that it is through *faith* that the followers of Christ in this age have been joined to Christ's death and resurrection, thus producing "the contrast of 'already' and 'not yet.'"[2] For example, nowhere does Paul proclaim more clearly than in Ephesians and Colossians that Christ has triumphed over the powers that stand against him, but also that the people of God in Christ must continue to stand against these powers.

> God has disarmed [the opposing powers] in Christ, made a public example of them, and harnessed them to his triumphal chariot (Col 2:15; cf. Eph 1:20ff; 4:8ff.). Through him God has reconciled, pacified, subjected all things to himself (Col 1:20). On the other hand it continues to hold for the church as well that it has to wage war not against flesh and blood, but against the principalities, the powers, the world rulers of this darkness, the evil spirits in the heavenly places (Eph 6:12). The powers, however much already vanquished in Christ, have not yet become harmless. But in order to be able to contend against them suitably, the church has received an armor from God, so richly furnished that it is able to continue to stand (Eph 6:13ff.).[3]

The basis on which Paul urges Colossian Christians to conduct their lives is the *already* of Christ's triumph over sin and death: "So if you have been raised with Christ, seek the things that are above, where Christ is, seated at the right hand of God. Set your minds on things that are above, not on things that are on earth, for you have died, and your life is hidden with Christ in God. When Christ who is your life is revealed, then you also will be revealed with him in glory" (Col 3:1–4). Because of their union with Christ *through a living faith*, believers can begin to grasp that they are *already* raised with Christ and hidden with him on high. Yet because Christ's earthly servants live by faith and not yet by sight, they continue to exercise their God-given responsibilities of this age in anticipation of Christ's return, a return that has *not yet* taken place.

Paul is not playing games with words and creating an unnecessary linguistic paradox. The relation of this age to the coming age is not reducible to a "before and after" in sun-and-moon time. There is, to be sure, the before and after of our lives as God's sixth-day creatures and that is why we look ahead to *future* developments. But from the point of view of what God has already done, and is still doing, in Christ, there

---

Christ" who is the one who opens the apocalyptic imagination to us. Braaten, "The Recovery," 31–32.

2. Ridderbos, *Paul*, 392.

3. Ridderbos, *Paul*, 392.

has been a definitive achievement in this age, which at the same time also transcends earthly time in the same way that the seventh-day of creation transcends the first six days and that Christ's resurrection transcends the mere resuscitation of an earthly body. The risen Christ is fully human, born into the generations of the first Adam, yet God's raising him from the dead to a new order of life has made him *already* the last Adam of seventh-day resurrection life for all who believe. At stake here, in other words, is not a paradox of time, but rather temporal language forced to deal with a reality that is not confined to temporal categories. God's days are not our days: the difference between this age and the coming age, between our sixth-day mode of life and resurrection life in God's day of rest transcend temporal categories.

The language of *already* and *not yet* is the language we must use to speak about the fulfillment of the creation in Jesus Christ, a fulfillment that, from our earthly point of view, has been secured but not yet completed. A similar use of temporal language that also sounds paradoxical is Jesus's words, "Very truly, I tell you, . . . before Abraham was, I am!" (John 8:58). The words of God's self-identification to Moses were, "I am." As the apostles later spoke of Jesus, they identified him as the one through whom all things were created, the one who transcends Abraham and Moses, and the one who transcends all of time as the Alpha and the Omega (Rev 1:8). We need to speak in a similar way about the relation of earthly time to the transcendence of God's seventh-day rest, which encompasses the whole creation. That kingdom, which we often speak of as reaching fulfillment in the age to come, is not going to be just another event in historical time but the culmination of all times in God's fully revealed kingdom. The seven days of creation are God's days and cannot be understood or measured in temporal terms.

Our temporal language of "already" and "not yet" is required because we are temporally bound creatures, and Jesus, the Son of God, became one with us in this age. Yet because God raised Jesus from the dead to a mode of resurrection life that transcends our earthly mode of existence, we may, through faith, see ourselves already incorporated in him. That means we may now begin to experience the renewing power of Christ in and through our earthly mode of existence. Through faith, hope, and love we are being redeemed through the last Adam for life in this age and not only for life in the age to come. The difference between the already and the not yet is thus, in part, the difference between living in Christ *by faith* now and living with him *by sight* in the new resurrection bodies of the age to come. As Paul puts it, "For now we see in a mirror, dimly, but then we will see face to face. Now I know only in part; then I will know fully, even as I have been fully known" (1 Cor 13:12).

Resurrection life does not refer to a miraculous return from death to the same earthly life we lived before death. The resurrection life of which Paul is speaking is life in God's everlasting kingdom where those raised from the dead put on immortality—a new mode of existence (1 Cor 15:49–57). The resurrection, as Hebrews expresses it, means entrance into God's sabbath rest, the seventh-day fulfillment of the whole creation, in which we will find rest from our labors (Heb 4:10). God hallowed that day from the beginning as the climax of his creation week. The seventh day is already a reality. It is the day in relation to which all the generations of humankind are oriented and toward which they should be directing their lives by lifting up the fruits of their labors, day-by-day, year-by-year, in thanksgiving to God. The prayer for God's kingdom to come and his will to be done on earth as it is in heaven (Matt 6:10) should envelope and drive all earthly responsibilities. In that way, we are praying with Moses that God will establish the work of our hands (Ps 90:17). Living by faith in Christ, we experience the forgiveness of sins and the renewing power of God's redeeming love so that we may live fruitfully now as the creatures God made us to be—stewards and developers of all that God has already put under the feet of the King of kings.

To live at present as disciples of Christ does not mean waiting around to enter another world in the future while feeling alienated from this world. As Wright puts it, life in Christ at present is not "a matter of merely marking time."[4] The "not yet" of Christ's return and the fulfillment of God's kingdom "does not mean hanging around with nothing to do."[5] The age to come will, in Christ Jesus, validate and fulfill the lives and labors of this age, not cast them aside. Gaffin believes that the closest parallel to Hebrews 4:10 (the promise of resting from our labors in God's rest) may be Revelation 14:13. "Believers, the Spirit says in Revelation, 'will rest from their labor, for their works will follow them.' Or, as Hebrews says, 'God is not unjust so as to forget' their works" (6:10).[6] Christ Jesus is God's righteous and approved sixth-day servant, the one who has already ascended to reign at the right hand of the Father in fulfillment of God's creation purposes (Rom 8:1–4; Phil 2:8–11; Heb 1:3; Rev 5:1–14). In him our labors will not be forgotten but rather commended and blessed.

AMBIGUITY IN N. T. WRIGHT

Recognizing God's seven-day creation order can, I believe, help to resolve an ambiguity I find in Wright's interpretation of the "already/not yet" in Paul. For Paul, according to Wright, "the present time is characterized by a mixture of fulfillment and expectation, of 'now' and 'not yet,' pointing towards a future in which what happened at the first Easter will be implemented fully and the true God will be all in all."[7] Elsewhere he writes, "The people who are called to stand at the crossroads of time, the strange interval between the 'now' and the 'not yet,' the present and the future, are also called to stand at the intersection of heaven and earth, sharing the pains and puzzles of the present creation but sharing also in the newly inaugurated life of the spirit."[8] Wright's

4. Wright, *Paul and Faithfulness*, 1115.

5. Wright, *Paul and Faithfulness*, 1113.

6. Gaffin, "A Sabbath Rest," 46.

7. Wright, *Resurrection*, 333.

8. Wright, *Paul and Faithfulness*, 1127.

language of "now and not yet," of "present and future," it seems to me, does not quite get at the relation between the "already" of Christ's ascension and enthronement and the "not yet" of our resurrection into the presence of the glory of God. Historically speaking, Jesus *did* die and *was* raised, but his death, resurrection, ascension, and enthronement cannot be captured adequately using the past tense. We need to speak of the living and reigning Lord with language of the "already" transcendent—the Lord of heaven and earth from beyond this age, yet directly related to all of its times. The question is how to emphasize that transcendent, eschatological reality in a way that the temporal tenses of our language do not do.

Wright's ambiguity in that respect is related to another difficulty. When Wright discusses the relation of the already to the not yet, he often draws on passages in Paul that emphasize the antithesis between the sinfulness of life in this darkened age and the righteous way of life in Christ. Paul, according to Wright, "understands the Messiah's people to have been liberated from the 'old evil age', to have entered the 'new age', to be 'daytime people' charged with living by the standards of light even though the world around is still in darkness" [Eph 5:11–14; 1 Thess 5:4–11].[9] In practice, according to Wright, this means learning to put sinful practices behind them, recognizing that "there are certain lifestyles which are simply incompatible with being part of that future."[10] The contrast Wright draws here is within the experience of believers—the contrast between sinful lives in the old evil age and "daytime" righteousness, which is part of the new-age future. This suggests that, for Wright, the "already" is evident when believers exhibit (or begin to exhibit) their liberation from this sinful age, while the "not yet" of the the future is when daytime people will be completely liberated from the old nature.

The problem with this way of putting things is not only its temporal confinement, focusing on the past, present, and future experience of believers in relation to the old evil age and the new righteous age. The problem is also the identification of this age with sin and darkness while overlooking the fact that this age and its human generations are part of God's good creation. Surely it is not God's good creation, including human life in this age that needs to be put behind us but only the sins that weigh us down and alienate us from God and one another. Wright misses the relation of the good creation of God's first six days, including humans, to creation's fulfillment in the age to come. The "already and the not yet," in other words, are not first of all about the temporal present and future of the salvation and sanctification of believers, but rather about Christ having *already* entered into creation's fulfillment beyond this age and his relation to the *not yet* of our continuing life in this age. The new life that Christians begin to experience in this age comes from Christ by the Spirit through *faith*, by which believers see themselves already united with Christ in the age to come. Through that faith they are to continue to grow in newness of life here and now in

9. Wright, *Paul and Faithfulness*, 1111.

10. Wright, *Paul and Faithfulness*, 1113.

their earthly labors, even as they look with anticipation to the resurrection of their bodies. The death and darkness of human faithlessness and disobedience are what must be overcome, not this age of God's creation as such.

Consider also the way Wright identifies the "standards of light" by which Christians should live. Living by those standards, he writes, is to be part of a future that is incompatible with the darkness of this evil age. But what does that imply about the meaning of God's good creation and the covenant way of life to which God called humans from the beginning? Would it not be more accurate to say that Christ has overcome the death and darkness caused by human sinfulness in order to set right (rectify, reconcile) and fulfill the good creation, including its standards of covenant life that have held humans accountable from the very foundation? Wouldn't this mean that God's blessings and curses on the human generations have clarified the difference between righteous and unrighteous actions throughout this age? Wright, it seems to me, conflates the contrast between darkness and light with the contrast between the present and the future of human experience. That makes it difficult to distinguish between God's good purposes for humans in this age, on the one hand, and the consequences of human sinfulness that distort and degrade the good creation, on the other hand. It hinders understanding of the distinction between the light God has always shed on the human generations in this age and the full light of God's fulfilled kingdom in the new Jerusalem (see John 1:9 and Rev 21:23–24).

Wright's comments on Colossians 3 bring to the fore this ambiguity that hints at a misleading dualism. "The Messiah's resurrection," he says, "has brought about total change. Those who have died and been raised with him have a new identity; patterns of behavior which belong with the old life must simply be killed off. There is a to-and-fro implied here between what is already true at one level ('you *have* stripped off the old human nature') and what must become true by sheer, new-creational moral effort ('you *must* kill off')."[11] Part of the difficulty with this phrasing is that Wright fails to emphasize that our present experience of dying and rising with Christ is *by faith*. At present we have a "new identity"—the righteousness of the risen Christ—only through faith-union with him; being fully clothed with that new identity will come only when we are raised in him into the face-to-face presence of God. The "already" is *Christ's* resurrection into the age to come, which has "not yet" been our experience. In our present mode of existence, everything has not yet been totally changed. Those who have been united with Christ by faith can anticipate their own resurrection because they can "see" themselves in Christ. They can and should, by the power of the Spirit, turn from their sinful ways to live as disciples of Christ in the exercise of all their responsibilities in this age.

The human condition, or mode of life, in which we now experience the Spirit-empowering drive to repent of our sins is the condition of being God's sixth-day image and likeness in the generations of the first Adam. Consequently, followers of Christ

11. Wright, *Paul and Faithfulness*, 1103.

live by faith (not yet by sight) in the resurrected and ascended last Adam. Moreover, the "old nature" that Wright says we are to "kill off" is that of faithless hearts and sinful habits that have resulted from disobedience toward the one who has created us. The "old nature" to which Paul refers when emphasizing the sinful way of life should not be confused with our creaturely identity as the image of God, as if everything about this age is evil. Moreover, in my reading of Paul, the "new" that must become true for us is certainly not something we will bring about by "sheer, new-creational moral effort." The effort believers are to make in this age, by the power of the Spirit, is the faithful discipleship of Christ in all of our earthly callings as we live in the joy of his gift of life through his victory over sin and death.

I also want to point out that Wright does not always associate life in this age with "pains and puzzles" and evil lifestyles.[12] He says, for example, that the age of the new covenant will fulfill the "Torah's promise of life; and within that eschatological frame-work, based on the Messiah and energized by the spirit, the behaviour which Paul expects of those 'in the Messiah' is precisely Israel-behaviour, fulfilled-Torah behaviour."[13] Here, it seems to me, Wright properly points to God's norms and standards that do not originate, temporally speaking, from the *risen* Christ, but were articulated at least as early as the covenant with Israel. Moreover, it is clear enough in Scripture that the standards of righteousness originate with God's covenant with creation. To love God with all our heart, mind, and strength, and to love our neighbors as ourselves are creation-order standards, not something new for Christians. Those torah standards of behavior have not fallen from heaven following Christ's ascension to the right hand of God on high. They are grounded in the creation of all things through the Son of God who is the firstborn over all creation, the one in whom, from the beginning, all things hang together. In Christ Jesus, by the Spirit, therefore, the way of life characterized by torah-fulfillment is the kind of life that all humans, including Christians, should be living in this age as they store up treasures in heaven for the creation's fulfillment in the age to come. Christ is indeed the redeeming light that overcomes the darkness of sin and death, and by his grace we are restored to fellowship with God. Yet that to which we are being lifted in him is the fulfillment of creation, including human life in this age, rather than something pitted against life in this old age.

What is required in order to overcome the ambiguity in Wright, it seems to me, is to recognize God's seven-day creation as the ground for the three distinctions just noted. The first distinction is that between two ages of human life with God, the time of the sixth-day generations of the first Adam and the time of the seventh-day mode of life of the last Adam. That distinction is the basis of the second one between the exercise of human responsibilities in this age according to standards of right living that are given with creation and reaffirmed by God's covenants, on the one hand, and on the other hand, the fulfillment of all human labors in and through the righteousness

12. Wright, *Paul and Faithfulness*, 1116.

13. Wright, *Paul and Faithfulness*, 1111.

of Christ who is reconciling all things to God for God's sabbath with creation. The third distinction, not to be conflated with the first two, is that between the sinful disobedience of the generations of the first Adam and the cleansed, reconciled, and fulfilled life of Christ Jesus, the last Adam, and all who are raised with him to life in the age to come.

Due to human sinfulness, all of our responsibilities have indeed been darkened, twisted, and misdirected in dishonor of God and neighbors, with the consequence that, apart from the grace of God, all hope of right living now and fulfillment in God's kingdom is lost. But in Christ Jesus, our brother, life in this age has been recovered and renewed through his faithfulness, and God has blessed his faithfulness by raising him from the dead to the new mode of resurrection life. Therefore, all who trust and follow Christ participate in his redemptive redirection of their earthly lives on the way to the completion and reward of eternal life in God's sabbath glory. The "already" of Christ's resurrection from the dead establishes the condition for new life in him now through faith, lived in anticipation of what is still "not yet"—the resurrection into imperishable life with him.

IN CONCLUSION

Ridderbos writes that the real content of Paul's gospel is the "revelation of the mystery" (Rom 16:25–26; Col 1:25–26; Eph 3:2–3).[14] The mystery "has reference to the purpose of God with a view to the fullness of the times (Eph 1:9, 10). Standing over against the 'kept secret for long ages,' 'hidden for ages and generations,' etc., is again and again the 'now' of the revelation, the end of the waiting ages, the ultimate intervention of God according to his counsel and promise."[15] Yet this end, this final revelation, this eschatological completion of God's purposes, which is *now* revealed in Christ, has *not yet* been fully disclosed. According to Ridderbos, "The revelation of the mystery, the summary and the fundamental pattern of Paul's whole proclamation of Christ, will not be completed before Christ shall have been manifested in glory with all his own (Col. 3:4), the last mystery shall have been disclosed (1 Cor 15:51; Rom 11:25), and the creation now groaning and in travail shall have been redeemed from the bondage of corruption into the liberty of the glory of the children of God. It is for the revelation of that great day that the Spirit himself prays and groans and comes to the help of the church in its weakness (Rom 8:21ff)."[16]

The incarnate Son of God became one with us in Jesus, in our present (sixth-day) mode of existence. The mode of existence that characterizes the risen Christ, the last Adam, is that of resurrection fulfillment in God's (seventh-day) presence. The "already" is apparent in Christ Jesus because he—the incarnate Son of God—has

14. Ridderbos, *Paul*, 47.

15. Ridderbos, *Paul*, 47.

16. Ridderbos, *Paul*, 90.

lived, died, and been raised from the dead to eternal life. Our identity with Christ—in Christ—is now grasped by faith, empowered by the Spirit, who "prays and groans" with us in our longing for fulfillment and gives us a foretaste of what is to come.[17]

17. Ridderbos, *Paul*, 66.

21

Israel and the Prophets

EXODUS AND SABBATH

THE SEVEN-DAY WEEK OF God's creation constitutes reality. That is the ground of the revelatory disclosure in this age of the *already* and the *not yet*. God's sabbath rest has, from the foundation, been hallowed for the consummation of creation. That is why, in this age of human generational unfolding, Jacob could catch a glimpse in a dream of the *already* transcendent glory of God's throne room and why Isaiah could hear God declare that *already* "heaven is my throne and the earth is my footstool" (Isa 66:1). That is why Ezekiel and Daniel could speak in advance about the resurrection of the dead, and why Abraham was looking ahead to a city beyond anything humans could establish (Heb 11:10).

In the exodus from Egypt, Israel experienced God's saving deeds and promises of more to come. Dwelling in the security of God's redeeming love, Israel celebrated release from slavery with a gift God gave them of a day of rest each week (Deut 5:15). Yet that day of rest always opened to the next week of labor and to the continuing arrival and passing away of days and weeks and years. The pattern of weekly sabbaths pointed ahead in anticipation to a sabbath year that had not yet arrived. Each sabbath year stirred hopes for the year of jubilee. From tabernacle wanderings to temple establishment, from temple destruction to the exile, and from exile to the return of a remnant, the faithful of Israel were enveloped by God's *already* even while they continued to look ahead to the fulfillment of God's promises that had *not yet* been fulfilled. Israel's experience of God was rooted not only in the remembrance of God's past deeds but in the dependability and steadfastness of the Lord's promises of greater things to come. The presence of God with Israel instilled confidence of divine justice and mercy that would establish God's kingdom once and for all.

For this reason, says N. T. Wright, it is not surprising that we find evidence of hope for the resurrection of the dead emerging in the Old Testament. That emerging hope is based not on anything in the human make-up (e.g. an "immortal soul"), but on YHWH and him alone. Indeed, YHWH is the substance of the hope, not merely the ground: he himself is the "portion," i.e. the inheritance, of the righteous, devout Israelite. At the same time, it is his power alone that can make alive, as some ancient prayers have it. "With you is the fountain of life," sang the Psalmist; "in your light we see light" [Ps 36:9]. When this strong faith in YHWH as the creator, the life-giver, the God of ultimate justice met the apparent contradiction of the injustices and sufferings of life, at that point there was . . . a chance of fresh belief springing up . . . [I]f YHWH was the inheritance of his people, and if his love and faithfulness were as strong as Israel's traditions made out, then there was no ultimate bar to seeing death itself as a beaten foe.[1]

Even before Ezekiel and Daniel began to speak of a transfiguring resurrection, Israel was learning that God's sabbath promises are rock solid. Hope for what is not yet revealed grew from the soil of God's fulfilled promises. Israel's hope was grounded in God's continuing, never-failing faithfulness, which confirmed anew each morning that God was, is, and will always be celebrating the fulfillment of the "very good" creation in sabbath glory, the celebration of the final and everlasting jubilee.

TEMPLE, JERUSALEM, AND THE WORLD TO COME

Jewish scholar Jon Levenson points to the importance of the temple in Israel's experience of God's presence in their midst. It was, he argues, the foundation of an emerging belief in resurrection from the dead. Ezekiel's oracle in 28:11–19, according to Levenson, identifies "the Temple on 'God's holy mountain' with 'Eden, the garden of God'" (vv. 13–14), and that "builds in turn, upon the conception of the Temple as paradise."[2] We noted in earlier chapters that the temple, like the tabernacle before it, represented God's dwelling with Israel. Everything about it was revelatory of God's creation order—the macrocosmic temple—and thus it spoke of the *already* of God's salvation of Israel and the assurance of the fulfillment of God's kingdom, which had not yet arrived. The temple stood "as a prototype of the redeemed world envisioned by some to lie ahead," says Levenson. "It connects the protological and the eschatological, the primal and the final, preserving Eden and providing a taste of the World-to-Come."[3] "The rabbinic notion of the World-to-Come envisions a mode of existence that has elements of continuity and elements of discontinuity with this world, with this life," Levinson told interviewer Sharon Goldman. "Therefore, any effort to envision the World-to-Come necessarily entails mythopoetic language, while attempts to account for this mode of being rationalistically and empirically come across as silly, in my view.

1. Wright, *Resurrection*, 107–8.
2. Levenson, *Resurrection and Restoration*, 85.
3. Levenson, *Resurrection and Restoration*, 90.

Levinson continues, "We have to remember that these ideas are inseparable from a vision of the redemption and utter transformation of the world. When mythopoetic or liturgical language is flattened into propositional or empirical affirmations, something crucial is lost in the translation."[4]

Another student of ancient Israel, Eric Voegelin, would agree with Levenson about the legitimacy of biblical writers using "mythopoetic" language to speak of God's transformation of the world. But unlike Levenson, Voegelin believes that such symbolic language, as found in apocalyptic literature, should not be read to suggest the actual coming of a radical change of the cosmic order, as some of the prophetic language implies. Voegelin is leery of any belief that reality as we now experience it can be transfigured. He uses the Greek word "metastasis" to refer to belief in the kind of radical change of, or escape from, the world that humans presently experience.[5] If a prophet's metastatic vision is understood to be mythopoetic in referring to what God might reveal to humans in history, Voegelin believes it can be constructive for the deepening of our understanding of God's ordering of history. But if a metastatic vision implies belief in an escape from the history of this world's order under God, then the consequences can be dangerous. "If the prophets, in their despair over Israel [because of its failure to keep covenant with God], indulged in metastatic dreams, in which the tension of historical order was abolished by a divine act of grace," they stood on the edge of danger, in Voegelin's view. But, he continues, "at least they did not indulge in metastatic nightmares, in which the *opus* [the work of abolishment] was performed by human acts of revolution."[6]

As we will see in the next chapter, Voegelin's leeriness of metastatic visions also leads him to reject the apostle Paul's vision of the transfiguration of reality through the resurrection of Christ. Voegelin recognizes that a radical change in human consciousness and historical development did take place with God's covenant with Israel. Israel's experience led to the movement away from cosmological myths that shaped empires like those in Egypt and Babylon and toward a new understanding of the order of history revealed by God. After "the world-transcendent God had revealed himself," there was no going back. "One could not pretend to live in another order of being than the one illuminated by revelation. And least of all could one think of going beyond revelation replacing the constitution of being with a man-made substitute. Man exists *within* the order of being; and there is no history *outside* the historical form under revelation."[7]

However, we may ask, what if the covenantal order God established with Israel disclosed the wider and deeper truth that cosmic reality is constituted as a seven-day creation order? What if Israel's experience of sabbath days, sabbath years, and a

---

4. Goldman, "World Repaired," 82.

5. Voegelin, *Israel and Revelation*, 452–54.

6. Voegelin, *Israel and Revelation*, 465.

7. Voegelin, *Israel and Revelation*, 465.

sabbatical jubilee led them to anticipate a fulfillment of life with God beyond this age? In other words, what if the order of creation entails the orientation of all things toward God's sabbath rest, the fulfillment of which entails the transfiguration of human experience through the resurrection of the dead? If the Bible speaks in this way, then Voegelin's understanding of Israel's experience misses the significance of Levenson's account of the development of Israel's belief in the resurrection.

Return with me to Levenson's interpretation of the meaning of the temple for Israel. He reads the short Psalm 133 about the blessing of brothers living together in unity and of everlasting life on Mount Zion as an illumination of the meaning of the temple in the temple city. The psalm, he writes, presents "a paradigm that is spatial: death is the norm outside Zion and cannot be reversed, but within the temple city, death is unknown, for there God has ordained the blessing of eternal life."[8] A journey to the temple, therefore, was understood as a movement toward redemption. "This conception of the Temple as paradise, the place rendered inviolable by the pervasive presence of God, explains one of the more striking features of Temple-oriented devotion in the Hebrew Bible. I am referring to the longing to remain in the Temple so often expressed by the psalmists."[9]

Wright says something similar about Psalm 73, for when the psalmist goes into God's sanctuary he realizes that God's destruction of the wicked is certain; it's as if it has already been accomplished. "But that is not all," says Wright. "The Psalmist himself discovers that he is grasped by a love that will not let him go, a power that even death, and the dissolution of the body, cannot thwart."[10] The psalmist expresses God's *already* with the words "I am always with you; you hold me by my right hand" (v. 23) and "God is the strength of my heart and my portion for ever" (v. 26). The *not yet* of the psalmist's experience comes through in the words, "and afterward you will take me into glory" (v. 24); as for now, "I have made the Sovereign Lord my refuge; I will tell of all your deeds" (v. 28). It seems clear, says Wright, that the words "and afterward" in verse 24 refer "not to an event that will take place later on within the present life, but to a state which will obtain after the present life of being guided by God's counsel."[11]

According to Levenson, the hope of resurrection to eternal life did not appear suddenly from out of the blue late in Israel's history. That hope and vision grew from the ways—and the long history—of God's revelatory dealings with Israel. When the

> expectation of resurrection arises, resurrection is still only the prelude to something greater and more permanent. This is "eternal life," as the book of Daniel puts it (12:2), or, to use the familiar rabbinic expression, life in the World-to-Come. Since this new life is thought to follow upon resurrection, it perforce entails embodiedness: people come back in the flesh. But the flesh

8. Levenson, *Resurrection and Restoration*, 92.

9. Levenson, *Resurrection and Restoration*, 92.

10. Wright, *Resurrection*, 106.

11. Wright, *Resurrection*, 106.

in which they come back is necessarily different from the kind they knew in their mortal life, for now they have become immune to death and the bodily infirmities associated with it. There is no second death for those granted eternal life. . . . Their new life is thus not a mere continuation of the old but rather a radical transformation of it, a perfecting of the self in a world distinguished from this one by its perfection.[12]

What Levenson helps us see is that the Hebrew Bible expresses an understanding of life that is not confined to the coming and passing away of the human generations (and the generations of other living creatures) in this age. By faith, believers saw something beyond life in this age. Since everything is related to God, and because Israel lived by God's covenant goodness and promises, the faithful came to believe that their lives in this world are dependent entirely on the God who is above at all times, as well as in their time. It is the *already* of God's position and accomplishments "from everlasting to everlasting" that nurtured the anticipation of a resurrection that had *not yet* come.

From a Christian point of view, the reality of such a resurrection into a new mode of eternal life has been made definite in Christ's resurrection and ascension. Yet the experience of Christians living in this age by faith is not functionally different from the experience of those who lived by faith in God before the coming of Christ. That is because the creation-order basis for the relationship of the already/not yet is God's seven-day creation. This is why the New Testament letter to the Hebrews can cite Old Testament figures from Abel to Samuel, David, and the prophets as examples of faithfulness for Christians. For the faithful of all generations know that "faith is being sure of what we hope for and certain of what we do not see" (Heb 11:1).

As Levenson says in a published interview, if we are to understand what the Bible says about Israel's experience of God, we cannot stand within the framework of a closed naturalistic view of the world. To say, for example, as many would today, that death is the final act in human life, "reveals the limitation of a worldview predicated on our [modern] deterministic and mechanistic understanding of the normal course of things . . . If you're committed to a totally naturalistic universe without a personal

---

12. Levenson, *Resurrection and Restoration*, 106–7. In Levenson's discussion of Dan 12, he expands on this point. It would be a mistake, he says, "to imagine that the 'eternal life' the deserving receive is simply a restoration to their old quotidian reality, only without the pain and injustice. To 'be radiant like the bright expanse of sky' (Dan 12:3) is (if the pun may be pardoned) light years away from having to reinhabit one's old body for all eternity. This is worth noting because scholars often present the issue as if the only alternatives are immortality of the soul, on the one hand, and resurrection of the body, on the other. Doing so is to neglect the key fact that resurrection was thought to yield a transformed and perfected form of bodily existence and thus a state of being both like and unlike any we can know in the flesh. To glance ahead to later historical periods, one thinks, for example, of the Christian apostle Paul's comment on the resurrection of the dead: 'It is sown a physical body (*sōma psuchikon*); it is raised a spiritual body (*sōma pneumatikon*)' (1 Cor 15:44)." Levenson, *Resurrection and Restoration*, 189. Levenson also emphasizes, "The classical Jewish belief in the resurrection of the dead is not simply the notion that departed individuals will eventually receive their due. It is the confidence that God will in the end fulfill his outstanding promises to Israel, even to those worthy members of Israel who sleep in the dust." Levenson, *Resurrection and Restoration*, 200.

creator God, an active God who actually does things, then the best you can do with the resurrection of the dead is to say that it's a symbol of hope, but a hope that ends at the grave."[13] In tune with Levenson, I believe the already and the not yet of a closed naturalistic view reduces the meaning of life to this: the end of all things is *already* determined. It is death, and nothing lies beyond it. Consequently, day-to-day existence is conducted in anticipation of nothing greater than one's own death, which has *not yet* taken place.

CONCLUSION

Crucial for an understanding of Christ's resurrection and the resurrection of the faithful is a recognition of God's seven-day order of creation. The age to come is not a post-fall invention by God to provide an escape from this fallen world. The revelation of the mystery in Christ is the revelation of God's purposes for creation from beginning to end, namely to reveal the glory of God in and through Israel's Messiah in company with all his brothers and sisters. The key, then, to understanding the relation between the redemptive-*historical* unfolding of God's revelation, on the one hand, and the fulfillment of the creation's seven-day *order*, on the other, is recognizing that human life in this age—our sixth-day mode of existence—has never been the end and goal of creation. The creation order does not reach its completion with the life and achievements of the human generations. The present mode of our existence, along with everything God has created, has always been revelatory in anticipation of a greater climax. The human generations, like all other creatures, exist at God's disposal for a purpose that culminates beyond this age. The historical life, death, resurrection, and ascension of Jesus Christ is the beginning of the revelation of the mystery that encompasses all time and will fill the creation full in God's sabbath *with* creation—the seventh-day consummation of God's kingdom-temple. Faith in Christ, therefore, entails more than learning to stand in a tradition that looks back to the historical life and death of Jesus and interpreting him in the context of God's covenant promises to Abraham, Isaac, and Jacob. Living by faith in Christ means living for, and towards, the fulfillment of all things through the new covenant in him that speaks God's final word (Heb 1:1–2).

The inescapable fact is that humans have been created to live by faith and not by sight throughout their generations. We are the sixth-day image of God and our humanness, by its very nature, is ordered toward a goal beyond itself that cannot be seen or grasped fully in this age. That is why our choice is not between living by faith and living without faith; rather, the choice is either to live by faith in the true God or to try to live by faith in false gods. Consequently, every biblical reference to new life in Christ as a *present* experience—something that is "now" and "already"—speaks of a way of life *by faith* that is not yet *by sight*.

13. Goldman, "World Repaired," 78.

22

To Exit or Remake the World?

ERIC VOEGELIN'S WORRY ABOUT PAUL

MORE THAN SIXTY YEARS ago, noted political philosopher and biblical scholar, Eric Voegelin, wrote an essay titled "The Pauline Vision of the Resurrected,"[1] which bears directly on our discussion of the *already* and the *not yet*. In the essay, he calls into question the apostle Paul's vision of the transfiguration of reality through the resurrection of Christ.

Voegelin was a remarkably wide-ranging and profound thinker who developed a penetrating critique of ancient Gnosticism and its influence on both Christianity and various modern philosophies and ideological movements. In various expressions of Gnosticism, which flourished around the time of Christ, a central element, writes Voegelin, was "the experience of the world as an alien place into which man has strayed and from which he must find his way back home to the other world of his origin."[2] A gnostic prayer would read like this: "'Deliver us from the darkness of this world into which we are flung.' The world is no longer the well-ordered, the cosmos, in which Hellenic man felt at home; nor is it the Judaeo-Christian world that God created and found good."[3] For the gnostics, the instrument of salvation is *gnosis*—knowledge. Voegelin explains that since the gnostics believed "entanglement with the world is brought about by *agnoia*, ignorance, the soul will be able to disentangle itself through knowledge of its true life and its condition of alienness in this world."[4] A sharp antithetical dualism is apparent here between the dark world of bodily entrapment and ignorance, on the one hand, and the good world of true knowledge through which the soul can find its true home, on the other.

---

1. Voegelin, "Pauline Vision," 239–71.
2. Voegelin, *Science, Politics and Gnosticism*, 9.
3. Voegelin, *Science, Politics and Gnosticism*, 9.
4. Voegelin, *Science, Politics and Gnosticism*, 11–12.

Major councils of the ancient church declared Gnosticism a heresy. But its influence was not expunged from Christian circles. Some converts to Christianity came to identify Christ as the answer to the gnostic prayer for release from this alienating world. They saw Christ as the illuminating light that brings the kind of knowledge that will allow the soul to escape from this world and return to its true home. Some of the disputes that arose in those circles were about timing: is true knowledge available "already," even during life in this world, or is it something to be hoped for only after the body dies and the soul is released to its true home, which has "not yet" come to pass?

Although Voegelin does not believe the New Testament is a gnostic text, he does worry that Paul came too close to the dangers of Gnosticism when he envisioned a *transfiguration* of reality through the resurrection of Christ. Paul's vision of the resurrected Christ, Voegelin contends, could and did lend support to the belief that this world is a dark and alien place of death from which the soul needs release. Unlike Plato and Aristotle, who accepted the present order of the cosmos as a given and sought to attune their souls *within* that order, Paul, according to Voegelin, believed that in Christ one can find salvation *from* the world's disorder. Paul supposedly believed that, with the second coming of Christ and the resurrection of the dead, a new world order would appear, that the perishable would put on the imperishable, that death would be swallowed up in life. For Voegelin, that idea was dangerous because it led people to disparage the present life and world order rather than to seek true understanding of themselves within it.

Whereas Plato and Aristotle sought to understand the order of the cosmos and their relation to the divine from within it, Voegelin argues that Paul believed in, or at least suggested hope for, an "exodus from [the] structure" of reality.[5] What is central in Paul's letters, says Voegelin, is "the history of faith," the "meaning *of* history, because he knows the end of the story in the transfiguration that begins with the

---

5. Voegelin, "Pauline Vision," 258. According to Voegelin, there are parallels between Paul and Plato/Aristotle, but with Paul, the emphasis "has decisively shifted from the divinely noetic order incarnate in the world to the divinely pneumatic salvation from its disorder, from the paradox of reality to the abolition of the paradox, from the experience of the directional movement to its consummation. The critical difference is the treatment of *phthora*, perishing. In the noetic theophany of the philosophers, the *athanatizein* [immortalizing] of the psyche is kept in balance with the rhythm of *genesis* and *phthora* in the cosmos; in the pneumatic theophany of Paul, the *athanasia* [death] of man is not to be separated from the abolition of *phthora* in the cosmos. Flesh and blood, the *soma psychikon*, cannot enter the kingdom of God; it must be changed into the *soma pneumatikon* (1 Cor 15:44, 55); for the perishing (*phthora*) cannot take possession of the imperishing (*aphtharsia*) (v. 50). The change of reality to the state of *aphtharsia* is the Pauline exegesis of the *mysterion* (vv. 51–52) . . . Paul [in contrast to Plato] is fascinated by the implications of theophany so strongly that he lets his imagery of a *genesis* without *phthora* interfere with the primary experience of the cosmos. In 1 Corinthians 15 he lets his exultation rise to the apocalyptic assurance that 'we shall not sleep, but we shall all be changed, in a moment, in the twinkling of an eye, at the last trumpet. For the trumpet will sound and the dead will be raised imperishable, and we (who have not yet died) shall be changed.' The *aphtharsia* is an event to be expected in the lifetime of his readers and himself. The metastatic expectation of the Second Coming has begun its long history of disappointment." Voegelin, "Pauline Vision," 241.

Resurrection."[6] Paul, in other words, gave some encouragement to the gnostic influence in Christian circles. Some of Paul's teaching showed signs of *noetic* disturbance or aberration ("noetic" is the adjective of the Greek word "nous," meaning "rational soul"). Those Christians who thought in terms of the darkness of this world versus another world of light were inclined to understand Paul's interpretation of Christ's resurrection as implying belief in an exodus from this dark world into the other world of true enlightenment.

The way to overcome this predicament, according to Voegelin, is to reject every gnostic temptation. With respect to Paul's teaching, it would mean accepting the profound insight into divine transcendence brought on by his vision of Christ, while rejecting the idea that a vision of the resurrected Christ implies an actual forthcoming transfiguration of the cosmic order. From Voegelin's point of view, true knowledge is not a special gnosis leading to a release of the soul from this world, but rather a clear understanding of who we are within this world in relation to the divine. For Voegelin, humans may legitimately share in Paul's *noetic* experience of divine transcendence, but should refuse to accept Paul's belief that an actual transfiguring exodus from this reality is possible.

Voegelin's criticism of Paul arises from his conviction that cosmic order does not allow for a radical change in the human condition. What is wise and correct in Plato and Aristotle, from Voegelin's point of view, is that they accepted the human condition as an existence "in between" (*metaxy*)—between time and timelessness, between that which is naturally embodied and that which is rational and tuned to timeless transcendence. Human existence must not be identified with, or reduced to, either the temporal or the timeless. Nor can humans escape their own nature characterized by existence in the "in between."[7] Voegelin lauds Paul and other New Testament writers for the advance they made in articulating the profound experience of being pulled by God's revelation toward divine transcendence. The danger arose when Paul's vision of the resurrected Christ led him to believe that humans could eventually experience an exodus from the "in between" which, for Voegelin, is an unchangeable part of the structure of cosmic order.

6. Voegelin, "Pauline Vision," 258.

7. Michael Morrissey explains, "Voegelin reminds us that the symbols of immortality are not informative; they are evocative. They are not descriptive but exegetic, for they refer not to entities in the external world but rather to the movement of the soul within the *metaxy*. They are not concepts with an external referent but indices of language arising from the religious experience of the eternal as consciousness becomes aware of its movement toward the ground. Their meaning can only be understood if they evoke in the listener or reader the corresponding movement of participatory consciousness as experienced by their original authors, that is, in the experience of the loving quest for the divine Beyond." Morrissey, "Voegelin, Religious Experience," 21. According to Voegelin, under the pressure of noetic distress, people disassociate "this world" of existence in time from the "other world" of the timeless. That is a mistake, for "we 'exist' in neither the one nor the other of these worlds but in the tension between time and the timeless . . . [Consequently,] the dissociation of the 'world' transforms us into 'strangers' to either one of the hypostatized worlds." Voegelin, "Immortality," 235–79; 269.

While I believe Voegelin is fundamentally mistaken in his criticism of Paul, he nonetheless offers some worthy insights into the nature of Gnosticism and its influence on Christianity. I agree with him that to imagine an antithetical dualism between this world and another world is gnostic, but I do not believe Paul articulated or even encouraged acceptance of such a dualism. Rather, for Paul, the resurrection of Christ leads to the *fulfillment* of God's one and only creation order understood in biblical terms, not ancient Greek philosophical terms. The entire seven-day order of creation is the order of reality. Through Christ, the creation is fulfilled, not destroyed, by God's judgment of sin and redemption of sinners. Salvation in Christ constitutes a recovery, a cleansing renewal, reconciliation, and consummation of God's good creation. For example, Paul's words to the Colossians quoted earlier, "Set your mind on things that are above, not on things that are on earth" (3:2–3), should not be read as evidence of a gnostic tendency. The point is that, by faith in Christ, one's life is now hidden with the resurrected Christ in anticipation of what is still "not yet." Paul is not telling believers to live as if their souls have *already* escaped (or can eventually escape) from their evil bodies in this dark world to enter a timeless world of light. To the contrary, the present experience of dying and being raised with Christ comes through faith-identity with Christ. Our position now, in relation to Christ Jesus, is not antithetical to the creation order and does not call for an escape from it or a revolutionary revolt against it. Rather, it is a relation in which, by the power of the Holy Spirit, we are enabled to learn habits of repentance from sin within this world and to live in accord with our creaturely responsibility as the image of God. From a Christian point of view, our responsibility is exercised before the face of God in and for this world in anticipation of its fulfillment, not its demise.

Christ's death and resurrection affirm, uphold, and renew life in this age of God's good creation by forgiving sins and defeating all that stands against God's love for us and for the whole creation. Through faith in the risen Christ, our "not yet" is tied intimately to Christ's "already." Yet this means that, in service to him now, our responsibility is to get on with the important affairs of life in this age. This world is not an evil entrapment from which our souls need an escape. It is the revelatory reality in which we are to work out our salvation with fear and trembling in every vocation. That is precisely what Paul admonishes the Colossian Christians to do, namely, to live in peace with one another, forgiving one another, being gentle, kind, humble, patient and compassionate in all that they do (Col. 3:12–14). This is how husbands and wives are to love one another (vv. 18–19), how parents should raise their children (vv. 20–21), and how servants and masters should relate to one another (vv. 22–24). There are things about our sinful patterns of disobedience in this world that need to be changed and from which we need to turn away in repentance (vv. 5–10), but our bodily life is not evil and we have no need to seek an exit from family life, work, and building just communities. Those whom Paul sees as already "hidden with Christ in God" are human beings in the line of the first Adam, now forgiven and being renewed through Christ in anticipation of bodily resurrection and fulfillment in the age to come. All of this takes place within the order of God's one and only seven-day order of creation.

Belief in the kind of transfiguration Paul is speaking of has to do with Christ's resurrection with his brothers and sisters into face-to-face fellowship with God, when "this perishable body puts on imperishability" (1 Cor 15:54). For Paul, there are indeed two different modes of human existence in God's order of creation: the first is that of earthlings—the generations of the first Adam (the seed that is planted); the second is that of resurrected bodies—the resurrection mode of existence to which the life-giving Spirit, the last Adam, raises us (the living plant). Biblically speaking, these two modes of existence are not associated with two different worlds, one of dark, ignorant materiality and the other of immaterial, timeless knowledge and light. Therefore, it seems to me that Voegelin starts with a fundamentally different understanding of reality than Paul did, and that is why Voegelin misunderstands Paul.[8]

WHAT CAN WE LEARN FROM VOEGELIN?

Having challenged Voegelin's interpretation of Paul's vision of the resurrected Christ, we should not take leave of him too quickly. His insight into the dangers of Gnosticism leads in two constructive directions.

First, Voegelin's desire that we should take the meaning of life within the structure of this world seriously stands as a warning against any misunderstanding of Christianity that treats our present life and its responsibilities lightly or negatively. Christians have all too easily accommodated themselves to elements of a gnostic mindset when they think that Christian faith means simply enduring the pains (alienations) of this world while awaiting entrance into another one. As we've emphasized throughout this book, the fulfillment of life found in Christ is a fulfillment of the revelatory responsibilities of life in this age. The way to live by faith in Christ is by engaging with utmost seriousness in the relationships and responsibilities we bear now, because it is precisely through obedient faithfulness as earthlings that we invest in the kingdom that will be revealed in its fullness when Christ returns. As Paul says of those who are in Christ, "For we are what he has made us, created in Christ Jesus for good works, which God prepared beforehand to be our way of life" (Eph 2:10).

Learning to turn away from sinful patterns of degradation and destruction in this age and toward the development of wise, just, and loving patterns of life is exactly the way we are to live by faith and hope now. Life in this age is directly related to the

---

8. Another New Testament text, the epistle to the Hebrews, has also been interpreted as a gnostic—or Platonic-influenced writing. A primary proponent of that interpretation was Ernst Kasemann's *The Wandering People of God*. Critical evaluations and rejections of Kasemann and those who shared his view can be found in Long, *Hebrews*, 62–64, 84–94; Adams, "Cosmology of Hebrews," 122–39; Schenck, *Cosmology and Eschatology*, 55–57; and Schenck, "God Has Spoken," 329–31.

creation's coming fulfillment. In Christ, the works of the faithful will follow them (Rev 14:13). Why else would God have become one with us in this age in order to reconcile all things to God? The *already* of Christ's ascension to the throne of glory is not a signal to look for an exit from this world. Our present mode of existence may continue for decades and generations to come, and if so, it means that the responsibilities of God's royal stewards in this age have not yet been completed.

The second helpful direction in which Voegelin's criticism moves is to an exposure of Gnosticism's modern, inverted perversions. Under the impact of gnostic-influenced Christianity, a number of early modern thinkers and movements inverted the desire to escape from life in this dark world by imagining that humans can radically reconstruct this world by their own knowledge and power to achieve their utopian hopes. What these revolutionaries sought and still seek, Voegelin argues, is to exit this unjust world not by escaping from it but by reconstructing it from within, acting as if they are re-creator gods. They try, as Voegelin famously put it, to "immanentize the eschaton"—to bring heaven down to earth.[9] They reject God and any transcendent purposes requiring a god and replace them with autonomous human knowledge that can reconstruct the world by eliminating ignorance, inequality, and pain. That is the meaning of all attempts to "immanentize the eschaton."

Voegelin believes there is a direct line from Paul's vision of a transfigured world to the modern political revolutionaries who want to reconstruct reality to fit their utopian ambitions. The modernist tendency was already apparent, says Voegelin, "when Petrarca (1304–1374) symbolized the age that began with Christ as the *tenebrae*, the dark age, that now would be followed by a renewal of the *lux* [light] of pagan antiquity."[10] By Hegel's time, says Voegelin, the "Logos of Christ" was interpreted as having finally found its "full incarnation in the Logos of Hegel's 'absolute knowledge.'"[11] Although Voegelin does not blame Paul for Hegel, Marx, and many other modern humanists, he does see lines of influence from Paul's Christ to modern messianic Gnosticism.

> The transfiguration that had begun with the theophany [manifestation of God] in Paul's vision of the Resurrected was now completed in the egophany [manifestation of the ego] of the speculative thinker. The Parousia [second coming] at last, had occurred ... We have not moved so far away from Christianity as the conflict between the Church and modernity would suggest. On the contrary, the modern revolt is so intimately a development of the 'Christianity' against which it is in revolt that it would be unintelligible if it could not be understood as the deformation of the theophanic events in which the dynamics of transfiguration was revealed to Jesus and the Apostles.[12]

9. In critique of modern Gnosticism, see Voegelin's *From Enlightenment to Revolution*, and Voegelin, *New Science*, 107–90. See also O'Regan, *Gnostic Return*.

10. Voegelin, "Pauline Vision," 268.

11. Voegelin, "Pauline Vision," 268–69.

12. Voegelin, "Pauline Vision," 269. A different, and I believe more adequate, account of modern

What Christians can learn from Voegelin is to examine themselves from a biblical point of view to consider the extent to which they mistakenly maintain ancient and/or modern gnostic tendencies in the way they live and think in relation to God and to one another. In this regard, Jürgen Moltmann says something significant about how the Christian celebration of the Lord's supper—the Eucharistic feast—should help Christians move away from gnostic and modern utopian tendencies to a more coherent and faithful way of life as Christ's followers. "In act and in the Word of promise," writes Moltmann, "the shared meal calls to remembrance Christ's death and anticipates his coming in glory . . . [T]hose who have shared the supper of the Lord should live in the fellowship of Christ and lead their whole life in his Spirit."[13] Sharing the Lord's Supper in the communion of the saints, as the body of Christ, is a bodily act of expectation and anticipation of Christ's bodily return. It is a communal meal of remembering and looking forward that gives direction to the whole of life in this age. In speaking against sexual immorality in 1 Corinthians 6:19–20, for example, Paul writes, "do you not know that your body is a temple of the Holy Spirit within you, which you have from God, and that you are not your own? For you were bought with a price; therefore glorify God in your body." Paul's words carry implications that reach far beyond the responsibility of maintaining sexual purity. The hope and longing for Christ's return, says Moltmann, does not represent a desire to take flight from the world. "Nor does it provide any foundation for hostility towards the body. On the contrary, it makes people prepared to remain true to the earth, and to honour the body." Life in hope reaches out "to the active shaping of life. It is life in anticipation of the coming One, life in 'expectant creativity.'"[14]

Through our labors in this age, we legitimately long for that which is not yet, and our longing should be expressed by the redoubling of efforts to serve God faithfully in this age because of what God has already given us. It is precisely through our persevering earthly stewardship, even in face of death, that God is fashioning Christ's followers to be the house of God. The Spirit is working through God's people right now to shape them into the "living stones" that will compose that house (1 Pet 2:4–5). You must go on, says Paul, "by the mercies of God, to present your bodies as a living sacrifice, holy and acceptable to God" (Rom 12:1). Therefore, remember always the Lord's death till he comes by sharing in the meal that he has given us with his own body and blood. The disciples of Christ are to use the gifts given them in this age "to do what is noble in the sight of all . . . [to] live peaceably with all," not taking revenge on others but leaving that in God's hands and seeking to overcome evil with good (Rom 12:17–21).

That kind of service means we must take all of our earthly responsibilities seriously, working to stop and reverse destructive, unjust human practices of persons

---

humanism's derivation and departure from ancient and medieval cultures is developed by Herman Dooyeweerd in *Roots of Western Culture* and *In the Twilight*.

13. Moltmann, *Way of Jesus Christ*, 338, 339.

14. Moltmann, *Way of Jesus Christ*, 340.

and institutions. It means working for social, economic, and political reformation, because such institutions are part of our responsibility as the sixth-day image of God, and they are meant to reveal something of God's ways with us. We should be working, as Hebrews put it, to "provoke one another to love and good deeds . . . all the more as you see the Day approaching" (Heb 10:24–25).

23

Incorporation into Christ

CONSUMMATING THE COVENANT BOND

WHILE THERE ARE A variety of ways to speak about the "already" and the "not yet" of God's kingdom, and about the relation of Christ to those who belong to him, a major simile is "incorporation." The relation of the faithful to the risen Christ is marked by their union with him as a corporate body. What does that mean?

Thus far in part 5, we have worked with the distinction between (1) faith-union with the risen and ascended Christ and (2) face-to-face union with God when the resurrection harvest is complete. We've argued that the already/not yet drama is not first of all a temporal movement from the present to the future, but the drama of the sixth-day human generations in relation to God whose seventh-day rest orients creation throughout all generations. The unfolding drama of God with creation culminates in the revelation of the Son of God in this age in Jesus, whose death, resurrection, and ascension reveal him to be the Christ, the life-giving Spirit of the age to come. For the human generations, the movement is from their sixth-day mode of existence, extending from the first Adam, to the seventh-day mode of imperishable life in the last Adam.

The meaning of incorporation is closely related to God's covenantal bond with creation in judgment and blessing. God's new covenant in Messiah Jesus is the climax of all earthly covenants that build toward it. Christ is the one through whom all things have been created and hang together. He is the Alpha as well as the Omega. For human creatures to be incorporated into Christ's death and resurrection is thus to be joined with believers of all ages in the new covenant in Christ that fills all things full to the glory of God.

The Bible highlights many of our creaturely relationships that reveal something of the meaning of God's covenant bond with creation and incorporation into Christ. That bond and that incorporation are like the union of a bride and bridegroom in marriage; like a tightly knit family; like citizens and government servants bound together in a just political community; like a grand palace constructed of building materials crafted perfectly together; or like an orchestra and conductor performing together in perfect unity. In the present age, by the power of the Spirit, the body of Christ requires maturation through the faithful exercise of all the responsibilities that belong to the image of God—God's royal priesthood. We should not think that a relationship with God in Christ is operative in only one sphere of life. Life is whole, and every part—all members of the orchestra—should play together in tune with God in the revelatory and anticipatory terms of honor and hospitality, commission toward commendation, and covenant for community. Everything that is revelatory of God in this age is constitutively anticipatory of the fulfilled covenant community—the divine-human marriage, the body of Christ, the family of God, the new Jerusalem, the kingdom of God. Consequently, the experience of life in Christ by faith in this age moves toward its consummation in face-to-face communion with him in the age to come. We are not yet there, but in the resurrected and ascended Christ—the Messiah of Israel and Lord of the world—God's sabbath has already been opened and entered by the righteous human acceptable to God. Incorporation of the faithful into Christ, therefore, envelopes them throughout this age on into the age to come.

A REDEMPTIVE-HISTORICAL DISTINCTION

Herman Ridderbos argues that the distinction between the already and the not yet, when considered from the viewpoint of life in this age, is a redemptive-historical distinction.[1] What has been revealed in Christ's resurrection and ascension is the first fruits of the resurrection harvest and fulfillment of creation. Christ's finished work envelopes all times, past, present, and future. As Paul accounts for it, according to Ridderbos, "the old" stands over against "the new," "not first of all in a personal and ethical sense, but in a redemptive-historical, eschatological sense."[2] It is not in the first place about what has to be changed in the believer, but about what has been done to sinful humanity on the cross in the "new man," Christ. "Because the old man was condemned and put to death in Christ's death on the cross, the body of sin, the flesh, the old mode of existence of sin, has lost its dominion and control over those who are in him." Therefore, in "Christ's death and resurrection they have been transferred to the new order of life—the life order of the new creation, the new man."[3] The transfer is real and at the same time not yet fully realized.

Wright's distinction between a "literal" and a "metaphorical" resurrections does not quite capture the redemptive-historical dynamic that Ridderbos points to in the relation between the risen Christ, on the one hand, and his disciples in this age united with him by faith, on the other. By "literal," Wright means the actual resurrection

1. Ridderbos, *Paul*, 39–43.

2. Ridderbos, *Paul*, 63.

3. Ridderbos, *Paul*, 63.

that Jesus has already experienced and that believers will experience in the future. By "metaphorical," he means "the new life of the baptized believer, whose concrete referent is the communal and personal new life in which the shackles of sin have been broken."[4] "The literal resurrection of Jesus sets the context for the metaphorical resurrection of believers as the anticipation of their own literal resurrection . . . both the literal and the metaphorical meanings have concrete referents, the literal referring to bodily resurrection and the metaphorical referring to practical holiness and service."[5]

With this language, it seems to me, Wright is interpreting Paul's teaching about the resurrection in a way that focuses on the time of exiting the grave. In other words, Jesus already emerged from the tomb, while believers, whether dead or living now, have not yet experienced bodily resurrection. Wright sees an equivalence in the "literal" resurrection of Jesus (already) and of believers (not yet). At some time in the future, believers will also rise from the dead as Jesus did. Thus, when the apostle Paul describes the way of life that believers should follow now, Wright tags it "metaphorical," because believers have not yet experienced literal resurrection. Their new life should be like resurrection in a metaphorical way with its "referent" being "practical holiness and service" in this age.

However, with Ridderbos, I hear something different from Paul. Paul's reference to the risen Christ does not focus on Jesus having left the tomb (though that is true), but on his having become the "last Adam," "a life-giving spirit," through whom God brings eternal life (1 Cor 15:45; Rom 5:21, 6:10). "Now," says Paul, "if we died with Christ, we believe that we will also live with him" (Rom. 6:8). The mode of resurrection life that is to characterize believers now is not a "metaphor" that anticipates the "literal" rising from death. It is a life lived by faith in the risen Christ in whom we are incorporated and with whom we anticipate living in the presence of God's sabbath glory. The risen Christ, who is seated at the highest place of authority, is not simply alive from the dead but elevated to a new mode of existence beyond the mode of life we now live. Believers will be transfigured to that new mode of life through union with Christ's resurrection. That is what we are now anticipating through our faith-bond with him by the power of the Holy Spirit. So it seems to me that rather than the term "metaphorical," it would be better to use the words "revelatory" and "anticipatory" to describe the way Christians should live in this age, empowered by and maturing through the work of the Spirit.

The risen Christ in glory is the referent *now* for the community of his disciples, and only as a consequence of that does the community of the faithful work out its salvation together with fear and trembling in "practical holiness and service." The latter is not a metaphor of a future exit from the grave but evidence of the way God's sixth-day human creatures are literally being restored by Christ to the responsibilities they should always have been exercising in this age as they store up treasures in heaven in

4. Wright, *Resurrection*, 253.

5. Wright, *Resurrection*, 255.

anticipation of fulfillment in God's sabbath with creation. In faith-union with Christ, we can now live joyfully, lovingly, thankfully, and with perseverance as God's earthly stewards because we understand by faith that all of life on earth will be fulfilled in the age to come. To be alive in Christ by faith means that believers may and must learn the habits of repentance, turning from sin back to the path of right living exemplified by Jesus. Practical holiness and service is not a metaphor but a revelatory exhibition of the work of Christ in and through us to do his good work in all that we do now.

Ridderbos writes, "it is the redemptive-historical transition, effected in Christ's death and resurrection, that is working itself out" in the process of God's transformation of descendants of the first Adam into the fulfilled humanity of the last Adam. "And it all rests on their being-in-him, as the second Adam." This is why Paul can speak of humans as being renewed in accordance with the image of their creator (Col 3:9–17). These are all Adam categories referring to the redeemed being recreated in Christ, the new Adam (Eph 2:10). And, "as they have borne the image of the first (earthly) Adam, so, by virtue of this same corporate relationship, they will bear the image of the last (heavenly) Adam (I Cor. 15)." This corporate unity with Christ so dominates the idea of the "new man," writes Ridderbos, that believers, as the one body of Christ, can be called "the one new man" (Eph 2:15). Paul can say of them together—as one community or body—that they "will be permitted to attain to 'the perfect man,' the mature man in Christ (Eph 4:13)."[6]

IN CHRIST, BY FAITH, HOPE, AND LOVE

With regard to the "now" of life in this age, Ridderbos urges us to take note of the way "Paul alternates the expressions 'in Christ' and 'in the Spirit' with 'in the faith' or 'by faith.'" What in one place "is called living, walking, standing in Christ (Rom 6:11; Col 2:6; Phil 4:1; 1 Thess 3:8), and elsewhere living, walking, in or by the Spirit (Gal 5:25; Rom 8:4), can also be called living, walking, standing in or by faith (Gal 2:20; 2 Cor 5:7; Rom 11:20; 1 Cor 16:13; 2 Cor 1:24). In another place, to walk in Christ signifies the same thing as to be established in the faith (Col 2:6, 7); the comfort of the apostle through the faith of the church finds its ground in the fact that they stand in the Lord (1 Thess 3:7, 8)."[7] To live, walk, and stand in Christ now by the power of the Spirit means growing in the understanding of our corporate identity in him. The "in" and "with" does not mean for Paul some kind of mystical experience or simply a way of speaking about a personal awareness of Christ's presence, encouragement, and friendship.

The "corporate" language depends very much on Paul's contrast between the first Adam and the last Adam. Paul speaks of humans as bearing the likeness of the first Adam—earthy, natural creatures (1 Cor 15:49)—and also as being dead in Adam

6. Ridderbos, *Paul*, 64, and for more on "incorporation" see 207–14, 399–406.

7. Ridderbos, *Paul*, 233.

through the sin that marks them all (1 Cor 15:22; Rom 5:12). In a similar and parallel way, he speaks of those living by faith in Christ as having been buried and raised with him and of bearing the likeness of the last Adam in whom they will be raised to a new mode of spiritual, heavenly existence (1 Cor 15:42–49). Paul draws a contrast between what we might call two corporate representatives. But in this case, the word "representative" means something more profound than when we speak of a legislative representative or someone who represents an organization. "Adam" stands for all of humankind; we are all Adamic, children of the first Adam. The "last Adam" stands for the whole family of the redeemed. The first Adam (and all humans) is mortal, natural, and, because of sin, unrighteous and alienated from God. The last Adam (and all who belong to him) is, in his resurrected and ascended life, immortal, spiritual, and righteous. Therefore, if we live, walk, and stand in Christ, we become one with him through faith even as we continue to live as mortal creatures. Incorporation into Christ by faith will become face-to-face communion in the resurrection mode of existence. When we were born, we began life in the human family, bearing all the characteristic marks of the generations of humankind. To enter the family of Christ Jesus, we must be born again, not by entering our mother's womb a second time but by faith, leading to habits of repentance and a redeemed life. All who are born again in Christ Jesus are last-Adam people.

Closely connected to *faith*, as a characteristic of life in this age, is *hope*. As Hebrews puts it, "Now faith is the assurance of things hoped for, the conviction of things not seen" (Heb 11:1). Paul says, it is in the hope of the redemption of our bodies that "we were saved. Now hope that is seen is not hope. For who hopes for what is seen? But if we hope for what we do not see, we wait for it with patience" (Rom 8:24–25). Living with hope should characterize the entire life of Christians, and we are able to have such hope because the "first fruits of the Spirit" have already been given to us (Rom 8:23). We do not yet see the fulfillment that is still to come, for we have not yet experienced our resurrection; but through faith and hope we know that God by the Spirit has already joined us to Christ's death and resurrection. And if we "hold firm the confidence and the pride that belong to hope," says Hebrews, we will discover that we are, in fact, being built into the very house of God, incorporated into the body of Christ (Heb 3:6).

It is with regard to hope that Moltmann has made one of his most distinctive contributions. "Faith binds man to Christ," he writes. "Hope sets this faith open to the comprehensive future of Christ. Hope is therefore the 'inseparable companion' of faith." And "faith is the foundation upon which hope rests, hope nourishes and sustains faith."[8] Paul and Peter speak of our sufferings as sharing in Christ's sufferings (Rom 8:15; 1 Pet 4:13), yet even in their suffering, they could rejoice in joy of the Lord. Moltmann relates this to the meaning of Christian hope. If we can only hope for what we do not have, doesn't that cheat us out of "the happiness of the present?" No, he

8. Moltmann, *Theology of Hope*, 20.

argues. "How could it do so! For it is itself the happiness of the present. It pronounces the poor blessed, receives the weary and heavy laden, the humbled and wronged, the hungry and the dying, because it perceives the parousia of the kingdom for them." This is why, says Moltmann, "that living without hope is like no longer living."[9]

Rather than thinking like Karl Marx that Christian hope is an opiate that drugs people into a stupor and keeps them from trying to change this world, we should recognize that hope in Christ actually motivates life now in anticipation of its eschatological fulfillment. "The hope that is continually led on further by the promise of God," writes Moltmann, "reveals all thinking in history to be eschatologically oriented and eschatologically stamped as provisional."[10] That is why our labors are not in vain, because their provisional nature points ahead to their fulfillment. That was the confidence Moses expressed in Psalm 90:17: even though our earthly lives are like grass that grows and then fades away, we count on God to "establish the work of our hands."

Finally, as we know so well from Paul, it is *love* that should most deeply characterize the faithful in Christ. In fact, faith and hope will no longer be needed when all things are filled full, but love will endure forever (1 Cor 13:13). We might say that God's love in Christ, which engenders our love, is the glue that binds together this age and the coming age of God's seven-day creation. Love is God's covenant bond with creation through the Son whom God loves. Love is the oil of gladness that flows in and through Christ's bond with us and our bond with one another. Love is the driving force of the covenantal, redemptive-historical drama. God's love in Christ holds on to his own throughout the "not yet" of this age and carries them in the bond of Christ's "already" into the consummation of the entire creation.

BAPTISM AND THE SPIRIT

A final point of entry into the covenantal bond of incorporation in Christ is the New Testament's teaching of baptism into Christ by the Spirit.

In Romans 6, Paul speaks of the baptism of believers into Christ's death, which entails their dying to sin. "Baptism," writes Gaffin, "is 'into Christ' (cf. Gal 3:27); that is, baptism signifies union with Christ . . . Hence baptism into Christ means union with him in his death" (Rom. 6:3–5).[11] Yet Christ did not stay in the grave; consequently, baptism also means union with him in his resurrection *from the dead* to the new mode of imperishable life. Consequently, baptism encompasses the entire transition from this age to the coming age, from the earthly mode of first-Adam existence to the new mode of imperishable, last-Adam existence, from sin and death to life eternal. This

---

9. Moltmann, *Theology of Hope*, 32.

10. Moltmann, *Theology of Hope*, 33.

11. Gaffin, *Resurrection and Redemption*, 45. For more on baptism and the Lord's Supper, see Ridderbos, *Paul*, 396–428. On the relation of the covenant signs of circumcision and baptism, see the in-depth study by Kline, *By Oath Consigned*.

is so because baptism into Christ locates believers within God's covenantal embrace of the entire creation. Being in Christ, according to Ridderbos, does not refer to "a communion that becomes reality only in certain sublime moments, but rather of an abiding reality determinative for the whole of the Christian life, to which appeal can be made at all times, in all sorts of connections, and with respect to the whole church without distinction."[12] It is the death and resurrection of Christ to which we are joined by faith that Paul refers to repeatedly when he speaks of baptism. Being incorporated into Christ, says Ridderbos, means being baptized into "the life-context represented by Christ as the last Adam," and thus into the fulfillment of all things.[13]

With reference to Paul's metaphor of the resurrection "harvest" (1 Cor 15:20–23), of which Christ is the firstfruits followed by those who belong to him when he returns, Gaffin underlines the connection "between Christ as firstfruits and Christ as life-giving Spirit. Since Christ's resurrection is the indispensable foundation for others to share in resurrection life, he functions as life-giving Spirit only on the basis of his resurrection, only in his resurrected state. Specifically the resurrected Christ is the life-giving Christ."[14] There are several references in the New Testament, particularly in Paul, that connect baptism with the "bestowal" and "sealing" of the Spirit. This connection, says Ridderbos, "does not consist specifically in an incidental outpouring of the unusual gifts of the Spirit," but to the transition into the new life of Christ. God has anointed us, set his seal of ownership on us, and "put his Spirit in our hearts as a deposit, guaranteeing what is to come" (2 Cor 1:21–22). Having heard the word of truth and having believed, Paul tells the Ephesians, "you were marked with the seal of the promised Holy Spirit; this is the pledge of our inheritance toward redemption as God's own people, to the praise of his glory" (Eph 1:13, 14).[15]

In the "already" and the "not yet" of God's revelation in Christ, we see the same dynamics at work as in the relation of the first Adam to the last Adam. Both of these, I have argued, presuppose the seven-day order of God's creation, which exists in and through Christ. The drama of God's covenantal disclosure of reality unfolds in our experience through the course of history, the history of the human generations. That history is related in all respects, at all points, and in all times to God the creator, judge, and redeemer of creation. That drama, which may present us with apparent paradoxes, such as the simultaneous "already and not yet," needs to be understood on its own terms. When the Son of God takes on the flesh of the first Adam and atones for the sins of the world through death on a cross, and is then raised to the

---

12. Ridderbos, *Paul*, 59.

13. Ridderbos, *Paul*, 207.

14. Gaffin, *Resurrection and Redemption*, 88.

15. Ridderbos, *Paul*, 400–1. "We must conclude," writes Ridderbos, "that to have died and been buried with Christ neither comes about in baptism in the sense of the mystery theology, nor becomes an actual occurrence in baptism in the sense of the doctrine of contemporaneity, but that dying with Christ has been given with incorporation into Christ, and is thus appropriated to the one baptized as a given reality by baptism as the rite of incorporation." Ridderbos, *Paul*, 408–9.

new mode of existence of the last Adam, we are enveloped in a mystery that cannot be fathomed from the standpoint of our present mode of existence. For God's new covenant in Christ is not just one more historical covenant; it is the covenant that sums up and fulfills all the times of God's covenantal dealings with humankind and the whole creation.

The reality of Christ's life, death, resurrection, and ascension cannot be adequately captured by the temporal categories of human thought and speech. From the viewpoint of Christ's resurrection, we may speak of "already." But from the viewpoint of our life in this age, and the unfolding of the generations of the first Adam, we must say "not yet." Instead of trying to resolve the apparent paradox in a way that fits temporal categories, we should accept the reality of God's creation order, which is not grounded in time but instead establishes time. The mystery of creation and God's relation to it did not pose problems for the biblical writers. The language of "resurrection harvest," "incorporation," a "seed planted," the "splendor of perishable bodies," "death being swallowed up in victory," and many other words, phrases, and arguments are sufficient to convey what Paul calls "the mystery." That mystery is now being unveiled, though we still understand it only in part and see it only through a glass darkly. We do not yet know as we are known. We have not yet entered (become) the heavenly tent. We have not yet put on the clothing of our heavenly dwelling. What remains mysterious need not deter us, for we live now by faith and hope through which to rest in the Lord while concentrating on loving one another.

PART 6

Israel and the New Covenant

24

A New Covenant God Will Make

ISRAEL AND THE COVENANTS

IN JEREMIAH WE READ, "The days are surely coming, says the Lord, when I will make a new covenant with the house of Israel and the house of Judah" (Jer 31:31). How does that divine promise relate to the original covenant God made with Israel? If Jesus is the embodiment of that new covenant, as Christians believe, how does that fulfill God's promise to "the house of Israel and the house of Judah"?

In this chapter, we introduce the argument that will be developed in the next three chapters that God's covenants with Noah, Abraham, Israel, and David build on one another in a revelatory unfolding process that anticipates the new covenant promised by God in Jeremiah. Our approach is different from those who assume that the new covenant displaces the ones that preceded it. Instead, it assumes that the earlier covenants, including God's covenant with Israel, continue, even now, to bear witness to, and anticipate the fulfillment of, the new covenant God promised to make with Israel and Judah.[1] To understand this, we need to recognize, in biblical terms, that even today God's new-covenant promises have not yet been entirely fulfilled. Messiah Jesus has come but has not yet returned. God's kingdom has not yet been fully unveiled. In the new covenant that God promised through Jeremiah, no one will any longer need to teach one's neighbor to know the Lord, because "they shall all know me, from the least of them to the greatest" (Jer 31:34). That promise also has not yet been fully realized. Thus, we need to look again at how the new covenant is related to the earlier covenants.

God's covenants with Abraham on through to David entailed many promises that would be fulfilled in the future, along the way. Think, for example, of God's promise

---

1. In part, I am drawing here on the idea introduced by Elmer Martens that a comprehensive biblical theology should speak of "cumulative revelation" rather than "progressive revelation." Martens says, this approach "leaves in place all disclosures as constitutive in some way of the 'total revelation.'" Martens, "Reaching," 93–94.

to Abraham that through his seed all nations would be blessed (Gen 12:2–3; 18:18; 22:18; 26:4; 28:14). That was before any child had been born to Abraham and Sarah. Moreover, the same promise was repeated to Isaac and Jacob. There is great mystery here, yet the pattern of promise and anticipated fulfillment is clear. The covenants with Abraham, Isaac, and Jacob looked ahead to the time when God would fulfill those promises to them and their offspring. We also know from the prophets that many of God's promises, which included curses as well as blessings, have been fulfilled while many others have not yet come to pass. That is why the questions that arise in almost every discussion of God's covenants, old and new, tend to focus on the timing and the meaning of their fulfillment. For example, God promised to establish David's throne forever and to restore Israel and Judah to right standing with God, yet it does not appear today that a son of David sits on a throne of Israel or that Israel and Judah have been fully restored to righteousness before God.

If we are to believe what is written in the Old and New Testaments, therefore, we must struggle with the question of when and how God fulfilled, is fulfilling, or will fulfill the covenant promises to Israel. If Jesus is the promised Messiah through whom God is establishing the new covenant, how does (how will) that new covenant reach fulfillment? Recall the final conversation that the risen Jesus had with his disciples before ascending to heaven (Acts 1:1–8). They asked him, "Lord, is this the time when you will restore the kingdom to Israel?" (v. 6). Jesus did not reject their question as irrelevant to his mission. He told them it was not for them to know the times and dates God sets, but "you will receive power when the Holy Spirit has come upon you; and you will be my witnesses in Jerusalem, in all Judea and Samaria, and to the ends of the earth" (vv. 7–8). The disciples's question to Jesus is still awaiting a final answer. The dates of fulfillment are for God to decide. So again we ask, how are God's covenants with Noah, Abraham, Isaac, Jacob, and David related to Jesus?

Ben Witherington draws together in the following way some of the questions we've been raising. When Paul says in Romans 9:6 that "not all who are descended from Israel are Israel," he "does not speak of a 'new Israel,' nor does he speak of the *replacement* of one Israel by another here. His argument is about the way the one true people of God have developed through history. He does, however, redefine who the people of God are, countering both popular Jewish notions about the claim Jews had on God because of their physical descent . . . but at the same time countering attitudes that some Gentile Roman Christians seem to have had that suggested that Gentiles had replaced Jews as God's chosen people (11:19)."[2] How does Paul understand the relation of Israel to Christ and his disciples? How can God remain faithful to Israel and at the same time do something so new, so final and climactic, that it redefines the people of God?

---

2. Witherington, *Jesus, Paul*, 116.

CREATION, ELECTION, AND COVENANT PROMISES

To get our bearings, look with me for a moment at the Bible's opening chapters together with the openings of John's Gospel, Hebrews, and Colossians. For we cannot grasp the meaning of God's covenant with Israel and its relation to the revelation of Messiah Jesus apart from God's creation purposes. According to the biblical witness, all things have been created through the Son of God who became flesh in Jesus Christ. All things hold together in him (John 1:1–4; Col 1:15–20; Heb 1:1–3). God's creation order and purposes stand at the foundation of all the judgment-redemption covenants of the Old Testament and the New. "Part of the point of covenant renewal," writes N. T. Wright in reference to Paul's letters, "is that this was God's intended way of renewing creation itself; this is the larger framework of thought within which Paul is operating."[3]

In the Genesis account of creation, we can recognize an originating covenant[4] in the sense that it is God's bond with the creation, which includes the terms of God's commissioning of Adam and Eve to serve as the stewards, rulers, prophets, and priests in creation. Humans are appointed to love and walk with God throughout their generations, exercising the responsibilities God has given them. The orientation of their lives and the whole creation moves toward the praise of God whose sabbath blessing will be their inheritance when all has been fulfilled in righteousness (see Heb 4:1–12). In their disobedience, however, the human generations have become estranged from God and subject to the curse of death rather than becoming joyful stewards and recipients of God's blessings. Yet God does not immediately carry out the full penalty of death (Gen 3), which would have cut off the unfolding generations of humankind. Instead, God mercifully upholds the human generations in order to bring the creation to fulfillment (Gen 3:21–24).

The great flood-judgment (Gen 6–8) nearly accomplished God's curse of death on unrighteous humanity, but in the act of saving the righteous man Noah (a second Adam), God establishes a creation-renewal covenant with him, promising new blessings for the continuation of humankind's earthly stewardship and the creation's continued fruitfulness (Gen 9:8–17). God's election of Noah and his generation makes possible a fresh start in the exercise of human responsibility in accord with the original creation covenant (Gen 9:1–7). This again opens the way for the human generations to anticipate fulfillment in God's consummation of creation. Nevertheless, the disobedience of Adam has not yet been overcome, and the generations of Noah soon show themselves to be as unfaithful to God as the earlier generations were.

In God's covenants with Abram/Abraham we see the next "calling out" (election) of a representative from among the nations, but this time it does not go hand-in-hand with the destruction of all others, as when God saved only Noah. God's purpose in

---

3. Wright, *Resurrection*, 303. See also Wright's *Climax*, 17–40.

4. See particularly Hahn, *Kinship by Covenant*, 95; Wright, *Paul in Fresh Perspective*, 21–39; Dumbrell, *Covenant and Creation*; and Robertson, *Christ and Covenants*.

electing Abram is again to create a people—a great nation—marked by trust in God and serving as a channel of God's blessing to all nations on earth (Gen 12:1–3; Ps 47).[5] God's election of Abraham forces the next question: what now comes of God's earlier promises to Noah for all of humanity, including those not in the line of Abraham? Abraham is clearly a son of Noah, not a replacement for Noah. God's covenant with Abraham builds on the Noachian covenant, which was a reaffirmation of God's faithfulness to the creation as a whole. The Abrahamic covenant does not abrogate either the Noachian or the Adamic covenants, but builds on them as part of God's continuing judgment and redemption of creation and blessing of the nations (see Isa 54:9).

From the seed of Abraham only Isaac is elected for God's covenantal line, but that does not mean God's covenant with Abraham is abrogated when Isaac is born or that all who are not of Isaac are damned for all eternity. Ishmael, too, is protected and blessed by God (Gen 21:8–21). Then, from the seed of Isaac, only Jacob (Israel) is chosen. Yet that does not mean the elimination of Esau from God's purposes for Israel and the nations. Nor does it mean that God's covenant with Isaac is superseded when Jacob is elected. All too soon the children of Israel find themselves enslaved in Egypt, and when God liberates them from captivity, he sets them up as a nation whose covenant elaborates the true way of life for the redeemed, which is to shine as a light for all nations. As Wright puts it, "Israel is to be God's royal nation of holy priests, chosen out of the world but also for the sake of the world. Israel is to be the light of the world: the nations will see in Israel what it means to be truly human, and hence who the true God is. For this purpose, Israel is given Torah."[6] In choosing Israel to be his people, God remains true to—and continues to fulfill promises made to—Isaac, Abraham, Noah, and Adam.

These revelatory covenants do not answer all the questions we might ask about God's ultimate disposition of every individual person. The election of Jacob and not Esau does not imply that every child of Esau is bound for hell for all eternity and that every child of Jacob is saved for eternity. That is not what this covenantal history is all about. God's election of Abraham does not imply that every person outside Abraham's bloodline is condemned to inherit God's wrath for all eternity. Stanley Stowers offers a helpful comment in this regard. "Paul's point [in Romans 9] is not that Ishmael and Esau were damned. They were not. Rather, Isaac and Jacob were made instruments 'so that God's purpose of election might continue' (9:11) . . . Thus chapter 9 tells us that one cannot find membership in a lineage by works. Rather, God decides on the lines of descent, and membership in the lineage comes by birth."[7] There is much about God's election of covenant partners that remains a mystery to us. Yet the Scriptures are clear

---

5. To understand the meaning of God's covenants, it is necessary to grasp the generational and kinship character of the relation God establishes with figures such as Noah and Abraham. Hahn explains this in systematic detail in his *Kinship by Covenant*.

6. Wright, *Paul in Fresh Perspective*, 109.

7. Stowers, *Rereading of Romans*, 301.

that God's election of Israel had in view other nations, the whole creation, and the revelation of God's glory above all (see, for example, Isa 34–35 and Jer 46–51).

In the wilderness after the exodus and in the promised land, Israel showed that despite God's special covenant with them, they too continued in the line of sinful Adam and Noah. Part of the Sinai covenant is God's promised curses as well as blessings of the chosen people, depending on how they responded to God's will for them (Deut 6–8; Lev 26:1–46; Josh 23:14–16; Pss 50; 78; Isa 1:27–28; Jer 16:10–15; 17:5–8). After God's judgment of Israel by the Assyrians, only Judah and Benjamin were spared for a time. In other words, even before the exile of Judah, not all of Israel continued as "Israel"; God kept only Judah and Benjamin in the land. Judah was not all of Israel, nor was Israel all of humanity, but each was chosen for the sake of God's acts of judging, saving, and consummating creation to reveal the glory of God. The Jews as descendants from Israel continue to bear the marks of God's special covenant with Israel (as Paul emphasizes in Rom 9:4–5). But the full meaning of God's faithfulness to that covenant has included judgment of Israel's covenant-breaking disobedience.

Again and again, God's faithfulness to the covenants with Abraham on through Israel at Sinai is evident in the cutting off of some and in the saving of a remnant in fulfillment of God's promises. Covenant history unfolds historically under God's protection and judgment, under God's blessings and curses. Moreover, God's covenants with Abraham, Isaac, and Jacob point with promise to a consummation of creation beyond this age and not only to certain future events in this age (see for example Isa 54–58). Therefore, God's covenant with Israel continues to bear witness to that which God has been doing and will continue to do in fulfillment of it. It stands as a living witness to the new covenant that God will make with the houses of Israel and Judah.

In Jacob's dream, he caught a glimpse of the divine throne room (Gen 28:10–22). When God met with Moses, the glory of the Lord was so great that Moses was not allowed to see God's face (Exod 33:12–23), and, thereafter, Moses had to wear a veil in the presence of the people because his own face was so radiant (Exod 34:29–35). God called Moses to lead Israel out of Egypt and into the promised land, yet God did not allow Moses to enter the land. Moses saw it only from a distance (Deut 32:48–52). What he saw and had come to expect of God was more than the promised land could ever deliver (Heb 3:1–6).[8] Even in building the temple, which David was not allowed to build, Solomon was aware that it could not truly contain God. "Even heaven and the highest heaven cannot contain you [Lord], much less this house that I have built" (1 Kgs 8:27). When the Lord blessed Solomon and promised to "establish your royal throne over Israel forever, as I promised your father David, saying, 'There shall not fail you a successor on the throne of Israel'" (1 Kgs 9:5), we again hear the promise of an eternity. But within several generations, the kings of both Israel and Judah are

---

8. Paul's contrast (in 2 Cor 3:7–18) of the glory of the Sinai covenant reflected in Moses' face with the greater glory of the new covenant in Christ adds weight to our judgment here. See the interpretations of this passage by Wright, *Climax*, 175–92, and Witherington, *Jesus, Paul*, 109–11.

destroyed or taken captive, and Israel and then Judah are driven into exile. The reason for God's judgment against Israel is offered in God's pledge to Solomon: "If you turn aside from following me, you or your children, and do not keep my commandments and my statutes that I have set before you, but go and serve other gods and worship them, then I will cut Israel off from the land that I have given them; and the house that I have consecrated for my name I will cast out of my sight; and Israel will become a proverb and a taunt among all peoples" (1 Kgs 9:6–7).

Nonetheless, God's promise to restore a remnant and to establish David's kingdom forever still rings out from the Psalms and the Prophets. God's ways are not our ways and they reach beyond the confines of our earthly generations. It is not for us to know "the times or periods that the Father has set by his own authority" (Acts 1:7). The future king that God promised through the prophets will be more than any human king could ever be: "May he live while the sun endures, and as long as the moon, throughout all generations . . . May he have dominion from sea to sea, and from the River to the ends of the earth . . . May all kings fall down before him, all nations give him service" (Ps 72:5, 8, 11). Isaiah, called by God to announce judgment upon Israel, also holds out the hope of an heir of David who will save his people. "His authority shall grow continually, and there shall be endless peace for the throne of David and his kingdom. He will establish and uphold it with justice and with righteousness from this time onward and forevermore. The zeal of the Lord of hosts will do this" (Isa 9:7). In the midst of Jeremiah's prophecies of judgment on the nations, including Judah and Jerusalem, the Lord swears on his "covenant with the day and my covenant with the night" (Jer 33:20): "The days are surely coming, says the Lord, when I will fulfill the promise I made to the house of Israel and the house of Judah. In those days and at that time I will cause a righteous Branch to spring up for David; and he shall execute justice and righteousness in the land. In those days Judah will be saved and Jerusalem will live in safety. And this is the name by which it will be called: 'The Lord is our righteousness'" (Jer 33:14–16). Just as God assured Abraham and Sarah, who were well past the childbearing age, that they would have a son (Gen 18:10–14), so too God sees through and beyond the desolation of Israel and the destruction of throne and temple to the fulfillment of covenant promises made long ago to those chosen from among the nations.

According to the New Testament witness, God's covenant in Christ is the new covenant prophesied by Jeremiah and Ezekiel. It is also clear that the new covenant builds on and fulfills the old; it does not discard the old as irrelevant to the new. Even after the coming of Jesus and his death and resurrection, the end has not yet come. Paul and the other apostles of Messiah Jesus, just like Abraham, Moses, David, Solomon, Isaiah, and Jeremiah, saw with eyes of faith something that is still not yet complete, something that in its fullness transcends the time and scope of both genealogical and historical possibilities (see Heb 11).

The revelation of Jesus as Israel's Messiah, the seed of Abraham through whom all nations will be blessed, began with his incarnation, death, resurrection, and ascension. But the fullness of God's promised new covenant has not yet been disclosed. Jesus has not yet returned. The climactic fulfillment of the revelation of the glory of God is still something we anticipate by faith. And all the while, the testimony of God's creation order, the rainbow sign to Noah, God's covenant promises to Abraham and the children of Israel, and the promise that David's throne will endure forever—all of these continue to bear testimony to God's covenant faithfulness, which now, in Christ Jesus, is approaching fulfillment.

25

Supersession or No?

ISRAEL AND THE CHURCH

THE GOSPELS AND OTHER writings of the New Testament profess that Jesus is the Messiah of Israel, son of David, son of Abraham (Matt 1:1).[1] John the Baptist heralds the Messiah's coming (Mark 1:1–12; John 1:6–9). Luke emphasizes that the line of Jesus goes back not only through Israel to Abraham but also through Shem to Noah and Adam (Luke 3:23–38). John's Gospel reaches back even before and beyond Adam, declaring Jesus to be word of God through whom all things were created (John 1:1–5). The Letter to the Hebrews begins much the same way as John's Gospel, professing that Jesus Christ is the mediator of both the creation and a *new covenant*, the climactic and eternal covenant that both underlies and fulfills God's covenant with Israel (Heb 1:1–3; 7:17–28; 8:1–13). Paul proclaims Jesus Christ to be the last Adam (1 Cor 15:45) and the one through whom God's promise of blessing to all nations is being fulfilled (Eph 2:11–22; Gal 3:6–9). Jesus is identified as the suffering servant foretold by Isaiah (Isa 53), and both the lamb of God who is sacrificed to take away the sins of the world and the great high priest who offers himself as that sacrifice to God (Luke 24:26; Heb 9:26—10:14; 1 Pet 2:21–25; Rev 5:9–14). Through him, the wall between Jews and gentiles has been torn down, reconciling the entire creation to God (Eph 2:14–18; 2 Cor 5:17–21). Finally, Messiah Jesus is the one who, through resurrection from the dead, has become not only the everlasting king of Israel (in David's line) but also thereby the king of the whole world, the one who inaugurates the kingdom of God that brings the creation to fulfillment in God's sabbath rest (Matt 28:18; Phil 2:5–11; Heb 1:3; 4:1–11).

Can one draw from this brief summary the conclusion that, after the coming of Jesus, the Christian church takes the place of—or supersedes historically—Israel as God's chosen people? In the light of these Scriptures, how are we to understand the relation of Jesus Christ to God's covenant with Israel? In Christian circles for most of the past 2,000 years, the chief arguments about this have revolved around the *already*

1. For a good overview of the relation of Jesus to Israel and to Israel's messianic expectations, see Wright, *Knowing Jesus.*

and the *not yet* of God's coming kingdom. Christ has already come but he has not yet returned, as promised. Were God's covenants with Israel fulfilled completely with Christ's first coming, or will they be fulfilled only after Christ's second coming and the culminating revelation of God's kingdom? Is the church now, already, God's newly chosen people, or will God reveal the chosen people in its entirety only after Christ returns? Is it biblical to believe that God continues to uphold the covenant with Israel alongside the new covenant in Christ, or are the Jews now properly related to God only through the church?

From early in the church's history, most of its authorities have argued that the death, resurrection, and ascension of Jesus brought an end to God's covenant with Israel. In other words, the church, historically speaking, *superseded* Israel because God's covenant with Israel culminated in Christ who became the head of a new people of God, the church.[2] The history of this age, from that point of view, is divided into a "before" and "after": before the coming of Jesus, God's saving work was revealed through Israel; after Christ's coming, God's work of salvation comes through the church. God, in other words, has made a *new covenant,* which establishes the church and supersedes the old covenant with Israel.

One consequence of the commitment to *supersessionism,* though not a necessary one, has been the long history of anti-Semitism and persecution of the Jews. Recently, however, largely motivated by the horrors of the Holocaust, there has been a significant revision of judgment by a number of church bodies, calling for repentance from anti-Semitism. In support of those calls for repentance, a number of theologians and ethicists have developed systematic criticisms of supersessionism as well as some new interpretations of the relevant biblical texts.[3]

One of the contemporary anti-supersessionists is R. Kendall Soulen who summarizes the supersessionist argument as follows: "God chose the Jewish people after the fall of Adam in order to prepare the world for the coming of Jesus Christ, the Savior. After Christ came, however, the special role of the Jewish people came to an end and its place was taken by the church, the new Israel."[4] Building on the work of Michael

2. For background on the formation of supersessionist doctrine in the ancient church, see Fredriksen, *Augustine and Jews,* and Carroll, *Constantine's Sword.* For brief introductions to medieval, Reformation-era, and more recent supersessionist thinking, see Bader-Saye, *Church and Israel,* 70–80, and Soulen, *God of Israel,* 25–106. Note also, Pak, "A Break," 7–28.

3. The literature of anti-supersessionist (or nonsupersessionist) thinking is by now quite extensive. For an introduction, see Kinzer, *Post-Missionary Messianic Judaism*; Harink, *Paul Among Postliberals*; Yoder, *Jewish-Christian Schism*; Bader-Saye, *Church and Israel*; Holwerda, *Jesus and Israel*; Stowers, *Rereading of Romans*; and Rosenberg, *Christian Problem.*

4. Soulen, *God of Israel,* 1–2. Harink argues that N. T. Wright is a supersessionist because "Wright's entire project" is built on the "conviction that in Jesus Christ 'the promises of Israel's restoration had in fact been fulfilled.'" Harink, *Paul Among Postliberals,* 154. Harink, however, retains a historically restricted perspective that hinders attention to the eschatological (history-transcending) meaning of Christ's death and resurrection in the way Paul explains it. Thus throughout his evaluation of Wright (153–84), Harink locates everything Wright says in "a linear 'covenant-historical' narrative in which he says for Wright there is a divinely driven linear movement from Israel, to Christ, to the church, in

Wyschogrod and Charles Wood, among others, Soulen argues that supersessionism is incompatible with a truly Christian theology. Instead, "Christians should acknowledge that God's history with Israel and the nations is the permanent and enduring medium of God's work as the Consummator of human creation, and therefore it is also the permanent and enduring context of the gospel about Jesus."[5] Robert Jenson agrees: "Israel *must* continue separately from the church, precisely from the church's point of view."[6]

The mistake of the church, as Soulen sees it, has been to interpret "redemption in Christ as deliverance from God's history with Israel and the nations."[7] Instead, he believes, the faithful in Christ are not saved by a deliverance from God's history with Israel and the nations but are saved by participation through Israel in God's consummation of the creation.[8] The whole of history since God's covenant with Israel, including the coming of Christ and Christian history, is encompassed by "the permanent and enduring medium" of God's covenant with Israel. For Soulen, the "hermeneutical center of the Scriptures" is not Jesus Christ but "the God of Israel's eschatological reign, conceived as the final outcome of God's work as the One who consummates the human family in and through God's history with Israel and the nations."[9] Christ comes later in history to gather gentiles into God's consummating purposes for Israel and the whole human family.[10]

Scott Bader-Saye also understands God's covenant with Israel to be the foundational and enduring expression of God's covenant faithfulness. He writes, "neither the Jews of Israel's Scripture nor the Jews today need Jesus in order to trust that God will be faithful to God's promises. The irrevocability of the covenant [with Israel] is the abiding assurance of God's election, which is eternal and unconditional."[11] "There can be no separation of God's reign from the people whom God has chosen to embody it," Bader-Saye writes. "When seen in this light, Israel's constitution as the elect people of God becomes the church's principal political claim."[12] After quoting from Jeremiah 31:35–37, where God promises to establish a new covenant with Israel, Bader-Saye writes, "God's faithfulness to Israel is as solid as creation itself, and God's rejection

---

which historical Israel's role after Christ simply ceases to be of any theological significance." Harink, *Paul Among Postliberals*, 161. This is a partial misunderstanding of Wright. Harink's historicist reductionism misses Wright's more-than-historical understanding of the incarnation, death, resurrection, and promised return of Christ.

5. Soulen, *God of Israel*, 110. Wyschogrod's major work is *Body of Faith*. Wood's book is *The Formation*.

6. Jenson, "Toward a Christian Doctrine," 3.

7. Soulen, *God of Israel*, 110.

8. Soulen, *God of Israel*, 112.

9. Soulen, *God of Israel*, 113.

10. Soulen, *God of Israel*, 110.

11. Bader-Saye, *Church and Israel*, 82.

12. Bader-Saye, *Church and Israel*, 94.

of Israel is as impossible as the measuring of the heavens."[13] The way in which Christ functions for Bader-Saye and Soelen, therefore, is as the mediator to the gentiles of God's covenant with Israel.

The argument of the anti-supersessionists that we have summarized thus far is, like the supersessionist argument, very much historically linear, the starting point of which is God's covenant with Israel. For this reason it seems to me that Soulen, Bader-Saye, and others not only miss what preceded God's covenant with Israel, but also underestimate the trans-historical orientation of the New Testament proclamation of God's covenant in Christ. In order to avoid any slippage into historical supersessionism, Bader-Saye feels compelled to treat references to a "new" covenant in the New Testament as essentially the promised historical consummation of God's covenant with Israel. In that regard, he is even ready to reject parts of the New Testament that he believes teach supersessionism. The language of "new covenant" appears frequently in Hebrews (Heb 8:8, 13; 9:15; 12:24), he writes, and for that reason, by implication, the letter is deficient. Unlike Paul's reading of Jeremiah 31, Hebrews uses this language in a deeply supersessionistic way, according to Bader-Saye. The author of the letter speaks of Jesus' bringing a "better covenant" (Heb 7:22, 8:6). The letter continues, "In speaking of 'a new covenant,' he has made the first one obsolete. And what is obsolete and growing old will soon disappear" (Heb 8:13).[14] Despite this "misunderstanding" evident in Hebrews, Bader-Saye believes Hebrews is otherwise remarkable for what it *does* say about Israel. "For instance, the author makes clear in the invocation of Jeremiah 31 that the 'new covenant' is made with 'the house of Israel' and 'the house of Judah' (8:8). Further, in 11:40 the point of the new covenant is not to undo the promises of God or to call into question the faithfulness of Israel—indeed the whole chapter is a recitation of Israel's faithfulness—but rather to proclaim that the fulfillment of God's promises to Israel miraculously awaited the inclusion of the Gentiles (not replacement by the Gentiles)."[15]

Jenson emphasizes more emphatically than some of the other anti-supersessionists the eschatological, trans-historical fulfillment of creation that both Israel and the church are anticipating. "The Eucharist depicted in the book of Revelation in which the tribes of Israel lead the gentiles in praise of the Lord will be celebrated only in the

---

13. Bader-Saye, *Church and Israel*, 99.

14. Richard Hays also contends that Hebrews is a supersessionist document and quite different in that respect from the writings of Paul. Hays, *Echoes in Paul*, 98–99. Much of what Hays writes here is relevant to, and largely supportive of, the anti-supersessionist point of view; see especially 87–121. With reference to Heb and 1 Pet, Mark Boda makes a point sympathetic to our argument about the developmental unfolding of revelation. The New Testament, he writes, "teaches the cumulative and progressive character of revelation. After highlighting the revelation of God through the prophets 'long ago,' Heb 1:1–3 is careful to note that 'in these last days' revelation has now come 'in His Son.' Second Peter 1:18–21 speaks of 'the prophetic message *made* more sure.' Revelation must not be treated as all on the same level but rather as what accumulates and progresses in significance as history unfolds." Boda, *Heartbeat*, 163.

15. Bader-Saye, *Church and Israel*, 99–100.

New Jerusalem; the people of God to which the gentiles are gathered must wait for that city."[16] The new covenant in Christ is closely connected to the new Jerusalem, anticipated during this age by faith through the celebration of the Eucharist. In the meantime, during the time between the two comings of Christ, the Jews remain as God's people. "For the church as she is, without the enveloping Jewish matrix, cannot by herself provide God with a *people*. The church in the meantime as she is can only *hope* to be a people, not having in herself the connections of the flesh and the givenness they create."[17]

Why does Jenson elevate Israel's "connections of the flesh" above the bonds of faith in defining the "people of God"? In what sense does the givenness created by Israel's connections of flesh make it more of a people than the community that is being made into the *body* of Christ? To ask it in a somewhat different way, isn't Israel as much a people of promise and faith as it is a people of blood ancestry? Paul tells the Galatian churches, "consider Abraham: 'He believed God, and it was credited to him as righteousness.' Understand, then, that those who believe are children of Abraham. The Scripture foresaw that God would justify the Gentiles by faith, and announced the gospel in advance to Abraham: 'All nations will be blessed through you.' So those who have faith are blessed along with Abraham, the man of faith" (Gal 3:6–9; Gen 15:6; 12:3; 18:18; 22:18). Jenson lays emphasis on the Israel of flesh rather than the children of Abraham by faith, but doesn't God's covenant with Israel follow from God's covenant promises to Abraham and Abraham's response of faith? And doesn't God's covenant with Israel call the people to the same faithfulness and trust in God exhibited by Abraham?

Jenson introduces another difference between Israel and the church with his idea of a detour. "The time of the church," he says, "is a time within the advent of the Christ to fulfill Israel's history." When Jesus came, the messianic expectations were not fulfilled all at once. God instituted the church "by not letting Jesus' Resurrection be itself the End" but instead by "appointing the famous 'delay of the Parousia.'" Consequently, Israel's anticipation of God's messianic kingdom would, from a Christian point of view, have to continue as anticipation until the second coming of Christ. "The straight line route to the Kingdom is broken, and a side trip through the church with its mission is ordained."[18] As Jenson sees it, the church is now a people only insofar as by faith and the sacraments she lives in anticipation of the fulfillment of God's promises to Israel. Even after his resurrection from the dead, Christ "is present to faith and not to sight."[19] "The Lord's return will restore his people to the main road, ending the

---

16. Jensen, "Toward a Christian Doctrine," 16.
17. Jensen, "Toward a Christian Doctrine," 16.
18. Jensen, "Toward a Christian Doctrine," 10–11.
19. Jensen, "Toward a Christian Doctrine," 20.

detour. But that is to say, his return will terminate the separation between the church and Israel according to the flesh."[20]

JÜRGEN MOLTMANN

Moltmann is another of the anti-supersessionists. He believes that "Israel has an enduring 'salvific calling,' parallel to the church of the Gentiles, for God remains true to his election and his promise (Rom. 11.1f.) . . . Christianity is God's 'other community of hope,' parallel to Israel, and over against Israel. Parallel to the people of God [i.e., Israel], [the church] is the missionary and messianic church of the nations. It can therefore only remain true to its own hope if it recognizes Israel as the older community of hope alongside itself."[21] How long do the two communities continue separately alongside one another historically? According to Moltmann, Israel (the Jews today) will not turn to Christ through faith; instead, at the end of history they will be converted, as Paul was, "by seeing Christ." That "seeing" will take place when Christ returns to rule the earth for a millennium. Moltmann reads passages in Revelation to say that the martyrs identified in Revelation 7 as "the hundred and forty-four thousand 'sealed out of every tribe of the sons of Israel'" will be raised from the dead and "joined by 'a great multitude from every nation, from all tribes and peoples and tongues . . . who have come out of the great tribulation' (7.9 and 14)." Those martyrs will constitute an Israel-centered kingdom of Christ on earth—a millennial kingdom that "forms the organic transitional link between the present state of the world and the completion of the world that will one day come about."[22] Israel's "life from the dead" at that point will not be "identical with the eschatological 'resurrection of the dead' on the Last Day, but is in line with the resurrection of Christ from the dead and the resurrection 'from the dead' of those who live and suffer with Christ (Phil 3.11)."[23]

The church, therefore, does not supersede Israel in the course of history, according to Moltmann, and it is a mistake even to think of Christ's millennial reign in ordinary temporal terms. Time itself will be different then. "The whole situation of the world will change. It is therefore wrong to fit the messianic kingdom into calendar time, for that is the time of this transitory world."[24] Yet, in Moltmann's terms, Christ's millennial kingdom that joins Jewish martyrs and gentile Christians together in the service of Christ *by sight* will not be the beginning of the new creation beyond history. Moltmann thus seems to understand the transitional reign of Christ as something that will be neither temporal in the current sense nor supra-temporal in the new-creation sense. What kind of "third thing," then, will it be?

20. Jensen, "Toward a Christian Doctrine," 20.

21. Moltmann, *Coming of God*, 197–98.

22. Moltmann, *Coming of God*, 199.

23. Moltmann, *Coming of God*, 198.

24. Moltmann, *Coming of God*, 199–200.

According to Richard Bauckham, most of Moltmann's writings prior to his book, *The Coming of God,* do not mention the millennium. Why then did he introduce the idea of a millennial, pre-eschatological end of history in his later work? "It seems," writes Bauckham, "that Moltmann now thinks only the millennium, as a this-worldly future prior to the new creation," can supply the motivation for Christian life in this world. "Without millenarian hope," writes Bauckham, quoting Moltmann, "the Christian ethic of resistance and consistent discipleship lose their most powerful motivation."[25] Moreover, as Moltmann sees it, there is a goal in this for Israel, "for whom the millennium represents resurrection and redemption, the fulfillment of the messianic promises . . . The millennium consummates history; the eschaton ends history."[26] For Moltmann, God's covenant with Israel apparently reaches its goal, its consummation, at the end of history prior to the revelation of the new creation.

Of the anti-supersessionists we have considered, Jenson and Moltmann argue for two covenantal tracks through history after the coming of Jesus as a way to maintain Israel's independent covenantal relation to God. For Jenson that means, from a Christian point of view, a historical detour until God fulfills the covenant promises to Israel. The end of that detour will be found in the eschatological consummation. For Moltmann there is no detour, though Israel and the church follow separate covenantal tracks in relation to God. But the end of the separation comes in two stages for Moltmann. The first stage will be the millennial reign of Christ at the end of history with Jewish martyrs raised from the dead to join a company of faithful gentiles. The second stage will be the trans-historical eschatological fulfillment of all peoples in the new creation.

What shall we make of these anti-supersessionist arguments? Must we choose between supersession and anti-supersession, or is there a way to reconcile them or transcend the divide between them?

A DIFFERENT PERSPECTIVE ON THE SUPERSESSIONIST DEBATE

The weight of the biblical testimony, it seems to me, suggests that it is a mistake to take God's covenant with Israel as the starting point for considering God's relation to Israel and the nations. This means, among other things, that we should not confine biblical interpretation within a linear-historical point of view that begins with Israel. There is indeed a historical unfolding of God's covenantal disclosure of reality to and through the sixth-day human generations, and it includes God's covenant with Israel. Yet, historically speaking, God's covenant with Israel is not the beginning of God's covenantal disclosures; the covenant with Israel follows from God's covenant with Abraham that follows after, but does not displace, the Noachian covenant. Moreover, the revelatory drama of God's relation with the human generations, and particularly

25. Bauckham, "Millennium," 135.
26. Bauckham, "Millennium," 139.

the generations of Abraham, Isaac, and Jacob, has always had an orientation toward the fulfillment of God's promises in both the historical future and the transcendent (seventh-day), trans-historical consummation of God's kingdom.

When Jesus was revealed historically as Israel's Messiah, son of David, son of Israel, son of Abraham, he was also proclaimed the Son of God through whom all things are created. And looking forward, we are told that the whole creation will be filled with the glory of God because of Christ. From all of this it is clear that, with Christ's first coming, God did not cancel the preceding covenants and discard Israel to start a second history with the church. I agree with the anti-supersessionists on this point. All of the earlier covenants were and are being confirmed as true and revelatory witnesses to God's covenant faithfulness throughout this age in anticipation of fulfillment. Consequently, God's covenantal commitment to Israel continues to bear witness to God's faithfulness. However—and this is where I want to qualify and break through the linear-historical confinement of much anti-supersessionist thinking— God's covenant with Israel is, at root, dependent on, and a witness to, all that God is doing in and through creation from its foundation to its seventh-day culmination.

Soulen is right to speak of the God of Israel as the consummator of creation, but that consummation will be more than the historical fulfillment of God's covenant promises to Israel. God's relation to Israel is not the beginning and the end of history, though nothing about God's covenant with Israel will go unfulfilled. In that regard, Soulen's criticism of Barth misses the point, it seems to me, when he says, "Despite Barth's exegetically brilliant association of God's consummating work with God's election of Israel, his vision of consummation ultimately collapses into the single person of Jesus Christ, who threatens to absorb all biblical substance into himself."[27] According to the biblical narrative, however, God's covenants do not "collapse" into Christ but are confirmed and fulfilled in him in a trans-historical, seventh-day culmination that is not yet complete. Jesus Christ does not "threaten to absorb all biblical substance into himself" in the sense of discarding and superseding all earlier covenants. Instead, he is disclosing that everything of biblical, covenantal substance from the beginning of creation has born testimony to him and continues to bear testimony to God's faithfulness. God's covenant with Israel has not been abrogated in history with the first coming of Christ but is being validated by Christ in a way that has not yet reached its fulfillment.[28] In the consummation of all things, Christ will not stand alone apart from

27. Soulen, *God of Israel*, 21.

28. The quotation from Heb 8:13, interpreted by Bader-Saye (*Church and Israel*, 99–100) as a demonstration of the supersessionist perspective of Heb, does not at all suggest that to be the case. The entire letter, and particularly the whole of Heb 8, speaks of the contrast between the trans-historical (heavenly) covenant of Christ in contrast to the earthly covenant with Israel. Insofar as the risen Christ has ascended into the "true tabernacle," which the earthly tabernacle imaged, the author speaks of him having made the first covenant "obsolete" but not as a completed historical action at Christ's first coming or upon his ascension. The author of Hebrews completes verse 8:13 with, "what is obsolete and growing old will soon disappear." However long the time period suggested by "soon," it does not indicate the church's displacement of Israel at a point within history. Christ has indeed come, but

all that God invested in the historical covenants, but will unveil the entire company of the resurrected people of God, the new Jerusalem, God's family, the bride of Christ, and his brothers and sisters. That will be the fulfillment of God's covenant with Israel, not the abrogation of it. Yet in the eschatological sense of the biblical language, God's sabbath consummation of creation will fulfill, in a transfiguring way, the whole of God's first six creation days.

The difficult matter of timing, as Jenson helps to explain, is that the appearance of the Messiah in the person of Jesus did not bring about the consummation of all things in a historical moment. The Messiah, he says, has not yet come in such a way "as to complete Israel's story." Or as I would prefer to say, Jesus Christ has not yet finished coming in all the ways the Messiah has been promised to come to consummate the creation in God's kingdom and sabbath rest. Therefore, congregations of the household of Christian faith do not replace the Jews in a historical displacement sense, any more than the Jews replaced Israel, or Israel cut itself off from Abraham, or Abraham superseded God's promises to Noah. As I understand the Scriptures, the supersessionists are mistaken to think that God's covenant bond with Israel lasted only during the period, or dispensation, from Moses to the first coming of Christ. Yet I also believe the anti-supersessionists are mistaken in trying to uphold the validity of God's covenant with Israel by making it the starting point and the "permanent and enduring medium" of, or the "eternal and unconditional" witness to, God's faithfulness through all of history.

Dispensational detours, two-track covenant trajectories, a millennial resurrection from the dead, and the subordination of Christ to a role within God's covenant with Israel are all unnecessary and misleading if we take fully into account the seven-day order of creation and the "already" and the "not yet" of God's kingdom coming. From the expansive perspective being proposed in this book, we can see that God's unfolding covenant revelations in history do not displace one another in sequential supersession. Instead, they keep mounting up and building on one another in a cumulative way as anticipatory witnesses to the fullness that is coming. The culmination of the whole creation in God's seventh-day rest is, and will be, the celebration of all that God has done in covenant faithfulness throughout history. The New Testament's testimony is that the completion of the coming of the resurrected Jesus, the Messiah (Christ), will confirm and consummate all God's covenants with Israel and the nations.

---

the fulfillment of the "new" covenant through him is something the letter speaks of as still to come from the viewpoint of those living in this age by faith. To grasp the force of the letter, one must accept the relation of an "already" recognized through eyes of faith and a "not yet" that can now only be anticipated.

26

Romans 9–11

GOD IS JUST

WE TURN NOW TO the dense argument of the apostle Paul in Romans 9–11 about God's covenant with Israel in relation to which Messiah Jesus has been revealed as the *telos* (end, goal, culmination) of the law (Rom 10:4). The first thing to emphasize is that these three chapters are an integral part of Paul's entire letter to the Romans, and Paul also deals with the same subject in other letters, especially Galatians and Ephesians. In addition, the book of Acts offers many details about Paul's work with Jews and gentiles. So we have a wider New Testament context, not to speak of the Old Testament context, in which to read Romans 9–11.[1]

Paul begins his letter to the Romans with a focus on God's dealings with all nations. God's covenant with Israel is not the beginning of the story of God's creating, judging, and redeeming purposes. Paul makes clear that his mission is to the gentiles (Rom 1:5; 15:15–16). At the same time, he is writing to Christians in Rome as a Jew who has been transformed by the revelation of Jesus, whom he believes is the long-promised Messiah (Christ) of Israel. Jesus is the promised seed of Abraham through whom all nations will be blessed.[2] This is the good news Paul shares with the Romans. "For I am not ashamed of the gospel; it is the power of God for salvation to everyone who has faith: to the Jew first and also to the Greek. For in it the righteousness of God

---

1. On the larger context of Rom 9–11 and its interpretations, see Stowers, *A Rereading of Romans*, 141, 285–329; Witherington, *Jesus, Paul*, 99–128; Wright, *Paul and Faithfulness*, 1043–265; Wright, *Paul in Fresh Perspective*, 108–29; Wright, *Climax*, 231–57; and Aageson, "Typology, Correspondence," 51–72. For an unusual Jewish interpretation of Rom 9–11 that stresses the importance to Paul of the distinction between the natural order and the order of the Spirit (and thus the distinction between Israel of the flesh and the Israel of faith), see Taubes, *Political Theology*, 23–54; 117–42.

2. Wright, as we shall see, emphasizes the priority of God's covenant with Abraham over the covenant with Israel. The former is the foundation of the latter. This, he argues, is the case throughout Paul's epistles. Hahn agrees, saying of Gal 3–4, "in Paul's view of salvation history, the Abrahamic covenant has chronological priority and ontological primacy over the Mosaic." Hahn, *Kinship by Covenant*, 238.

is revealed through faith for faith; as it is written, 'The one who is righteous will live by faith'" (Rom 1:16–17). The good news is that God is now bringing all of history, all the promises of the covenants, and the entire creation to fulfillment in the revelation of God's glory (Rom 5:9–11; 8:14–25, 37–39; 11:36; 13:10–4; 16:25–27).

It is important at the outset to emphasize this *telos* or climax of creation, which has been such a long time in coming. Wright indicates, "There can be no smooth crescendo from the call of Abraham to the new creation. The call of Abraham must be the call of a people through whom God would deal with the evil that had infected the world."[3] Nevertheless, God's dealing with sin and evil through the call of Abraham, the covenant with Israel, and the coming of Jesus is not solely or even primarily to deal with evil. God's condemnation and judgment of disobedience is necessary to redeem and reconcile the creation to God for its fulfillment in the revelation of divine glory. Nonetheless, much of Romans does focus on God's judgment of unrighteousness.

In fact, in the very next verse after Paul announces his mission to the gentiles, he addresses, in the starkest terms, the human predicament, namely, that "the wrath of God is revealed from heaven against all ungodliness and wickedness of those who by their wickedness suppress the truth" (Rom 1:18). Paul's litany of human wickedness is extensive, including acts of judging others for their wickedness while doing evil oneself. The warning extends to everyone, including the Jews, because all are sinners. "There will be anguish and distress for everyone who does evil, the Jew first and also the Greek, but glory and honor and peace for everyone who does good, the Jew first and also the Greek. For God shows no partiality" (Rom 2:9–11). If circumcised Jews "break the law," Paul says, "your circumcision has become uncircumcision." And "if those who are uncircumcised keep the requirements of the law, will not their uncircumcision be regarded as circumcision?" (Rom 2:25–26). The universal, impartial reach of God's righteousness is fundamental for all humanity.

However, if that is true, what advantage is there to being a Jew and practicing circumcision? "Much, in every way." Paul answers. "For in the first place the Jews were entrusted with the oracles of God. What if some were unfaithful? Will their unfaithfulness nullify the faithfulness of God? By no means! Although everyone is a liar, let God be proved true" (Rom 3:1–4). If our unrighteousness brings out God's righteousness more clearly, does that mean God is unjust in bringing his wrath on us? Certainly not! "For then how could God judge the world?" (Rom 3:5–6). Paul emphasizes the unique covenantal status of Israel among the nations, including God's words to them promising curses as well as blessings (see Deut 30:11–20). In a few quick sentences, Paul seems to have turned from his affirmation of the Jewish advantage back to the reaffirmation of equality of all people in face of God's righteousness. "What then?" he asks. Are Jews any better off? "No, not at all; for we have already charged that all, both Jews and Greeks, are under the power of sin" (Rom 3:9).

---

3. Wright, *Paul and Faithfulness*, 1190.

In these opening chapters, Paul has set the stage for his mission to Rome to preach the gospel to the gentiles. The God of Israel has indeed been doing something special through his covenant with Israel, but it is God's righteousness and salvation that constitute that specialness. It is not the righteousness of the children of Israel that causes God to make the covenant with them; rather, it is God's righteousness that is the foundation of the covenant with Israel.[4] What Paul goes on to say, then, is essentially a defense of God's righteousness in relation to all nations, including Israel. Paul will appeal to God's promises to Abraham that preceded and grounded the covenant with Israel. He will explain why gentile inclusion with Jews in God's blessings was intended from the beginning, just as the certainty of judgment (the curses) against all wickedness by Jews and gentiles was promised. The entire book of Romans, says Wright, is primarily about God, especially Romans 9–11. Here we find "the question of God's word, God's children, God's promise, God's purpose in election, God's call, God's love (and hatred), God's justice (or injustice), God's mercy, God's power, God's name, God's sovereignty, God's will, God's rights as the potter over the clay, God's wrath and power, God's patience, God's glory and God's people."[5] "The whole of Romans 9–11," in Wright's view, "is an exposition of how the one God has been faithful, in Jesus Christ, to the promises he made to Abraham."[6]

Paul's firm belief is that Messiah Jesus was anticipated by the testimony of the Law and the Prophets. If Jesus is the *fulfillment* of the law, then God has not dealt unjustly with Israel but instead has fulfilled the promises made to Abraham, Isaac, and Jacob. To understand how God is doing this, it is necessary to understand the nature

4. Ridderbos, *Paul*, 343.

5. Wright, *Paul and Faithfulness*, 1157.

6. Wright, *Climax*, 234. While my reading of Rom 9–11 is generally in tune with that of Wright, I find a problematic ambiguity at some points in his interpretation of Paul. According to Wright, Paul preaches that the "Messiah has done that for which Israel was chosen in the first place. His [the Messiah's] death . . . has made the atonement through which all nations are redeemed. God's faithfulness is therefore fully and finally unveiled on the cross. The Messiah has done for the world what Israel was called to do. He has done *in Israel's place* what Israel was called to do but could not, namely to act on behalf of the whole world." Wright, *Paul in Fresh Perspective*, 120. Wright seems to be arguing that Israel was supposed to be God's sacrifice unto death for the sins of the world in order to redeem the nations, but Israel failed at that task because it did not act on behalf of the whole world. The Messiah then takes the place of Israel to do what Israel was supposed to do. But surely Wright does not mean that Israel was called by God to be the redemptive sacrifice for the world's sin; God is the redeemer of Israel and the world, and redemption can now be understood to have come through the shed blood and resurrected body of Israel's Messiah, Jesus. If, however, Wright means that Israel was supposed to be the prime human exhibit—the fruit—of *God's* saving grace and righteousness, then that seems right. Israel failed even to be the faithful witness to God's mercy by failing to keep covenant with God. Consequently the gentiles were unable to see the evidence and hear the good news of God's blessing of the nations in keeping with God's promise to Abraham. This second way of reading Christ's relation to Israel makes biblical sense, but the first way does not. Wright is much less equivocal when he says in another context that Israel "is the people of God rescued at the exodus, whose law was the way of life for a people already redeemed," Wright, *Justification*, 243. Israel and all those whom God is saving are to be exhibits of God's saving grace through the blood sacrifice of the lamb of God. Israel was not called to be that redeemer.

of God's covenant promises to Israel, rooted in the covenant with Abraham, for Paul passionately desires that his fellow Jews recognize and put their trust in Jesus as God's promised Messiah to Israel (Rom 9:1–5).[7] In his expression of this deep desire, Paul does not treat fellow Jews as if God's covenants with their ancestors are no longer relevant. To the contrary, it is precisely in terms of those covenants that Paul makes the case that his fellow Jews may be in danger of God's wrath. God's wrath is not a failure on God's part to keep covenant with Israel: "It is not as though the word of God had failed" (Rom 9:6). After all, God's gifts to Israel are still relevant and can in no way be denied or taken back, for "to them belong the adoption, the glory, the covenants, the giving of the law, the worship, and the promises; to them belong the patriarchs, and from them, according to the flesh, comes the Messiah, who is over all, God blessed forever. Amen" (Rom 9:4–5).[8] The challenge Paul faces is to show from the Law and the Prophets that God has been faithful to Israel all along and that the culminating revelation of that faithfulness in Jesus Christ confirms God's continuing commitment to, and fulfillment of, his covenant with Israel.

FROM ABRAHAM TO CHRIST

Turn with me now to Romans 9–11. From the time of God's covenants with Abram/Abraham, Paul says, it has been clear that "not all who are descended from Israel are Israel" (Rom 9:6). What does Paul mean by this? On the one hand, God has given Israel irrevocable gifts, as we just noted in Romans 9:4-5. The Israel of which he is speaking is the ancestral line leading to Jesus himself, a son of Israel. At the same time, God's promises have never depended on or arisen *from* that ancestry. God's promises to Abraham predated the ancestry of Israel and the giving of the law; the former are the foundation of the law. Moreover, not all of Abraham's descendants were identified as the *children* of God's *promise* (Rom 9:7). God's promises to Abraham were to pass down through Isaac, not through his earlier son, Ishmael, even though God blessed Ishmael, and Abraham circumcised him and all other males in his family (Gen 16:10–14; 17:20–27). God told Abraham, "It is through Isaac that descendants will be named for you" (Rom 9:7, 29).[9] The same thing happened with God's blessing of Isaac:

7. According to Stowers, writing about Paul's expression of anguish over fellow Jews not recognizing the Messiah (Rom 9:1–4), "the passage sounds a paradigmatic echo of Moses pleading with God to have his name erased from the book of life in exchange for the salvation of the people of Israel (Exod 32:32; Num 11:15). Nothing in the Pauline corpus prepares the reader for this. Paul often speaks to his gentile communities about his suffering for their benefit in the likeness of Christ's suffering. But here he would forfeit life in Christ for the sake of his fellow Jews." Stowers, *Rereading of Romans*, 292.

8. On the subject of God's exclusive gifts to Israel, see Hays, *Echoes in Paul*, 47–48; and for extended commentary on Rom 9–11 as a whole see 63–83.

9. Wright elaborates on this passage in greater detail: "The argument of 9:6–29 is held together by the mention of the 'seed' in 9.7 and 9.29." Paul then "re-introduces the distinction between 'children of flesh' and 'children of promise'; only the latter are *sperma* [seed]." Then Paul reiterates the point that many gentiles are also called through faith to be children of Abraham. Wright, *Paul and Faithfulness*,

Isaac's wife Rebecca had twin boys, but God's covenant promises went to and through Jacob, not through Esau (Rom 9:10–12). In other words, the generations of Jacob are only one of the lines of descent from Isaac, who was only one of the descendants of Abraham.

Did God's election of Isaac and Jacob rather than the others make God unjust? Of course not, Paul argues, for God's covenants establish the terms on which God deals with Israel and the nations. He will have mercy on whom he will have mercy (Rom 9:15). There are no terms or standards above God's righteousness and mercy by which to judge God's actions in establishing covenants.[10] In keeping with the terms of the covenant with Abraham, God extended its promises to Isaac and to Jacob without doing any injustice to Ishmael or Esau. Moreover, God's election of Jacob happened before the birth of the twins, so it is impossible to argue that there was anything about the deeds of Jacob or Esau that caused God to favor Jacob (Rom 9:11–13).

Now, if we keep in mind that God's covenants with Abram/Abraham included the promise that through his seed all nations would be blessed (Gen 22:18), then surely God is also justified in choosing people from among the gentiles to be "objects of mercy" (just as he called out some from among the descendants of Israel to be objects of his mercy), "prepared beforehand for glory" (Rom 9:23–26). Here, Paul quotes from four passages in Hosea and Isaiah in support of his exposition (Hos 2:23 and 1:10; Isa 10:22–23 and 1:9). Yet on what terms does God include gentiles as objects of his mercy? That is the next question Paul addresses (Rom 9:30—10:13): is it possible for gentiles, who were not party to God's covenant with Israel, to obtain righteousness "through faith," while children of Israel, "who did strive for the righteousness that is based on the law, did not succeed in fulfilling that law" (Rom 9:30–31)?

That is indeed what Paul says is happening, and he picks up from an earlier argument in the letter (Rom 3:19–31). He is not pitting faith against God's covenant with Israel. Rather, he is arguing that the law of the covenant itself attests to righteousness obtained through faith—for Jew and gentile alike. This means that neither physical descent from Abraham nor the effort to obtain righteousness by keeping the law is what makes one a member of the community of faith exhibited by Abraham. Hays interprets Romans 3:19–31 this way: "Paul wants to argue that Judaism itself, rightly understood, claims its relation to Abraham not by virtue of physical descent from him (*kata sarka*) but by virtue of sharing his trust in the God who made the promises. In that sense, the gospel, which invites all people, including Gentiles, into right relation

---

1187–88. See also Ridderbos, *Paul*, 343–45.

10. According to Stowers, "the whole discussion in 9–11 supposes that God consistently acts for the greater good of those (Israel and the gentile peoples) to whom he has committed himself by promise. But human observers stand in no position to judge why God acts in the way he does (cf. 11:33–36). Paul connects this theme of God's inscrutable ways to the theme of human works . . . Even the righteous with their best intentions cannot use their own good efforts as a guarantee that God will do things the way that seems best to them. God cannot be bribed, even with works of righteousness." Stowers, *Rereading of Romans*, 300.

with God through faith, confirms the Law; it is consistent with the real substance of the Law's teaching."[11]

From Romans 9:30 on into the next chapter, Paul focuses on the human response to God's promises. Those of Israel who have not attained righteousness are in that position, says Paul, "because they did not strive for it on the basis of faith, but as if it were based on works" (Rom 9:32). Paul's fellow Jews are zealous, he says, but in their zealousness to keep the law, they have been trying thereby either to establish or to prove their own righteousness. That shows their ignorance because it is clear from God's covenant history going back to Abraham that righteousness is God's gift, just as the law itself is God's gift. Righteousness—right standing before God—is not something that a person can earn by trying to achieve it (Rom 10:2–13).

The contrast Paul is drawing here is not simply between *faith* and *works*, but between *God's righteousness* (now made manifest in Messiah Jesus), on the one hand, and on the other hand, the *righteousness* that many *Jews are striving to achieve by trying to keep the law*.[12] Abraham's *response in faith* to God's promise was credited to him as righteousness, whereas those who tried to establish their own righteousness did not obtain it. Paul writes, "I can testify that they [his fellow Jews] have a zeal for God, but it is not enlightened. For, being ignorant of the righteousness that comes from God, and seeking to establish their own, they have not submitted to God's righteousness" (Rom 10:2–3).

Ridderbos makes an important point here about Paul's understanding of faith, namely, that it entails obedience. "Faith as obedience is of central significance for Paul's conception and is repeatedly defined as such in his epistles. He says immediately at the beginning of the Epistle to the Romans that he has received his apostleship unto 'obedience of faith' among all the gentiles." The "obedience of faith" means surrendering to and trusting the God who establishes people in his righteousness. Ridderbos continues, "Unbelief means therefore not being obedient, being disobedient to the gospel (Rom 10:16; cf. 11:30; 2 Thess 1:18). Faith and obedience belong together and can be employed as interchangeable ideas (cf. Rom 1:8 and 16:19; 1 Thess 1:8 and Rom 15:18), as can unbelief and disobedience (cf. Rom 2:8; Eph 2:2; 5:6)."[13] Living by faith is not living lawlessly but living in accord with trust in the God whose righteousness and promises are the spring from which an obedient life flows.

---

11. Hays, *Echoes in Paul*, 54–55.

12. Israel's fault in Paul's view, says Wright, is not that she pursued righteousness by trying to keep the law, "but that, pursuing it in the wrong way, she did not attain to it (9:31–32)." Wright, *Climax*, 244. This is what Paul argued in Gal 2. "Paul's doctrine of justification by faith," says Wright, "refers to the way in which God's people have been redefined. 'We,' affirms Paul, 'are by birth Jews, not gentile sinners' yet we know that one is not justified by works of Torah, but through the faithfulness of Jesus the Messiah; thus we too have believed in the Messiah, Jesus, so that we might be justified by the faithfulness of the Messiah and not by works of Torah, because through works of Torah no flesh will be justified.'" Wright, *Paul in Fresh Perspective*, 111.

13. Ridderbos, *Paul*, 237.

As Paul understands it, "Christ is the end of the law so that there may be righteousness for everyone who believes" (Rom 10:2–4). Or as Paul states it earlier in the letter, no one will be judged righteous in God's sight by observing the law, "for through the law comes knowledge of sin. But now, apart from the law, the righteousness of God has been disclosed, and is attested by the law and the prophets, the righteousness of God through faith in Jesus Christ for all who believe. For there is no distinction, since all have sinned and fall short of the glory of God; they are now justified by his grace as a gift, through the redemption that is in Christ Jesus, whom God put forward as a sacrifice of atonement by his blood, effective through faith" (Rom 3:20–24).

God elected Abraham, Isaac, and Jacob before they could act to prove themselves righteous before God. Now, in Jesus, that righteousness of God is being revealed and offered freely in messianic finality in fulfillment of all God's covenant promises to Abraham, Isaac, and Jacob, including the promise that through their seed, all nations will be blessed. The righteousness of Israel's Messiah is reckoned to all who put their faith in him: "'No one who believes in him will be put to shame.' For there is no distinction between Jew and Greek; the same Lord is Lord of all and is generous to all who call on him. For, 'Everyone who calls on the name of the Lord shall be saved'" (Rom 10:11–13).[14] Paul posed and answered the following question earlier in the letter: "Then what becomes of boasting? It is excluded. By what law? By that of works? No, but by the law of faith. For we hold that a person is justified by faith apart from works prescribed by the law. Or is God the God of Jews only? Is he not the God of Gentiles also, since God is one; and he will justify the circumcised on the ground of faith and the uncircumcised through that same faith. Do we then overthrow the law by this faith? By no means! On the contrary, we uphold the law" (Rom 3:27–31).

A REMNANT

And yet . . . and yet . . . if not all of Israel is Israel, the question comes up again: does this mean God has rejected Israel or been unfaithful to his covenant with them? (Rom 11:1). Paul's answer, again, is no. This time, he begins with himself and, by implication, with other Jews who are followers of Jesus. "I myself am an Israelite," says Paul, "a descendant of Abraham, a member of the tribe of Benjamin. God has not rejected his people whom he foreknew" (Rom 11:1–2). Remember Elijah who became convinced

14. Paul quotes Moses saying that righteousness in keeping the law amounts to this: "The person who does these things will live by them" (Rom 10:5). The meaning of Paul's argument, according to Wright, is that the *doing* of Torah is actually fulfilled "when anyone, be they Jew or Gentile, hears the gospel of Christ and believes it. Each of the three verses in Deuteronomy quoted here end with the phrase 'so that you may do it'; *this*, Paul is asserting, is the true 'doing' of the Torah, of which Leviticus speaks. This is how God will give her [Israel] a new heart, so that she will find the Torah 'on her lips and in her heart': and, just as with the stumbling stone of 9:33, Christ and Torah are fused together, so that when Christ is preached and believed, Torah is being paradoxically fulfilled." Wright, *Climax*, 245.

that he was the last one of Israel to trust in God? God assured Elijah that there were still 7,000 who had not bowed the knee to Baal. Regardless of how small or large the number of Israel's offspring who put their trust in God's righteousness, "there is a remnant, chosen by grace. But if it is by grace, it is no longer on the basis of works" (Rom 11:5–6). God's commitment to Israel through the covenants that reach all the way back to Abraham is confirmed and made evident by those in the lineage of Israel who, like Abraham, have trusted God's promises, putting their confidence and faith in God's righteousness.

"What then? Israel failed to obtain what it was seeking. The elect obtained it, but the rest were hardened" (Rom 11:7). Yet even in this case of *faith* on the one hand and *hardening* on the other, did those who stumbled over God's righteousness stumble "so as to fall? By no means!" says Paul. "But through their stumbling salvation has come to the Gentiles, so as to make Israel jealous" (Rom 11:11; Deut 32:21). *This is a new turn in Paul's argument.* It goes beyond the distinction between faithless Israel and a faithful remnant. Why have those who stumbled not fallen beyond recovery? We might expect Paul to answer that God's mercy and love for Israel will lead fallen ones to repent of their sins and turn back in faith to God. Paul will affirm just that, but his answer includes a more complicated twist, namely, that the stumbling of Israel has made room for salvation to come to the gentiles, and that, in turn, will make hardened Israel jealous and lead them back to the God of their fathers through Messiah Jesus.[15] Here is Paul's statement: "Now I am speaking to you Gentiles. Inasmuch then as I am an apostle to the Gentiles, I glorify my ministry in order to make my own people jealous, and thus save some of them. For if their rejection is the reconciliation of the world, what will their acceptance be but life from the dead! If the part of the dough offered as first fruits is holy, then the whole batch is holy; and if the root is holy, then the branches also are holy" (Rom 11:13–16).

How do the metaphors of dough and branches elucidate Paul's point about the rejection and then the acceptance of Israel? Paul is connecting God's rejection of unbelieving Israel with God's making room for the grafting in of gentiles. That idea was not explicit in God's promise to Abraham that all nations would be blessed through his seed (Gen 22:18), but the idea is present in Deuteronomy 32:21, which Paul quotes in 10:19 and 11:11. Paul continues his argument by saying that the inclusion of gentiles because of the rejection of stumbling Israelites brings reconciliation to the world (overcoming the divide between Jews and gentiles; see Eph 2:11–12). God's acceptance again of those once rejected means life from the dead. Such reconciliation

---

15. There are many signs in Rom 9–11, writes Witherington, that "Paul is presenting an argument based on an apocalyptic revelation from God." Witherington, *Jesus, Paul*, 112. At the same time, these chapters "reflect a profound meditation upon numerous Old Testament texts and is not simply the record of an apocalyptic vision." Witherington, *Jesus, Paul*, 222. "In fact more than half of all the Old Testament quotes in Romans occur in 9–11 and about 40 percent of those are from Isaiah. Almost a third of all the verses in these chapters involve a quote or paraphrasing of the Old Testament." Witherington, *Jesus, Paul*, 113.

and new life mean that the entire tree and the whole lump of dough are thus made holy. The great future of "life from the dead" of which Paul speaks, says Ridderbos, will not dawn "without the pleroma [the fullness] of Israel; all nations will be blessed with Abraham's seed. The holy root of Israel continues to support all, the holy leaven permeates all, and the gentiles are grafted into the olive tree of Israel (Rom 11:24)."[16]

But whom does Paul have in mind as the holy first fruits of the dough and the holy root of the branches? The answer to that question is not yet stated explicitly.

ROOT AND BRANCHES

Paul continues in the verses that follow with the root and branch metaphor. Some of the natural (original) branches of the tree of God's covenant with Israel have indeed been broken off because of their unbelief. Branches from a wild olive tree (gentiles) have been grafted into the tree whose root is holy. Those wild branches "now share the rich root of the olive tree" (Rom 11:17). But Paul immediately warns the grafted-in gentiles not to think of themselves as superior to the natural branches. Remember, "it is not you that support the root, but the root that supports you" (Rom 11:18). The branches broken off were to make room for you, but the reason for their removal was their unbelief, and you are now alive in the root only through faith, not because of anything that makes you superior to those who were cut off. "So do not become proud, but stand in awe," Paul writes, "For if God did not spare the natural branches, perhaps he will not spare you" (Rom 11:18–21).

Consider, then, "the kindness and the severity of God," Paul continues, "severity toward those who have fallen, but God's kindness toward you, provided you continue in his kindness; otherwise, you also will be cut off. And even those of Israel, if they do not persist in unbelief, will be grafted in, for God has the power to graft them in again" (Rom 11:22–23). Here, Paul's development of the metaphor brings the story into sharp focus. The chief actor in all of this is the God of Abraham, Isaac, Jacob, and Messiah Jesus. God is the one who grafts in and cuts off. The root of the living tree is God's righteousness that was accredited to Abraham because of his faith, and that righteousness has now been revealed in the person of the Messiah, the one whom John's gospel identifies as the vine on which living branches flourish (John 15:1–8). Paul puts it this way later in his letter: "For I tell you that Christ has become a servant of the circumscribed on behalf of the truth of God, in order that he might confirm the promises given to the patriarchs, and in order that the Gentiles might glorify God for his mercy" (15:8–9). Paul then quotes from several passages of scripture, concluding with this one: "The root of Jesse shall come, the one who rises to rule the Gentiles; in him the Gentiles shall hope" (Rom 15:12; see Isa 11:1, 10).

16. Ridderbos, *Paul*, 360.

As long as it is still today, therefore, the drama of cutting off and grafting in (and regrafting in) continues to unfold as the good news of God's fulfillment of covenant promises is proclaimed and exhibited in the obedience of faith. The natural branches of the tree are the descendants of Israel, some of which continue in faith while others are cut off because of their unbelief. And many gentiles are now turning to God in faith through the righteousness of Messiah Jesus and are being grafted into the same root that has supported Israel from the beginning. While some of those among the gentiles are cut off because they do not continue in God's kindness, many among the Jews who were cut off are grafted in again. "For if you [gentiles] have been cut from what is by nature a wild olive tree and grafted, contrary to nature, into a cultivated olive tree, how much more will these natural branches be grafted back into their own olive tree" (Rom 11:24). God is reconciling Jews and gentiles through the Messiah's righteousness, making them a single covenant family. Paul can thus refer to the living olive tree as Israel's *own* because the covenants with the patriarchs made the children of Israel God's chosen people, the family of promise. The root of that tree has now been revealed as Israel's long-promised, long-anticipated Messiah, Jesus.

The metaphor of the olive tree, according to Wright, "is a metaphor of Israel itself . . . The whole point of the image is that there is—just as in Galatians 3—a single family; a family rooted in the patriarchs and the promises God made to them; a family from which, strangely, many 'natural branches' have been broken off, but into which many 'unnatural branches' have been grafted." Clearly then, "there are not two 'peoples of God', one for gentiles to be incorporated into and one for Jews to remain within."[17] There is only one tree, and only one root on which the one family depends.

The Son of God incarnate in Jesus, the son of David, son of Israel, son of Abraham, and son of Adam, has lived among us, suffered death through crucifixion,[18] been raised from the dead, and now sits at the right hand of majesty on high until the time of the human generations is full and God's kingdom is established on earth as it is in heaven. This unfolding drama as we now experience it constitutes both an *already* and a *not yet*. The Messiah has come but has not yet completed all that his coming promises. The culmination of the kingdom is already at work but is not yet fully manifest. The resurrection harvest has begun with the resurrection of Christ, the first fruits, but the harvest is not yet complete (1 Cor 15:20). Consequently, now is the time of God's

17. Wright, *Paul and Faithfulness*, 1214.

18. Hahn's summary of Paul's argument in Gal 3–4 shows that the passage follows the same track as the argument in Rom 9–11: "Jesus Christ, the 'only Son' of the Father who is sacrificed on the mountain 'upon the wood,' takes on himself the Deuteronomic covenant curses at the cross, thus enabling the blessings of the Abrahamic covenant-oath to flow once again to the Gentiles. Thus Jesus fulfills the sacrifice of the Abrahamic covenant typified and prefigured at the Aqedah by Abraham's one 'seed,' Isaac. Paul sees at the center of this whole process the reality of divine sonship. God has acted as a father toward Israel, bringing him to life as a son (Exodus and Sinai covenant), subjecting him to the pedagogy of the Law (Levitical and Deuteronomic codes), and bringing him to maturity through the coming of the one Son (the New Covenant) while opening the way for the other nations of the human family also to enter into this filial relationship." Hahn, *Kinship byCovenant*, 276–77.

cutting off and (re)grafting in. God's covenant promises to Abraham, Israel, and David have not yet been fulfilled in their entirety. Yet Paul's gospel—God's good news—is that the Messiah in and through whom all those promises are grounded and secured has been revealed, and through him God's seventh-day glory will be celebrated by the great family of God.

There is a mystery here, says Paul, and he does not want the gentile Christians in Rome to be ignorant of it and imagine that they have surpassed or superseded the Jews as God's chosen people. There is a historical dynamic at work here within the transcendent, culminating purposes of God. "As regards the gospel," writes Paul, "they [the Jews] are enemies of God for your sake; but as regards election they are beloved for the sake of their ancestors; for the gifts and the calling of God are irrevocable" (Rom 11:28–29). The gospel of Christ is being proclaimed in fulfillment of God's covenant with Israel, not as a displacement of it. There is a love of God for the patriarchs of Israel to whom much was promised, and God's gifts and call to them are irrevocable.

Part of the mystery of God's revelatory purposes remains to be unveiled. The hardening experienced by part of Israel is for a time, "until the full number of the Gentiles has come in" and God's grafting in again of those previously cut off is completed (Rom 11:25, 23). In this way, "all Israel will be saved"(Rom 11:26).[19] Paul's summary

19. My interpretation of Rom 11:26 is close to, but not identical with, the interpretations of Wright and Witherington. According to Wright, "when Paul says 'all Israel shall be saved' in 11.26 he is consciously echoing 'all who call on the name of the Lord shall be saved' in 10:13, which is offered as the answer to the question of 10.1 about the salvation for presently unbelieving Jews. As he says in 11.23, they can be grafted in *if they do not remain in unbelief*." Wright, *Paul in Fresh Perspective*, 126–27. Witherington writes, "Neither Paul nor Jesus speak (sic) of the displacement or replacement of *all* Jews by some new entity called Israel. Nor is there any evidence that either Jesus or Paul envisioned two different peoples of God existing simultaneously. For Paul the Israel of God made up of Jew and Gentile united in Christ is the true or legitimate development of Israel in the present, but non-Christian Jews are not broken off from the true people of God forever. The crucial point then is that God is not finished with Israel yet." Witherington, *Jesus, Paul*, 226–27.

Quite in contrast to Wright and Witherington stand those who read "all Israel" to mean all Jewish people. Kinzer, for example, connects this view with the idea that the temporary lack of faith in Jesus (as the Messiah) among Jews may be "paradoxically, a participation in Yeshua's [Jesus's] vicarious, redemptive suffering." Kinzer, *Post-Missionary*, 133. Kinzer believes that, in Rom 9–11, "Paul sees the community of Israel, even in its state of unbelief (in Yeshua), as a holy people, a nation in covenant with God . . . He believes that the Jewish People retain their position as the heirs of God's promises and is certain that those promises will ultimately be realized in their national life" Kinzer, *Post-Missionary*, 140. For Douglas Harink, "all Israel" is the Israel of national descent ("fleshly"). The "chosen remnant part of Israel (those who have attained the righteousness from faith) suffices to stand in for the whole elect people. The chosen remnant is not to be understood as the 'saved' minority portion of Israel over against the 'lost' majority. The remnant is rather the representative part of the whole, the very means by which the whole of Israel (including the hardened portion) is already made holy." Harink, *Paul Among Post-Liberals*, 174. The representative minority of fleshly Israel thus serves, in Harink's interpretation, as the savior of the whole of fleshly Israel regardless of any hardening or lack of faith among them. Paul, who is a fleshly Jew, "together with a larger remnant of fleshly Jews, stands in for the whole of fleshly Israel, already rendering the whole body of Israel holy and pointing toward its final salvation (Rom 11:16). It is this God who demonstrates faithfulness to fleshly Israel who can also

for the followers of Christ in Rome goes like this: "Just as you were once disobedient to God but have now received mercy because of their disobedience, so they have now been disobedient in order that, by the mercy shown to you, they too may now receive mercy. For God has imprisoned all in disobedience so that he may be merciful to all" (Rom 11:30–32). The fullness of Israel, the complete Israel, will constitute the complete family of God, including the grafted-in gentiles of faith. Jews and gentiles are reconciled and joined together through Jesus in fulfillment of God's promises to Abraham. Does mystery remain here? Indeed it does. It is situated, Ridderbos writes,

> in the manner in which this fullness of Israel is to be saved: in the strange interdependence of the salvation of Israel and that of the gentiles. Israel, which was chosen from among the gentiles, must, contrary to every human expectation, first give way to the gentiles. But as Israel because of its disobedience has become a cause of salvation for the gentiles, so now the gentiles must provoke Israel to jealousy. There is thus an interaction. God grants no mercy to Israel without the gentiles, but neither does he do so to the gentiles without Israel. As he first shut up all under disobedience, so will he have mercy on all. The whole argument of Romans 11:1–32 leads to the indication of this mutual relationship of dependence, of this undulatory movement of salvation (cf. vv. 30–32), and on this, too, the doxology of the depth of the riches, wisdom, and knowledge of God and of the inscrutableness of his ways is founded (vv. 33–36).[20]

Paul concludes chapter 11 in awestruck praise: "O the depth of the riches and wisdom and knowledge of God! How unsearchable are his judgments and how inscrutable his ways! 'For who has known the mind of the Lord? Or who has been his counselor?' 'Or who has given a gift to him, to receive a gift in return?' For from him and through him and to him are all things. To him be the glory forever. Amen" (11:33–36).

SUMMARY

If we have correctly followed the flow of Paul's gospel message in Romans 9–11, we can summarize it as follows: the gospel of Jesus Christ that Paul is proclaiming to the gentiles finds them at odds with Israel because gentiles have not been part of God's covenant with Israel. That covenant, with all the gifts entailed in it (Rom 9:4–5), still stands because of God's faithfulness to the patriarchs—Abraham, Isaac, and Jacob. Yet the dynamic, revelatory process that God set in motion with the call of Abraham is one in which gentiles, who were at one time disobedient to God, are now being included as recipients of God's mercy and promised blessings. The reconciling breakthrough

---

finally be trusted faithfully to show mercy to all, both Israel and the nations; indeed, to the nations only in and through fleshly Israel, from whom, 'according to the flesh, comes the messiah, who is over all' (Rom 9:5)" Harink, *Paul Among Post-Liberals*, 183.

20. Ridderbos, *Paul*, 359–60.

has come through the revelation that Israel's Messiah is Jesus. Through faith in Messiah Jesus—the seed of Abraham—gentiles are being grafted into the tree of covenant promise. Moreover, all the living branches of the tree, whether Jew or gentile, live only because of God's righteousness, mercy, and love. "God has imprisoned all in disobedience so that he may be merciful to all" (Rom 11:32). The righteousness with which Jews and gentiles alike can find favor with God is God's righteousness revealed in Christ Jesus and credited to them through faith, as was the case with Abraham when he put his trust in God.

Abraham's response of faith took place before God established the covenant sign of circumcision and long before the Sinai covenant, so right standing with God comes not by the law and works of the law but by God's gift of righteousness credited to those who put and keep their trust in God. God's righteousness, the root of the tree, is none other than Messiah Jesus. That is why the word of God [quoting Deut. 30:14] "is near you, on your lips and in your heart" (Rom 10:8). Consequently, God's gracious, merciful gift is this, that "if you confess with your lips that Jesus is Lord and believe in your heart that God raised him from the dead, you will be saved. For one believes with the heart and so is justified, and one confesses with the mouth and so is saved" (Rom 10:9–10).

27

Becoming Bethel

Completion of the Covenant Community

COVENANT FOR COMMUNITY, THE pattern introduced in chapter 9, has been abuilding in the dynamic development of God's bond with creation, particularly the bond with the sixth-day human generations. After Jacob saw in a dream the stairway to heaven and called the place where he slept "Bethel"—the house of God—recipients of God's promises have looked with anticipation to dwelling with God. Along through the course of history, even when they were unaware of it, those who followed God's lead were being shaped into the building blocks of that house (Gen 28:10–22; 1 Pet 2:4–5; Heb 3:5–6; 11:10).

The Alpha and the Omega of this covenant community has now been revealed in Messiah Jesus. The new covenant in his blood is the culminating seal of all earthly covenants that point toward it in *revelatory anticipation*. According to Paul, central to the mystery of disclosing the covenant community through Christ is the reconciliation of Jew and gentile to become the one family of God, the one bride of Christ, the citizens in God's one kingdom. Addressing gentile believers in Ephesus, Paul sums up this good news as follows. Remember gentiles, you who from birth were called "uncircumcised" by those who call themselves "the circumcision"—

> remember that you were at that time without Christ, being aliens from the commonwealth of Israel, and strangers to the covenants of the promise, having no hope and without God in the world. But now in Christ Jesus you who once were far off have been brought near by the blood of Christ. For he is our peace; in his flesh he has made both groups into one and has broken down the dividing wall, that is, the hostility between us. He has abolished the law with its commandments and ordinances, that he might create in himself one new humanity in place of the two, thus making peace, and might reconcile both groups to God in one body through the cross, thus putting to death that hostility through it. So he came and proclaimed peace to you who were far off

and peace to those who were near, for through him both of us have access in
one Spirit to the Father (Eph 2:12–19).

As a consequence of all that God has accomplished, Paul continues, "you are no longer
strangers and aliens, but you are citizens with the saints and also members of the
household of God, built upon the foundation of the apostles and prophets, with Christ
Jesus himself as the cornerstone. In him the whole structure is joined together and
grows into a holy temple in the Lord; in whom you also are built together spiritually
into a dwelling place for God" (Eph 2:11–22). The long-developing hope for God to
dwell with his people has been confirmed with the revelation of the cornerstone of
that house, Christ Jesus. This means that through him the *honor and hospitality* of the
image of God is elevated and blessed. And the Father's blessing of his Son, by raising
him from the dead and welcoming him into the throne room on high, trumpets the
good news that all of God's people have become Bethel.

Christ Jesus does not ascend to God's sabbath joy alone; he is drawing with him
the full company of his brothers and sisters from all the generations of humankind
(John 15:9–17; 17:1–26). In the hope of that fulfillment, we who are still alive in this
age are to continue to walk in faith, hope, and love, following him until the construction of that holy temple is completed. In response to the revelation of this mystery, the
apostles break forth in thanksgiving and praise:

"Now to God who is able to strengthen you according to my gospel and the proclamation of Jesus Christ, according to the revelation of the mystery that was kept
secret for long ages but is now disclosed, and through the prophetic writings is made
known to all the Gentiles, according to the command of the eternal God, to bring
about the obedience of faith—to the only wise God, through Jesus Christ to whom be
the glory forever! Amen" (Rom 16:25–27).

"Blessed be the God and Father of our Lord Jesus Christ! By his great mercy he
has given us a new birth into a living hope through the resurrection of Jesus Christ
from the dead, and into an inheritance that is imperishable, undefiled, and unfading,
kept in heaven for you, who are being protected by the power of God through faith for
a salvation ready to be revealed in the last time" (1 Pet 1:3–5).

"And I heard a loud voice from the throne saying, 'Look! God's dwelling place is
now among the people, and he will dwell with them. They will be his people, and God
himself will be with them and be their God. He will wipe every tear from their eyes.
There will be no more death or mourning or crying or pain, for the old order of things
has passed away'" (Rev 21:3–4, TNIV; see Isa 25:6–8; 65:17–19).

BLESSINGS IN ABUNDANCE AND CURSES NO MORE

During the continuation of this age, God's covenant with Israel continues to bear witness to God's promised blessings and curses that fall upon covenant breakers. It is no

longer only the children of Israel who are subject to the sternness of the covenant. By God's mercy in Jesus, gentile branches are being grafted into the covenant tree, but those who do not continue in God's kindness will be cut off (Rom 9:2; 10:21–24). God has now "imprisoned all in disobedience so that he may be merciful to all" (Rom 11:32). All of us, in our sin, now stand before the messianic judge and redeemer of Israel, the Lord of all nations. All authority in heaven and on earth has been given to him (Matt 28:18). The urgent message of the apostles, then, is this: repent and believe the good news that the Messiah has suffered God's judgment for the sins of the world. Do not continue in the ways of death. Repent, turn around to trust and follow the one who gives life (Mark 1:4–5; Acts 2:36–38; 17:30–31; Rev 2:4–5) and puts an end to God's covenant curses.

Covenant-breaking did not begin with Israel. It began with Adam and continued with Noah and the generations thereafter. The generations of the first Adam were to be God's family, God's household, God's dwelling place, but all have sinned and fallen under God's judgment, as Paul makes clear in the first chapters of Romans. Into that darkness God spoke to Abram, calling him to put his trust in God. Through the seed of Abram/Abraham, God promised immeasurable reward. The covenant with Israel then spelled out for all to hear and to see the meaning of both the blessings and the curses God promised for those whom he saved from Egypt as his chosen people. In confrontation with Israel's repeated disobedience, the prophets warned of God's curses and explained the meaning of them when they fell on the people.

Yet, even when the prophets spoke of God's condemnation, they also told of God's enduring love, comfort, and coming restoration through a new covenant he would make with them. Then, from within the remnant of Judah and Benjamin, from the house of David, a child was born to become the King of the Jews, though his kingship would come through suffering. The seed of Abraham, a son of Israel, the promised Messiah suffered God's curse of death to make atonement for the sins of Israel and the whole world. "He was despised and rejected by others; a man of suffering and acquainted with infirmity . . . But he was wounded for our transgressions, crushed for our iniquities, upon him was the punishment that made us whole, and by his bruises we are healed (Isa 53:3–6; see Rom 3:25–26; Heb 9:1–28).

We should not think of Israel's disobedience and of the sins of the nations only in terms of evil deeds of individuals who violate specific rules and regulations of the law. Human disobedience has become engrained in cultural patterns that engender and perpetuate corruption, neglect, blindness, selfishness, and every manner of degradation. Such evil is institutional as well as personal, leading people and their cultures into ways of death. The prophets' words of condemnation show this again and again, directed toward so many of Israel's (and other nations') patterns of economic, familial, political, and cultic injustice toward God and neighbors. And the same is evident throughout history. A white American Christian today may say that he has never maligned an African-American and yet be unconscious of the debilitating evil of America's slave system, the consequences of which continue to infect the habits and institutions of American society to this day. A Dutch or French Christian might say that her grandparents never betrayed Jews to the authorities that sent them off to the gas chambers, yet she may remain oblivious to the weight of anti-Semitism that still infects the culture of which she is a part. A Christian who is an executive in a bank, or oil company, or commercial franchise might say that she never committed a fraudulent act or mistreated an employee at work yet ignore misleading advertising or unfair compensation patterns in her institution that have contributed to banking crises, price-fixing, and social conflicts that plague the society in which she lives. The list of direct and indirect patterns of fraud, discrimination, maltreatment, and murder could be extended beyond the length of this book to include countless stories from societies, cultures, and civilizations throughout the history of the world. All of this stands under God's condemnation—the divine curses.

We are guilty! We have all sinned! We deserve God's righteous condemnation. It is only by the grace and mercy of God that Noah was preserved, that Abraham followed God in faith, and that Israel was chosen to be God's people of promise and witness. And it is only by God's grace and mercy that while all were yet sinners, Messiah Jesus died for us (Rom 5:6–8). That is the good news announced ahead of time by Isaiah, Jeremiah, and other prophets, and the good news proclaimed by the apostles. The light has shined in the darkness and the darkness will not overcome it (John 1:1–5; Isa 60:1–3); no one on earth can hide from the Spirit's conveyance of God's kindness and sternness (Jn. 16:5–16; Isa. 59:1–21; 63:7–10). This Messiah will return, and the question is whether he will find faith on the earth (Luke 16:6–8; Isa 66:12–24).

The good news is that Jesus Christ has borne the sins of the world and thereby buried all curses, including the curse of death.

THE TIME OF TESTING

The time between the ascension of the risen Messiah and his return in glory is the time of the Spirit's testing, sifting, judging, calling, cutting off, and grafting in. We are living in the last days of this age, according to the prophet Joel, when God is pouring out his Spirit on all people. "In these last days . . . your sons and your daughters shall prophesy, and your young men shall see visions, your old men shall dream dreams. Even upon my slaves, both men and women, in those days I will pour out my Spirit; and they shall prophesy" (Acts 2:17–18; Joel 2:28–29). This is the time when both the good plants and weeds grow together in the field of the world until harvest time (Matt 13:36–43). No authority on earth is given authority to clean up the field and pull out the weeds, and God's mercy and patience continue until God's angels are sent to harvest the field and separate every evil thing from the good so that "the righteous will shine like the sun in the kingdom of their Father" (Matt 13:43). The complete covenant community that God is drawing together from among the living and the dead of all generations has not yet been revealed. But the Spirit of God is at work and this is the time to hear and understand the parable of the weeds.

The last days are upon us because the ascension of the Son of Man to resurrection fulfillment has unleashed the Spirit on earth (John 16:1–16; Acts 2:21). Now is the time of the Spirit's cutting off and grafting in, though not yet the day of final judgment and fulfillment in glory. This is the time when the question of Jesus's disciples still hangs in the air: is it now, Lord, when you will restore the kingdom to Israel (Acts 1:6)? Jesus responded to that question by saying, "it is not for you to know the times or periods the Father has set by his own authority." The Spirit will come upon you and you will go out in his power to be my witnesses in Jerusalem, and in all Judea and Samaria, and to the ends of the earth (Acts 1:7–8). The implication appears to be, as the apostles work it out, that the time of Israel's hopes for kingdom fulfillment will come when the whole earth is shown to be the kingdom of God, when God's will through Christ Jesus is done on earth as it is in heaven, and thus when the completed Israel of Jews and gentiles is revealed to be the bride of Christ, the family of God, the Bethel of God with his people.

The good news about Messiah Jesus is this: God exalted him to the throne on high, "and gave him the name that is above every name, so that at the name of Jesus every knee should bend, in heaven and on earth and under the earth, and every tongue should confess that Jesus Christ is Lord, to the glory of God the Father" (Phil 2:9–11). The time of the final disclosure of the glory of God and the bending of every knee at the name of the exalted Jesus has not yet come in its fullness. But now is the time for those living to bow and confess his name, to show by faith, as Abraham did, the obedience of faith that anticipates the fulfillment God has promised. John the baptizer and the apostles called out: repent and believe the good news of the one God who has made Messiah Jesus the cornerstone of the house of righteousness.

In contrast to the argument of Robert Jenson, whom we considered in chapter 25, I would not call the time in which we now live, between the first and second comings of Christ, a "detour" anymore than I would call it a "parenthesis" as many dispensationalists do. We live in the time of the extended coming of Christ Jesus, who is being revealed to the nations in fulfillment of God's promises to Abraham, Israel, and David. Even now, all authority in heaven and earth belongs to him and he is ruling with mercy, patience, and long-suffering until the time is full. This is why Paul's testimony to Christ's resurrection is of such great importance. Jesus Christ was not just another prophet in the historical line of Israel's prophets or simply a highly respected rabbi who spoke with great authority in affirming the integrity of God's covenant with Israel. At the heart of Romans 9–11, Paul quotes Leviticus 18:5 and Deuteronomy 30:12–14 to say that God's making of a new covenant, which will fulfill all God's promises to Israel and the nations, has been evident in the drama of the coming of Messiah Jesus. Now, says Paul, the "doing of Torah" is to be found in the obedience of faith—in confessing that "Jesus is Lord" and that "*God raised him from the dead*" (Rom 10:9).

The Sinai covenant and Israel's entrance into the promised land did not bring about the end of history and eternal rest with God. God chose Israel to be the historically specific, uniquely revelatory community of anticipation of fulfilled humanity, God's chosen people. Ancient Israel and the Jews were not predecessors of another people who would take their place at a particular point of time in history. God's covenant with Israel amounts to more than that. Messiah Jesus is a son of David, son of Israel. The faithful in Christ are being grafted into the root of the tree of Israel as joint heirs of God's promises to Abraham. The full household of faith is being drawn by means of a second birth into Israel's Messiah—the last Adam—to become fellow citizens of God's kingdom, members of the one community of God's sabbath-blessed humanity.

Worshipping God today in these last days does not have as its orientation a final goal in this age but rather the goal of God's transcendent sanctuary, Mount Zion. The author of Hebrews reminds his listeners that they have not come to a mountain "that can be touched, a blazing fire, and darkness, and gloom, and a tempest, and the sound of a trumpet, and a voice whose words made the hearers beg that not another word be spoken to them" (Heb 12:18–19). No, you are not now standing where the children of Israel stood and Moses said, "I am trembling with fear" (Heb 12:21; see Deut 9:18–21). Instead, says the author, "you have come to Mount Zion and to the city of the living God, the heavenly Jerusalem, and to innumerable angels in festal gathering, and to the assembly of the firstborn who are enrolled in heaven, and to God the judge of all, and to the spirits of the righteous made perfect, and to Jesus, the mediator of a new covenant, and to the sprinkled blood that speaks a better word than the blood of Abel" (Heb 12:22–24). All of those descriptive qualifiers speak of Bethel fulfilled, of the covenant community celebrating in joyful assembly. *Through eyes of faith* the people of God can recognize and understand that in their worship today, in this age, they are gathering around that mountain of God's sabbath celebration. And their deeds, in every sphere of human responsibility, should follow from and lead to such worship.

> Therefore, since we are receiving a kingdom that cannot be shaken, let us give thanks, by which we offer to God an acceptable worship with reverence and awe; for indeed our God is a consuming fire. Let mutual love continue. Do not neglect to show hospitality to strangers, for by doing that some have entertained angels without knowing it. Remember those who are in prison, as though you were in prison with them; those are being tortured, as though you yourselves were being tortured. Let marriage be held in honor by all . . . Keep your lives free from the love of money, and be content with what you have; for he has said, "I will never leave you or forsake you." So you can say with confidence, "The Lord is my helper; I will not be afraid. What can anyone do to me?" (Heb 12:28—13:3).

PART 7

The Way, the Truth, and the Life

28

Running the Race

IF GOD'S SEVEN DAYS of creation do indeed constitute the whole of reality, and if the Bible is the written witness to God's covenantal disclosure of reality, then we might sum up the responsibility of earthlings this way: "run your race along the right path faithfully and wisely." The words "right path," "faithfully," and "wisely" depend entirely on the great love commands, as Jesus articulated them: "'Hear, O Israel: the Lord our God, the Lord is one; you shall love the Lord your God with all your heart, and with all your soul, and with all your mind, and with all your strength.' The second is this, 'You shall love your neighbor as yourself.' There is no other commandment greater than these" (Mark 12:29–31).

God's sixth-day human creature, the image of God, has been created to live by *faith*—faithfully, trustingly—in all of life's labors, throughout their generations. In order to run such a race, humans need to become mature in *wisdom* to exercise their responsibilities properly before God. Living wisely by faith as God's royal stewards entails a distinctive *way of life*—following the right path—by walking with God in righteousness on the way to the creation's fulfillment.

The best-known and best-loved Psalm 23 captures the spirit of running this race. It is a song of faith from the shepherd-king David who praises God for guiding him along paths of righteousness and blessing him with comfort and abundance even when he is surrounded by enemies. David is sure that following that wise path all the days of his life will guide him into the house of the Lord forever. With Psalm 23 in mind, listen to a few of the admonitions and encouragements offered by followers of Jesus. The author of the letter to the Hebrews expresses disappointment that so many of his readers remain immature, like infants still needing milk to drink when they should be eating solid food as mature adults. What is the difference between the immature and the mature? The immature, says Hebrews, are unacquainted with the teaching about righteousness, whereas the mature are "those whose faculties have been trained by practice to distinguish good from evil" (Heb 5:13–14; Prov 9:6). Maturity of that kind is an exhibition of wisdom. The apostle Paul counsels the faithful in Thessalonica, "test everything; hold fast to what is good; abstain from every form of evil" (1 Thess 5:21). The apostle James, "a servant of God and of the Lord Jesus Christ," writes to the twelve tribes dispersed among the nations (Jas 1:1), asking them, "Who is wise and understanding among you? Show by your good life that your works are done with gentleness born of wisdom" (Jas 3:13).

To grow in wisdom through faith in Christ arises from following in the way of Christ, nurtured by the Spirit. Very early in the emergence of Christian communities, they were referred to as followers of the way.[1] Jesus referred to himself as the way, the truth, and the life after saying to his disciples that he was leaving to go to prepare a place for them. They asked him where he was going and how they could know the way (John 14:1–6). This was not an odd question from the disciples or an unfamiliar statement by Jesus. The statement and the question were right in line with Israel's experience of following God in the exodus, of God giving them the pillar of cloud and the pillar of fire to guide them in the wilderness into an uncertain future. Much later David asked the Lord, "Teach me your way, O Lord, that I may walk in your truth" (Ps 86:11; see also Exod 18:20; Deut 1:33). The wise father about whom Proverbs speaks says to his son, "I have taught you the way of wisdom; I have led you in the paths of uprightness," and urges him to "keep hold of instruction; do not let go; guard her, for she is your life" (Prov 4:11, 13).

Just as Jesus identified himself, or was identified by the apostles, as the bread and water and light of life, so his followers understood his claim to be the way and the truth of life. The New Testament authors urge their readers to hold onto Christ who is your life and walk in his way so you will live. Tremper Longman explains that the new covenant in Christ is not presented in the New Testament as a replacement for the old covenant, but as the fulfillment of the old.[2] Jesus is the originating word of God who came to dwell among us; in him all things have been created and hold together; the wisdom of God revealed in Christ is intimately related to God's wisdom for Israel.

There are many counsels of "faithfulness, wisdom, truth, and the way" in the New Testament, and they follow the long line of Old Testament *faith-wisdom-and-the-way* teachings. Paul tells Roman Christians, "Do not repay anyone evil for evil, but take thought for what is noble in the sight of all . . . Beloved, never avenge yourselves, but leave room for the wrath of God" (Rom 12:17, 19). Paul did not invent a new Christian formula for right living in this case but was quoting ancient wisdom from God, as we can read in Proverbs: "Do not say, 'I will repay evil'; wait for the Lord, and he will help you" (Prov 20:22). Psalm 101, another of David's psalms, begins, "I will sing of loyalty and of justice; to you, O Lord, I will sing. I will study the way that is

---

1. See Acts 9:2; 18:25; 19:9, 23; 22:4; 24:14, 22. Wright, *Resurrection*, 556, 566.

2. Longman, *Fear of the Lord*, 167.

blameless. When shall I attain it?" (Ps 101:1–2). David sings this song as he follows the path along which God is leading him: "I will walk with integrity of heart within my house; I will not set before my eyes anything that is base . . . I will look with favor on the faithful in the land, so that they may live with me; whoever walks in the way that is blameless shall minister to me" (Ps 101:2, 6).

David is following the commandments the Lord gave to Israel when preparing them for entrance into the promised land. Moses said to the people, "See, just as the Lord my God has charged me, I now teach you statutes and ordinances for you to observe in the land that you are about to enter and occupy. You must observe them diligently, for this will show your wisdom and discernment to the peoples, who, when they hear all these statutes, will say, 'Surely this great nation is a wise and discerning people!' For what other great nation has a god so near to it as the Lord our God is whenever we call to him? And what other great nation has statutes and ordinances as just as this entire law that I am settling before you today?" (Deut 4:5–8).[3]

Job asks, "But where shall wisdom be found?" and realizes, "God understands the way to it, and he knows its place . . . And he said to humankind, 'Truly, the fear of the Lord, that is wisdom; and to depart from evil is understanding'" (Job 28:12, 23, 28). This, too, is an echo of the covenant commands God gave Israel at the start: "So now, O Israel, what does the Lord your God require of you? Only to fear the Lord your God, to walk in all his ways, to love him, to serve the Lord your God with all your heart and with all your soul, and to keep the commandments of the Lord your God and his decrees that I am commanding you today, for your own well-being" (Deut 10:12–13). In Proverbs we read, "When the ways of people please the Lord, he causes even their enemies to be at peace with them. Better is a little with righteousness than large income with injustice" (Prov 16:7–8); "The righteous know the rights of the poor; the wicked have no such understanding" (Prov 29:7; cf. Jas 5:1–6). To do justice, to treat others with the honor and respect due them, is to walk in the way of wisdom; it is to practice—to exhibit in life—the truth. It is to know and to keep faith with God, the creator, judge, and redeemer.

The laws of life given to Israel are to be acted upon and kept with open, trusting hearts, not simply acknowledged with words and perfunctory practices of piety. Amos conveyed the following admonition from God to Israel and Judah:

> I hate, I despise your festivals,
>> and I take no delight in your solemn assemblies.
> Even though you offer me your burnt offerings and grain offerings,
>> I will not accept them;
> and the offerings of well-being of your fatted animals
>> I will not look upon.
> Take away from me the noise of your songs;

---

3. For in-depth commentary on Proverbs 27–29 and the responsibility of rulers to be wise in searching out the demands of justice, see Van Leeuwen, "Proverbs," 233–47.

> I will not listen to the melody of your harps.
>> But let justice roll down like waters,
>>> and righteousness like an ever-flowing stream (Amos 5:24).[4]

The foolishness of pride and mistreatment of others, particularly the poor and oppressed, cannot be hidden from God's sight by pious words and attendance at worship services. The way of life is more than a way of worship.

Longman emphasizes how closely biblical wisdom in Israel is tied to the order of creation and God's covenant with Israel.[5] Unusual in a book that discusses Israel's wisdom literature is Longman's attention to a little-noticed passage in Ezekiel 28, which is an oracle against the king of Tyre. The oracle lauds the wisdom the king had gained but then compares him negatively with Adam in the garden of Eden. The comparison mocks the pride (and in some respects the foolishness) of the king of Tyre. Longman points out that Adam and the king both had wisdom but lost it because of their pride. The "object lesson" of the oracle, then, is that "wisdom comes only in submission to God."[6] In regard to the origin of wisdom, the oracle is parallel to the teaching of Proverbs 8 about lady wisdom who was present when God set the heavens in place and marked out the foundations of the earth (Prov 8:27–29). True wisdom for humans derives from the creator and the very order of creation. To gain wisdom and hold it requires humility and the fear of the Lord.

PATHWAY AS JOURNEY

William Brown explains that the picture of a pathway—of life as a journey—is one of the most important underlying metaphors of the Psalms, and, I would add, of much of the rest of the Scriptures. Moreover, the picture of walking on the right path—running the race—is closely connected with heeding God's word and *doing* what God instructs.[7] Perhaps the most familiar use of this metaphor is in Psalm 119:105: "Your

---

4. Diane Bergant points to the important influence of wisdom teaching on several of the prophets, including Isaiah, Amos, Hosea, and Micah. "Although Isaiah clearly condemns human wisdom for its claims of excellence and independence of divine wisdom (cf. 5:8–14, 21; 29:14), the prophet stands within the tradition of wisdom perspectives and articulates his vision of the future in wisdom imagery. Unlike earlier prophets who only sparingly employed sapiential vocabulary, Isaiah makes extensive use of words such as 'wise,' 'know,' 'understanding,' and 'counsel.' However, it is in his image of the future that his appropriation and application of sapiential themes is most evident. In the eschatological passages 9:1–6 and 11:1–9, the future leader is called 'Wonder-Counsellor' (9:5) and is endowed with 'the spirit of wisdom and of understanding, a spirit of counsel and of strength, a spirit of knowledge and of fear of the Lord' (11:2b)." Bergant, *What Are They Saying*, 79.

5. Longman, *Fear of the Lord*, 127–46, 163–75. See also Perdue, *Wisdom and Creation*.

6. Longman, *Fear of the Lord*, 96–100.

7. Brown, *Seeing Psalms*, 31–53. Commenting on Ps 119 in particular, but taking in many other psalms by implication, Brown writes, "Poetically speaking, the metaphor of the pathway 'maps' both God's *tora* and the speaker's response to *tora*, imbuing them with a sense of dynamic, mutual engagement. Nothing is static about God's commandments and one's adherence to them. God's 'word' is a

word is a lamp to my feet and a light to my path." Following the right path by heeding God's illuminating word is also closely related to the readiness to receive God's discipline. One of the Proverbs reads, "My child, do not despise the Lord's discipline or be weary of his reproof, for the Lord reproves the one he loves, as a father the son in whom he delights" (Prov 3:11–12). The New Testament letter to the Hebrews quotes this proverb when encouraging believers not to lose heart when God disciplines them (Heb 12:5–6; see also Prov 13:18).

A close connection between our words and deeds is demanded throughout the New Testament, as it was in the Old. John says that the one who claims to know God "but does not obey his commandments, is a liar, and in such a person the truth does not exist" (1 John 2:4). True love of, and faith in, God is expressed in action: "We know love by this, that he [Jesus Christ] laid down his life for us—and we ought to lay down our lives for one another" (1 John 3:16). James asks, "What good is it, my brothers and sisters, if you say you have faith but do not have works? . . . So faith by itself, if it has no works, is dead" (Jas 2:14, 17).

How is it possible to gain the kind of wisdom needed to run the race of life in this age? It is possible, according to the New Testament, through faith in Jesus Christ, who embodies the very wisdom of God from the beginning to the end of creation. Upon Jesus's ascension to the majesty on high, the Holy Spirit descended on the world. The Spirit's coming, made possible by the reconciliation of all things to God through Jesus Christ, is twofold: to draw people to life in Christ and to convict the world of its guilt due to sin (John 14:15–27; 15:26–27; 16:5–15). Not surprising, then, is Paul's frequently used phrase (a verb) describing the Christian way of life as "walking by the Spirit." Gordon Fee explains that the verb "to walk" "was common in Judaism to refer to a person's whole way of life. Paul adopted it as his most common metaphor for ethical conduct (17 occurrences in all). All other imperatives proceed from this one. The primary form that the walking takes is living 'in love' (Eph 5:2; cf. Gal 5:6), hence love is the first-mentioned 'fruit of the Spirit' (Gal 5:22; cf. 5:14; Rom 13:8–10)."[8]

These few verses from the Old and New Testaments represent just the tip of the iceberg of the Bible's faith-and-wisdom-for-the-path encouragements and admonitions. Again and again we read the mandates to love God above all and our neighbors as ourselves, to do justice, to act with humility, to care for the poor and oppressed, to give ourselves to others in love, to become mature as wise persons able to discern and act on the difference between right and wrong in every relationship and responsibility we have. To live and love through Christ by faith is to exhibit the fruits of communion and cooperation with God in the governance and development of creation. Wisdom is required for maturity in conducting our family affairs and employments, in the

---

lamp to illuminate the psalmist's 'path' (v. 105), and the way of God's precepts is part of God's ongoing 'wondrous work' (v. 27)." Brown, *Seeing Psalms*, 34. See also Bartholomew and Goheen, *Drama of Scripture*.

8. Fee, *God's Empowering Presence*, 879–80.

execution of justice in law courts and government offices, and in teaching young people how to relate to their enemies as well as to their friends. Maturity and wisdom are evident in those who are walking in the Spirit by love in cooperation with others.

The Gospels and Epistles address whole persons and communities in the full scope of their lives. Disciples of Jesus are ordinary earthlings who grow in wisdom by walking with the Lord in faith. The followers of Jesus live from out of the Hebrew Bible and from all that God revealed to Israel along the way. In John's Gospel, especially, the wisdom texts of the Old Testament are evident in presenting the good news of Jesus. The followers of Jesus Christ have been called from death to life and therefore they should produce much fruit during their lives as they follow the path the Spirit opens to them (John 15:5–8).[9] If we are truly alive by *faith* in Jesus Christ—the last Adam— then it means that the Spirit of the Lord is drawing us into *the way* of discipleship marked out by God's love, wisdom, and righteousness.

TO HOMESTEAD OR TO SOJOURN

Contrasting metaphors that appear through much of the Bible are helpful here in capturing the drama of life. The contrast to which I am referring is between settling down and moving on, between putting down stakes and wandering, between taking possession of the land and living as strangers in exile. Let's call it the contrast between *homesteading* and *sojourning*. God made us for this world, for this creation, for the sixth-day life of royal-priestly service. The generations of the image of God belong here, not elsewhere. Life on earth is not foreign territory for us. Therefore, we should indeed live as homesteaders, as people who put down stakes and invest our lives in the place and the work God has given us, walking along the good path of life as good stewards of the world God loves so much.

At the same time, biblically speaking, we can say that our homesteading should be done as sojourners, knowing that the end in view for all earthly labors is God's sabbath rest—fulfillment in the seventh-day consummation of creation. There is a destination beyond this age toward which God is directing us, a destination we can "see" now with eyes of faith. Yet the meaning of that goal is disclosed precisely through ardent homesteading here and now, because the path toward God's rest runs right through this age, not around it or away from it (see Heb 11:8–10). The creation's seventh-day fulfillment is precisely the fulfillment of the whole creation, including all of our sixth-day responsibilities.

9. James Charlesworth makes the case that John's Gospel presents Jesus as a new Moses (in John 6:1–14), a portrait that is then enlarged so we can see Jesus as the manna God provided to Israel in the wilderness (bread from heaven; John 6:47–49). Later, John pictures Jesus as the tree of life whose branches (disciples) are to bear much fruit (John 15:8). These images and metaphors and many others appear in the wisdom literature of the Old Testament. Charlesworth, "Lady Wisdom," 103–4, 109. One can also see in John the way that discipleship in this age refers back to God's ordering of creation through the one who became incarnate in Jesus. See Culpepper, "Creation Ethics," 62–90.

Now look from the other side of the paired metaphors: we should sojourn as homesteaders. Our longing for fulfillment, for God's blessed benediction and the sha-lom of the promised land, must never be pitted against life in this age. The meaning of fulfillment, of rest and celebration comes only as the culmination of earthly lives of love and service. To be sure, our manifold sinfulness—self-serving habits, disregard and destruction of others, failure to love and serve God with all of our talents and responsibilities—leads us astray and calls for God's condemnation. True life demands that we turn from our wicked ways to follow the light that illumines the path on which we are to walk. Yet earthly life is not a problem that needs to be overcome; sin is the problem that derails both our homesteading and sojourning. Life in this world, in this age of creation, is not evil, and gives us no excuse for a desire to escape from it. Sin is the evil that makes life uncomfortable and destructive, so what is required is repentance, a turn away from sin and the foolish ways we are trying to homestead and sojourn.

Edward Adams comments on the "sojourning" image in Hebrews 11:13–14 (about the faithful who "admitted that they were aliens and strangers on earth") by saying that the author is not demonizing life on earth here. The "cosmological ethos of the epistle to the Hebrews, as I read it, is decidedly *pro*-creational."[10] It is true that misdirected, unrighteous lives on earth alienate us from God and can make us feel like strangers in a world not oriented to God as it should be. Moreover, the faithful can already see by faith the city of God that is coming. No wonder they long for it. The picture in Hebrews is like Paul's in Romans, "that the whole creation has been groan-ing in labor pains until now; and not only the creation, but we ourselves, who have the first fruits of the Spirit, groan inwardly while we wait for adoption, the redemption of our bodies" (Rom 8:22–23). It is also true that as sixth-day creatures we know that life in this age is not the ultimate end and goal of life. The more we see the fulfillment coming, the more we long for its arrival.

Nevertheless, the biblical answer to darkness and death in this age is to show and tell of the light God is shining in the darkness right now—the light and life for creation in Christ Jesus, the light of the world. In this age, therefore, we should look ahead to the age to come not by turning away from this life but by casting off deeds that weigh us down, and put on the armor of life offered by Christ. "The announce-ment of God's coming, the coming of the kingdom, his righteousness and his glory," Moltmann writes, "opens up for the people touched by it not just a new future, but the way into that future too."[11] "In the Old Testament and Judaism we find the same link between God's future and the ethical awakening of the people concerned: 'Keep justice and do righteousness, *for* soon my justice will come and my righteousness be revealed' (Isa 56:1). And—even more unambiguously—at the end of the book of Isaiah (60:1): 'Arise, *become* light, for your light *is coming* and the glory of the Lord is rising upon

---

10. Adams, "Cosmology of Hebrews," 138–39. Schenck is even more emphatic about this: *Cos-mology and Eschatology*, 52–59.

11. Moltmann, "Liberation of Future," 266.

you."[12] As Hebrews puts it, "let us consider how to provoke one another to love and good deeds . . . all the more as you see the Day approaching" (Heb 10:24–25).

The intricately interdependent seven days of God's creation require that sixth-day human creatures homestead as sojourners and sojourn as homesteaders. The commission God has given us is to be good stewards of all that is in our hands to do in anticipation of the Master's benedictory blessing in the age to come. That is Jesus's message in the parable of the talents (Matt 25:14–30). This world, life in this age, is the home in which God has placed us to develop and grow in our royal-priestly vocations on the way, by God's grace, to the supreme blessing of face-to-face celebration of God's glory in unending Jubilee. This also means that our present home is a tent, a tabernacle, soon to be transfigured into the permanent palace and royal estate of God's kingdom.[13] In the life of the risen Christ, who is the way, the truth, and the life, we can see by faith that we are *already* seated with him at the right hand of majesty on high (Heb 1:3), *already* hidden with Christ in God (Col 3:3). For that reason, we are to homestead all the more diligently as developers, caretakers, and governors of creation, building up the body of Christ, which the Spirit is knitting together to be God's house (see Heb 3:6). Surely, this is part of what John conveys in the opening of his Gospel when he says that the word of God "tented" among us (John 1:14). The word of God took on flesh in Jesus to homestead with us in this age without reserve (Heb 2:14–18). Yet his homesteading consisted of giving himself up in service to God (as our homesteading should lead us to do) and shepherding us through death and resurrection to life in our permanent home (see 1 Cor 15:54 and 2 Cor 5:1–10).[14] To run the race set before us, we are free in Christ to spend ourselves, to give up all that we are and do in loving service to God and neighbors.

---

12. Moltmann, "Liberation of Future," 266. See also Goheen, *Light to Nations*.

13. Moltmann puts it this way, using theological terms: "Every human christology is a 'christology of the way,' not yet a 'christology of the home country,' a christology of faith, not yet a christology of sight." And further, "Every confession of Christ leads to the way, and along the way, and is not yet in itself the goal." Moltmann, *Way of Jesus Christ*, xiv, 33. See also Wright, *New Heavens, New Earth*; and Marshall and Gilbert, *Heaven is Not My Home*.

14. See Culpepper, "Creation Ethics," 62–90. Charlesworth, writes that wisdom teaching, picked up in the opening section of John's Gospel, presents the Word or logos of God as antedating creation, being with God in heaven, and the agent of creation. He is the one who "brings life and light into the world and into the hearts of humans. Like Wisdom, the Word or Logos according to the prologue tented among humans; but, according to the following chapters in the Fourth Gospel, Jesus . . . returned to heaven to be with God his Father." Charlesworth, "Lady Wisdom," 118. For more on John's use of the wisdom tradition, see Witherington, *John's Wisdom*. On the identification of Jesus with the wisdom of Prov in Col, see Wright, *Climax*, 107–19.

29

Trusting the True God

MANY FAITHS, MANY GODS

FOR MANY CHRISTIANS, THE word "faith" means the Christian faith, faith in Christ. Many assume that those who are not Christians live without faith. It is also popular today to speak of "people of faith"—those who practice one or another of a variety of religions. What seems clear in the Bible is that those who do not live by faith in the God of Israel and Jesus Christ are not without faith. Their faith may be placed in someone or something different from the biblical God, but they nonetheless live by faith. To be human is to live by faith. From a biblical point of view, living by faith is part of what it means to be the sixth-day image of God, created by and dependent on the creator of all things. What does that mean?

The answer is both simple and complex. Put simply, none of us lives in complete "self-possession," as Marcel Gauchet speaks of it.[1] We do not exist in a condition of self-created self-sufficiency such that we are independent of everything beyond ourselves. In this life, we are always on the move from a past we cannot hold onto toward an unknown future we cannot create or control. Consequently, we necessarily find ourselves living by faith, trusting that there will (or will not) be life tomorrow, that life does (or does not) make sense, that each new day will (or will not) open to the prospect of food, a parent's love, meaningful work, and the joy of reward. Regardless of whether faith rests in the true God or a false god, we make decisions every day guided by what we believe, by what we trust for the meaning of things.

Many people today live by faith in freedom and individual autonomy made possible, in part, by the progress of science and technology that offer hope of gaining mastery over disease and other limitations on life, freedom, and greater happiness. Yet the progressive development of science and technology may also be pointing in the opposite direction. Some scientists and philosophers with the greatest faith in science believe that humans may be nothing more than physically, chemically, and

1. Gauchet, *Disenchantment*, 191–207.

biologically determined animals. Well-known philosopher Daniel Dennett, for example, whose recent book is titled *From Bacteria to Bach and Back*, told an interviewer in a conversation about robots, "I've been arguing for years that, yes, in principle it's possible for human consciousness to be realized in a machine. After all, that's what we are . . . We're robots made of robots made of robots. We're incredibly complex, trillions of moving parts. But they're all non-miraculous robotic parts."[2] Another author who spoke in depth with Dennett explained, "Dennett does not believe that we are 'mere things.' He thinks that we have souls, but he is certain that those souls can be explained by science. If evolution built them, they can be reverse engineered. 'There ain't no magic there,' he told me. 'Just stage magic.'"[3]

British philosopher Mary Midgley responds to the arguments of Dennett and others of his persuasion by saying that in the final analysis this mode of reductive reasoning leads to the conclusion that humans *as persons* are "an illusion." She quotes Francis Crick, one of the discoverers of DNA, who explained, "'You, your joys and your sorrows, your memories and your ambitions, your sense of personal identity and free will, are in fact no more than the behaviour of a vast assembly of nerve cells and their attendant molecules.'"[4]

Thomas Nagel, an atheistic philosopher, agrees with Midgley. The naturalistic belief that everything is reducible to energized particles, he writes, is "an assumption governing the scientific project rather than a well-confirmed scientific hypothesis." Those who criticize him for raising doubts about reductive naturalism do so "because almost everyone in our secular culture has been browbeaten into regarding the reductive research program as sacrosanct, on the ground that anything else would not be science."[5]

The paragraphs above should not be taken to imply that I believe most modern scientists and philosophers embrace the naturalistic beliefs of Dennett, Crick, and others. Perhaps a large majority of them do, but many such as Midgley, and Nagel, do not.[6] The point I am making about reductive naturalism is simply that it depends on the fundamental, unexamined assumption that reality is a self-contained physical, chemical, biotic conglomerate. That basic belief is at odds with other basic beliefs, including the fundamental presupposition of the biblical texts that everything is God's creation, made for a revelatory relationship with God. Consequently, disagreements among philosophers and scientists often arise not, first of all, in the practice of science, but at the level of basic beliefs and underlying assumptions. For that reason,

2. Thornhill, "Philosopher Daniel Dennett."

3. Rothman, "A Science of Soul," 49.

4. Midgley, *Are you an Illusion?*, 22. Closely related to Dennett in point of view is Richard Dawkins, whose book *The God Delusion* does to God what Midgley thinks Dennett does to the human person. For a critique of Dennett, Dawkins, and others, see Plantinga, *Where Conflict Lies*.

5. Nagel, *Mind and Cosmos*, 11, 7. For more from Nagel, see his *Secular Philosophy*.

6. The circle of anti-reductionists also includes Clouser, *Myth of Religious Neutrality*; Klapwijk, *Purpose in the Living World*; and Plantinga, *Where Conflict Lies*.

naturalism as a basic belief and reductive naturalism as the presumed basis for doing science demonstrate the inescapable reality that humans live by faith. What we choose to believe in is not always simple and unitary. Many (and probably most) of us try to hold on to competing beliefs, even incompatible basic beliefs about the nature of reality, including our human identity and purpose.

Strong faith, weak faith, divided faith, doubt, or radical skepticism—those appear to be the only options. Human life offers no possibility of achieving the kind of self-anchoring self-possession that would allow us to transcend our faith-dependent existence. For that reason, and in the face of so many competing beliefs, many have come to believe that there is no universal ground for faith but only a variety of choices, viewpoints, and commitments that each person or culture fashions for itself, all of which may be equally valid or invalid. Yet that conviction also functions as a basic faith, namely, believing that nothing is or can be universally valid and dependable.[7] However, one can never be certain that fundamental relativism is true. To believe that all is relative among autonomous individuals and cultures is to depend on a very basic assumption, which is to live by faith.

Every way of life that humans have tried to follow depends on and grows from faith. And that is where complexity comes to the fore in the unfolding of human experience. On the basis of deep cultural faiths, humans shape and build trust in relationships and institutions, at least until those faiths weaken or crumble due to cultural and institutional breakdown. Living by faith entails the need to trust or to doubt certain people (and institutions) with whom we are intricately intertwined, including family

7. A good example of an argument grounded in the basic assumption of human autonomy is that of legal philosopher Ronald Dworkin. Most of us, Dworkin says, think there must be more to life than simply trying to satisfy our drives, instincts, tastes, and preferences. But, why should we "want a life that is good in a more critical sense: a life we can take pride in having lived when the drives are slaked or even if they are not"? Dworkin's answer is, "we can explain this ambition only when we recognize that we have a responsibility to live well and believe that living well means creating a life that is not simply pleasurable but good in that critical way. You might ask: responsibility to whom? It is misleading to answer: responsible to ourselves . . . We must instead acknowledge an idea that I believe we almost all accept in the way we live but that is rarely explicitly formulated or acknowledged. We are charged to live well by the bare fact of our existence as self-conscious creatures with lives to lead. We are charged in the way we are charged by the value of anything entrusted to our care. It is *important* that we live well; not important just to us or to anyone else, but just important." Dworkin, "What is a Good Life?" para. 17, 18.

This argument, it seems to me, ends in emptiness, devoid of meaning. It is not a moral argument to say that to live a good life is important because it is important. Dworkin uses the morally loaded words, "responsibility," "charged," "value," "good," "entrusted," "important"—words rooted in the language of human *vocation*, of being *called* (charged) by our creator to exercise various responsibilities in cooperation with fellow humans in accord with standards that humans do not create. Yet Dworkin has emptied those terms of all moral meaning. What is left is the "feeling" that we all supposedly accept that we ought to live well because it is important. His phrases, "in a more critical sense" and "critical way," suggest something normative that transcends self-seeking pleasure, but the reference is to nothing beyond each autonomous person's critical judgment. The verbs "charged" and "entrusted" are in the passive voice, leaving entirely unidentified the person, institution, or normative principle that gives the charge or does the entrusting.

members, friends, employers, fellow workers, school teachers, pastors, bankers, and government officials. The wide diversity and complexity of relationships provides the context in which we pursue our ways of life, whether the American way of life or a communist way of life, a Christian way of life or a rationalist way of life, a libertarian way of life or a trust-in-science way of life. In fact, we inevitably find ourselves living with confidence (or uncertainty) that life in the society where we find ourselves does (or does not) have meaning in the long run and that our current purpose in life is (or is not) sufficiently clear and trustworthy to support the decisions we have to make every day.[8]

The fact that our ways of life, which are bound up with countless institutions and organizations, depend on faith shows that the deepest and most important questions about the meaning of our lives, cultures, civilizations, and history are ultimately questions of faith. This is evident in the way parents raise their children, in the reasons public officials give for making decisions, in the goals businesses set for themselves, and in the aims that shape school curricula. The fact that humans everywhere live by faith is especially evident when fundamental differences among basic beliefs clash within our hearts and minds and within and between nations and civilizations.[9]

Guiding faiths set the course for following different ways of life. In the nineteenth century, one of the founders of modern sociology, Auguste Comte, called for a new "religion of humanity" to displace the Christian religion, which he and others believed was out of date.[10] Early in the twentieth century, John Dewey argued that social habits needed to catch up with the progress of science. For that to occur, a radical change was necessary in education and social practices, he argued. A new covenant of reason was required—a comprehensive democratic way of life, a society-wide common faith, something like a secular religion of democracy.[11] It matters not whether personal conviction or mass public opinion follows the path of a religion of humanity or democracy, of secular materialism or Aryan supremacy, of nationalism or individual freedom; they all depend on basic assumptions, on faith and trust. All of them are competing for our allegiance. The modern dogma that a secular way of life is not religious because it does not appeal to a transcendent deity is now recognized by many scholars and ordinary people to be a sleight of hand (or a sleight of language and thought). Ways of life not guided by faith in a god beyond this world are not thereby

8. The literature now available on religions and attempts to live by faith or without faith, is voluminous. Here is a small sample. Calhoun, et al., *Rethinking Secularism*; Nagel, *Secular Philosophy*; Kearney, *Anatheism*; Taylor, *A Secular Age*; Clouser, *Myth of Religious Neutrality*; Benson, *Graven Ideologies*; Gauchet, *Disenchantment*; Cogley, *Religion*; Dooyeweerd, *Twilight*.

9. See, for example, Smith, *Sacred Project*; Huntington, *Clash of Civilizations*; Kolakowski, *Modernity*; Lukacs, *Confessions*; Voegelin, *From Enlightenment*; Dooyeweerd, *Roots*; Rundell, *Origins*.

10. Comte, *Catechism*. On Comte see Voegelin, *From Enlightenment*, 136–94.

11. See, in particular, John Dewey's books, *My Pedagogic Creed*, and *Democracy and Education*. On Dewey, see Selznick, *Moral Commonwealth*, 17–36, 172–75, 522–25; and Berkowitz, "Religion of Democracy," 133–39.

nonreligious, for they depend on something else as the ground of faith. We can speak quite legitimately, therefore, of *secular* religions, such as Comte's religion of humanity, Dewey's religion of democracy, or, in Luc Ferry's words, "the humanism of humanity made God."[12]

FAITH IN THE COVENANT-MAKING GOD

Hundreds of millions of people today live by faith in the God of the biblical covenants—the creator, judge, and redeemer of life, the beginning and end of all things. Hear O Israel, the Lord our God is one: "you shall have no other gods before me. You shall not make for yourself an idol, whether in the form of anything that is in heaven above, or that is on the earth beneath, or that is in the waters under the earth" (Exod 20:3–4). The biblical proverbs teach that the fear of the Lord is the beginning of wisdom (Prov 15:33). Wisdom that comes from accepting our dependence on God and walking with God is what opens hearts and minds to the path of life: "Trust in the Lord with all your heart, and do not rely on your own insight. In all your ways acknowledge him, and he will make straight your paths" (Prov 3:5–6). Without trust in God, according to Proverbs, one will become foolish rather than wise. Without fear of the Lord, one's path will be crooked and lead to death.[13]

The Bible knows of no bifurcation between "religious" and "non-religious" realms of life. It recognizes the difference between worship and work, between sacramental acts and farming or parenting. But it does not recognize a distinction between a part of life that is lived in relation to God and other parts that are unrelated to God. All of life is related to God, lived in relation to God. Van Leeuwen comments, "We moderns tend to exclude the divine mystery from history, leaving only natural connections between acts and consequences. But ancient Israel saw God as the hidden actor even in the mundane."[14] Von Rad put it this way: "It was perhaps her [Israel's] greatness

---

12. The quotation is from Ferry, *Man Made God*, 131. Ferry's book, Gauchet's *Disenchantment,* and Eagleton's *Culture and Death of God* are good examples of contemporary thinkers who recognize the impossibility of living without faith.

13. According to Von Rad, "When Jeremiah says that that man is blessed who trusts in Yahweh (Jer 17.7), then he is, as far as his thinking is concerned, wholly within the sphere of the sentence which states that the fear of Yahweh is the beginning of knowledge (Prov 1.7; etc.). The 'fool' was not simply an imbecile, but a man who resisted a truth which presented itself to him in creation, who, for whatever reasons, did not trust in an order which would be beneficial for him, but which now turns against him." Von Rad, *Wisdom in Israel*, 298. That is the understanding Paul expressed in his letter to the Romans about God's condemnation of the "godless," who are without excuse for their ignorance and foolishness. It's not that they never knew about God and therefore had an excuse for not trusting God, "for though they knew God, they did not honor him as God or give thanks to him, but they became futile in their thinking, and their senseless minds were darkened. Claiming to be wise, they became fools; and they exchanged the glory of the immortal God for images resembling a mortal human being or birds or four-footed animals or reptiles" (Rom 1:21–23).

14. Van Leeuwen, "Proverbs," 135. For some profound insights along these lines see Smit, "Divine Mystery," 223–46.

that she did not keep faith and knowledge apart. The experiences of the world were for her always divine experiences as well, and the experiences of God were for her experiences of the world."[15] For Israel, life with God encompassed the whole of life, everything that goes on in the realm of human responsibility—family life and agriculture, war and worship, buying and selling, eating and drinking. In the everyday world of human relationships and care for the earth, Israel was called to follow in the way of the Lord. True faith meant full trust in God. To live by faith entailed trusting the way of the Lord.

From a standpoint inside the drama of the creation's natural and historical development, we might say with Van Leeuwen that the meaning of life comes to focus in the relation between "divine mastery and responsible human freedom,"[16] or perhaps we could say, between divine mystery and human responsibility. The relation between God and the human generations in this age remains something of a mystery from our human point of view. However, there is a fundamental difference between biblical Christianity and modern, naturalistic secularism, which starts with the assumption that the natural world of human experience is not dependent on a creating and caring God. Those who live by that faith seem to hope that whatever life's unknowns might be, they will be uncovered and dealt with by human reason; religious myths are of no help. It is easy to see, therefore, why secular religions challenge the basic presuppositions of biblical religion with its belief in an all-embracing relationship between God and human creatures.

Several lines in Proverbs 15 and 16 may sound paradoxical or contradictory to modern ears, but they make an important point about God's relation to humans. The Bible testifies to the intricate and all-embracing relation between the creator and creaturely life while at the same time showing that God's ways are above human ways. According to the proverbs, "The human mind plans the way, but the Lord directs the steps" (Prov 16:9); "The eyes of the Lord are in every place, keeping watch on the evil and the good" (Prov 15:3); "The Lord has made everything for its purpose, even the wicked for the day of trouble" (Prov 16:4). Our first reaction to these proverbs might be to ask: if the Lord determines everything, then how can the wicked be responsible for their wickedness? If the Lord directs each person's steps, does that mean the plans people make are illusory or useless?

Questions like those arise from a mistaken assumption that the Lord's decisions and our decisions function on the same plane of cause and effect: either God or the wicked person is responsible for wickedness; either God or the one who makes plans is responsible for the steps a person takes. It cannot be both, we say; it must be either/

15. Von Rad, *Wisdom in Israel*, 62. Von Rad goes on to say, biblical faith "does not—as is popularly believed today—hinder knowledge; on the contrary, it is what liberates knowledge, enables it really to come to the point and indicates to it its proper place in the sphere of varied, human activity. In Israel, the intellect never freed itself from or became independent of the foundation of its whole existence, that is its commitment to Yahweh." Von Rad, *Wisdom in Israel*, 68.

16. Van Leeuwen, "Proverbs," 195.

or. But that misses the biblical context of meaning in which humans are made for a comprehensive relation to God; they are created in God's very image and likeness. The mystery of God's relation to human beings is built into the seven-day order of creation in which humans exercise genuine responsibility under God's sovereignty. God's actions do not undermine or displace human responsibility, but relate to it by upholding its genuineness and accountability; God created humans to exercise just such responsibility. In this age, we must plan our course of action and bear responsibility for our decisions whether we act wisely or foolishly, righteously or wickedly, justly or unjustly. At the same time, God's ways and purposes are always higher than our ways, doing more than we can imagine or fathom, for God is the Lord of all seven days of creation, of everything that exists. Those who live by faith in this God can count on wise counsel, corrective discipline, light on their path, and loving care to guide their decision making. Humans are neither autonomous nor automatons; they are made for the exercise of real responsibilities in partnership with God.

The presentation of divine mystery and human freedom in the Bible is not confined to the Old Testament. It is deeply imbedded in the New Testament's message about what it means to live by faith. In Paul's letters, as Gaffin explains, there is what might seem to us to be an odd relation between his *indicatives* and his *imperatives*, between what he observes and explains, on the one hand, and what he admonishes or commands, on the other.[17] By faith, according to Paul, Christians can speak of themselves as *already* united with the resurrected Christ. Paul speaks of that union as a fact, using the indicative: "So if you have been raised with Christ . . ." That phrase is then followed by an imperative directed to human responsibility: "seek the things that are above, where Christ is, seated at the right hand of God" (Col 3:1). That may sound backward to us. If we have already been raised with Christ, why would Paul urge us to seek what is above (where he said we already are)? Why would he not reverse the order and urge us to set our hearts on things above *in order that* we might be raised with Christ. To understand Paul's language, we need to recognize that the indicative arises from Christ's bond with his people. Christ, our brother, who is our life, has already been raised and already sits at the right hand of majesty on high, and we who live *by faith* see ourselves united with him. That is why, in the arena of our present responsibilities, we should (imperative) act in keeping with (the indicative of) Christ's life and position. Our responsibilities continue in this age in the confidence that we are joined with Christ all the way into the age to come.[18]

17. Gaffin, *By Faith*, 68–69. Additional examples of this indicative/imperative relationship can be found in Rom 6:2, 12; 1 Cor 5:7; Gal 5:1, 25; Eph 5:8; and Col 3:9–10.

18. Gaffin, *By Faith*, 71. "If according to Jesus' gospel the kingdom of God is 'close,'" writes Moltmann, commenting on Matt 3:2 and parallel passages, "then it is already *present*, but present only as the *coming* kingdom," not yet as the completed and fully revealed kingdom. Moltmann, *Way of Jesus Christ*, 97. For Wright's interpretation of Paul on the relation of God's completed kingdom to the continuing exercise of human responsibility in this age, see *Paul and Faithfulness*, 1078–128. Cf. Moloney, "God, Eschatology," 197–219.

Here, as in the Old Testament's proverbs (and other texts), there is a mystery about the relation between God's actions and human actions, between what God does and what we continue to be responsible to do. The relation between God's actions and ours, between God's revelation *in Jesus Christ* and the responsibilities that belong to his followers in this age, cannot be fully explained from within the temporal categories and language of our present mode of experience. The God of the biblical covenants calls us, in Christ, to trust the Lord for the meaning of life because life in its fullness is beyond our fathoming even though God is opening it to us. With humility and wisdom, therefore, we should put our trust in the God that leads us as a good shepherd along the path of life.

FROM FAITH TO SIGHT

Paul's indicatives and imperatives make sense if we accept that we have been created to live by *faith* and *trust* in God. Biblical faith entails trusting the God who has already raised Christ to the throne on high. In this age, our comprehension of those divine actions will always be limited. That is why we are to seek the wisdom God has for those who walk faithfully and humbly with the Lord. Rather than be frustrated by the limits of our understanding, we should accept and relish the mystery of being the creature God made us to be, created in God's image for the highest level of responsibility of service to God. We should be awestruck every day with the realization that we have been commissioned to serve as God's royal stewards, as the rulers and developers of the earth, able to anticipate the day when we will know as we are known and live with God face-to-face in sabbath celebration. In following this way of life, we will discover that all of our vocations, including the work of science and philosophy, open to the service of God and to learning more and more about both God and ourselves.

Quite in contrast to the mystery of trust in the true God is the mystery of why we turn away from trust in God's faithfulness toward trust in ourselves. In our sin we become increasingly unable to see, hear, and understand even what God has clearly revealed in this age. We try to live by following myths of our own making, thinking we are wise and can solve our own problems. In our disobedience and wickedness we become blind and deaf to the truth all around us, as Paul explains in the first chapter of Romans. Those who choose not to live by the wisdom that comes from trusting and serving God are not in fact able to free themselves from dependence on God. Instead, they become trapped in the foolishness of serving false gods that will only fail. In order to live truly, rightly, fruitfully, and wisely, therefore, we need to be cleansed of our unrighteousness so we can learn to love wisdom instead of foolishness and to follow paths of love, justice, and good stewardship rather than paths of hatred, wastefulness, and degradation. That is precisely what Christians confess that God is doing for fallen humanity in Jesus Christ.

This is the good news of Paul's message in Romans 8:18–24. The new humanity in Christ's resurrection lives now in anticipation of the transfiguring redemption of the whole creation. According to Paul, Wright explains, "the creation itself . . . will be set free from its bondage to decay 'unto the freedom of the glory of the children of God.'"[19] The larger picture within which Paul's vision of resurrection makes sense is that God's good creation, liberated from the corruption and decay brought on by human sinfulness, will celebrate with resurrected humans the glory of the kingly rule of the Messiah. And that vision and hope of resurrection, grasped now by faith, calls for those still at work in this age to present their bodies a living sacrifice to God (Rom 12:1–2), offering up the fruits of all their labors as gifts to God.

Throughout this book we have been arguing (on the basis of an acknowledged faith in the biblical God) that all people, without exception, whether they acknowledge it or not, live in God's world completely dependent on the Lord of heaven and earth. Every person shares the identity of the image of God, made for life in God's seven-day creation. We have all been made to exercise God-given responsibilities that depend on faith-communion with the creator who loves us and commissions us for this service. As creatures who bear real responsibility, therefore, we face a choice: 1) live by trust in the true God, the source and illuminator of life's meaning that is now reaching fulfillment through Jesus Christ, or 2) try to live by trust in ourselves and in the gods we create for ourselves to try to achieve the goals and purposes we choose and work for. In each case, to live is to live by faith, trusting in the God or gods we serve.

If everything that exists is the creation of God, then it is not possible to appeal to some standard of evidence outside of God and creation to prove that the biblical story of life is true or false. In fact, it is impossible for humans to *prove* that any story (or argument) about human identity and purpose is true or false, judged by criteria that transcend all stories and arguments. We have all been created to live by faith, and only the consummation of creation will validate the truth or error of the paths we have chosen to follow in our earthly lives. Proof comes with the confirmation of faith, with the fulfillment of life, not before. And if it is true that the whole of reality is God's seven-day creation and not a closed "nature" of inexplicable origin and destiny, then the different faith-guided ways of life will have consequences and yield evidence along the way that indicate what is wise and what is foolish, what is good and what is detrimental, what is a blessing and what is a curse. In particular, if we accept that everything about our earthly lives is revelatory of God and that our very identity as God's royal stewards calls us to invest our lives in loving cooperation with one another, then we will discover that the life of service to God and neighbors through Jesus Christ is the pathway that rewards its followers with wisdom and joy even in the toughest and most troubling of times.

19. Wright, *Resurrection*, 258.

In this book, I have been writing from the standpoint of faith in the Lord of the biblical drama, the God who made us in the divine image, male and female in our generations. We have explored only a little of what it means to live by faith in dependence on the words and actions of the biblical God whom we have come to know as the patient, longsuffering, covenant-keeping Lord of Abraham, Isaac, Jacob, and Jesus. Messiah Jesus is not a private god who belongs to the Christian community or a household god with whom we can bargain in times of need or overwhelming crisis. In biblical terms, Christ Jesus is the Alpha and the Omega, the one with whom every person and every people must come to grips. He is the judge and redeemer who addresses every tribe and nation. He has come and is coming again to fulfill God's promises, to complete God's judgment-redemption of this sin-darkened creation, reconciling all things to God. In the end, says Paul, every knee will bow and every tongue confess that Christ is the Lord of all (Phil 2:10–11). He is the way, the truth, and the life. His Spirit continues even now to lead the faithful into all truth (John 14:15–21) while also "convicting the world of guilt in regard to sin and righteousness and judgment" (John 16:8–11). We do not belong to ourselves; we do not own ourselves. Those who seek to hold onto their lives will lose them, but those who give themselves up in service to God and neighbors will receive them in a new and fulfilling way.

Moltmann says the expectation that God's kingdom will fill the earth is closely connected to Israel's practice of sabbath celebration every week, every seventh year, and especially in the year of Jubilee. In Israel's experience, "the sabbath rest is already a foretaste of the redeemed world. Consequently in Israel the sabbath has always been especially close to God's expected Messiah . . . The sabbath rest links the experience of God *in* history with the messianic hope in God *for* history."[20] Thus, when Jesus began his public teaching by reading the Jubilee Year announcement from Isaiah in a synagogue in Nazareth (Luke 4:16–21; Isa 61:1, 2), there could be no doubt that he was announcing the messianic presence of God in history and calling people to repent and to turn to God in faith because the kingdom of God is at hand.

20. Moltmann, "Liberation of Future," 280.

30

Maturing in Wisdom

WISDOM IS WHAT WE need if we are to live rightly, rewardingly, justly, and lovingly with one another, with all other creatures, and with God. Wisdom begins with recognizing reality for what it is: God's revelatory creation. This means conducting our lives with the conviction that our honor and dignity come from the one who created us in the divine image. The overriding and all-embracing purpose of human life through all generations is to worship, love, and serve God as royal, priestly stewards of creation. To live wisely in this age is to cooperate in investing our talents and energies in God's creation-wide building program, which is drawing together everything good from the generations of humankind and all creatures into a climactic revelation of the divine-human community that will fill creation full. If the meaning of life in this age is to be disclosed by giving ourselves wholeheartedly to God's revelatory-anticipatory building program, then the wisdom we need for the exercise of our responsibilities is the kind that is fit for precisely that kind of life—life as the sixth-day image of God in God's seven-day creation.

Wisdom also demands of us an open acknowledgement that our pride and arrogance make us fools rather than wise persons. In that condition, we are unable to please God or find fulfillment. But how can stubborn, arrogant fools gain the kind of wisdom and self-understanding they need? To desire such wisdom and to turn to God for it indicates a willingness to repent of our foolishness and arrogance. Yet how is such repentance possible for fools? It is possible because repentance and wisdom are gifts from a merciful God who loves us and has opened the way to reconciliation and fulfillment. In fact, that is precisely what the biblical story tells us. God's judging and redeeming work has been carried forward through long ages of covenantal mercy revealed through Noah, Abraham, and Israel, and now through the new covenant in Christ's blood, by which all things are being reconciled to God. Through the wisdom of God embodied in Christ Jesus we can begin to live again, *here and now*, by turning from arrogance to humility and from ignorance to understanding to follow the one whose humility, faithfulness, maturity, and love embody and exhibit the true way of life.[1]

DOES WISDOM ELEVATE LIFE OR CONSTRICT IT?

The teaching of Ecclesiastes, however, seems to cast doubt if not downright scorn on the value of wisdom. The reader might even wonder why that book is in the Bible. In some parts of it, the teacher (*Qoheleth* in Hebrew) does laud wisdom, saying for example, "Then I saw that wisdom excels folly as light excels darkness. The wise have eyes in their head, but fools walk in darkness" (Eccl 2:13–14). However, the passage from which we have just quoted quickly takes a different turn, raising a crucial question about whether to pursue wisdom or even to trust God. For the teacher observes, "'What happens to the fool will happen to me also; why then have I been so very wise?' And I said to myself that this also is vanity[2]. For there is no enduring remembrance of the wise or of fools, seeing that in the days to come all will have been long forgotten. How can the wise die just like fools?" (Eccl 2:14–16).

According to Van Leeuwen, Ecclesiastes and parts of the books of Job and Proverbs open up complexities, apparent contradictions, and mysteries that demonstrate how limited human wisdom is.[3] Perhaps, then, the teacher of Ecclesiastes is simply recognizing those limits to the human quest for wisdom. Yet that is not always the tone of Qoheleth. It is certainly true, the teacher observes, that the wise person and the fool will both die and that very few human beings are remembered for very long after they die. Does it then make any difference whether a person seeks wisdom or pursues a life of foolishness? If life should be judged only by the similar way it ends for every person, then perhaps we should just eat, drink, and be merry for as long as we live. If everything is vanity—meaningless or unfathomable—why bother trying to gain wisdom?

Before going further with that line of thought in Ecclesiastes, consider the similar-sounding words of Psalm 90:

1. For more on Jesus as the Wisdom of God who comes as the reconciling redeemer of sinners and Lord of life, see Wright, *Jesus*, 311–16; Wright, *Resurrection*, 281–94; Longman, *Fear of the Lord*, 243–56; and Witherington, *Jesus the Sage*.

2. In his commentary, *Ecclesiastes*, Craig Bartholomew generally uses the words "enigmatic" and "incomprehensible" to convey the meaning of the Hebrew word translated in many versions of the Bible as "vanity" or "meaningless." For a somewhat different yet complementary approach, see Greidanus, *Preaching Christ*.

3. Van Leeuwen, "Proverbs," 17–264.

> You [Lord] sweep them away; they are like a dream,
> > they are like grass that is renewed in the morning;
> in the morning it flourishes and is renewed;
> > in the evening it fades and withers . . .
> For all our years pass away under your wrath;
> > Our years come to an end like a sigh.
> The days of our life are seventy years,
> > or perhaps eighty, if we are strong;
> even then their span is only toil and trouble;
> > they are soon gone, and we fly away (Ps 90:5–6, 9–10).

One can easily imagine that the next verse of the psalm might read, "This too is vanity, unfathomable, enigmatic." Yet the psalm does not continue that way. The words just quoted are from the middle of the psalm. Moses actually begins with praise to the Lord, the creator of everything, who has been "our dwelling place in all generations" (v. 1). Moses concludes with a prayer that is both a plea and an expectation: O Lord, "satisfy us in the morning with your steadfast love, so that we may rejoice and be glad all our days . . . Let the favor of the Lord our God be upon us, and prosper for us the work of our hands—O prosper the work of our hands" (Ps 90:14, 17).

One can see from the comparison of these texts that while Moses and Qoheleth both recognize the common earthly passing of wise and foolish persons, Qoheleth frequently stops after that observation and draws the conclusion that all is vanity or meaningless. Moses, on the other hand, continues with a confident appeal to God who is active beyond human fathoming yet at the same time gives us shelter and the assurance of the enduring value of our labors. Moses asks God to do what only God can do, namely, make something out of our human frailty beyond the length of our days in this age. God has always been Israel's dwelling place and therefore God can be trusted to continue as our dwelling place to the end and forever. Even though at death we seem to fly away like withering grass, Moses pleads with God to prosper the work of his hands, confident that God can do it. Moreover, as the author of Hebrews says, the life and accomplishments of Moses have indeed been established as part of the very house that God is building through Messiah Jesus (Heb 3:1–6).

Returning to Ecclesiastes, we hear the teacher say that when he was king over Israel, he applied his "mind to seek and to search out by wisdom *all that is done under heaven*; it is an unhappy business that God has given to human beings to be busy with. I saw *all the things that are done under the sun*; and see, all is vanity and a chasing after wind" (Eccl 1:12–18, italics mine). In searching for wisdom, the teacher had focused on what is seen under the sun, but God's actions and purposes are not confined to what happens under the sun. Consequently, gaining true wisdom requires more than an understanding of what takes place under heaven. True wisdom demands humility before God who is above all things and assesses our lives day by day in relation to more than what can be observed under the sun.

Despite the differences in the quotations from Psalm 90 and Ecclesiastes, the teacher does eventually reach a conclusion that resonates with the overall message of Psalm 90. Even though it might appear, from one point of view, that choosing between the way of wisdom and the way of foolishness makes no difference, there is something too restrictive about that judgment. In fact, despite the expressed frustration that everything is vanity, "Qoheleth never offers folly as an option," says Roland Murphy. "He condemns folly at several points (5:3; 6:11; 10:12–15)."[4] After finishing what he wants to say about the limits of his quest for wisdom, the teacher comes to the following "conclusion of the matter:" "Fear God, and keep his commandments; for that is the whole duty of everyone. For God will bring every deed into judgment, including every secret thing, whether good or evil" (Eccl 12:13–14).

What we can never know in this age, the teacher concludes, are the secret, hidden things. Only God can "bring every deed into judgment." The ultimate decision that every person must make, therefore, is whether or not to trust God and keep his commandments throughout life in this age. The teacher thus expresses the conviction that all is not meaningless when we regard life from the viewpoint of God's transcendent wisdom and sovereignty. There is more to life, and more to our relationship with God, than we are able to see in this age of our sixth-day generations. Only God has the wisdom to make the final determination about the goodness and evil of our deeds. Leo Perdue writes that for the teacher of Ecclesiastes, "Humanity is not the center of reality, nor are humans the measure of all things. God, not humanity, rules over creation and directs history, though in utter secrecy."[5] As Van Leeuwen puts it in his discussion of Proverbs,

> Not even the wise can comprehend all the contradictions and mysteries of life, of God and cosmos. The wicked can prosper, especially in a time of chaos, and the righteous can suffer unjustly. (These themes are developed more extensively in Job and Ecclesiastes.) Still, Proverbs insists that it is better to be poor and godly than rich and wicked . . . Ultimately Proverbs is a book of faith (1:7), insisting on the reality of God's justice and righteousness, even when experience seems to contradict it (see Hebrews 11). God's justice often remains hidden, since much of life—and God's own self—is beyond human grasping . . ."[6]

4. Murphy, "Israel's Wisdom," 18.

5. Perdue, *Wisdom and Creation*, 242. Commenting on Proverbs 16:1–9, Van Leeuwen writes, "In God's freedom and sovereignty, human wisdom—for all its goodness and indispensability—finds its radical limits. In the mystery of world and humankind, the sages encountered the mystery of God, who answers finally to no one else. God is not answerable to us humans, nor subject to our manipulations and theological demands (cf. Rom 3:3–8; 11:33–36)." Van Leeuwen, "Proverbs," 163.

6. Van Leeuwen, "Proverbs," 25. Von Rad concludes his study of wisdom in Israel by saying that "the presupposition for coping with life is trust in Yahweh and in the orders put into operation by him. Particularly characteristic of the fact that in the teachings of the wise men everything comes from Yahweh and is, in the last resort, directed towards him, was the theme of proper trust, a theme to which the wise men return again and again, and the warning against false trust." Von Rad, *Wisdom*

Wisdom is not something humans can achieve simply by observing what appears, or by a rational effort to penetrate behind what appears. Wisdom is not something we can gain by mental effort or a will to power.[7] It is a gift from God that grows in the hearts and minds and conversations of those who work at obedience, who seek to *do* the truth in humility before God. Wisdom is required for, and arises from, wholehearted engagement with the responsibilities of this life that God has given us, and that is why trusting in a false god and misunderstanding the reality of which we are a part will lead to foolishness, not to wisdom. Speaking from the perspective of Proverbs, Perdue writes, "Through the study of and love for wisdom, the life-sustaining, ordering power of creation is made accessible to humans. Indeed, the wisdom tradition in its continuing and dynamic formulation is grounded in the life-giving order of the cosmos. Wisdom comes to humans as both a divine gift . . . and the result of human study and desire. Wisdom must be given by God; it cannot be grasped. Yet wisdom cannot be attained, unless it is desired."[8]

Wisdom is what parents need in order to nurture loving families through many stages of development and unanticipated crises. When Paul tells children to "obey your parents in the Lord" (Eph 6:1) and tells fathers not to "provoke your children, or they may lose heart" (Col 3:21), he speaks not only from the fifth commandment (Exod 20:12), but also from proverbial wisdom: "A wise child loves discipline, but a scoffer does not listen to rebuke" (Prov 13:1), and "Train children in the right way, and when old, they will not stray" (Prov 22:6). Wisdom is what government officials need in order to conduct sound statecraft and to uphold justice (see especially Prov 28–29). Wisdom is what responsible farmers, engineers, teachers, artists, scientists, and entrepreneurs need for the development and practice of their distinctive crafts, the organizing of interrelated disciplines, and for training apprentices who will eventually be able to go beyond their mentors in creative and fruitful achievements.

Wisdom is not first of all a tool for survival, but the fuel for flourishing in God's creation as we learn to know ourselves ever more truly in the process of coming to know God ever more profoundly. When humans conduct their affairs worthily, build sound institutions as well as trustworthy relationships, and do right by one another and other creatures, then they reveal something of the wisdom and glory of God that

---

in Israel, 307.

7. In a fascinating article on Martin Heidegger's late writings, David Bentley Hart explores Heidegger's assessment of the western philosophical quest for wisdom. Heidegger believed that by the twentieth century that quest had led to nihilism, making it "all but impossible for humanity to dwell in the world as anything other than its master." Human reasoning, given over to science and technology, is now "simply a narrow and calculative rationalism that sees the world about us not as the home in which we dwell, where we might keep ourselves near to being's mystery and respond to it; rather, the world for us now is mere mechanism, as well as a 'standing reserve' of material resources awaiting exploitation in the projects of the human will." Heidegger, according to Hart, says that we now live "in a very deep twilight indeed; ours is the time of the 'darkening of the world and the flight of the gods.'" Hart, "A Philosopher," 44–51.

8. Perdue, *Wisdom and Creation*, 84.

anticipates the full disclosure of that glory in the age to come. Participating in that mode of revelation, we come to know more of God and thereby come to know more of who we are as the image of God. The two go hand-in-hand, as John Calvin stated so emphatically.[9] In the long historical course of God's covenantal dealings with humankind, more and more of the wisdom humans need for serving God has been disclosed. Finally, in Jesus, the humanly embodied wisdom of God has been revealed in a preeminent way.[10] For men and women to mature in wisdom is part of what it means to grow up in the life-giving Spirit of Jesus Christ.

WISDOM AND THE REVELATORY PATTERNS OF CREATION

One way to show what wisdom means and how it works is to explore it in relation to the revelatory patterns of creation we introduced in chapter 4.

Honor and Hospitality

The first pattern is that of *honor* and *hospitality*. The honor of human creatures is found in our identity as the image of God, made for partnership and fellowship with God in developing and governing the earth. Men and women have the honor of cooperatively exercising a wide range of responsibilities in caring for and governing creation, involving all of our talents and vocations.[11] The honor God bestows on us can be seen, as Psalm 8 puts it, in our crown of glory as rulers over the works of God's hands, including everything from gardening to home building, from parenting to engineering,

---

9. John Calvin is known for starting his *Institutes of the Christian Religion* with a discussion of the relation of self-knowledge to the knowledge of God, saying that all human wisdom and knowledge depends on the knowledge of God and of ourselves. But Brown makes a valuable observation about Calvin in this regard. In Calvin's disputes with Roman Catholics, he was very critical of the use of images, as were other Protestant iconoclasts. The problem, says Brown, is that "in his iconoclastic zeal, Calvin confused image and idol." In fact, the prophets "reveled in imagery: Hosea likened God to an 'evergreen cypress' (Hos 14:8); Jeremiah was fascinated with the image of the potter and his clay (Jer 18:1–12); and Malachi fashioned the effulgent image of the 'sun of righteousness' rising 'with healing in its wings' (Mal 4:2a [3:20a Heb.])." Brown, *Seeing Psalms*, 9–10.

10. Charlesworth observes that the Christology in John's Gospel is "quite unlike Job 28 and Baruch 3–4, according to which only God knows the place of Wisdom. For the Fourth Evangelist, Wisdom is embodied in Jesus, the Logos, and the Johannine community puts its stamp on the incarnation of Wisdom by stressing that 'we have seen his glory, glory as of the only Son from the Father' . . . As A. S. van der Woude points out, the purpose of Wisdom is to glorify God, and this task 'equals cultic sacrifices.' This idea in Judaism would have been appealing to the fourth Evangelist, who stands out among the evangelists in stressing the glory of Jesus." Charlesworth, "Lady Wisdom," 101–2. On Paul's interpretation of Colossians regarding Jesus as the embodiment of God's wisdom, see Wright, *Climax*, 107–19.

11. On Proverbs 26 Van Leeuwen writes, "'Honor' (or 'glory') designates one's place in society (26:1, 8). It encompasses such things as power, authority, position, office, prerogatives, and even wealth . . . God (Mal 1:6), kings (Ps 21:6), rulers (Gen 45:13), as well as ordinary men and women—all have a glory that is proper to them ([Prov] 3:35; 11:16; 15:33; 18:12; 20:3; 27:18; 29:23; Sir 10:23–24, 27–31)." Van Leeuwen, "Proverbs," 226.

from performing arts to public governance. Everything we do wisely and fruitfully enriches our experience of being in community with God as bride, family, disciples, priests, dwelling place, and kingdom citizens.[12] All of this is part of what allows us to serve as *hospitable* hosts of God as we lift up the creation in priestly service to him.

Honor and hospitality are related intrinsically as two sides of the same coin. Gaining dominion over the earth means that humans are developing their capabilities cooperatively in order to provide mutual benefits as well as thank offerings to God. Our honor is revealed in honoring God above all, and that requires love of one another and wise care of God's other creatures in keeping with the honor God has given each of them. To do this requires sound judgment based on keen insight. That depends on wisdom, for it is wisdom we need in order to give proper honor to God, to one another, and to every other creature. When we do justice in our position of ruling, stewarding, and blessing creation in the service of God, we thereby find satisfaction and delight in the hospitality we offer to God and to one another. There is nothing in all creation that does not find its place in this relationship of honor bestowed and hospitality provided.

Much of the law given to Israel indicates how to make correct distinctions in order to recognize the honor due to each creature. Leviticus 18 and 19 contain long lists of such distinctions. "Do not dishonor your father by having sexual relations with your mother" (Lev 18:7, TNIV). "You shall not have sexual relations with an animal and defile yourself with it" (Lev 18:23, TNIV). "Do not curse the deaf or put a stumbling block in front of the blind, but fear your God. I am the Lord" (Lev 19:14, TNIV). "Do not mate different kinds of animals. Do not plant your field with two kinds of seed. Do not wear clothing woven of two kinds of material" (Lev 19:19, TNIV). The lists touch on almost every kind of relationship among humans and between humans and other creatures.[13]

Two verses in Proverbs exemplify the pattern with respect to retributive justice. Proverbs 17:15 and 17:26 read, "One who justifies the wicked and one who condemns the righteous are both alike an abomination to the Lord," and "To impose a fine on the innocent is not right, or to flog the noble for their integrity." The scene here is a courtroom or prison and the issue is retributive justice. To acquit the guilty or to punish the innocent is exactly backwards, upside down, a violation of the principle that one should receive what one deserves or is owed. As Van Leeuwen says about Proverbs 28:5, "Without justice in human relations and society, there is no true knowledge of God (see [Prov] 29:7; Jer 22:13–16). Conversely, to seek God without seeking social

12. Van Leeuwen says that in Proverbs 8:27–31 the relation between "architect-adviser" (master workman) and the expression of delight can be understood by reference to other scripture passages. "A counselor who gives good advice is a source of delight to the one counseled: 'Your decrees are my delight, they are my counselors' (Ps 119:24). And Israel, pictured as a vineyard created by God's hard work, is called the 'garden of his delight' (Isa 5:7 NIV)." Van Leeuwen, "Proverbs," 95.

13. See Longman, *Fear of the Lord*, 109–75.

justice is an exercise in bad faith (Amos 5:46, 14–15)."[14] One can easily see from these few references why wisdom is closely connected with justice and righteousness. Wise people discern and build on what is right and just, leading them to do what is fitting, fruitful, and in tune with the honor and hospitality that belong to each of God's creatures and, above all, to God.

Commission Towards Commendation

When we look at the second pattern introduced earlier, we see that the human vocation—or commission—to develop and govern the earth requires the kind of wisdom that is generated from the ongoing conversation we are to have with God as we carry out our earthly responsibilities. Recall for a moment the observation Brown makes about two of the dominant metaphors in the Psalms: "pathway" and "refuge." Pathway is something taught, studied, and revealed, says Brown, appealing to passages in Psalms 16:11, 27:11, and 101:2. It suggests directed movement toward the accomplishment of a mission, seeking the right direction toward the right goal. "'Refuge,' by contrast, is neither revealed nor taught; it is, rather, a domain of existence established by and identified with God."[15] Yet, the two images reinforce one another in the Bible in ways that illuminate the pattern of commission toward commendation. God has commissioned humans with responsibilities that require wisdom in order to follow the right path to achieve what God has called us to do. Yet the purpose of life is not found in the endless following of a path, even a righteous path. Men and women want to complete their work, to enjoy the fruits of their labors, to offer them up to God, and to receive the reward of rest and celebration with the Lord (see Matt 25:14–30; Luke 19:17; Heb 4:9–11).

Psalms 5, 16, 23, 31, and 84, among others, bring these two metaphors together beautifully. The "pilgrimage song" of Psalm 84, says Brown, "integrates both movement and residence: those who set their face toward Zion to dwell in its courts are identified with those who 'walk uprightly'" (84:11b). "Indeed, the pilgrimage to Zion is a journey of the heart, within which is set the sanctuary route. As they 'go from strength to strength,' sustained along the way by the fructified land, they reach their final destination. The journey to Zion is rooted in both the will and emotive depth of one's being. The metaphor of the 'pathway' effectively directs desire, conjoins body and soul, and prepares the heart to enter God's domain."[16] The pathway, in other words, is the way of covenant faithfulness.

The biblical God is not the deists' god who supposedly got the world started and then stepped back to let it roll on by itself self-sufficiently like a self-winding clock. The biblical God is deeply involved with creation from beginning to fulfillment,

14. Van Leeuwen, "Proverbs," 237.

15. Brown, *Seeing Psalms*, 39; and see 15–30.

16. Brown, *Seeing Psalms*, 41. See also Lund, *Way Metaphors*.

taking delight in it, agonizing over its degradations, urging those on the wrong path to return to the way of life, and making covenants of blessings and curses to manifest the honor and loving purposes of God.[17] From a biblical point of view, wisdom is more than scientific and technological expertise that might lead to useful outcomes for the development and management of particular ventures in this age. Wisdom guides constructive insights and contributions of human reasoning, to be sure, but more profoundly it manifests itself in sound judgments about human conduct in all of life's relationships and responsibilities. Wisdom lies behind the maturation of love among family members, neighbors, friends, and even our enemies; it is central to mastering the arts of counseling, teaching, elder care, environmental protection, and governing. The apostle James asks, "Who is wise and understanding among you? Show by your good life that your works are done with gentleness born of wisdom . . . But the wisdom from above is first pure, then peaceable, gentle, willing to yield, full of mercy and good fruits, without a trace of partiality or hypocrisy. And a harvest of righteousness is sown in peace for those who make peace" (Jas 3:13, 17–18).[18]

Wisdom also teaches, therefore, that men and women should welcome God's correction, reproof, and discipline so they can stay on the right path or return to it. Quoting Proverbs 3:11–12, the author of Hebrews writes, "My child, do not regard lightly the discipline of the Lord, or lose heart when you are punished by him; for the Lord disciplines those whom he loves, and chastises every child whom he accepts" (Heb 12:5–6). God disciplines us "for our good, in order that we may share his holiness. Now, discipline always seems painful rather than pleasant at the time, but later it yields the peaceful fruit of righteousness to those who have been trained by it" (Heb 12:10–11). Without God's discipline, there can be no intimate, conversational, and creative walk with God that engenders the wisdom we need. Whether therefore we need correction or congratulation, condemnation or commendation, it is not possible to establish our own systems of assessment and reward sufficient to guide and judge the totality of our lives. That kind of discipline and commendation comes only from the one who made us and commissioned us for a calling greater than any we could devise for ourselves. It is from the good shepherd that we learn to be good shepherds.

Consider Van Leeuwen's commentary on Proverbs 27:23–27, a brief poem celebrating the pastoral life of sheep and their shepherd. There is a play here, says Van Leeuwen, on the metaphor of the shepherd as a king and the king as a shepherd. "The metaphor of the king as shepherd was widespread in the ancient world, including Israel (cf. Psalm 23) . . . Whether applied to a landholder or to a ruler, this little poem (27:23–27) reminds all people that God has given them a quasi-royal responsibility for a bit of this earth . . . Our stewardship requires that we know intimately those things, creatures, and persons entrusted to our care (27:23). Governments need to understand the people, the land, and justice. Teachers need to know and love their

---

17. See Perdue, *Wisdom and Creation*, 122.

18. For more on the wisdom of James, see Longman, *Fear of the Lord*, 252–54.

students and their subjects. Workers and artists need to know their materials and their craft."[19]

Many of the Proverbs and other biblical texts elaborate on this portrayal of human responsibility. Two proverbs offer the same wise insight: "Those who oppress the poor insult their Maker, but those who are kind to the needy honor him" (Prov 14:31). "Whoever gives to the poor will lack nothing, but one who turns a blind eye will get many a curse" (Prov 28:27). Poor people are easily ignored and pushed aside, and they certainly cannot afford to pay for an attorney to defend them. But just like rich persons, they have the same maker who has created them in the divine image to carry out God's commission of earthly governance and development. This connects "commission toward commendation" with "honor and hospitality." Failing to act as good shepherds of our neighbors in carrying out our responsibilities is to dishonor the creator. At stake here is not only the honor that belongs to every human person, rich or poor, but also the honor that belongs to God.

This is where we can hear the music of the good news of the new covenant: God's Son, the good shepherd stoops all the way down to dwell among us, taking on our sixth-day identity and responsibility as his own, giving up his life to provide purification for our sins, and calling brothers and sisters to follow him faithfully in the renewal of our responsibilities until our work is completed. Then, in the fullness of time and because of the faithfulness of Jesus, God's original decree of "very good" (Gen 1:31) will be realized and we will understand the words, "This is my Son in whom I am well pleased." Becoming one with us in this age, Jesus became the mediator who is reconciling all things to God, restoring the glory and the responsibilities of the image of God, and blessing the faithful with God's gracious gift of entry into the resurrection hospitality of God.

Revelation in Anticipation

The creature that reveals God most remarkably is the one made in the divine image. The wise exercise of human responsibilities, including the worship of God, is the chief medium through which we come to know God and ourselves in the covenantal conversation that constitutes our relationship with God. Commenting on Proverbs 2:5-9, Van Leeuwen writes, "Humans get to know God somewhat as they get to know a language, through interaction with parents and others who speak and act in the ordinary activities of life. As parents relate to God, world, and others, they communicate a certain understanding of God and reality. The child's business is gradually to take responsibility for his or her life in response to parents, [other] persons, the world, and God. The quest for wisdom is necessarily a quest for God, for wisdom comes from God."[20] It is precisely in and through marriage, family, friendship, industry, commerce,

---

19. Van Leeuwen, "Proverbs," 233–34.

20. Van Leeuwen, "Proverbs," 43.

education, governance, and worship that we grow in the knowledge of God and in self-knowledge.[21] Consequently, the development of all these divine-human relationships opens the way to an understanding of the deep, revelatory meaning of our honor and hospitality and of our commission from God that drives us forward in our high calling in Christ Jesus.

Through the creational pattern of anticipatory revelation we become especially aware of the relation between human wisdom and divine wisdom. True wisdom that we gain and exercise in this age is revelatory of divine wisdom. Human wisdom manifested in the exercise of just governance, family love, economic integrity, and care for other creatures reveals something of the divine wisdom that makes human wisdom possible. One of the most remarkable portrayals of wisdom in the Bible is the personification of wisdom as a woman worth more than gold and silver, as the pure wife who stands in obvious contrast to the prostitute, and as the diligent and productive person who epitomizes all that humans should be. The first of these personifications appears, for example, in Proverbs 3:13–15:

> Happy are those who find wisdom,
>   and those who get understanding,
> for her income is better than silver,
>   and her revenue better than gold.
> She is more precious than jewels,
>   And nothing you desire can compare with her.

The second personification of wisdom comes through in some of the Proverbs, Psalms, and the Song of Songs. In Proverbs a father advises his son,

> Let your fountain be blessed,
>   and rejoice in the wife of your youth,
>   a lovely deer, a graceful doe.
> May her breasts satisfy you at all times;
>   may you be intoxicated always by her love.
> Why should you be intoxicated, my son, by another woman
>   and embrace the bosom of an adulterer? (Prov 5:18–20)

---

21. Perdue comments on the importance of teaching and learning in the biblical wisdom tradition. Whether in the family, or an apprenticeship, or a school, disciplines were developed "through a course of study and a process of correction" (see Prov 1:2–3, 7–8; 15:33; 23:23). "Becoming wise is a way of life, a process that continues for a lifetime, as the wise person seeks to live in harmony with God, the cosmos, the social order, and a human nature, which requires the discipline and structure of teaching." Perdue, *Wisdom and Creation*, 73–74. This is at least part of the background to an understanding of Jesus's call for his disciples to follow him. It is clearly evident in the Hebrews passage about "the teaching of righteousness" learned by mature people "whose faculties by have been trained to distinguish good from evil" (Heb 5:13–14).

The third and especially striking portrait of lady wisdom comes in Proverbs 31:10–31.[22] Not only does this portrait show the importance of women in disclosing the image of God, but it also shows how this particular woman epitomizes wise humanity in a wide range of responsibilities. The wise woman here is like the faithful wife who, in many biblical passages, represents the whole of humanity in their role as the bride of God (see Isa 54:5–8; Hos 2:16–20), as the bride of Christ (Eph 5:25–33; Rev 21:1–4). The Proverbs 31 passage is too long to quote in full, but a few of its verses are illustrative:

> A wife of noble character who can find?
>   She is worth far more than rubies . . .
> She selects wool and flax
>   and works with eager hands . . .
> She considers a field and buys it;
>   out of her earnings she plants a vineyard.
> She sets about her work vigorously;
>   her arms are strong for her tasks . . .
> She opens her arms to the poor
>   and extends her hands to the needy . . .
> She speaks with wisdom,
>   and faithful instruction is on her tongue . . .
> Honor her for all that her hands have done,
>   and let her works bring her praise at the city gate.
> (Prov 31:10, 13, 16–17, 20, 26, 31, TNIV)

This woman's deserved praise "at the city gate" reminds us of the honor of governing justly. Earlier in this litany about the wise and valiant women, we are told, "Her husband is known in the city gates, taking his seat among the elders of the land" (31:23). That parallels Job's recollection of his finest hour, before his suffering began.

> When I went to the gate of the city
>   and took my seat in the square,
> the young men saw me and stepped aside
>   and the old men rose to their feet, . . .
> Whoever heard me spoke well of me,
>   and those who saw me commended me,
> because I rescued the poor who cried for help,
>   and the fatherless who had none to assist them. . . .
> I put on righteousness as my clothing; justice was my robe and my turban. . . .
> People listened to me expectantly, waiting in silence for my counsel"
> (Job 29:7–8, 11–12, 14, 21, TNIV).[23]

---

22. For excellent commentary on Proverbs 31:10–31, "Hymn to the Valiant Woman," see Van Leeuwen, "Proverbs," 259–64.

23. The pervasive concern of Prov 28 and 29, says Van Leeuwen, is for just rule. "Israelite rulers were responsible for justice, the righting of wrongs (2 Sam 14:4–11; 15:1–6). They especially were

Covenant for Community

Fourth and finally, the pattern of *covenant for community* illuminates the tightly woven interdependence of all four patterns. Humans—the very image of God—are created for community with God. In that regard, the seven days of creation are the all-embracing, covenantal context of that community. Humans are the creature God honors above all others—the creature made to develop, care for, and rule the earth in hospitable, thankful cooperation with God. The generations of sixth-day humankind are sent forth on a mission that will deepen, widen, and enrich communion with God in familial, educational, entrepreneurial, artistic, priestly, prophetic, and governmental ways.[24] Wisely and faithfully nurturing the talents and capabilities required for those responsibilities reveals something of God's nurturing care and confirms the high calling of the human generations and the covenantal integrity of creation.

We should not be surprised that the grand, complex expanse of creation, particularly of the long-developing human generations, has been made to serve as the host of the divine-human community. The great hymn of Colossians 1:15–20, which conveys much the same message as the opening verses of Hebrews and of Revelation 1:4–8, 12–18, presents a concentrated expression of the cosmic scope of the covenant for community brought to fulfillment through Christ Jesus:

> He [Christ] is the image of the invisible God, the firstborn of all creation; for in him all things in heaven and on earth were created, things visible and invisible, whether thrones or dominions or rulers or powers—all things have been created through him and for him. He himself is before all things, and in him all things hold together. He is the head of the body, the church; he is the beginning, the firstborn from the dead, so that he might come to have first place in everything. For in him all the fullness of God was pleased to dwell, and through him God was pleased to reconcile to himself all things, whether on earth or in heaven, by making peace through the blood of his cross (Col 1:15–20).

The seven-day order of creation, born through the wisdom of God is the dynamic context of God's relation to creation from beginning to fulfillment, from "Let there be light" to "Enter my rest." In God's climactic day of creation, the community of honor fulfilled through God's new covenant in Christ will become the hospitality center of

---

required to do justice for the poor, who have no earthly defender (see Prov 22:22–23; 23:10–11; 29:4, 14; Ps 72). For this purpose, God has given these rulers authority and power, and they are accountable to God in their exercise of that power (see Wis 6:1–9; Rom 13:1–7)." Van Leeuwen, "Proverbs," 239; see also 214.

24. Van Leeuwen writes that a person of important social status, a person with "weight" and/or wealth in ancient societies, was not necessarily the person who manifested true wisdom and integrity. In biblical terms, however, "becoming a human of 'weight' begins by submitting to the formative discipline of another self. Character formation requires parents, teachers, and mentors who know what makes a solid person and how to help others become solid people." Van Leeuwen, "Proverbs," 133.

divine joy. All anticipatory revelations throughout this age will be joined together as constitutive elements of the fully revealed city of God, the completed and resurrected community of Christ's body in the age to come. In that day of sabbath celebration, at home with God, we will be filled with wisdom in all that we do henceforth and forever.

31

Following the Right Path

CHARTING THE WAY

THE LETTER TO THE Hebrews in the New Testament presents a beautiful, compact, tough-love exposition of what it means to walk by faith with wisdom on "the way" of life. The letter begins with a celebration of the revelation of God's Son "in these last days," the climactic, definitive communication that will never be surpassed. For God's Son is the very "reflection of God's glory," the one "through whom" God created all things, and the one who sustains "all things by his powerful word." The extended passage that continues after that initial burst of praise is all about the preeminence of the Son of God who has taken on human flesh to fulfill God's purposes. In reading the first chapters of Hebrews, one is reminded of Jesus' words, "I am the way, the truth, and the life." To trust and follow him on the right path is life itself. Listen, then, to what God is saying through this Son.

According to Hebrews, the trajectory of the Son's journey moves from the foundations of creation to the fulfillment of all things.[1] Those whom God is addressing through the Son are enveloped by this revelation. Creatures made in the image of God are part of the universe created through the Son; they are the ones to whom the words of "these last days" are directed; they are the sinners for whom the Son has provided purification for sins; and they (we) now stand before him, enthroned now "at the right hand of the Majesty on high."

There is no creature, including angels, superior to God's Son. Verses 5–14 of chapter 1 explain the Son's superiority with quotations from the Psalms and other passages in the Old Testament. The angels are servants of the Son, called to worship him. He is the Davidic king whose throne God will establish forever, with righteousness "the scepter of your kingdom." Regarding the human generations, the author quotes Psalm 110, conveying God's word to the Son: "Sit at my right hand until I make

1. Reading Hebrews as narrative is developed in Schenck, *Cosmology and Eschatology*, 10–17, 182–90. See also Schencke, "Keeping His Appointment," 91–117.

your enemies a footstool for your feet." The Son of God introduced in the first chapter of Hebrews is the foundation of creation (the Alpha) and the divine-human ruler who now sits on the throne of God's completed kingdom (the Omega).

What does the preeminence of God's Son mean for the image of God, male and female, whom God commissioned to rule the earth under God? That is precisely the question the author answers in the next three chapters of the letter, and he urges readers to pay very close attention so they will not miss the good news and suffer "just punishment" for having ignored "such a great salvation." Following him on the right path by faith with wisdom is a matter of life itself.

CROWNED WITH GLORY AND HONOR

The letter's focus, beginning at Hebrews 2:5, shifts to the world to come, that is, the world seen from the viewpoint of the incarnate Son seated at the right hand of majesty on high. Because of that focus, we might feel jolted by the sudden transition in 2:5, where the author shifts from discussing the Son's superiority to discussing the position in which God originally placed humans in relation to the angels.[2] Here he quotes from Psalm 8, which in many ways is a rearticulation of Genesis 1: "What are human beings that you are mindful of them, or mortals, that you care for them? You have made them for a little while lower than the angels; you have crowned them with glory and honor, subjecting all things under their feet" (Ps 2:6–8). The letter then continues with the words, "Now in subjecting all things to them, God left nothing outside their control" (Ps 2:8b). We hear, in this quotation from Psalm 8, three themes that are tightly intertwined in Hebrews. First, there is the relation of humans to the angels—made a little lower than the angels, but not subject to them. Second, there is the high calling of humans to govern and develop the earth. Third, there is the relation of the Son to the men and women the psalmist says were crowned with glory and honor.

The climax of the Son's journey to the right hand of majesty on high is closely connected, as we can see, to the beginning of all things, because everything has been created through him. The Son moves from supremacy to supremacy, from authoritative originator and sustainer of all things to incarnate Lord of life enthroned at God's right hand. The surprising thing, as the quotation from Psalm 8 indicates, is that this appears to be the very trajectory for which God created humans (male and female) in the first place. For God made them "a little lower than the angels" yet crowned them with glory and honor, putting everything under their feet.

What then is the connection between the supreme Son and the sixth-day humans created in God's image? Have the humans of Genesis 1 and Psalm 8 now been displaced by God's incarnate Son? A difference between them is certainly indicated here. Humans, for example, are created through the Son and are not the ones through

---

2. Schenck deals with the relation of Heb 2 and Ps 8 in detail in *Cosmology and Eschatology*, 51–77.

whom God made the universe. God has crowned humans with glory and honor, but only the Son is "the reflection of God's glory and the exact imprint of God's very being" (Heb 1:3). Nevertheless, the verses in the second chapter that we just read show a common bond or identity between the Son and the humans of Psalm 8 and Genesis 1:26–30.[3] That close connection is explained in the remainder of chapter 2, verses 9–18, and the explanation has everything to do with a brief phrase that appeared earlier in 1:3: "when he had made purification for sins."

Immediately after the author of Hebrews quotes Psalm 8, adding, "God left nothing outside their control," he says, "we do not yet see everything in subjection to them" (2:8b). Evidently, God's assignment of humans to rule the earth has not yet been accomplished. The glory and honor that crowns humans is apparently not yet fully (if at all) realized. Why is that? The author begins to answer that question by pointing to what we *do* see in contrast to what we *do not* see. What we *do* see is *Jesus*! This is the first time in the letter the name of Jesus appears,[4] and he is identified with the humans of Psalm 8: "but we do see Jesus, who for a little while was made lower than the angels, now crowned with glory and honor" (Heb 2:9a). The common humanity of *Jesus* and the *humans* of Psalm 8 (and Genesis 1) shines through in the fact that the Son of God became fully human in Jesus.[5]

The sentence does not stop there, however. It continues with the explanation that he was crowned with glory and honor *because* he suffered death, so that "by the grace of God he might taste death for everyone" (Heb 2:9). Jesus's death is directly tied to "everyone"; he did not die for himself. Jesus is the one through whom God is "bringing many children to glory," and to do that "it was fitting that God, for whom and through whom all things exist . . . should make the pioneer of their salvation perfect through sufferings. For the one who sanctifies and those who are sanctified all have one Father. For this reason Jesus is not ashamed to call them brothers and sisters" (Heb 2:10–11). Scott Hahn writes, "The point is that Jesus does not regain the Adamic privileges for

---

3. Support for this interpretation comes, for example, from Bartholomew, *Introducing Biblical Hermeneutics*, 515–16; Long, *Hebrews*, 57–62; Wilson, *Hebrews*, 47–67; and Schenck, *Cosmology and Eschatology*, 55.

4. See Ellingworth, *Epistle to Hebrews*, 153.

5. Schenck suggests that the author of Hebrews understood Ps 8 to be about humans as well as Christ, with a "radical relationship" between them. "The psalm would then imply that the sons [the humans of Gen 1 and Ps 8] were destined for glory and honour like Christ, as well as to rule over the All like Christ. Indeed, it becomes possible to see Christ's glory as a solution to the problem of humanity's failed glory. Christ and humanity become identified with each other as [Heb] 2:9 now moves from the glory promised to human kind to the glory fulfilled in Jesus as the representative of his 'brothers.'" Schenk, *Cosmology and Eschatology*, 55. In other words, Jesus does not displace the "man" of Psalm 8:5 by pushing them (male and female) aside. To the contrary, Jesus is a man of the sixth-day human generations and takes on the full identity and responsibility of those generations. Moreover, as the letter explains, the suffering and crowning of Jesus is "for everyone." The Son—Jesus—who provides purification for sins and is elevated to the right hand of majesty in heaven does this on our behalf as our human brother who is "bringing many children to glory" after "tasting death for everyone."

himself only, but to share them with the rest of humanity."[6] Furthermore, as Hahn points out, "The 'brothers' of Christ are strikingly called his 'children' twice in this passage (vv. 13–14)." But how can Christ be both father and brother? "This becomes explicable," Hahn continues, "when we recall that in the ancient patriarchal family, the firstborn son inherited all the legal and cultic rights and responsibilities of the father, and thus became like a second father to his younger siblings."[7]

Hahn assumes that the suffering unto death of Jesus regains the Adamic privileges humans lost due to sin. But it is not clear from the passage that the honor of being created in God's image with the commission to govern the earth was lost and needs to be regained. Jesus affirmed the creaturely identity and responsibility of humans by becoming one with them; it is their purification from sin—the sin that has misdirected and dishonored them—that is needed. Humans have clearly broken troth with God and turned to their own way, failing to exercise their responsibilities faithfully. Humans mired in sin must be cleansed if they are to fulfill their Adamic calling, and Hebrews tells us that Jesus, the incarnate son, offered himself for precisely that purification.

In addition to human faithlessness as the reason we "do not yet see everything in subjection to them," another part of the reason is that not all of the human generations have yet been born. So the God-given vocation of the human generations must continue to develop. In any case, it is precisely the creation mediated through the Son that is being redeemed and fulfilled by the one to whom God said, "Sit at my right hand until I make your enemies a footstool for your feet" (Heb 1:13, quoting Ps 110:1). In other words, *everything about the earthly glory and honor of human life in God's creation is being perfected (brought to fulfillment) through Jesus,* who locks arms with his brothers and sisters in doing so. The glory and honor with which God crowned men and women has reflected God's glory in the Son from the beginning. The Son of God, by becoming one with us in Jesus, stands in for us and with us, and in so doing, he suffers death for everyone so he can bring many brothers and sisters (sons and daughters) to glory by making them holy, by cleansing them of sin. This is nothing less than the announcement of creation's redemption—creation reconciled and fulfilled through the one who sustains all things yet who stooped to become one with us, thereby making possible the fulfillment of the human vocation to govern the earth as God's vicegerrents.[8]

What we discover from Hebrews 2, in other words, is a multifaceted revelation in Jesus. He is not only a sacrificial lamb who makes propitiation for sin. He is the exemplar of what it means to be human, exhibiting how the image of God should live

---

6. Hahn, *Kinship by Covenant*, 286.

7. Hahn, *Kinship by Covenant*, 286. For Hahn's introduction to the meaning of kinship as the root of covenant bonds, see 37–48.

8. On the Levitical sacrificial background to the death of Jesus as covenant bonding see Polen, "Leviticus and Hebrews," 217–25.

on earth in faithful service to God. And it is only by fulfilling all that God has made humans to be and to do that their crown of glory and honor can be disclosed with everything properly ordered under their feet.[9] For Jesus to be honored for his death and suffering as a propitiation for sin certainly tells us that, at present, something is insufficient and degraded about the God-honored humans for whom he came to taste death. His sacrifice is for purification in order to reconcile all things to God. In that regard, the *incarnation* tells us that God decided it is fitting that the one who will make many sons and daughters perfect should himself be made perfect through suffering. The one who sanctifies them and those who are made holy are of the same family.

By becoming one of us, Jesus is able to serve as the kinsman redeemer of his brothers and sisters, thereby upholding and fulfilling the high calling for which God has created them. Jesus is the pioneer of life, the exemplar of how humans should live, the one who illumines the pathway and guides the travelers to the fulfillment of their creaturely vocation so that everything will be ordered to the praise of God. That is why the author can emphasize that we *do* "see Jesus." The author has already emphasized the destiny of this incarnate Son of God in 1:3: "When he had made purification for sins, he sat down at the right hand of the Majesty on high." The supreme Son, having become fully human, having accomplished all that is needed for the purification of sinners and the reconciling fulfillment of creation, sat down in kingly rule with everything properly ordered under his feet.

The flesh-and-blood humans, who are God's sixth-day creatures with a high calling that has not been taken from them, have fallen into a condition of slavery because of their fear of death (Heb 2:14–18). Their fear of death is apparently what leaves them subject to the devil who holds the power of death. They find themselves subject to the devil, they fear death, and therefore they are not living as they should be living in open, fearless service of God. This is precisely why at present "we do not see everything in subjection to them." In these circumstances, God does not come to help angels but to help the human creatures commissioned with responsibility and authority to rule the earth. In order to liberate men and women, God saw fit to make their redeemer perfect through suffering. Only a fellow human could make atonement for sin. And precisely as a man, Jesus took on that role of the merciful and faithful high priest.

THE WAY OF THE CROSS

Hebrews 1–2 touches again and again on the role of human beings created to govern the earth. Through the incarnation of the Son who redeems human beings with all their creaturely responsibilities, God upholds the honor, commission, and revelatory character of those created in God's image. That is who God made us to be; our earthly

---

9. The point I am making here could open to an extended discussion of the several metaphors that have characterized arguments over the meaning of Christ's atonement. For an introduction to that subject see Boersma, *Violence*, 99–201.

calling remains the same. Yet as long as we persist in stumbling along in the dark, alienated from God, destroying the earth and one another, we will be broken creatures gripped by the fear of death. Christ's atonement for sins overcomes what is wrong, carries sin away, and puts death and the devil under his feet.

Although Hebrews does not speak of "the way of the cross," the author clearly has the cross in view when discussing the atonement for sins through Jesus's suffering unto death. He has tasted death for everyone and thus can free them from the grip of the one who holds the power of death. Jesus calls us to follow him along the path he has traveled, the path of service to God and one another even if it leads to suffering and death, because through faith we know that, in Jesus, God assures us of life. As the author says later in the letter, "Remember those who are in prison, as though you were there in prison with them, those who are being tortured, as though you yourselves were being tortured . . . Through him, then, let us continually offer a sacrifice of praise to God, that is, the fruit of lips that confess his name. Do not neglect to do good and to share what you have, for such sacrifices are pleasing to God" (Heb 13:3, 15–16). Just as Jesus identified with us, we should put ourselves in the place of fellow humans who are suffering and serve them with deeds of loving sacrifice for their good. Following the way of the cross means learning to live as Jesus did. We must become willing—free of the fear of death—to give ourselves up for our neighbor's sake, not trying to hold on to our lives as if we could secure them against death.

Very much in tune with Hebrews, Paul explained Christ's death this way: "Indeed, rarely will anyone die for a righteous person—though perhaps for a good person someone might actually dare to die. But God proves his love for us in that while we still were sinners Christ died for us" (Rom 5:7–8). Paul urged the Philippian Christians to adopt the same attitude that Jesus exhibited in giving himself up to death on a cross for us. "Do nothing from selfish ambition or conceit, but in humility regard others as better than yourselves. Let each of you look not to your own interests, but to the interests of others" (Phil 2:3–4). Jesus himself instructed his disciples to love even their enemies and not just their friends (Luke 6:27–36).

What Hebrews 1–2 explains is that yielding to temptation and sin is not an alternate way of life for God's creatures; instead, it is the way of fear, slavery, and death. It is not a path along which one can actually walk and live without fear. It is not a way forward for those made in the image of God and crowned with glory and honor. That is why the author opens the second chapter with a reminder about those in the past who did not listen to the angels' message and received justifiable punishment for "every transgression or disobedience." If that is what happened to those who were warned by angels, says the writer, then "how can we escape if we neglect so great a salvation," which has now been announced by the very Son of God? (Heb 2:2–3; 1:1–2). The true way of life is the one for which God created us (Heb 2:5–8; Ps 8:3–8; Gen 1:26–30). It is the way of life Jesus has come to recover for us. Jesus gave up his life on the cross for that purpose and God raised him from the dead to sit at "the right hand of the Majesty on high." The way of life leads to crowning fulfillment.

Of course, following the way of the cross does not mean that we can make others perfect through our suffering or provide purification for their sins. That is what Jesus alone could do. It is in Jesus, not in those who follow him, that we see the "merciful and faithful high priest" who made atonement for the sins of the world. Our way of life is the way of thankfulness to God *in Jesus*, of giving ourselves over without reserve to the one who has set us free from the devil and the fear of death. That way of faithful living is precisely the one for which God created us, as shown in the life of Jesus. Wright says the gospel Paul preached can be "summarized under the word *katallage*, 'reconciliation,'" as articulated in 2 Corinthians 5:13—6:2. The whole of creation is being reconciled to God in Christ Jesus. The gospel is "the truth about the world, about its creator, about all of human life."[10] James Thompson makes the important point that the verb "to perfect" as used in Hebrews means "to bring to completion,"[11] or as I would put it, "to bring to fulfillment." The right path to perfection, completion, and fulfillment is the path from the beginning to the culmination of God's creation purposes in God's sabbath with creation.

GOD'S HOUSE-BUILDING PROJECT

The dominant image of the divine-human relationship in the first two chapters of Hebrews is familial in the patriarchal manner that characterized ancient times: father, son, and siblings (brothers and sisters), which is the basis of the images of ruling and priestly service. In the third chapter, the author moves to a second prominent image, that of a house or royal estate. The author urges the brothers and sisters of Jesus, who, because of him, now share in the heavenly calling, to "consider that Jesus, the apostle and high priest of our confession, was faithful to the one who appointed him" (Heb 3:1). That leads to a comparison of Jesus with Moses, whom the Israelites followed out of Egypt. Moses and Jesus, writes the author, were both appointed to serve in God's house-building program.[12] Moses was "faithful in all God's house," but "Jesus is

10. Wright, *Paul and Faithfulness*, 1488.

11. Thompson, *Hebrews*, 67.

12. When Stephen Dempster discusses New Testament typological interpretation of the Hebrew Bible, he writes that two meanings of "house" merge in the person of Jesus in the New Testament. The "house" of David (in the sense of a dynasty) and the "temple" both find fulfillment in Jesus Christ.

worthy of more glory than Moses, just as the builder of a house has more honor than the house itself" (Heb 3:3). Even though, historically speaking, Moses served prior to the coming of Jesus, Hebrews nonetheless speaks of Moses as having served in the house that God has been building through the Son all along, the Son whom we now meet in Jesus. Moses, in his day, was testifying "to the things that would be spoken later." Now, in these last days, we are witnessing the arrival of the builder and proprietor of the house. Here for the first time in his letter, without explanation or comment, the author uses the name "Christ" (Messiah): "Christ, however, was faithful over God's house as a son" (Heb 3:6).

Then, in a surprising metaphorical enlargement, the author makes this statement: "*and we are his house*, if we hold firm the confidence and the pride that belong to hope" (Heb 3:6b, italics added). The house that God has been building all along—from the time of Moses and Abraham (Heb 2:16) and even from the "foundations of the earth" (Heb 1:10)—is a human community, a family, a household. Bartholomew emphasizes the creational overtones of the imagery here. "As a Son, Jesus is the Davidic king who rules over all things, and we know from [Heb 1:2] that Jesus is the agent of creation and thus also 'the builder of all things'" (Heb 3:4).[13] We who are being made into God's house are now called sons and daughters of God through the suffering and glory of the brother who is making us into a holy dwelling for God. From the viewpoint of our sixth-day mode of experience, the building of that house is still going on today. It is not yet finished. *We* today are being made part of God's house "if we hold firm the confidence and the pride that belong to hope" (Heb 3:6). The Son over God's house is already seated at the right hand of majesty on high. He has been made perfect through suffering. He is now serving not only as lord of creation and high priest of God's people, but also as the Son and host of God's house. Those who hear and respond to what God is saying through his Son in these last days and do not ignore such a great salvation, but hold onto their great hope in Christ, are being crafted into the very dwelling place of God.

What the author sees overarches time in ways that are grammatically unfamiliar to us. The "Son of God," "Jesus," and the risen "Christ" are names spoken with the use of multiple verb tenses, past, present, and future. God is building a house, not yet complete, in which Moses was a servant of Jesus even though Jesus did not live on earth until long after Moses. Jesus sits enthroned, but the house over which he holds authority is not yet completed. With that vision before him, the author of Hebrews sees the unfolding generations of humankind continuing to carry out their responsibilities on earth through faith in Christ Jesus who is now seated on high in seventh-day glory.

Dempster, *Dominion and Dynasty*, 233. However, Dempster does not emphasize the Hebrew Bible's development of the ways in which tabernacle, temple, and other realities serve as revelatory anticipations of God's seventh-day dwelling with fulfilled Israel, who are, as Hebrews puts it, the house of God.

13. Bartholomew, *Introducing Biblical Hermeneutics*, 503. For more on the house and temple metaphor see Ellingworth, *Epistle to Hebrews*, 196–97.

What comes together in Hebrews is the close relationship among several images of fulfillment—the house, the promised land, God's rest, fulfillment of the human family, heaven, and God's glory.[14] All of these make manifest the revelatory character of creation, which keeps on mounting up toward fulfillment. As Wright says, "For Paul, the point was that the new creation launched with Jesus' resurrection was the renewal of creation, not its abolition and replacement."[15] Along the way, tabernacle, temple, and visions of the heavenly throne point ahead in anticipation to God's completed house. The ultimate promised land of rest with God is the goal of God's blessing of human faithfulness.

A WARNING IN VIEW OF THE SABBATH REST

At the same time that the author speaks of what God has completed in Christ, he urges the faithful to keep on being faithful, to hold onto their hope, which is grounded in what Jesus has done for them. Just as the author remembers all too well how the Israelites kept falling away from their hope, falling away from faithfulness in God's house, and thus incurring God's wrath, he does not want those now responding to the good news of God's revelation in Jesus to fall away from faith and hope. The remaining verses of the chapter focus on this theme, with important quotations from Psalm 95. And here, for only the second time, the author refers to the work of the Holy Spirit (Heb 3:7; 2:4), who is God at work in the distribution of gifts, warnings, discipline, and blessings among men and women on earth. In the same way that the Holy Spirit warned Israel (through the words of Psalm 95) not to harden their hearts, the author now delivers the same message, which continues to ring out as a living word for our day. "Take care, brothers and sisters, that none of you may have an evil, unbelieving heart that turns away from the living God. But exhort one another every day, as long as it is called 'today,' so that none of you may be hardened by the deceitfulness of sin. For we have become partners of Christ, if only we hold our first confidence firm to the end" (Heb 3:12–14).

This is the opening through which Hebrews leads us to see by faith the awesome vision of God's sabbath rest, which has been opened to us through Jesus, our elder brother and savior. This is the subject we introduced in chapter 3 when first considering God's seven days of creation in Genesis 1 and 2. Since Jesus, the resurrected Christ, has ascended to God's right hand and entered God's rest, God is drawing the earthlings whom Jesus has drawn to himself into that sabbath rest. The author of Hebrews sees God's day of rest as the climax of the story, the completion of the journey with all of its labors, the goal of the true way of life, the time without evening and morning when we will celebrate the glory of God, creator, judge, and redeemer.[16]

14. Schenck develops much of this brilliantly in *Cosmology and Eschatology*, 51–77, 144–81.

15. Wright, *Paul and Faithfulness*, 1491.

16. Wilson says that the word for sabbath rest (*sabbatismos*) used in Heb. 4:9–10 may have been

God's rest is the opened heaven where Christ Jesus sits with his brothers and sisters at the right hand of majesty (see Isa 66:1). God's rest—the seventh day of creation—is what the New Testament describes elsewhere as the new heavens and new earth. It is the eternal house and the new clothing that Paul speaks of in 2 Corinthians 5:1–5. It is the revelation of the glory of Father, Son, and Spirit in which we will participate, on bended knee, face-to-face. It is the new Jerusalem as portrayed by John on Patmos—the kingdom of God.

In view of all that has now been revealed in these last days, the author of Hebrews urges the faithful to open their hearts in faith and run their race to the end, cheered on by the "great cloud of witnesses" that have gone before. To those who have heard the message of so great a salvation, the author speaks with urgency, saying to his readers, "lay aside every weigh and the sin that clings so closely, and let us run with perseverance the race that is set before us, looking to Jesus the pioneer and perfecter of our faith, who for the sake of the joy that was set before him endured the cross, disregarding its shame, and has taken his seat at the right hand of the throne of God" (Heb 12:1–2). Caught up by the Spirit in that vision, the writer delivers this beautiful, climactic benediction: "Now may the God of peace, who brought back from the dead our Lord Jesus, the great shepherd of the sheep, by the blood of the eternal covenant, make you complete in everything good so that you may do his will, working among us that which is pleasing in his sight, through Jesus Christ, to whom be the glory forever and ever" (Heb 13:20–21).

---

created by the author himself. It does not indicate an event but "a sabbath-life," a sabbath way of life. Wilson quotes C. Spicq who describes the sabbath-life or sabbath-rest as "a participation in the very beatitude of God (Matt 25:21)." Wilson, *Hebrews*, 84. For additional detail on the word usage, see Lindars, *Theology of the Letter*, 49–50.

32

All the More as You See the Day Approaching

How then shall we live? The New Testament's answer is this: live as followers of the Way, as disciples of Jesus Christ (see Acts 22:4, 24:14, 22). Yet as we have seen in the foregoing chapters, the meaning of those brief phrases is loaded. Beginning to unpack them, we may add this: live faithfully as the creatures God made us to be—the sixth-day image of God commissioned to exercise the responsibilities of royal stewardship in the service of the Lord of all creation. That is the way of life that has been reopened through Jesus, God's faithful steward and high priest, who gave himself up for us and calls us to follow him in giving ourselves up in thankful service to God and neighbors. In other words, a righteous man—the Messiah of Israel—has come to stand in our place, a kinsman redeemer and sacrifice for our sins who is reconciling all things to God. That is the message summed up in four words in Hebrews 2:9: "but we see Jesus." We do not yet see the creation ordered properly under human governance, *but we do see Jesus*. The Son of God has become one with us in this age to overcome sin and darkness through his own death and to restore the human vocation to its service of glorifying God. That is the way of Jesus Christ, the way of God's mercy and love and righteousness, that we are to follow.

Our kinsman redeemer is none other than the incarnate Son of God, the Alpha and the Omega of all things, the one in and through whom all things are created and hang together. He is the last Adam through whom creation will be fulfilled in God's sabbath joy. That is why discipleship of Jesus Christ entails turning away from our disobedience and learning how to be faithful servants of God with all that we are and have.

THE DAY OF THE LORD

Now that the long history of God's covenant purposes has culminated in the revelation of Israel's Messiah (Christ) Jesus, we know that the kingdom of God is at hand, that the day of the Lord's final reckoning is upon us.[1] It is all the more urgent, then,

1. Thompson explains that "the Day" is an abbreviation for "day of judgment, and "day of the Lord

according to Hebrews, that we consider how to "provoke one another to love and good deeds." Don't give up gathering together, as some are doing, says the author, but encourage one another "all the more as you see the Day approaching" (Heb 10:24–25). Too many Christians seem to believe that when life in this world ends they will go to heaven, leaving behind all that occupied them on earth. They live as if this world and the next are disconnected. Gathering together, as they see it, means gathering for worship on Sunday and evangelizing the lost.

The writer to the Hebrews presents a different vision, the same vision held by other New Testament writers. Life in this age, by revelatory anticipation, is intimately and intricately related to life in the age to come. Listen to the way the author introduces the section of Chapter 10 that begins at verse 19. Given all that God has done through the new covenant in Messiah Jesus to offer the ultimate, once-for-all sacrifice for sins and to put the covenant laws in the hearts and minds of believers, the author writes, we can now "have confidence to enter the sanctuary by the blood of Jesus" (Heb 10:19). The words here presuppose something said earlier in the letter, namely that Israel's tabernacle (and temple) were representative anticipations of the completed and all-encompassing tabernacle of creation whose sanctuary is where God dwells with those purified through Christ. Christ Jesus, says the author, has opened "a new and living way . . . for us through the curtain (that is, through his flesh), and since we have a great priest over the house of God, let us approach with a true heart in full assurance of faith, with our hearts sprinkled clean from an evil conscience and our bodies washed with pure water" (Heb 10:20–22).

The author, in other words, sees the human generations of this age occupying the outer courts of the creation-wide tabernacle in which God's history with Israel and the nations has disclosed more and more of God's purposes for the entire creation. Everything God instituted for Israel in this age through the sabbath patterns, the priesthood, the tabernacle, the animal sacrifices, entrance into the promised land, and more points toward God's eternal temple, new Jerusalem, and the promised land of creation's fulfillment. Now, through faith in the risen and ascended Christ Jesus, we are called to live as those who are being cleansed and purified through his blood to be made the dwelling place of God. In Hebrews 13:11–14, the author adds this comparison: the high priest carries the blood of animals into the sanctuary as a sin offering, but the bodies are burned outside the camp. And so, "Jesus also suffered outside the city gate in order to sanctify the people by his own blood. Let us then go to him outside the camp and bear the abuse he endured. For here we have no lasting city, but we are looking for the city that is to come" (Heb 13:12–14).

Jesus." "Old Testament prophets spoke of the 'Day of the Lord' (cf. Isa 2:12; 13:6; Joel 1:15; 2:31; Amos 5:18; Zech 14:1), a day of divine judgment. Since early Christians called Jesus 'Lord,' they spoke of the return of Christ (1 Cor 5:5; 1 Thess 5:2) as 'the day of the Lord.' In some instances, they spoke of the 'day of the Lord Jesus Christ' (1 Cor 1:8), 'the day of the Lord Jesus' (2 Cor 1:14), and 'the day of Christ' (Phil 1:10; 2:16). In other instances that phrase is abbreviated to 'the day' (2 Tim 1:2, 18; 4:8; Heb 10:25)." Thompson, *Hebrews*, 207.

The sanctuary or most holy place that Jesus entered was not in the earthly tabernacle or the Jerusalem temple, but in the eternal temple of which its earthly representatives were revelatory shadows. So, in this case, when Christ died outside the gate, his priestly offering transcended all earthy sacrifices, opening the whole creation to fulfillment in the city that is to come—the eternal city of God's rest where there is no longer a need for sacrifices. Through Christ, the curtain in the sanctuary that symbolically separated God from the people has been ripped open, exposing the entire creation to the light of Christ and the redeeming power of his sacrifice. Through Jesus Christ, the entire creation is now being transfigured into the sanctuary of righteousness, the house of God at home with his people.[2]

LOVE AND GOOD DEEDS

That is why verses 24–25 of Hebrews chapter 10 are so important for the way we should live here and now. The "love and good deeds" that Hebrews urges us to practice are, by God's grace, being stored up as treasures for the seventh-day fulfillment of creation. What we do now relates directly to what is coming. Life in this age is intimately related to the next. Therefore, the more we see the day approaching, the more we should stir one another to action. That is the opposite of sitting back to wait for a train that will take us to another country, another world.

Yet one still might ask: what about those places in the Bible that say the day of the Lord will bring the end of this world, that the world will be burned up, destroyed, rolled up like a tarp and thrown away? Listen to Peter who warns, "the day of the Lord will come like a thief, and then the heavens will pass away with a loud noise, and the elements will be dissolved with fire, and the earth and everything that is done on it will be disclosed" (2 Pet 3:10). Hear the description of the new heaven and new earth in Revelation: "the first heaven and the first earth had passed away, and the sea was no more" (Rev 21:1); "the city [New Jerusalem] has no need of sun or moon to shine on it" (Rev 21:23). There are other passages that say similar things. What do they mean if not what they seem to say?

If we look closely at the whole of 2 Peter and the book of Revelation, we see that the discontinuities between this age and the coming age are rooted in the deeper continuity of God's covenant bond with creation from beginning to end. For example, Christ identifies himself as "the Alpha and the Omega," the beginning and the climax of all things (Rev 1:8), and Peter is encouraging believers to live righteously and faithfully *now* so they "will receive a rich welcome into the eternal kingdom of our Lord and Savior Jesus Christ" (2 Pet 1:11). Paul speaks of looking ahead to being clothed with immortality in the age to come (1 Cor 15:53) and of believers "longing

---

2 With a focus primarily on Heb 9, Schenck presents a thorough scholarly examination of the relation of the earthly tabernacle to the heavenly tabernacle. Schenck, *Cosmology and Eschatology*, 144–81.

to be clothed with our heavenly dwelling" (2 Cor 5:2). The same persons and the same God will enter into a new kind of relationship in the resurrection, but that relationship will be the fulfillment of what God has been doing with our lives and with the whole creation from the beginning. Paul would prefer to be with the Lord, he tells the Corinthians, but whether we are at home in the body of this age or away from it with the Lord, "we make it our aim to please him. For all of us must appear before the judgment seat of Christ, so that each may receive recompense for what has been done in the body, whether good or evil" (2 Cor 5:9–10; note also Jesus's parable in Matt 25:14–30). What we do on earth, in other words, matters to God for eternity, and our works will be judged by Christ, whether they are good or bad.

Language about the earth burning up or being destroyed should not be read as teaching that this creation will be cast aside and believers will enter another creation. The explanation offered by many biblical scholars is that the language of destructive fire is *apocalyptic* language that refers to climactic judgment of all that is evil. The sentence we quoted above from 2 Peter 3:10 concludes with the phrase, "and the earth and everything that is done on it will be disclosed." That follows from his words about the heavens disappearing with a roar and the elements being destroyed by fire. In other words, the earth and everything in it will be "disclosed," laid bare, exposed to its core, leaving no hidden corners of darkness. All of created reality and every human deed can then be seen for what it is. God's destruction of all that is evil is for the purpose of setting everything right again. Only what is good, clean, renewed, and righteous will come through the fire like refined gold. There will be a cleansing, or burning away, of what has been corrupted so that the change from one mode of creaturely existence into the resurrection mode of creaturely existence can be realized.

Consequently, we need to distinguish two meanings of discontinuity in God's good creation. The first and good kind of discontinuity is that between life in this age and life in the age to come. The second discontinuity is between the good creation (including human responsibility in this age) and the sinfully disfiguring corruption of life in this age. If we keep the latter discontinuity in mind when reading about God's judgment of sin, then we can recognize the validity of apocalyptic language about the "end of this world" in the fires of judgment so the good creation can be cleansed. However, we should not confuse the discontinuity between good and evil with the difference between the created goodness of our sixth-day human lives (in the line of the first Adam) and the fulfillment of creation through the last Adam in God's sabbath rest.

GATHERING TOGETHER

When Hebrews speaks of spurring one another to love and good deeds, urging believers not to give up meeting together, the latter phrase means much more than "don't forget to go to church on Sunday." The author is speaking here of why and how his readers should be practicing faithfulness in the bond of Christ. The context of the letter, and of this admonition in particular, is the covenant blessings and curses addressed to Israel so forcefully in Deuteronomy. It concerns the way believers should live and not only the way they should worship. It also alludes to God's message through Isaiah (and other prophets) when God was fed up with the people for continuing to offer sacrifices and prayers when at the same time they were violating their covenant obligations to do justice (Isa 1:7–17). God no longer wants to hear the prayers and smell the burning offerings offered by hypocrites. In Hebrews 10, the urgency is for believers to persist in following the way of life opened to them by Christ whom they confess as their savior from sin and a guilty conscience. To continue in the way of Christ entails doing what is right and good, which we should do by locking arms in cooperative efforts. The author, much like James, believes that faith without works is dead (Jas 2:14–17) and many if not most works require gathering together and organizing in order to do them.[3]

As we've argued throughout this book, the household of faith, the bride of Christ, is not merely an institutional worship community, in the sense of the denominational churches of today. Biblically speaking, the church is the body of Christ, the people of God—those called to follow Christ with their entire lives in every sphere of responsibility. All that God has given us to do in every kind of work and service is implicated in God's call to the sons and daughters of the first Adam to turn from their wicked ways and to follow Christ in all things. Living in this way is quite continuous with the way of life to which God called Abraham and Israel (see Hebrews 11). To think of the church simply as a "religious" organization alongside "secular" (non-religious) organizations is to misunderstand the identity of God's people. According to Stowers, it is a modern concept that religion is "an essentially private sphere of personal belief and activity separate from politics, law, economic activity, and ethnicity."[4] Jews in Paul's time understood God's covenant "as the religious-social-political-legal constitution of the Jewish people, a basis both for the temple state in Judea and for the Jewish communities in the diaspora . . . I am convinced that Paul understood the law in the same general way."[5] Discipleship of Christ, therefore, needs to be understood as an

---

3. For a detailed exegesis of the "rare" Greek word we translate "gathering together," or "assembling," see Ellingworth, *Epistle to Hebrews*, 527–30.

4. Stowers, *Rereading of Romans*, 26–27.

5. Stowers, *Rereading of Romans*, 35. On the relation between ethics for all of life in this age and

all-encompassing way of life, following on from the way of life to which God called Israel. Christ has come to fulfill all of God's covenant promises and obligations; he does not call his followers only to a new way of worship, but rather to a comprehensive way of righteous living on the way to creation's fulfillment.[6]

Another point to emphasize about "gathering together" is made by Paul Elling-worth. The rarely used Greek word we translate "gathering together" or "assembling" is only used in the Bible in "eschatological contexts." In other words, it connotes "the final assembling of God's people," the kind of assembling Hebrews speaks of in 12:26—"you have come to Mount Zion, to the heavenly Jerusalem, the city of the living God." This contrasts with Israel's assembly around the "mountain that can be touched and that is burning with fire" (Heb 12:18, TNIV),[7] and relates directly to what the author says at the beginning of Hebrews 12, urging the faithful to run the race with perseverance, fixing their eyes on Jesus, where he is seated at the "right hand of the throne of God" after having run his race, enduring the cross and scorning the shame it brought. David Hay offers important commentary here.

> Believers are summoned to guide their pilgrimage by looking to Jesus, con-sidering both his earthly career and his celestial glory. Their conduct should be modeled on his earthly perseverance; but they are also to meditate on his SESSION [his position at the right hand of God], the reward of that perse-verance. That the epistle's writer thinks that Christians can hope to share the SESSION is indicated by several facts. In Heb 4 a correspondence is developed between the "rest" (*katapausis*) which God entered (4.4) and that which be-lievers should labor to enter (4.11). In 10.12–13 and 12.2 Jesus' SESSION is interpreted above all as resting after the completion of his earthly task. . . . Fi-nally, the orientation of Heb 11.1—12.2 is hortatory and Jesus is presented as the supreme model of faith. His exaltation to the right hand is conceived here

---

creation's fulfillment through Christ in the age to come, see Moloney on ethics in the Gospel of John: "God, Eschatology," 197–219.

6. Wright, like Stowers, is a critic of the worldview guiding much of modern biblical criticism; he wants to emphasize, among other things, that Paul cannot be evaluated merely as a thinker. Al-though still using the contrasting terms "thinking" and "doing," Wright identifies thinking as one part of doing—the action of Christian communities to develop a new way of life. Paul's practical aim, Wright believes, was to promote the development of communities that "he regarded as the spirit-inhabited Messiah-people, constituted at least in his mind and perhaps also in historical truth as a new kind of reality, embodying a new kind of philosophy, of religion, and of politics, and a new kind of combination of those; and all of this within . . . a new kind of Jewishness, a community of new covenant, a community rooted in a new kind of prayer." Wright, *Paul and Faithfulness*, 1476. Although Wright mentions "politics" in this list, the broader range of human responsibilities as the image of God redeemed in Christ does not come into view. In his reference to a "new kind of Jewishness," the grounding of the covenant in creation does not shine through. One does not get a sufficient sense from passages like this that Wright connects "new creation" sufficiently with the actual creation of which we are now a part, though he often indicates, as we've noted, that there is continuity between old creation and new creation.

7. Ellingworth, *Epistle to Hebrews*, 528.

chiefly as a reward, and the logic of the whole passage points to an assumption that loyal Christians may expect like reward.[8]

FOLLOWING THE WAY

To understand Christians as a community of faithful servants giving themselves over to the Lord in anticipation of the reward of entering God's rest illuminates the revelatory pattern of "commission toward commendation" that we introduced in chapter 7. The disciples of Christ are the community of his followers in all that they do on earth. He has taken on our commission so that joined to him we might receive God's ultimate commendation. Identifying Jesus Christ as the bridegroom of his bride is one of the ways the New Testament describes the all-embracing relationship of God to his people. There is more to human society than the marriage bond, to be sure. Yet the marital relationship is not only intimate; it is also extensive, a bond that constitutes human identity in a way that even when spouses are exercising non-marital responsibilities in other spheres of life, they remain encompassed by their marriage, as do members of a family and extended families. Whether one emphasizes the relation of believers to Christ as that of brothers and sisters, his bride, his disciples, or his joint heirs, each of those relationships implies more than an organized worship function alongside institutions and responsibilities thought of as unrelated to Christ. That is why the mixed metaphor (Rev 21:2) of the new Jerusalem "coming down out of heaven from God, prepared as a bride adorned for her husband" is so powerfully revelatory.

How should those who constitute the bride of Messiah Jesus join together in order to provoke one another to love and good deeds? They should do so, as Hebrews says, by encouraging one another continually in the proper development of all their earthly vocations. The Christian way of life is a way of living thankfully and faithfully with wisdom in Christ's service using all the gifts and capabilities of the image of God. This is where the maturity of disciplined training in sound judgment is required (see Heb 5:11—6:3). What are the arenas in which we should be encouraging one another to turn away from doing wrong and to do what is right? The arenas are found in the full range of experiences and responsibilities for which God created us, as we have emphasized throughout. God has put all things under our feet and crowned us with glory and honor as cooperative participants in the revelation of God's glory. And all of this has now been secured in Christ Jesus, God's truly faithful servant.

To learn to follow the way of Jesus Christ entails learning to distinguish what is good from what is evil in every responsibility we exercise. And of course that demands growth in wisdom—in profound discernment. What is sound and healthy in our contemporary world exists because of God's gracious maintenance and redemption of the

---

8. Hay, *Glory at Right Hand*, 95–96.

good creation for the sake of Christ in whom all things hang together. What is wrong and evil in us and in our world is the deadly fruit of human selfishness, greed, hatred, and disregard of God and neighbors. Learning to distinguish good from evil in personal relationships and family life, in education and the arts and sciences, in industry, commerce, and government requires wise discernment to understand the creaturely meaning of every responsibility we bear.

There is no option of ignoring or fleeing from this world—the creation that God loves so much. The only living option is to repent and turn from the ways of death to the path of life. It is precisely in all spheres of human responsibility that we are to follow that path, for it is in them that the revelatory meaning of our humanity should shine through.[9] The struggle we face daily, therefore, is not with our created nature and the limits of life in this age but with the antithetical forces within each of us and throughout human culture that push and pull against the true way of life in Christ.

The way of life, in biblical terms, can be described from several vantage points: 1) as a journey of cultural development through which men and women exercise the responsibilities of sixth-day royal stewards commissioned to develop and govern the earth in praise of God; 2) as following the way of repentance from sin and turning back to the right path of life; and 3) as the way of the cross, the way of obedience even through suffering, learning to give ourselves up in service to our neighbors.[10] Together, these three perspectives show that followers of the way are on a journey of revelatory anticipation, glimpsing along the way what God has done and is doing to build the divine-human community. A return to the path of life, made possible by God's covenanting grace and forgiveness of sins, reaches its climax in the incarnation, death, resurrection, and ascension of Christ Jesus. And the Lord Jesus—our brother, teacher, bridegroom—has promised to come again to fulfill his pledge of love. Therefore, we, the beloved of the Song of Songs, may sing of our lover, "He has taken me to the banquet hall, and his banner over me is love" (Song 2:4, NIV). In response to God's love in Christ the writer of Hebrews sings this benediction:

9. This is not the place to try to articulate a philosophy of vocation in different arenas of human responsibility. However, such a task is necessary if we are to understand our discipleship as one of serving the Lord with all the gifts, capabilities, and responsibilities God has given us. Several perspectives on the meaning of work from a Christian point of view can be found in Witherington, *Work*; Volf, *Work in Spirit*; Hardy, *Fabric of This World*. See also Crouch, *Culture Making*; Edgar, *Created and Creating*; Naugle, *Reordered Love*; and Wolters, *Creation Regained*. From Kuyper, whose work we have discussed in various parts of this book, see his essays and speeches in *Abraham Kuyper* as well as *Our Program* and *Lectures on Calvinism*.

10. The three points of view I mention here are not intended to exhaust the meaning of following in Christ's path of living, dying, and rising again in victory over death. For an illuminating discussion of Christ's life, death, and resurrection as (1) model—moral influence; as (2) sacrifice—representative or substitutionary punishment; and as (3) royal victory over sin and death, see Boersma, *Violence*. Boersma discusses major theories of Christ's atonement that have been developed through church history and interrogates them in relation to contemporary theological concerns about the incompatibility of divine hospitality with a violent God. For a consideration of the atonement and blood sacrifices in Heb, see Long, *Hebrews*, 134–61.

Now may the God of peace, who brought back from the dead our Lord Jesus, the great Shepherd of the sheep, by the blood of the eternal covenant, make you complete in everything good so that you may do his will, working among us that which is pleasing in his sight, through Jesus Christ, to whom be the glory forever and ever. Amen (Heb 13:20–21).

Bibliography

Aageson, J. W. "Typology, Correspondence, and the Application of Scripture in Romans 9–11." *Journal for the Study of the New Testament* 31 (1987) 51–72.

———. *Written Also for Our Sake: Paul and the Art of Biblical Interpretation*. Louisville: Westminster John Knox, 1993.

Adams, Edward. "The Cosmology of Hebrews." In *The Epistle to the Hebrews and Christian Theology*, edited by Richard Bauckham et al., 122–39. Grand Rapids: Eerdmans, 2009.

Alexander, T. D. "From Adam to Judah: The Significance of the Family Tree in Genesis." *The Evangelical Quarterly* 61 (1989) 5–19.

Anderson, Bernhard. "Introduction: Mythopoeic and Theological Dimensions of Biblical Creation Faith." In *Creation in the Old Testament*, edited by Bernhard Anderson, 1–24. Philadelphia: Fortress, 1984.

Anderson, Gary A. *Christian Doctrine and the Old Testament*. Grand Rapids: Baker Academic, 2017.

Appiah, Kwame Anthony. *The Honor Code: How Moral Revolutions Happen*. New York: Norton, 2011.

Aterbury, Andrew E. "Abraham's Hospitality Among Jewish and Early Christian Writers." *Perspectives in Religious Studies* 30 (2003) 359–76.

Augustine. *The City of God*. Edited by Vernon J. Bourke. Translated by Gerald G. Walsh, SJ et al. Abridged ed. Garden City, NY: Doubleday, 1958.

Bader-Saye, Scott. *Church and Israel After Christendom: The Politics of Election*. Eugene, OR: Wipf and Stock, 1999.

Barker, Margaret. *The Great High Priest: The Temple Roots of Christian Liturgy*. New York: T. & T. Clark, 2003.

Barrett, C. K. "The Eschatology of the Epistle to the Hebrews." In *The Background of the New Testament and Its Eschatology*, edited by W.D. Davies and D. Daube, 363–93. Cambridge: Cambridge University Press, 1964.

Barth, Karl. *Church Dogmatics. 3/1: The Doctrine of Creation*. Edited by G. W. Bromiley and T. F. Torrance. Translated by J. W. Edwards et al. Edinburgh: T. & T. Clark, 1958.

———. *Church Dogmatics. 3/2: The Doctrine of Creation*. Edited by G. W. Bromiley and T. F. Torrance. Translated by Harold Knight et al. Edinburgh: T. & T. Clark, 1960.

Bartholomew, Craig G. "Covenant and Creation: Covenant Overload or Covenantal Deconstruction." *Calvin Theological Journal* 30 (1995) 11–33.

———. *Ecclesiastes*. Grand Rapids: Baker Academic, 2009.

———. *Introducing Biblical Hermeneutics: A Comprehensive Framework for Hearing God in Scripture*. Grand Rapids: Baker Academic, 2015.

Bartholomew, Craig G., Colin Greene, and Karl Moller, eds. *Renewing Biblical Interpretation*. Scripture and Hermeneutics Series 1. Grand Rapids: Zondervan, 2000.

Bartholomew, Craig G. et al., eds. *Canon and Biblical Interpretation*. Scripture and Hermeneutics Series 7. Grand Rapids: Zondervan, 2006.

Bartholomew, Craig G. and Michael W. Goheen. *The Drama of Scripture: Finding our Place in the Biblical Story*, 2nd ed. Grand Rapids: Baker Academic, 2014.

Bauckham, Richard. "The Millennium." In *God Will be All in All: The Eschatology of Jürgen Moltmann*, edited by Richard Bauckham, 123–47. Edinburgh: T. & T. Clark, 1999.

Beale, Gregory K. "The Garden Temple." *Kerux* 18 (2003) 3–50.

Begbie, Jeremy S. *A Peculiar Orthodoxy: Reflections on Theology and the Arts*. Grand Rapids: Baker Academic, 2018.

Benson, Bruce Ellis. *Graven Ideologies: Nietzsche, Derrida, and Marion on Modern Idolatry*. Downers Grove, IL: InterVarsity, 2002.

Bergant, Diane. *What Are They Saying About Wisdom Literature?* New York: Paulist, 1984.

Berkowitz, Peter. "The Religion of Democracy" *The Public Interest* (Winter 1996) 133–39. https://www.nationalaffairs.com/storage/app/uploads/public/58e/1a4/e8e/58e1a4e8 e5af2806578202.pdf

Berman, Harold J. *Law and Revolution: The Formation of the Western Legal Tradition*. Cambridge: Harvard University Press, 1983.

Berman, Joshua. *Created Equal: How the Bible Broke with Ancient Political Thought*. Oxford: Oxford University Press, 2008.

Bloch, Ariel, and Chana Bloch. *The Song of Songs: A New Translation*. New York: Random House, 1995.

Blocher, Henri. *In the Beginning: The Opening Chapters of Genesis*. Translated by David G. Preston. Downers Grove, IL: InterVarsity, 1984.

Boda, Mark J. *The Heartbeat of the Old Testament*. Grand Rapids: Baker Academic, 2017.

Boersma, Hans. *Violence, Hospitality, and the Cross*. Grand Rapids: Baker Academic, 2004.

Bouma-Prediger, Steven. *For the Beauty of the Earth: A Christian Vision for Creation Care*, 2nd ed. Grand Rapids: Eerdmans, 2010.

Braaten, Carl E. "The Recovery of Apocalyptic Imagination." In *The Last Things: Biblical and Theological Perspectives on Eschatology*, edited by Carl E. Braaten and Robert W. Jenson, 14–32. Grand Rapids: Eerdmans, 2002.

Brague, Remi. *The Law of God: The Philosophical History of an Idea*. Translated by Lydia G. Cochrane. Chicago: University of Chicago Press, 2007.

Bratt, James D. *Abraham Kuyper: Modern Calvinist, Christian Democrat*. Grand Rapids: Eerdmans, 2013.

Brettler, Marc. *God is King: Understanding an Israelite Metaphor*. London: Sheffield Academic, 1989.

Bright, John. *The Kingdom of God: The Biblical Concept and Its Meaning for the Church*. Nashville: Abingdon, 1953.

Brown, William P. *Seeing the Psalms: A Theology of Metaphor*. Louisville: Westminster John Knox, 2002.

Brueggemann, Walter. *Theology of the Old Testament*. Minneapolis: Fortress, 1997.

Bullinger, E. W. *Figures of Speech Used in the Bible*. Grand Rapids: Baker, 1968.

Burney, C. F. "Christ as the ΑΡΧΗ of Creation." *Journal of Theological Studies* 27 (1925) 160–77.

Burt, Sean. "'Your Torah is My Delight': Repetition and the Poetics of Immanence in Psalm 119." *Journal of Biblical Literature* 137 (2018) 685–700.

Byrne, Brendan, SJ. *The Hospitality of God*. Collegeville, MN: Liturgical Press, 2000.

Calhoun, Craig, Mark Juergensmeyer, and Jonathan Van Antwerpen, eds. *Rethinking Secularism*. Oxford: Oxford University Press, 2011.

Calvin, John. *Commentary on Genesis*. Grand Rapids: Baker, 1979.

Carroll, James. *Constantine's Sword: The Church and the Jews: A History*. Boston: Houghton Mifflin, 2000.

Charlesworth, James H. "Lady Wisdom and Johannine Christology." In *Light in a Spotless Mirror*, edited by James H. Charlesworth and Michael A. Daise, 92–133. Harrisburg, PA: Trinity Press International, 2003.

Childs, Brevard S. *Myth and Reality in the Old Testament*. Studies in Biblical Theology 27. London: SCM, 1962.

Clements, Ronald E. *One Hundred Years of Old Testament Interpretation*. Philadelphia: Westminster, 1976.

Clouser, Roy A. *The Myth of Religious Neutrality: An Essay on the Hidden Role of Religious Belief in Theories*, rev. ed. Notre Dame: University of Notre Dame Press, 2005.

Cogley, John. *Religion in a Secular Age*. New York: Praeger, 1968.

Comte, Auguste. *The Catechism of Positive Religion*. Translated by Richard Congreve. London: Kegan Paul, 1891, 1858.

Crawford, Michael. *The World Beyond Your Head: On Becoming an Individual in an Age of Distraction*. New York: Farrar, Straus and Giroux, 2015.

Crouch, Andy. *Culture Making: Recovering Our Creative Calling*. Downers Grove, IL: InterVarsity, 2008.

Culpepper, R. Alan. "The Creation Ethics of the Gospel of John." In *Johannine Ethics: The Moral World of the Gospel and Epistles of John*, edited by Sherri Brown and Christopher W. Skinner, 62–90. Minneapolis: Fortress, 2017.

Cummins, S. A. "Divine Life and Corporate Christology: God, Messiah Jesus, and the Covenant Community in Paul." In *The Messiah in the Old and New Testaments*. McMaster New Testament Studies, edited by Stanley E. Porter, 190–209. Grand Rapids: Eerdmans, 2007.

Currie, John. "Preaching by Faith, Not by Sight: A Sermon on 2 Corinthians 5:5." In *Resurrection and Eschatology, Essays in Honor of Richard B. Gaffin Jr.*, edited by Lane G. Tipton and Jeffrey C. Waddington, 555–64. Phillipsburg, NJ: P&R Publishing, 2008.

Dawkins, Richard. *The God Delusion*. Boston: Houghton Mifflin, 2006.

Dempster, Stephen. *Dominion and Dynasty*. Downers Grove, IL: InterVarsity Press, 2003.

Dennett, Daniel. *From Bacteria to Bach and Back: The Evolution of Minds*. New York: Norton, 2017.

Dewey, John. *Democracy and Education*. New York: Free Press, 1916.

———. *My Pedagogic Creed*. London: Forgotten Books, 1897.

De Witt, Calvin B. *Caring for Creation: Responsible Stewardship of God's Handiwork*. Grand Rapids: Baker, 1998.

Dooyeweerd, Herman. *Encyclopedia of the Science of Law: Introduction*. Edited by Alan M. Cameron. Translated by Robert N. Knudsen. The Collected Works of Herman Dooyeweerd A/8. Lewiston, NY: Edwin Mellen, 2002.

———. *In the Twilight of Western Thought*. Lewiston, NY: Edwin Mellen, 1999.

———. *Roots of Western Culture: Pagan, Secular, and Christian Options*. Edited by Mark Vander Vennen, et al. Translated by John Kraay. Lewiston, NY: Edwin Mellen, 2003.

Duff, Justin Harrison. "The Blood of Goats and Calves . . . and Bulls? An Allusion to Isaiah 1:11 LXX in Hebrews 10:4." *Journal of Biblical Literature* 137 (2018) 765–83.

Dumbrell, William J. *Covenant and Creation*. Nashville: Thomas Nelson, 1984.

———. "The Covenant with Noah." *The Reformed Theological Review* 38 (1979) 1–9.

———. *The End of the Beginning: Revelatioin 21–22 and the Old Testament*. Eugene, OR: Wipf and Stock, 2001.

———. *The Search for Order: Biblical Eschatology in Focus*. Grand Rapids: Baker, 1994.

Dworkin, Ronald. "What is a Good Life?" *The New York Review of Books* 58 (February 2011) 41–43. https://www.nybooks.com/articles/2011/02/10/what-good-life/.

Eagleton, Terry. *Culture and the Death of God*. New Haven: Yale University Press, 2014.

Edgar, William. *Created and Creating: A Biblical Theology of Culture*. Downers Grove, IL: IVP Academic, 2017.

Ellingworth, Paul. *The Epistle to the Hebrews*. The New International Greek Testament Commentary. Grand Rapids: Eerdmans, 1993.

Ellul, Jacques. *The Politics of God and the Politics of Man*. Edited and translated by Geoffrey W. Bromiley. Grand Rapids: Eerdmans, 1972.

Falk, Marcia. *The Song of Songs: A New Translation and Interpretation*. New York: HarperSanFrancisco, 1990.

Fee, Gordon D. *God's Empowering Presence: The Holy Spirit in the Letters of Paul*. Peabody, MA: Hendrickson, 1994.

Ferry, Luc. *Man Made God: The Meaning of Life*. Translated by David Pellauer. Chicago: University of Chicago Press, 2002.

Finer, S. E. *The History of Government*. 3 vols. Oxford: Oxford University Press, 1997, 1999.

Fishbane, Michael. *Biblical Interpretation in Ancient Israel*. Oxford: Oxford University Press, 1988.

Fredriksen, Paula. *Augustine and the Jews: A Christian Defense of Jews and Judaism*. New Haven: Yale University Press, 2010, 2008.

Frei, Hans W. *The Eclipse of Biblical Narrative: A Study in Eighteenth and Nineteenth Century Hermeneutics*. New Haven: Yale University Press, 1974.

Fretheim, Terence E. *God and World in the Old Testament*. Nashville: Abingdon, 2005.

Friedman, R. E. "The Tabernacle in the Temple." *Biblical Archaeologist* 43 (1980) 241–48.

Frye, Northrop. *The Great Code: The Bible and Literature*. New York: Harcourt, 1982.

Gaffin, Richard B. Jr. *By Faith, Not by Sight*. Bucks, UK: Paternoster, 2006.

———. "The Last Adam, The Life-Giving Spirit." In *The Forgotten Christ: Exploring the Majesty and Mystery of God Incarnate*, edited by Stephen Clark, 191–223. Nottingham, UK: Apollos, 2007.

———. *Resurrection and Redemption: A Study in Paul's Soteriology*. Phillipsburg, NJ: Presbyterian and Reformed, 1978.

———. "A Sabbath Rest Still Awaits the People of God." In *Pressing Toward the Mark*, edited by Charles G. Dennison and Richard C. Gamble, 33–51. Philadelphia: Committee for the Historian of the Orthodox Presbyterian Church, 1986.

Garner, David B. "The First and Last Son: Christology and Sonship in Pauline Soteriology." In *Resurrection and Eschatology*, edited by Lane G. Tipton and Jeffrey C. Waddington, 255–79. Phillipsburg, NJ: P&R, 2008.

Garrett, Duane. *Rethinking Genesis: The Sources and Authorship of the First Book of the Pentateuch.* Grand Rapids: Baker, 1991.

Gathercole, Simon. *Defending Substitution: An Essay on Atonement in Paul.* Grand Rapids: Baker Academic, 2015.

Gauchet, Marcel. *The Disenchantment of the World: A Political History of Religion.* Translated by Oscar Burge. Princeton: Princeton University Press, 1997.

Glanville, Mark. "The *Gēr* (Stranger) in Deuteronomy: Family for the Displaced." *Journal of Biblical Literature* 137 (2018) 599–623.

Glasson, T. Francis. "Theophany and Parousia." *New Testament Studies* 34 (1988) 259–70.

Goheen, Michael W. *A Light to the Nations: The Missional Church and the Biblical Story.* Grand Rapids: Baker Academic, 2011.

Golding, Thomas, A. "The Imagery of Shepherding in the Bible." *Bibliotheca Sacra* 163 (2006) 18–28.

Goldingay, John. *Old Testament Theology: Volume One: Israel's Gospel.* Downers Grove, IL: InterVarsity, 2003.

Goldman, Sharon. "The World Repaired, Remade: An Interview with Jon D. Levenson," *Harvard Divinity Bulletin* 35 (Winter 2007) 76–83.

Goppelt, Leonhard. *Typos: The Typological Interpretation of the Old Testament in the New.* Translated by Donald H. Madvig. Grand Rapids: Eerdmans, 1982.

Grant, Jamie A. *The King as Exemplar: The Function of Deuteronomy's Kingship Law in the Shaping of the Book of Psalms.* Academia Biblica 17. Atlanta: Society of Biblical Literature, 2004.

Green, Joel B., and Mark D. Baker. *Recovering the Scandal of the Cross.* Downers Grove, IL: IVP Academic, 2000.

Greidanus, Sydney. *Preaching Christ from Ecclesiastes.* Grand Rapids: Eerdmans, 2010.

Gunton, Colin. *The Actuality of Atonement: A Study of Metaphor, Rationality, and the Christian Tradition.* Grand Rapids: Eerdmans, 1989.

———. *Christ and Creation.* Grand Rapids: Eerdmans, 1992.

———. *Father, Son, and Holy Spirit.* New York: T. & T. Clark, 2003.

Hahn, Scott W. *Kinship by Covenant.* New Haven: Yale University Press, 2009.

Halbertal, Moshe, and Avishai Margalit. *Idolatry.* Translated by Naomi Goldblum. Cambridge: Harvard University Press, 1992.

Halbertal, Moshe, and Stephen Holmes. *The Beginning of Politics: Power in the Biblical Book of Samuel.* Princeton: Princeton University Press, 2017.

Hardy, Lee. *The Fabric of This World.* Grand Rapids: Eerdmans, 1990.

Harink, Douglas. *Paul Among the Postliberals: Pauline Theology Beyond Christendom and Modernity.* Grand Rapids: Brazos, 2003.

Hart, David Bentley. "A Philosopher in the Twilight." *First Things* (February 2011) 44–51.

Hay, David M. *Glory at the Right Hand: Psalm 110 in Early Christianity.* Nashville: Abingdon, 1973.

Hays, Richard B. *Echoes of Scripture in the Gospels.* Waco, TX: Baylor University Press, 2016.

———. *Echoes of Scripture in the Letters of Paul.* New Haven: Yale University Press, 1989.

———. *Reading Backwards: Figural Christology and the Fourfold Gospel Witness.* Waco, TX: Baylor University Press, 2014.

Heschel, Abraham Joshua. "The Sabbath." In *The Earth is the Lord's & The Sabbath*, 1–118. New York: Harper & Row, 1952.

Heslam, Peter S. *Creating a Christian Worldview: Abraham Kuyper's Lectures on Calvinism.* Grand Rapids: Eerdmans, 1998.

Hillers, Delbert R. *Covenant: The History of a Biblical Idea.* Baltimore: Johns Hopkins University Press, 1969.

Holwerda, David E. *Jesus and Israel: One Covenant or Two?* Grand Rapids: Eerdmans, 1995.

Hooker, Morna D. *From Adam to Christ: Essays on Paul.* Cambridge: Cambridge University Press, 1990.

Horton, Michael S. *Covenant and Eschatology: The Divine Drama.* Louisville: Westminster John Knox, 2002.

Huntington, Samuel P. *The Clash of Civilizations and the Remaking of World Order.* New York: Simon & Schuster, 1996.

Jaki, Stanley L. *Genesis 1 Through the Ages.* London: Thomas Moore, 1992.

Jenson, Robert W. "Toward a Christian Doctrine of Israel." *Reflections: Center of Theological Inquiry* 3 (2000) 2–21.

Kasemann, Ernst. *The Wandering People of God.* Translated by Roy A. Harrisville and Irving L. Sandberg. Minneapolis: Augsburg, 1984.

Kearney, Richard. *Anatheism: Returning to God After God.* New York: Columbia University Press, 2010.

Keiser, Thomas A. "The Divine Plural: A Literary-Contextual Argument for Plurality in the Godhead." *Journal for the Study of the Old Testament* 34 (2009) 131–46.

Kinzer, Mark. *Post-Missionary Messianic Judaism.* Grand Rapids: Brazos, 2005.

Klapwijk, Jacob. *Purpose in the Living World: Creation and Emergent Evolution.* Edited and translated by Harry Cook. Cambridge: Cambridge University Press, 2008.

Kline, Meredith G. *By Oath Consigned: A Reinterpretation of the Covenant Signs of Circumcision and Baptism.* Grand Rapids: Eerdmans, 1968.

———. *Images of the Spirit.* Grand Rapids: Baker, 1980.

———. *The Structure of Biblical Authority.* Grand Rapids: Eerdmans, 1972.

———. *Treaty of the Great King: The Covenant Structure of Deuteronomy.* Grand Rapids: Eerdmans, 1963.

Kolakowski, Leszek. *Modernity on Endless Trial.* Chicago: University of Chicago Press, 1990.

Kuyper, Abraham. *Abraham Kuyper: A Centennial Reader.* Edited by James D. Bratt. Grand Rapids: Eerdmans, 1998.

———. *Lectures on Calvinism.* Grand Rapids: Eerdmans, 1961.

———. *Our Program: A Christian Political Manifesto.* Edited and translated by Harry Van Dyke. Bellingham, WA: Lexham, 2015.

———. *Pro Rege: Living Under Christ's Kingship.* Edited by John Kok and Nelson D. Kloosterman. Translated by Albert Grootjes. 3 vols. Bellingham, WA: Lexham, 2016–2018.

———. *The Problem of Poverty.* Edited by James W. Skillen. Grand Rapids: Baker, 1991.

———. *The Revelation of St. John.* Translated by John Hendrik de Vries. Grand Rapids: Eerdmans, 1985.

———. *The Work of the Holy Spirit.* Translated by Henri de Vries. New York: Funk & Wagnalls, 1908.

LaCocque, André. "Cracks in the Wall." In *Thinking Biblically*, by André LaCocque and Paul Ricoeur, 3–29. Translated by David Pellauer. Chicago: University of Chicago Press, 1998.

———. "The Revelation of Revelations" In LaCocque and Ricoeur, *Thinking Biblically*. Translated by David Pellauer, 307–29. Chicago: University of Chicago Press, 1998.

Lakoff, George, and Mark Johnson. *Metaphors We Live By*. Chicago: University of Chicago Press, 2003.

Lee, Dorothy. "Creation, Ethics, and the Gospel of John." In *Johannine Ethics: The Moral World of the Gospel and Epistles of John*, edited by Sherri Brown and Christopher W. Skinner, 241–60. Minneapolis: Fortress, 2017.

Levenson, Jon D. *Resurrection and the Restoration of Israel*. New Haven: Yale University Press, 2006.

Lim, John T. K. "Explication of an Exegetical Enigma in Genesis 1:1–3." *Asia Journal of Theology* 16 (2002) 301–14.

Lindars, Barnabas, SSF. *The Theology of the Letter to the Hebrews*. Cambridge: Cambridge University Press, 1991.

Long, D. Stephen. *Hebrews*. Belief, A Theological Commentary on the Bible. Louisville: Westminster John Knox, 2011.

Longman, Tremper III. *The Fear of the Lord is Wisdom*. Grand Rapids: Baker Academic, 2017.

Lukacs, John. *Confessions of an Original Sinner*. New York: Ticknor & Fields, 1990.

Lund, Oystein. *Way Metaphors and Way Topics in Isaiah 40–55*. Tubingen: Mohr Siebeck, 2007.

Lundin, Roger. *Believing Again: Doubt and Faith in a Secular Age*. Grand Rapids: Eerdmans, 2009.

———. ed. *Disciplining Hermeneutics: Interpretation in Christian Perspective*. Grand Rapids: Eerdmans, 1997.

Marshall, Paul. *God and the Constitution*. Lanham, MD: Rowman and Littlefield, 2002.

Marshall, Paul, and Lela Gilbert. *Heaven is Not My Home*. Nashville: Thomas Nelson, 1999.

Martens, Elmer A. "Reaching for a Biblical Theology of the Whole Bible." In *Reclaiming the Old Testament: Essays in Honour of Waldemar Janzen*, edited by Gordon Zerbe, 81–101. Winnipeg: CMBC, 2001.

May, Gerhard. *Creatio Ex Nihilo: The Doctrine of "Creation Out of Nothing" in Early Christian Thought*. Translated by A. S. Worrall. London: T. & T. Clark, 2004.

McConville, J. Gordon. *Being Human in God's World*. Grand Rapids: Baker Academic, 2016.

———. "Old Testament Laws and Canonical Intentionality." In *Canon and Biblical Interpretation*, edited by Craig G. Bartholomew et al., 259–81. Scripture and Hermeneutics Series 7. Grand Rapids: Zondervan, 2006.

McDowell, Catherine L. *The Image of God in the Garden of Eden*. Winona Lake, IN: Eisenbrauns, 2015.

McFague, Sally. *Metaphorical Theology: Models of God in Religious Language*. Minneapolis: Fortress, 1982.

McFarland, Ian A. *From Nothing: A Theology of Creation*. Louisville: Westminster John Knox, 2014.

Middleton, J. Richard. *The Liberating Image: The Imago Dei and Genesis 1*. Grand Rapids: Brazos, 2005.

Midgley, Mary. *Are You an Illusion?* Durham, UK: Acumen, 2014.

Miller, Patrick D. "Deuteronomy and Psalms: Evoking a Biblical Conversation." *Journal of Biblical Literature* 118 (1999) 3–18.

———. "Divine Command/Divine Law: A Biblical Perspective." *Studies in Christian Ethics* 23 (2010) 21–34.

———. *The Way of the Lord: Essays in Biblical Theology*. Grand Rapids: Eerdmans, 2007.

Minear, Paul Sevier. *Christians and the New Creation: Genesis Motifs in the New Testament.* Louisville: Westminster John Knox, 1994.

Moloney, Francis J., SDB. "God, Eschatology, and 'This World': Ethics in the Gospel of John." In *Johannine Ethics: The Moral World of the Gospel and Epistles of John,* edited by Sherri Brown and Christopher W. Skinner, 197–219. Minneapolis: Fortress, 2017.

Moltmann, Jürgen. *The Coming of God: Christian Eschatology.* Translated by Margaret Kohl. Minneapolis: Fortress, 1996.

———. *God in Creation.* Translated by Margaret Kohl. New York: HarperSanFrancisco, 1991.

———. "The Liberation of the Future and Its Anticipations in History." In *God Will Be All in All: The Eschatology of Jürgen Moltmann,* edited by Richard Bauckham, 265–89. Edinburgh: T. & T. Clark, 1999.

———. *Theology of Hope: On the Ground and the Implications of a Christian Eschatology.* Translated by James W. Leitch. Minneapolis: Fortress, 1993.

———. *The Way of Jesus Christ.* Translated by Margaret Kohl. New York: HarperSanFranciso, 1990.

Morrissey, Michael P. "Voegelin, Religious Experience, and Immortality." In *The Politics of the Soul: Eric Voegelin on Religious Experience,* edited by Glenn Hughes, 11–31. Lanham, MD: Rowman & Littlefield, 1999.

Moye, Richard H. "In the Beginning: Myth and History in Genesis and Exodus," *Journal of Biblical Literature* 109 (1990) 577–98.

Murphy, Roland. "Israel's Wisdom: Dialogue between the Sages." In *Light in a Spotless Mirror,* edited by James H. Charlesworth and Michael A. Daise, 7–25. Harrisburg, PA: Trinity Press International, 2003.

Nagel, Thomas. *Mind and Cosmos: Why the Materialist Neo-Darwinian Conception of Nature is Almost Certainly False.* Oxford: Oxford University Press, 2012.

———. *Secular Philosophy and the Religious Temperament.* New York: Oxford University Press, 2010.

Nagle, John Copeland. "Playing Noah." *Minnesota Law Review* 82 (1998) 1171–260.

Nash, James A. *Loving Nature: Ecological Integrity and Christian Responsibility.* Nashville: Abingdon, 1991.

Naugle, David K. *Reordered Love, Reordered Lives.* Grand Rapids: Eerdmans, 2008.

———. *Worldview: The History of a Concept.* Grand Rapids: Eerdmans, 2002.

Naylor, Wendy Fish. "Abraham Kuyper and the Emergence of Neo-Calvinist Pluralism in the Dutch School Struggle." PhD diss., University of Chicago, 2006.

Nelson, Eric. *The Hebrew Republic: Jewish Sources and the Transformation of European Political Thought.* Cambridge: Harvard University Press, 2010.

Newbigin, Leslie. *The Gospel in a Pluralist Society.* Grand Rapids: Eerdmans, 1989.

O'Donovan, Oliver. *Resurrection and Moral Order: An Outline for Evangelical Ethics.* Grand Rapids: Eerdmans, 1986.

———. *The Ways of Judgment.* Grand Rapids: Eerdmans, 2005.

Ollenburger, Ben C. "Jubilee: 'The land is mine; you are aliens and tenants with me.'" In *Reclaiming the Old Testament: Essays in Honour of Waldemar Janzen,* edited by Gordon Zerbe, 208–34. Winnipeg, Manitoba: CMBC Publications, 2001.

Ong, Walter J., SJ. *The Presence of the Word.* Minneapolis: University of Minnesota Press, 1981.

O'Regan, Cyril. *Gnostic Return in Modernity.* Albany, NY: SUNY Press, 2001.

Pak, G. Sujin. "A Break with Anti-Judaic Exegesis: John Calvin and the Unity of the Testaments." *Calvin Theological Journal* 46 (2011) 7–28.

Paul, Ian. "Metaphor and Exegesis." In *After Pentecost: Language and Biblical Interpretation*, edited by Craig Bartholomew, Colin Greene, and Karl Moller, 387–402. Scripture and Hermeneutics Series 2. Grand Rapids: Zondervan, 2001.

Perdue, Leo G. *Wisdom and Creation*. Nashville: Abingdon, 1994.

Perry, T. A. *God's Twilight Zone: Wisdom in the Hebrew Bible*. Peabody, MA: Hendrickson, 2008.

Plantinga, Alvin. *Where the Conflict Lies: Science, Religion, and Naturalism*. New York: Oxford University Press, 2011.

Pohl, Christine D. *Making Room: Recovering Hospitality as a Christian Tradition*. Grand Rapids: Eerdmans, 1999.

Polen, Nehemia. "Leviticus and Hebrews . . . and Leviticus." In *The Epistle to the Hebrews and Christian Theology*, edited by Richard Bauckham et al., 213–25. Grand Rapids: Eerdmans, 2009.

Provan, Iain. *Discovering Genesis: Content, Interpretation, Reception*. Grand Rapids: Eerdmans, 2015.

———. *Seriously Dangerous Religion: What the Old Testament Really Says and Why it Matters*. Waco, TX: Baylor University Press, 2014.

Puffer, Matthew. "Human Dignity After Augustine's *Imago Dei*: On the Sources and Uses of Two Ethical Terms." *Journal of the Society of Christian Ethics* 37 (2017) 65–82.

Renckens, Henricus, SJ. *Israel's Concept of the Beginning: The Theology of Genesis 1–3*. Translated by Charles Napier. New York: Herder and Herder, 1964.

Ridderbos, Herman. *The Coming of the Kingdom*. Edited by Raymon O. Zorn. Translated by H. de Jongste. Philladelphia: Presbyterian and Reformed, 1973.

———. *Paul: An Outline of His Theology*. Translated by John Richard De Witt. Grand Rapids: Eerdmans, 1975.

Robertson, O. Palmer. *Christ and the Covenants*. Grand Rapids: Baker, 1980.

Rosenberg, Stuart E. *The Christian Problem: A Jewish View*. New York: Hippocrene Books, 1986.

Rothman, Joshua, "A Science of the Soul," *New Yorker*, March 27, 2017, 46–55.

Rundell, John F. *Origins of Modernity*. Madison: University of Wisconsin Press, 1987.

Santmire, H. Paul. "The Genesis Creation Narratives Revisited: Themes for a Global Age." *Interpretation* 45 (1991) 366–79.

Sarna, Nahum M. *Understanding Genesis: The Heritage of Biblical Israel*. New York: Schocken Books, 1966.

Schenck, Kenneth L. *Cosmology and Eschatology in Hebrews*. Society for New Testament Studies Monograph Series 143. Cambridge: Cambridge University Press, 2007.

———. "God Has Spoken: Hebrews' Theology of the Scriptures." In *The Epistle to the Hebrews and Christian Theology*, edited by Richard Bauckham et al., 321–36. Grand Rapids: Eerdmans, 2009.

———. "Keeping His Appointment: Creation and Enthronement in Hebrews." *Journal for the Study of the New Testament* 66 (1997) 91–117.

Schmemann, Alexander. *For the Life of the World: Sacraments and Orthodoxy*. Crestwood, NY: St. Vladimir's Seminary, 1973.

Schreiner, Thomas R. *The King in His Beauty: A Biblical Theology of the Old and New Testaments*. Grand Rapids: Baker Academic, 2013.

Seely, Paul H. "The Three-Storied Universe." *Journal of the American Scientific Affiliation* 21 (1969) 18–22.

Seerveld, Calvin. *Biblical Studies and Wisdom for Living.* Edited by John Kok. Sioux Center, IA: Dordt College Press, 2014.

———. *The Greatest Song: In Critique of Solomon,* rev. ed. Toronto: Tuppence, 1988.

Selznick, Philip. *The Moral Commonwealth.* Berkeley: University of California Press, 1992.

Skillen, James R. *Federal Ecosystem Management: Its Rise, Fall, and Afterlife.* Lawrence: University Press of Kansas, 2015.

———. *The Nation's Largest Landlord: The Bureau of Land Management in the American West.* Lawrence: University Press of Kansas, 2009.

Skillen, James W. *The Good of Politics: A Biblical, Historical, and Contemporary Introduction.* Grand Rapids: Baker Academic, 2014.

———. "Reengaging Figural Interpretation: The Impact of Erich Auerbach." *Calvin Theological Journal* 52 (2017) 181–203.

Skillen, John E. *Putting Art (Back) in Its Place.* Peabody, MA: Hendrickson, 2016.

Smit, M. C. "The Divine Mystery in History." In *Toward a Christian Conception of History,* edited by H. Donald Morton and Harry Van Dyke, 223–46. Lanham, MD: University Press of America and the Institute for Christian Studies, 2002.

Smith, Christian. *The Sacred Project of American Sociology.* Oxford: Oxford University Press, 2014.

Smith, David I., and Barbara Carvill. *The Gift of the Stranger: Faith, Hospitality, and Foreign Language Learning.* Grand Rapids: Eerdmans, 2000.

Soskice, Janet Martin. "Creation and the Glory of Creatures." *Modern Theology* 29 (2013) 172–85.

Soulen, R. Kendall. *The God of Israel and Christian Theology.* Minneapolis: Fortress, 1996.

Spykman, Gordon, J. *Reformational Theology: A New Paradigm for Doing Dogmatics.* Grand Rapids: Eerdmans, 1992.

Stek, John. "'Covenant' Overload in Reformed Theology." *Calvin Theological Journal* 29 (1994) 12–41.

———. "Psalm 103: Its Thematic Architecture." In *Text and Commentary: Essays in Memory of Bruce M. Metzger* 1, edited by J. Harold Ellens, 23–38. London: Sheffield Phoenix, 2007.

———. "What Says the Scripture?" In *Portraits of Creation: Biblical and Scientific Perspectives on the World's Formation,* edited by Howard J. Van Till et al., 203–65. Grand Rapids: Eerdmans, 1990.

Stowers, Stanley K. *A Rereading of Romans: Justice, Jews, and Gentiles.* New Haven: Yale University Press, 1994.

Strauss, D. F. M. *Philosophy: Discipline of the Disciplines.* Grand Rapids: Paideia, 2009.

Tannehill, Robert C. *The Narrative Unity of Luke-Acts: A Literary Interpretation.* 2 vols. Minneapolis: Fortress, 1990.

Taubes, Jacob. *The Political Theology of Paul.* Stanford, CA: Stanford University Press, 2004.

Taylor, Charles. *A Secular Age.* Cambridge: The Belknap Press of Harvard University Press, 2007.

Thiselton, Anthony C. *Hermeneutics: An Introduction.* Grand Rapids: Eerdmans, 2009.

Thompson, James W. *Hebrews.* Paideia Commentaries on the New Testament. Grand Rapids: Baker Academic, 2008.

Thornhill, John. "Philosopher Daniel Dennett on AI, Robots and Religion." *Financial Times*, March 2, 2017. https://www.ft.com/content/96187a7a-fce5-11e6-96f8-3700c5664d30.

Tierney, Brian. *The Idea of Natural Rights: Studies on Natural Rights, Natural Law, and Church Law, 1150–1625*. Emory University Studies in Law and Religion 5. Edited by John Witte Jr. Atlanta: Scholars Press, 1997.

Tigay, Jeffrey H. "Divine Creation of the King in Psalm 2:6." *Eretz-Israel* 27 (2003) 246–51.

Trotter, James M. "The Genre and Setting of Psalm 45." *Australian Biblical Review* 57 (2009) 34–46.

Turner, James. *Philology: The Forgotten Origins of the Modern Humanities*. Princeton: Princeton University Press, 2014.

Van Leeuwen, Raymond C. "The Book of Proverbs." In *The New Interpreter's Bible*, vol. 5, 17–264. Nashville: Abingdon, 1997.

———. "Cosmos, Temple, House: Building and Wisdom in Mesopotamia and Israel." In *Wisdom Literature in Mesopotamia and Israel*, edited by Richard J. Clifford, 67–90. Atlanta: Society of Biblical Literature, 2007.

Voegelin, Eric. *From Enlightenment to Revolution*. Edited by John Hallowell. Durham, NC: Duke University Press, 1975.

———. "Immortality: Experience and Symbol." *Harvard Theological Review* 60 (1969) 235–79.

———. *Israel and Revelation*. Order and History 1. Baton Rouge: Louisiana State University Press, 1956.

———. *The New Science of Politics*. Chicago: University of Chicago Press, 1952.

———. "The Pauline Vision of the Resurrected." In *Order and History: The Ecumenic Age*, vol. 4, 239–71. Baton Rouge: Louisiana State University Press, 1974.

———. *Science, Politics and Gnosticism*. Chicago: Henry Regnery, 1968.

Volf, Miroslav. *Work in the Spirit*. Eugene, OR: Wipf and Stock, 1991.

Von Rad, Gerhard. *Genesis: A Commentary*. Translated by John H. Marks. Philadelphia: Westminster, 1972.

———. *Wisdom in Israel*. Translated by James D. Martin. Nashville: Abingdon, 1972.

Walsh, Brian J., and J. Richard Middleton. *The Transforming Vision: Shaping a Christian World View*. Downers Grove, IL: InterVarsity, 1984.

Waltke, Bruce K., and Cathi J. Fredricks. *Genesis: A Commentary*. Grand Rapids: Zondervan, 2001.

Waltke, Bruce K., and M. O'Connor. *An Introduction to Biblical Hebrew Syntax*. Winona Lake, IN: Eisenbrauns, 1990.

Walton, John H. *The Lost World of Genesis One*. Downers Grove, IL: IVP Academic, 2009.

Welker, Michael. *Creation and Reality*. Translated by John F. Hoffmeyer. Minneapolis: Fortress, 1999.

Wenham, Gordon J. *Genesis 1–15*. Word Biblical Commentary 1. Waco, TX: Word, 1987.

Westfall, Cynthia Long. "Messianic Themes of Temple, Enthronement, and Victory in Hebrews and the General Epistles." In *The Messiah in the Old and New Testaments*, edited by Stanley E. Porter, 210–29. Grand Rapids: Eerdmans, 2007.

Williamson, P. R. *Sealed With an Oath: Covenant in God's Unfolding Purpose*. Downers Grove, IL: InterVarsity, 2007.

Wilson, R. McL. *Hebrews*. The New Century Bible Commentary. Grand Rapids: Eerdmans, 1987.

Witherington, Ben III. *Jesus, Paul and the End of the World: A Comparative Study in New Testament Eschatology*. Downers Grove, IL: InterVarsity, 1992.

———. *Jesus the Sage: The Pilgrimage of Wisdom*. Minneapolis: Fortress, 1994.

———. *John's Wisdom: A Commentary on the Fourth Gospel*. Louisville: Westminster John Knox, 1995.

———. *Work: A Kingdom Perspective on Labor*. Grand Rapids: Eerdmans, 2011.

Witte, John Jr. *Law and Protestantism: The Legal Teachings of the Lutheran Reformation*. Cambridge: Cambridge University Press, 2002.

———. *The Reformation of Rights: Law, Religion, and Human Rights in Early Modern Calvinism*. Cambridge: Cambridge University Press, 2007.

Wolters, Albert M. *Creation Regained: Biblical Basics for a Reformational Worldview*, 2nd ed. Grand Rapids: Eerdmans, 2005.

Wood, Charles. *The Formation of Christian Understanding: An Essay in Theological Hermeneutics*. Philadelphia: Westminster, 1981.

Wray, Judith Hock. *Rest as a Theological Metaphor in the Epistle to the Hebrews and the Gospel of Truth*. Society of Biblical Literature Dissertation Series 166. Atlanta: Scholars, 1998.

Wright, Christopher, J. H. *An Eye for an Eye: The Place of Old Testament Ethics Today*. Downers Grove, IL: InterVarsity, 1983.

———. *Knowing Jesus Through Old Testament Eyes*. Downers Grove, IL: InterVarsity, 1992.

———. *The Mission of God: Unlocking the Bible's Grand Narrative*. Downers Grove, IL: IVP Academic, 2006.

———. "Response to Gordon McConville." In *Canon and Biblical Interpretation*. Scripture and Hermeneutics Series 7, edited by Craig G. Bartholomew et al., 282–90. Grand Rapids: Zondervan, 2006.

Wright, N. T. *The Climax of the Covenant: Christ and the Law in Pauline Theology*. Minneapolis: Fortress, 1991.

———. *Evil and the Justice of God*. Downers Grove, IL: InterVarsity, 2006.

———. *Jesus and the Victory of God*. Minneapolis: Fortress, 1996.

———. *Justification: God's Plan and Paul's Vision*. Downers Grove, IL: IVP Academic, 2009.

———. *The Last Word: Scripture and the Authority of God—Getting Beyond the Bible Wars*. New York: HarperOne, 2006.

———. *New Heavens, New Earth: The Biblical Picture of Hope*. Grove Biblical Series B-11. Cambridge: Grove Books, 1999.

———. *The New Testament and the People of God*. Minneapolis: Fortress, 1992.

———. *The Paul Debate: Critical Questions for Understanding the Apostle*. Waco, TX: Baylor University Press, 2015.

———. *Paul and the Faithfulness of God*. Minneapolis: Fortress, 2013.

———. *Paul in Fresh Perspective*. Minneapolis: Fortress, 2005.

———. "Responding to Exile." In *Exile: A Conversation with N .T. Wright*, edited by James M. Scott, 305–32. Downers Grove, IL: IVP Academic, 2017.

———. *The Resurrection of the Son of God*. Minneapolis: Fortress, 2003.

———. "Yet the Sun Will Rise Again: Reflections on the Exile and Restoration in Second Temple Judaism, Jesus, Paul, and the Church Today." In *Exile: A Conversation with N. T. Wright*, edited by James M. Scott, 19–80. Downers Grove, IL: IVP Academic, 2017.

Wyschogrod, Michael. *The Body of Faith: God in the People of Israel*. San Francisco: Harper & Row, 1983.

Yoder, John Howard. *The Jewish-Christian Schism Revisited*. Edited by Michael G. Cartwright and Peter Ochs. Grand Rapids: Eerdmans, 2003.

Zuidema, S. U. "Common Grace and Christian Action in Abraham Kuyper." In *Communication and Confrontation*, 52–105. Toronto: Wedge Publishing Foundation, 1972.

Index